Thames Holocene

A Geoarchaeological Approach to the Investigation of the River Floodplain for High Speed 1, 1994–2003

by Martin Bates and Elizabeth Stafford

Thames Holocene

A Geoarchaeological Approach to the Investigation of the River Floodplain for High Speed 1, 1994–2003

by Martin Bates and Elizabeth Stafford

with contributions from

Hugo Anderson-Whymark, Alistair J Barclay, Catherine Barnett, Richard Bates, Edward Biddulph, Paul Blinkhorn, Nigel Cameron, John Crowther, Denise Druce, Emma-Jayne Evans, Damian Goodburn, Michael J Grant, Jessica M Grimm, Andrew Haggart, Phil Harding, Elizabeth Huckerby, Matt Leivers, Richard I Macphail, Lorraine Mepham, Sylvia Peglar, Mark Robinson, Rob Scaife, David Smith, Wendy Smith, Chris J Stevens, Lucy Verrill, John Whittaker and Sarah F Wyles

Illustrations by

Georgina Slater and Elizabeth Stafford

Oxford Wessex Archaeology

2013

ISBN 978-0-9545970-9-2

British Library Cataloguing in Publication Data
A catalogue record for this book is available from the British Library

Published by Oxford Wessex Archaeology,
a joint venture between Oxford Archaeology and Wessex Archaeology

Oxford Archaeology, Janus House, Osney Mead, Oxford OX2 0ES, Registered Charity No. 285627
Wessex Archaeology, Portway House, Old Sarum Park, Salisbury SP4 6EB, Registered Charity No. 287786

Typeset by K Lymer, Wessex Archaeology
Cover photograph: Queen Elizabeth II Bridge and the River Thames, from Ingress Park, Greenhithe © Owen Kemp
Printed and bound by Henry Ling (Dorset Press) Ltd, Dorchester

Contents

Part I
Introduction and Background

Chapter 1 Introduction 1

Chapter 2 Aims and Objectives of the Study 7

Chapter 3 Regional Background to the Route Corridor 9

Part II
Strategies and Methods

Chapter 4 A Regional Research Design 23

Chapter 5 Project Concepts 27

Chapter 6 Desk-top Investigation. 35

Part III
Field Investigation of the HS1 Corridor

Chapter 7 The Lea Valley 59

List of Figures

List of Plates

List of Tables

Abstract

The archaeological investigation of the route of High Speed 1 (HS1) (formerly known as the Channel Tunnel Rail Link), through the Thames Marshes, is not a conventional one, and this report is neither intended to be a complete landscape history of the Lower Thames, nor an exhaustive archaeological narrative of human occupation of the region. Rather, this work is primarily intended to present the methodological approach that was adopted for the investigation of approximately 18km (17%) of the HS1 route across an area of thick alluvium. By comparison with the remainder of the route, where conventional archaeological approaches to site location, assessment and, in some cases, excavation has been reported elsewhere (Booth *et al* 2011), the alluvial corridor of the Thames required a different approach.

From an early stage in the construction project (1994) it was determined that a geoarchaeological approach to the investigation of the alluvial corridor would be necessary because of the depth of sequences (in excess of 10m in many locations), and the relative invisibility of the archaeological resource in both the Historic Environment Record and to conventional survey. The project commenced with a thorough consideration of existing geotechnical and geo-morphological records. This allowed the construction of a geoarchaeological model for the alluvial corridor whereby different parts of the route were categorised as of low, medium and high potential based on a combination of archaeological and geomorphological inferences. Careful integration of the results of the geoarchaeological investigation were subsequently matched against engineering and route construction parameters in order to determine a cost-effective and logical approach to archaeological mitigation.

The field survey that was developed, following model construction, included geophysical investigation of buried sediment bodies, the use of boreholes, cone penetration testing and conventional test-pitting and trenching. These were deployed in key areas such as the Thames Tunnel portal in Swanscombe Marsh and the Ebbsfleet Valley. The project was successful in predicting the location of buried archaeological remains in a number of locations. Key amongst these are extensive remains excavated in the Ebbsfleet Valley (Andrews *et al* 2011a–b; Barnett *et al* 2011; Biddulph *et al* 2011; Wenban-Smith *et al* forthcoming), Mesolithic flint scatters at Tank Hill Road, Aveley (Leivers *et al* 2007) and Late Upper Palaeolithic and Neolithic scatters on Swanscombe Marsh (this volume). Other sites described here include an *in situ* Early Neolithic flint scatter on Rainham Marsh, close to the Neolithic site at Brookway Allotments (Meddens 1996), and evidence of seasonal Roman and medieval activity, including concentrations of pottery, animal bone and marine shell. The medieval activity, dated to the 11th to 13th centuries AD, may be associated with a phase of marshland reclamation and the building of sea-banks in the area of the former Wennington Creek.

Overall the investigation also confirmed, where fieldwork took place, that those areas of the route corridor considered of low archaeological potential did not contain significant evidence for human activity. The success of the project can therefore be measured not only in the prediction of zones of different archaeological potential but also in the fact that the project delivered a robust and well-structured archaeological response to specific construction impact, and in the process caused no major delays to the completion of HS1. This report makes the case for adopting a geoarchaeological approach to mitigating the impacts caused by future major construction projects in alluvial environments.

Résumé

L'investigation archéologique de la ligne à grande vitesse (High Speed 1, HS1) (autrefois connue comme Channel Tunnel Rail Link, liaison ferroviaire rapide avec le tunnel sous la Manche), traversant les marais de la Tamise, n'est pas une investigation conventionnelle. Ce n'est pas l'intention de ce rapport de présenter une histoire de paysage de la basse Tamise, ni un compte-rendu archéologique exhaustif de l'occupation humaine de la région. L'intention de cette étude est principalement de présenter l'approche méthodologique qui était abordée pour l'investigation sur à peu près 18km (17%) de la route HS1 traversant une région d'alluvion profonde. Par comparaison avec le reste de la route, en quel cas les approches archéologiques conventionnelles concernant la localisation des sites, l'évaluation et, parfois, l'excavation ont étaient publiées ailleurs (Booth *et al* 2011), le corridor d'alluvion de la Tamise nécessite une approche différente.

On a décidé très tôt pendant le projet de construction (1994) qu'un approche géoarchéologique serait nécessaire pour l'investigation du corridor d'alluvion à cause de la profondeur des strates (plus de 10m dans beaucoup de localités) et l'invisibilité de la ressource archéologique, autant dans l'inventaire de monuments historiques que pendant la prospection conventionnelle. Le projet commençait avec un examen approfondi des archives géotechniques et géomorphologiques existantes. Cela permettait la construction d'un modèle géoarchéologique du corridor d'alluvion, de catégoriser comme faible, moyen ou fort, le potentiel des éléments divers du tracé en raison d'une combinaison des inférences archéologiques et géomorphologiques. L'intégration méticuleuse des résultats de l'investigation géoarchéologique a été, par la suite, accordée avec les paramètres d'ingénierie et de construction de la route afin de déterminer une approche économique et logique des mesures d'atténuation archéologique.

La prospection de terrain réalisée à la suite de la construction du modèle inclut l'investigation géoarchéologique des couches de sédiments fossiles, des forages, de l'épreuve du pénétromètre cône, et des fosses et tranchées de sondage conventionnelle. Ces méthodes étaient appliquées aux sites importants comme le portail du tunnel sous la Tamise à Swanscombe Marsh et la vallée de l'Ebbsfleet. Le projet a réussi à prévoir ou se trouvaient des vestiges archéologiques dans plusieurs localités. Parmi les découvertes les plus importantes il y a les nombreux vestiges dégagés dans la vallée de l'Ebbsfleet (Andrews *et al* 2011a–b; Barnett *et al* 2011; Biddulph *et al* 2011; Wenban-Smith *et al* forthcoming), des dispersions de silex mésolithique à Tank Hill Road, Aveley (Leivers *et al* 2007), et les dispersions paléolithiques supérieurs finals ainsi que néolithiques à Swanscombe Marsh (ce volume). Autres gisements publié dans le tome incluent une dispersion *in situ* des silex du Néolithique ancien à Rainham Marsh (près du site néolithique à Brookway Allotments; Meddens 1996). Également, le témoignage d'activités saisonnières romanes et médiévales révèlent des concentrations de poterie, des restes d'ossements d'animaux et de mollusques marins. L'activité médiévale, datée du 11eme au 13eme siècle, pourrait être associée avec une phase de conquête des terrains dans les marais et à la construction de digues dans la zone de l'ancien ruisseau Wennington Creek.

Au total, les investigations ont aussi confirmé, dans les zones fouillées, que ces zones du corridor de la ligne à grande vitesse, censées avoir un potentiel archéologique faible ne révélaient pas d'activité humaine significative. Il est donc possible d'estimer le succès du projet, non seulement à la prévision des zones à potentiel archéologique divers mais aussi au fait que le projet a fourni une réponse archéologique robuste et bien structurée à un effet spécifique de construction. De plus, ce projet n'a pas provoqué de retards significatifs à l'achèvement de la ligne à grande vitesse. Ce rapport avance l'argument qu'il faille adopter une approche géoarchéologique sur l'effort d'atténuer les conséquences des grands projets de construction dans les environnements alluviaux.

Traduction: Jörn Schuster

Zusammenfassung

Die archäologische Untersuchung des Abschnitts der Hochgeschwindigkeitsstrecke High Speed 1 (HS1; ehemals Channel Tunnel Rail Link) durch die Themsemarschen, kann nicht als konventionell bezeichnet werden, und daher soll mit diesem Band weder eine vollständige Landschaftsgeschichte der unteren Themse vorgelegt werden, noch soll ein umfassender archäologischer Abriss der menschlichen Besiedlung der Region geboten werden. Vielmehr ist das Hauptanliegen dieser Arbeit die Beschreibung der Methodik für die Untersuchung des etwa 18km (17%) langen Abschnitts der HS1-Trasse durch eine Zone mit tiefgründigen alluvialen Sedimenten. Im Vergleich zum Rest der Trasse, über deren konventionelle archäologische Untersuchungsansätze wie Fundstellenlokalisierung, Voruntersuchung und, in einigen Fällen, Ausgrabung bereits andernorts berichtet wurde (Booth *et al* 2011), erforderte der alluviale Korridor der Themse eine andere Herangehensweise.

Schon kurz nach Beginn des Bauprojekts (1994) wurde entschieden, dass die Untersuchung des alluvialen Korridors wegen der Mächtigkeit der Schichtabfolgen (an vielen Stellen mehr als 10m) und der relativen Unsichtbarkeit archäologischer Befunde, sowohl in der archäologischen Landesaufnahme als auch bei konventionellen Prospektionen, eines geoarchäologischen Ansatzes bedürfte. Am Anfang des Projekts stand ein sorgfältiges Studium des vorhandenen geotechnischen und geomorphologischen Archivmaterials. Dies erlaubte es, ein geomorphologisches Modell des alluvialen Korridors zu erstellen, in dem das Potenzial der verschiedenen Abschnitte der Trasse aufgrund von archäologischen und geomorphologischen Überlegungen als niedrig, mittel und hoch eingestuft wurde. Die umsichtig integrierten Ergebnisse der geoarchäologischen Untersuchungen wurden daraufhin mit den technischen und konstruktiven Belangen der Strecke abgeglichen, um zu einem kosteneffektiven und logischen Ansatz für die archäologischen Ausgleichsmaßnahmen zu gelangen.

Im Rahmen der Geländeprospektionen, die der Erstellung des Modells folgten, wurden geophysikalische Untersuchungen fossiler Sedimentkörper und Drucksondierungen durchgeführt, und Bohrlöcher sowie konventionelle Testgruben und –schnitte angelegt. Diese Methoden kamen in Schlüsselbereichen wie dem Portal des Themsetunnels in Swanscombe Marsh und dem Ebbsfleet Tal zur Anwendung. Mit Hilfe des Projekts konnten obertägig nicht sichtbare archäologische Denkmale auf einer Reihe von Fundstellen erfolgreich lokalisiert werden. Von besonderer Bedeutung sind u. a. die umfangreichen Fundbereiche im Ebbsfleet Tal (Andrews *et al* 2011a–b; Barnett *et al* 2011; Biddulph *et al* 2011; Wenban-Smith *et al* forthcoming), die mesolithischen Flintstreuungen in der Tank Hill Road, Aveley (Leivers *et al* 2007), sowie die spät jungpaläolithischen und neolithischen Streuungen in der Swanscombe Marsh (in diesem Band). Weitere hier beschriebene Fundstellen umfassen eine *in situ* gefundene frühneolithische Flintstreuung in der Rainham Marsh (in der Nähe des neolithischen Fundplatzes Brookway Allotments; Meddens 1996), und Hinweise auf jahreszeitlich bedingte Aktivitäten kaiserzeitlicher und mittelalterlicher Zeitstellung, angedeutet u. a. durch Fundkonzentrationen von Keramik, Tierknochen und Meeresmuscheln. Die mittelalterliche Aktivität, die in das 11. bis 13. Jh. datiert, steht möglicherweise in Zusammenhang mit einer Landgewinnungsphase und dem Bau eines Seedeichs im Bereich des ehemaligen Priels Wennington Creek.

Insgesamt bestätigten die Untersuchungen, zumindest in den untersuchten Bereichen, dass Trassenabschnitte, für die ein geringes archäologisches Potenzial prognostiziert wurde, auch keine bedeutenden Hinweise auf menschliche Aktivität enthielten. Der Erfolg des Projekts lässt sich daher nicht nur anhand der Genauigkeit der Vorhersage des unterschiedlichen archäologischen Potenzials in verschiedenen Bereichen messen, sondern auch anhand der Tatsache, dass mithilfe des Projekts eine robuste und gut strukturierte Reaktion auf spezifische konstruktionsbedingte Beeinträchtigungen möglich war, und so größere Verzögerungen bei der Fertigstellung der HS1-Trasse vermieden werden konnten. Dieser Bericht liefert Argumente für einen geoarchäologischen Ansatz für die Ausgleichmaßnahmen der Beeinträchtigungen, die von zukünftigen Großbaustellen in alluvialen Bereichen zu erwarten sind.

Übersetzung: Jörn Schuster

Acknowledgements

The High Speed 1 (HS1; formerly the Channel Tunnel Rail Link) massive engineering and construction project commissioned a major programme of archaeological works, one of the largest ever undertaken in Britain. Rail Link Engineering's (RLE) in-house archaeology team which comprised Helen Glass, Jay Carver, Steve Haynes, Mark Turner and Brigitte Buss, project-managed all aspects of the work on behalf of Union Railways Ltd, the client organisation for the High Speed 1, during construction. Oxford and Wessex Archaeology would like to acknowledge and thank them individually and collectively for their constant assistance and support throughout all phases of the programme of archaeological work. They are further acknowledged, along with Lis Dyson of Kent County Council (KCC), for agreeing to the incorporation of results of the contiguous, KCC-funded excavation for the STDR-4 link road, in the Ebbsfleet Valley, into this publication.

The entire HS1 archaeology programme has been monitored by archaeologists from Kent County Council, Essex County Council and English Heritage and, in particular, thanks go to John Williams (KCC), Lis Dyson (KCC), Richard Havis (ECC), Peter Kendall (EH), Deborah Priddy (EH), Peter Murphy (EH), Dominique de Moulins (EH) and Jane Sidell (EH) for providing us with the benefit of their tremendous knowledge and advice. Professor Martin Bell, is thanked for reviewing the volume.

The joint venture was overseen by the chief executives of Wessex and Oxford Archaeology, Sue Davies and David Jennings, together with Clive Burrows and Simon Palmer. The management team was composed of John Dillon and Bob Williams.

The dedication and professionalism of all the archaeologists who worked on HS1 as part of the site team is gratefully acknowledged, particularly those who withstood the wettest winter on record in 2000–01. Although, it is not possible in this publication to name all of the participating technicians and assistant supervisors who worked so hard to complete recording work ahead of construction, the following contributions are highlighted.

The investigations at Temple Mills in the Lea Valley were managed for Wessex Archaeology by Andrew Crockett, and directed by Phil Harding and Hilary Valler.

The watching brief at Ripple Lane Tunnel Portal, Dagenham was managed for Wessex Archaeology by Mick Rawlings and directed by Hilary Valler.

The extensive watching brief on the service diversions across the North Thames marshes was managed for Oxford Archaeology by Stuart Foreman. The site director was Elizabeth Stafford, assisted by Iain Williamson, Mike Simms, Richard James, John Payne, Anna Wesley, Lorna O'Gorman, Wayne Sawtell, Ryan Whalley and Hugo Pinto.

The excavations at Tank Hill Road, Aveley, were managed for Wessex Archaeology by Andrew Crockett, evaluations were directed by Phil Harding, excavations by Jamie Wright and watching briefs by Mike Dinwiddy.

The excavation and watching brief at the Thames Crossing, Swanscombe were managed for Wessex Archaeology by Andrew Crockett, and directed by Caroline Budd, Hilary Valler and Dave Godden.

Excavations in the Lower Ebbsfleet Valley at Northfleet villa were managed for Oxford Archaeology by Stuart Foreman and Richard Brown. The Project Officer was Paul Murray. On-site production of digital mapping was carried out by Laura Hindmarsh, environmental processing by Richard James and finds management by Claire Rawlings and Rob Radford. Supervisors on the villa site were Emily Glass, John Payne, Simon Greenslade, Emma Noyce, Gerry Thacker and Mike Simms. The 'mill team' comprised Iain Williamson, Simon Pickstone, Simon Sworn, Stuart Milby and Neil Wigfield. Dana Goodburn-Brown (AMTEC) provided much conservation advice and on site specialist recording of the waterlogged wood was provided by Damian Goodburn (Museum of London Specialist Service).

Excavations in the Upper Ebbsfleet Valley at Springhead were managed for Wessex Archaeology by Mick Rawlings. Phil Andrews directed work on both the Sanctuary site and the Roadside settlement, with Mike Trevarthen acting as Project Officer on the latter. Amongst those who deserve special mention are Barry Hennessy, Hilary Valler, Neil Fitzpatrick, Steve Thompson and Nick Cooke. Rob De'Athe, John Martin and Barry Hennessy undertook various parts of the watching briefs at Springhead as well as in the surrounding area in 2002–3. Several of the site staff were present for substantial periods of the fieldwork and deserve mention, in particular Andrew Armstrong along with Emma Davidson and Howard Brown, as well as Rebecca Fitzpatrick, Claire Gannon, Richard Kelleher, Nick Plunkett, Gareth Thomas and the late Gary Wickenden.

Excavations for STDR-4 in the Ebbsfleet Valley were managed for Oxford Archaeology by Stuart Foreman. The Project Officer for the evaluation stage was Steve Lawrence and for the excavation, Andrew Mayes.

The lengthy and equally complex programme of post-excavation work for HS1, beginning in 2005, and undertaken by the Oxford Wessex Archaeology Joint Venture, was managed by Andrew Crockett of Wessex Archaeology. It is appropriate here at the outset to warmly thank all of the specialists and illustrators who have made contributions to the publication of the work and these are listed individually on the title page. The post-excavation team would like to specifically highlight and acknowledge the following contributions:

The co-ordination of much of the programme of finds assessment and analysis was undertaken by Lorraine Mepham and Leigh Allen. The programme of environmental assessment and analysis was co-ordinated by Catherine Barnett and Elizabeth Stafford, and assisted by Sarah Wyles, Hayley Clark, Dawn Irving and Luke Howarth. The post-excavation team are particularly grateful to Georgina Slater, principal illustrator for the project, for gathering together and ordering the large number of figures and plates and ensuring consistency in their style and quality. The worked flint from the Thames Crossing at Swanscombe, the Ebbsfleet Valley and Springhead was drawn by Sarah Lucas and Sophie Lamb. The Ebbsfleet Ware bowl from the STDR-4 investigations was photographed by Lucy Martin. The Tank Hill Road flints and the worked antler from Thames Crossing, Swanscombe were photographed by Elaine Wakefield.

Figures 1, 32–3, 40, 45–7, 50, 52, 54, 59–60, 78, 80, and 85 contain Ordnance Survey Data © Crown copyright and/or database right 2010. All rights reserved, Ordnance Survey Licence no. 100028190. Figures 17, 19, 21, 23, 25, 27, and 29 are based on 1:25,000 mapping reproduced by permission of Ordnance Survey on behalf of HMSO, © Crown copyright and database right 2013. All rights reserved, Ordnance Survey Licence no. 100028190. Figure 30 is based on 1:10,000 mapping reproduced by permission of Ordnance Survey on behalf of HMSO, © Crown copyright and database right 2013. All rights reserved, Ordnance Survey Licence no. 100028190. Figures 1–2, 4–6, 17, 19, 21, 23, 25, 27, 29–30, 59, 78–79 and 94 reproduced by permission of the British Geological Survey © NERC. All rights reserved. CP13/047. Plate 1 is reproduced courtesy of HS1; Plate 2 is reproduced courtesy of Richard Bates; Plate 3–4, 6, and 9 are reproduced courtesy of Martin Bates; Plate 5 is reproduced courtesy of Pre-Construct Archaeology.

Figure 6 is based on material first published in Miall 1996, fig. 8.18; Brown 1997, fig. 1.1; Walker and Catt 1984, fig. 2, and Figure 9 is based on illustrations first published in Dalrymple *et al* 1992, figs 7 and 14; Dalrymple 1992, figs 12 and 23.

Location of the archive

The HS1 archives associated with the Thames Holocene study will in due course be housed in accordance with the location of each contributing Event Code, as follows: all Event Codes within Greater London will be housed with the Museum of London's Archaeological Archive and Research Centre, Mortimer Wheeler House, 46 Eagle Wharf Road, London, N1 7ED; all Event Codes within the County of Essex will be housed at Thurrock Museum, Thameside Complex, Orsett Road, Grays, Essex, RM17 5DX under the accession code THK 4037; and all Event Codes within the County of Kent will be temporarily stored by Kent County Council at Dover Eastern Docks, pending resolution of museum storage provision within that county. It should be noted that in order to keep the records of the single Event Code ARC TMS00 (Thames Crossing) in one location, and on the basis of the relative significance of discoveries during the project, it has been agreed that all records for the project, which examined both the Essex and Kent Thames riverbank, will be held with the Kent archive. It is intended that the entire digital archive will, in due course, be deposited and made accessible via the Archaeology Data Service.

Part I
Introduction and Background

Chapter 1

Introduction

High Speed 1 (HS1; formerly the Channel Tunnel Rail Link), is the new high-speed railway linking London to the Continent via the Channel Tunnel (Fig 1). The route of HS1 passes through Kent in south-east England, connecting the tunnel portal at Folkestone via Ashford International to, Ebbsfleet International in north Kent, crossing under the Thames at Swanscombe and then through Essex and East London, via Stratford International to St Pancras International.

The massive engineering and construction project necessitated a major programme of archaeological works, one of the largest ever undertaken in Britain. Desk-based assessment (URL 1994) was followed by an extensive programme of evaluations comprising field walking, trial trenching, test pitting and borehole investigation, largely undertaken between 1994 and 1997. These investigations assessed the impact of the route on archaeological resources, with the aim of mitigating the impact of construction on this finite resource. Where archaeological sites could not be avoided or preserved *in situ* excavations were undertaken in advance of construction. The principal archaeological work for Section 2, commissioned by HS1 (as Union Railways North Ltd at that time), took place between September 2000 and March 2003, and formed part of an extensive programme of archaeological investigation, analysis and reporting carried out in advance of, during and after the construction of HS1.

This study, entitled Thames Holocene, focuses on the alluvial deposits that HS1 passes both over, and indeed through, not only within the River Thames floodplain, but also major tributaries of the Thames, including the Lea, Mar Dyke and Ebbsfleet.

The investigation of alluvial wetland areas within the UK (Coles and Coles 1996) can be traced back into the 19th century (eg, the discovery of the Brigg Raft

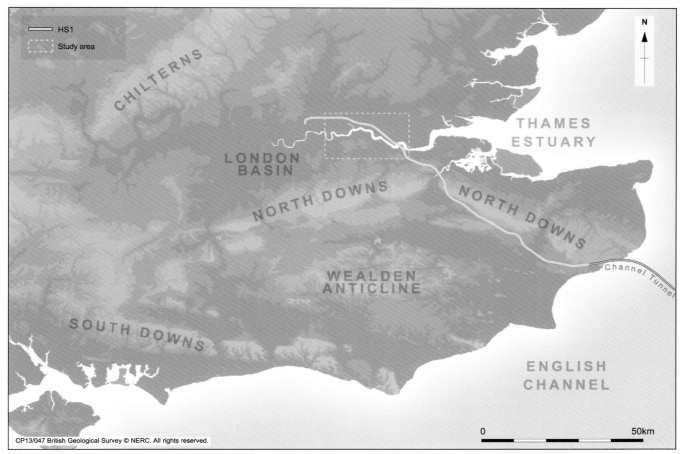

Figure 1 The route of HS1 through Kent and into London

– McGrail 1990) but it was only in the 1960s that wetland archaeology as a specialist area of study was first recognised (Van de Noort and O'Sullivan 2006). Since then nearly 50 years of archaeological research into wetland regions have been undertaken in the UK and foremost amongst these are studies focusing on the large, well-preserved prehistoric landscapes of the Somerset Wetlands (Coles and Coles 1986), the Fenland (Hall and Coles 1994), the North West Wetlands (Cowell and Innes 1994), the Humber Wetlands (Van de Noort and Davies 1993) and the Severn Levels (Bell 2007). By contrast, investigation of the Thames Estuary has been piecemeal and usually limited to the London Thames (eg, Milne *et al* 1997; Sidell *et al* 2000; 2002), although this picture is now changing (Seel 2001; Sidell 2003; Haughey 2003; 2007; Batchelor 2009). In most cases these studies have considered the landscape and stratigraphic context of the contained archaeological sites where it is the presence of waterlogged remains, often in undisturbed contexts and in association with the environmental archaeological evidence, which increases the significance and importance of these areas (Coles 1995).

Despite the numerous studies in these wetlands the prediction of locations where archaeological sites may exist beneath the alluvium remains difficult (Coles 1995; Deeben *et al* 1997; Bates 1998; Fulford *et al* 1997; Wilkinson and Bond 2001; Bates 2003; Challis and Howard 2003; Peeters 2006). In these wetland situations, considerable logistical and strategic problems are often encountered where the sequences may exceed 20m or more in depth and contain or bury sediments that potentially contain archaeological material from the last 12,000 years. As a result the sites are often beyond the reach of conventional survey and evaluation strategies for assessing likely sub-surface archaeological potential and their subsequent excavation (Bates *et al* 2000a; Peeters 2006). Coupled with the practical issues of working in such circumstances there are also conceptual issues to resolve regarding the nature of the buried resource and its remote identification.

It is precisely such difficulties that were faced during the construction of High Speed 1 (HS1, formerly known as the Channel Tunnel Rail Link) through the Thames and Medway Marshes, where approximately 18km (17%) of the total HS1 route length rests on alluvium deposited during the last *c* 12,000 years (Figs 1 and 2). The remainder of the HS1 route through Kent has been documented elsewhere (Booth *et al* 2011). These alluvial deposits were always considered likely to contain archaeological material but little was known of the true archaeological potential of these deposits (URL 1994). Consequently, the project faced considerable difficulties in attempting to devise a strategy to evaluate, identify and mitigate any archaeology buried within the footprint of the route corridor, which might include tunnel excavations, cut and cover operations, bridge foundations, piling and service diversions among the engineering impacts. In these circumstances it was therefore determined that a geoarchaeological approach

to the alluvial corridor would be adopted, through which commonly occurring relationships between sedimentary contexts and archaeology could be highlighted in order to allow predictions regarding the nature and the spatial distribution of areas of high archaeological potential. This process would rely heavily on extant geotechnical information (including that collected by project engineers for design of the scheme) for the route corridor linked to knowledge from previous archaeological and geological discoveries. The findings of the modelling would then inform the project team of the location of areas of high archaeological potential along the route corridor in advance of determining both detailed archaeological investigation and mitigation strategies and construction.

The project should also be viewed in the context of an on-going process of investigation associated with the infrastructure of the rail-link and the Channel Tunnel as well as development within the Thames corridor. Since the construction of the Channel Tunnel started in the late 1980s, geoarchaeological work has been associated with developments that included works at the Folkestone site of Holywell Coombe (Preece and Bridgland 1998) as well as the eastern part of HS1 (Booth *et al* 2011). At the same time, other projects in the Thames Estuary were also adopting a geoarchaeological approach to investigation including work on the Jubilee Line in Central London and in Southwark (Sidell *et al* 2000; 2002) and work on the A13 in East London (Stafford *et al* 2012).

This report describes the methods and approaches used in the project as well as the findings of elements of that survey. Unlike the many wetland archaeological projects recently undertaken in the UK (Coles and Coles 1986; Van de Noort and Davies 1993; Cowell and Innes 1994; Hall and Coles 1994; Bell 2007), where attempts to document regional archaeological histories are made, it is the objective of this volume to describe the methodology that was adopted to tackle these issues, to identify the location of any archaeology beneath the floodplain and to outline the nature of the results. The volume has been written in a manner that describes the way in which the project was undertaken from desk-top inception through strategy design and fieldwork to assessment and analysis. This structure was adopted in order to allow the authors to retrospectively critique the methods and approaches and critically evaluate the success of the project that had a lifespan of some 16 years, during which time methodologies and approaches to alluvial archaeology have seen significant changes. It is our hope firstly that the target audience for this volume is not just the alluvial archaeologist working in the lower reaches of river valleys in NW Europe, but the curators and consultant archaeologists currently in positions of responsibility who may learn from the successes and failures of our approach to this unique set of circumstances. Through this process of self-analysis more robust approaches to alluvial archaeology of lowland rivers and estuaries can be developed in the future. The success or otherwise of the project is measured both in terms of correctly identifying the location of buried archaeological material and confirming the absence of material from those areas of the route considered unlikely to contain archaeological material. That this has been achieved in specified locations along the route corridor (eg, at Tank Hill Road and Thames River Crossing) appears to be justification for this approach. However, we do not restrict ourselves to purely methodological approaches and consequently in the final chapter a consideration is made of the information gained regarding human activity within the route corridor, the palaeoenvironmental data pertaining to landscape evolution, and an evaluation of the success of the approach. The reader is cautioned that this volume is not an attempt to produce a narrative for the development of the Lower Thames in geological and archaeological terms over the last 12,000 years.

This publication is also part of an overall strategy to publish results from the rail link project and should be read in conjunction with the site focused reports (Andrews *et al* 2011a; Leivers *et al* 2007; Barnett *et al* forthcoming; Wenban-Smith *et al* forthcoming). Two sites or areas investigated within the Thames alluvial corridor area are omitted from detailed discussion in this report. The excavation of a major archaeological site at Tank Hill Road (Fig 2; Leivers *et al* 2007) was deemed sufficiently important to form a detailed, stand-alone publication and only an outline summary of the results from this site are presented here. Secondly the Ebbsfleet Valley (Fig 2; Andrews *et al* 2011a; Wenban-Smith *et al*

forthcoming) was identified as being a highly complex area in which Pleistocene and Holocene deposits were closely linked and a variety of archaeological materials were present. For this reason only outline summaries are given here.

A further note should be made regarding the duration and nature of the process of investigation undertaken during the lifetime of the project. The complex, varied and fragmentary nature of many of the sequences sampled and recorded, across the 18km of the alluvial corridor, during the 10 years or so between inception of the project and the final phases of field investigation have resulted in a fragmentary archive of data collected by a number of organisations. As a consequence it has been difficult for any one individual to have and maintain an overview of the project from start to finish. One of the authors (MB) has, however, followed the project from an early stage (1994) and has attempted to integrate and provide a seamless overview, the other author (ES) being involved in the HS1 fieldwork for Oxford Archaeology from 1998. Additionally, it should be noted that because of the long duration of the project the initial development of models and ideas used to drive the project began in 1994 and as a result the models used are based on data available in the middle 1990s. Another key issue regarding the data presented in this volume is the nature of the post-excavation strategy adopted in the project. In many cases investigation of samples from interventions consisted of study to assessment level only. This is typically the

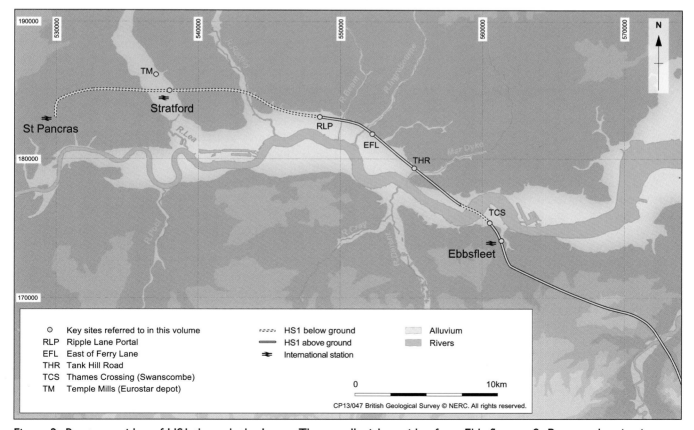

Figure 2 Route corridor of HS1 through the Lower Thames alluvial corridor from Ebbsfleet to St Pancras showing its position relative to alluvial and non-alluvial

case where archaeological material was absent or deemed to be of low significance. As a consequence, detailed analysis level studies were only carried out at Temple Mills and the Thames River Crossing. Elsewhere information (where relevant) is presented from assessment investigations only. Because of the geoarchaeological approach adopted by this study, key factors of importance were to determine environments of deposition for sedimentary units and (where possible) to ascribe age to the sequences. Assessment level investigation in most cases documented these traits to an adequate level to test the robustness of the original desk-top model. This approach reduced the need to investigate in detail the large number of sampling points investigated and limited the inherent expense in undertaking analysis on these numerous sequences. However, it should be made clear that the individual sequences investigated only to assessment level cannot be fully detailed or understood without further analysis. The requirement for such analysis has been prioritised by the degree of relationship with archaeological remains, where known, and with the key aims of this study against the availability of finite resources.

The Route Corridor Described

The route corridor linked to the Thames alluvium consists of four main areas (Fig 2) (the areas of bored tunnels within the bedrock towards St Pancras are not considered in this report and the results of investigations within those areas have been published elsewhere (eg, Emery and Wooldridge 2011). These are:

- The Lea Valley region; associated with the Stratford International Station (Stratford Box) and the Temple Mills engineering works;
- The North Thames Marshes; the main alluvial corridor from the Ripple Lane Portal to Purfleet;
- The Thames Crossing sector; either side of the Thames tunnel;
- The Ebbsfleet Valley.

Today much of the area occupied by HS1 crosses marshland that has seen recent industrial use either as factories, warehousing or hard standing, or it occupies land adjacent to existing rail corridors. The Lea Valley area represents an area of intense urban activity including domestic and rural activity since at least the mid-19th century, and most recently the site of the Olympic Park. By contrast, much of the main alluvial corridor area along the north bank of the Thames has seen predominantly industrial activity only in the last 200 years. Prior to the early 19th century both areas will have been predominantly rural with occasional small settlements and ephemeral activity associated with exploitation of the marshland and localised wharfs along the river frontage.

The location of much of the route across the estuarine alluvium is significant because such tracts of land are a microcosm of much of our coastal wetland areas on which significant pressures currently exist. These areas (particularly in the south-east) are at risk from greenfield industrial and dock development (eg, the new development at London Gateway near Stanford-le-Hope, Biddulph *et al* 2012), brownfield regeneration, replacement and up grading of sea defences in response to global warming, modernisation of the transport networks and the construction of energy installations. In all cases archaeological responses to development would be similar at times and therefore the present study provides a testing ground for the approach, methodology and models required for many of these other developments.

Engineering of the Route Corridor

The route corridor east from the St Pancras terminal lies in tunnels until Stratford is reached where the tunnels come to the surface. The excavations for the station at Stratford were known as the Stratford Box and included cut and cover excavations at either end to allow access to tunnelled sections west to the terminus and east towards Ripple Lane. Stratford Box was 1070m long, up to 50m wide and 16–22m deep. Tunnels carry the line eastwards to Ripple Lane where the tracks emerge through Ripple Lane Portal onto a surface lain formation.

The formation along the north bank of the Thames rests on a piled foundation that runs parallel to existing tracks of the London, Tilbury and Southend Railway for much of the distance. Crossings of north bank Thames tributaries such as the Ingrebourne (Rainham Creek) and Mar Dyke are made on viaducts with extensively piled foundations. Between the Thames Marshes at Mar Dyke and the approaches to the Thames tunnel the rail corridor crosses the Purfleet Anticline via a cutting before exiting the cutting on a steeply graded viaduct descending towards the cut and cover approach to the Thames tunnel.

The Thames crossing is a 3.55km long alignment that is dominated by a 2.5km bored tunnel with a 140m long cut and cover and 160m long retained wall at the north end and a 590m long cut and cover and 150m long retained wall at the south end. Exiting the cut and cover on the south bank the formation climbs passing below the North Kent Line and through a shallow cutting through Chalk and superficial deposits to enter the Ebbsfleet Valley and Ebbsfleet International. Beyond the station the railway crosses the Ebbsfleet and proceeds in a south-easterly direction to form a junction with the branch southwards that carried the line towards Waterloo Station before the high-speed line was completed.

Archaeological Concerns

The principal archaeological issues of concern within the route corridor were highlighted early in the project history when it was recognised that the original desk-top assessment of historic and cultural effects (URL 1994) contained limited information regarding archaeology from the alluvium. Although little information was available from the alluvial sectors of the route corridor it was recognised that potential existed within the wet marshland areas to produce archaeological remains.

These concerns were addressed through the gradual development of a geoarchaeological programme of works initially associated with desk-top data sources for specific sites already identified as problematic, that were subsequently developed into field surveys and assessments. For example, an early desk-top survey of the Purfleet cutting area was followed by initial borehole and trial pit excavations along the line of projected impact. Similar small-scale investigations were undertaken in the Ebbsfleet Valley. However, the early recognition of the problem led to a project focused on using the archive of geotechnical data collected and held at the Geotechnical Management Unit (GMU) within the engineering division of the design team. Investigation of these sources led directly to the production of a geoarchaeological evaluation of the route corridor that was produced by one of the authors (MB) for Oxford Archaeology in 1999 (URN and URS 1999).

In parallel with the emerging geoarchaeological approach to the route corridor, scheme wide project research objectives were being developed (URS 1997) that focused attention on generic issues related to regional and period specific agendas. Together these twin approaches formed the basis for the archaeological response and it is to the former, geoarchaeological, approach that the current volume is based around.

The Alluvial Corridor

The focus of this publication is the alluvial corridor of HS1 within the Thames area, broadly between Ebbsfleet and Stratford International stations (Fig 2). At this point consideration needs to be given to the definition of this term particularly with reference to those areas of HS1 omitted from this study (ie, non-alluvial areas). The term alluvium is used in British Geological Survey (BGS) mapping to define areas of deposit where fine-grained sediments deposited by water (river) action predominate. However, although useful and widely accepted, it is a problematic term, as it frequently confuses several issues. No specific textural properties or sediment properties are implied by this term and those deposits mapped as alluvial sediments in southern England (including the HS1 corridor) might include coarse gravels and sands (channel fills), sands and silts (channel margins and levees), silts and variably sandy or clayey silts (flood overbank deposits). Additionally, peats and other organic deposits (eg, tufa, calcareous marls, etc) may be present. There is also frequently assumed to be a depositional connection between alluvium and a riverine depositional system which is often tenuous,

indeed, borehole logs often describe all fine grained sediments as 'alluvial' where they may be estuarine, lacustrine, or even marine in depositional origin.

In geological mapping, alluvium, as a lithostratigraphic term, is often confused with a chronostratigraphic definition of being deposited in the Holocene (the last 11,700 years; *sensu* Walker *et al* 2009). This is unsatisfactory as it then renders subsurface coarse clastic deposits difficult to map. For example, Pleistocene river gravels are 'alluvial' in origin but variably mapped as 'Terrace Gravels' or 'Floodplain Gravels' in the Thames area. River gravels located underlying silty-clay Holocene deposits may be variably interpreted as either Pleistocene or Holocene in age by loggers without evidence for age being presented. This has significant archaeological implications.

These issues combine to make conventionally mapped 'alluvium' as mapped by the BGS of limited value for predicting either facies characteristics (the term facies is used in geology to refer to a body of rock or sediment with specified characteristics that reflect the process and environments of deposition that control sedimentation) or archaeological potential. Further problems pertain to the conjunction with valley floor topographic locations. While much alluvium may be proximal to active stream/river networks this need not be the case particularly where historic drainage has occurred or seasonal 'winterbourne' streams are ephemerally active in Chalk/Limestone geology. In some areas, colluvium as mapped may be relic alluvium from formerly more extensive floodplains.

Also, while deposition from water may typify the process origin of the deposit it should be noted that most river floodplain deposition is i) episodic ii) may involve periodic incursion into an otherwise well-drained cultivated or wooded landscape and iii) does not preclude other forms of deposition (eg, deposition of aeolian dusts). Therefore, while much of a lithostratigraphic alluvial sequence may appear to be characterised by deposition from a water-body, for much of the time period (chronosequence) represented by the alluvial sediments the area of deposition may be both suitable for occupation and attractive for subsistence over prehistoric timescales.

The focus of this study is the alluvium of the River Thames, defined by the limits of alluvium as mapped by the BGS (including marine or estuarine alluvium) or the floodplain of the river. It is recognised that under this broad classification sediments will be present that were deposited by a range of processes and indeed probably bury older Pleistocene sands, gravels and finer sediments (possibly including Pleistocene alluvium in places). Consequently, while the focus of this study has been on the Holocene sediments, elements of the record preserved beneath the floodplain relate to Late Devensian times (and possible older phases within the Late Pleistocene) are also dealt with. Omitted from this study are older alluvial deposits including Head, Brickearth and River Terrace Deposits (*sensu* BGS mapping) present above the river floodplain area.

Chapter 2

Aims and Objectives of the Study

The archaeological investigation of the alluvial tract of HS1 (Fig 2) was undertaken in a phased way that was determined by the perceived difficulties in evaluating and investigating the alluvial sequences as well as restrictions imposed by the engineering constraints of the construction project (see Chap 1, *Engineering of the route corridor*). Initial concerns regarding a perceived lack of archaeological potential of the alluvial tract were raised early in the project lifetime due to the apparent absence of archaeological material identified from the areas of alluvium within the route corridor (URL 1994). Consequently, it was recognised that the results of the historical and cultural resource evaluation of this area would require further consideration and the conclusions require additional investigation before they were resolved. Although this work had highlighted the paucity of data pertaining to the archaeological sequences of the alluvial zones where, with the exception of occasional sites of known prehistoric age (eg, in the Rainham area), only relatively recent (post-medieval) features were noted from these areas. In response an alternative strategy for evaluation was devised (Barham and Bates 1994; 1995) commencing with a detailed desk-top evaluation of extant geotechnical results. The outcome of the desk-top evaluation (URN and URS 1999) was a report detailing the anticipated nature and thickness of the alluvium along the route corridor. Linked to this was the construction of a geoarchaeological model including an assessment of the likely areas of high archaeological potential. The aims of the desk-top evaluation (1999) were to:

- Examine evaluation strategies commonly used within areas containing deeply stratified alluvium;

- Examine the likely relationship between archaeological sites and sedimentary contexts within such areas;

- Examine the likely nature of the stratigraphy within the alluvial areas of HS1 with particular reference to determining the age of the sediment sequences and the nature of the 3-D stratigraphic architecture of the sequences.

Following production of the report, a series of appropriate strategies were developed to address the issues raised in the desk-top evaluation. These strategies varied along the route corridor in relation not only to the perceived nature of the archaeological potential but also to the impact of the construction. In particular attention was paid to the relationship between the construction impact/nature and depth and location of the potential archaeology. A variety of approaches were adopted that are described in this report.

The aims and objectives of the study were developed through an academic framework (*Archaeological Research Strategy*) based on the sub-division of HS1 into a series of distinct landscape zones with an identifiable historical character as well as period specific time slices. This was placed along-side the engineering and geotechnical issues to refine the project aims and objectives.

Chapter 3

Regional Background to the Route Corridor

The Lower Thames extends from Blackfriars to the Shorne Marshes and forms the inner part of the Thames Estuary (Fig 3; Pl 1). The estuary of the Thames is classified as a tide dominated estuary (*sensu* Dalrymple *et al* 1992) with major sand bars within the outer estuary area (marine dominated zone) and an inner mixed energy zone with tidal meanders. The floodplain associated with HS1, which is coincident with the mixed energy zone of tidal meanders, is widest between the north bank Roding and Ingrebourne tributaries where a maximum distance of some 4.5km is attained (Fig 2). Today the Thames Estuary extends 100 miles (*c* 161km) from the tidal limit at Teddington to the estuary mouth at Sunk Head where it is 49 miles (*c* 79km) across between Margate and Orford Ness.

Presently the floodplain is managed to prevent flooding during high tides and the history of marshland reclamation is of the sequential construction of sea walls and drying out of the protected land since at least Norman times. The first real evidence of river wall embankments comes from the 13th century (Sturman 1961). Maintenance of the marshlands became an increasing concern over time, yet, despite concerted efforts, many occurrences of breaches in the sea wall are noted throughout the medieval and post-medieval periods (Whitaker 1889). Continual adaptation of the sea walls has seen its most recent manifestation in the construction of the Thames Barrage and 300km of associated sea defences have resulted in the present situation where extensive development is being encouraged in the low lying areas behind the sea wall. This area of the floodplain is today dominated by urban or industrial development, with increasing grassland and agricultural areas, and especially pasture, towards the estuary mouth in the east. Intertidal mudflats fringe the modern channel and expose relics of former floodplains at low tide, which are subject to increasing amounts of erosion associated with the industrial and leisure use of the river. Today the estuary experiences sediment input from both the freshwater riverine and marine zones. Active erosion is also taking places within the area (where permitted to do so).

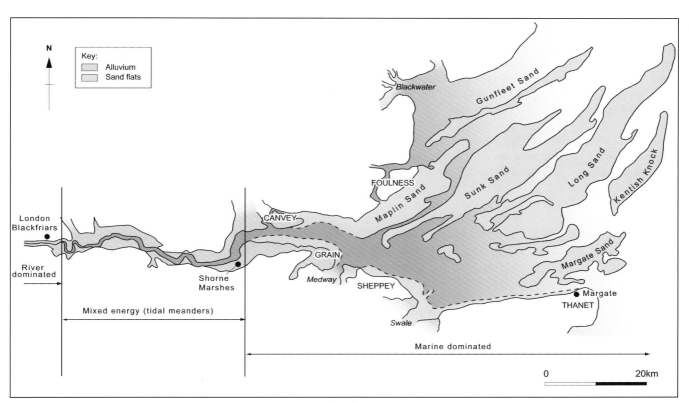

Figure 3 Sub-division of the Thames Estuary and location of different estuary zones

Bedrock Geology

South-east England includes the London Basin and the Weald (Sherlock 1947; Gallois 1965; Sumbler 1996; Ellison 2004) (Fig 4). The Chalk escarpment forming the Chiltern Hills, trending from south-west to north-east through Berkshire and Hertfordshire, dominates the London Basin. The basin is bounded by the North Downs chalk to the south and the Chilterns to the north. In the centre of the basin, within the area of the present day Thames Valley, younger Eocene sediments fill in the axis of the synclinal feature (Sherlock 1947; Sumbler 1996; Ellison 2004).

Bedrock geology within the study area of the London Basin is likely to have played an important role in the formation of the superficial sediments of the route corridor. For example, the soft Eocene sediments (such as the clays of the London Clay) provide the source for the clays and silts forming much of the Holocene lithologies throughout the estuary area (Kirby 1969; 1990). Conversely, the harder chalks of the Chilterns and North Downs have provided source areas for the flints that form most of the Pleistocene gravels now preserved along the valley margins and beneath much of the alluvium. Other factors relating to differences in bedrock type include both the influence on local topography and geomorphology as well as preservation potential within the deposited sediment stack. For example, sediments accumulating close to Chalk outcrops are more likely to contain carbonate based fossils than sequences distant from carbonate sources where ground pH is lower. Structural controls on river behaviour are also noted (for example the position of the Purfleet anticline has influenced the position of the Thames channel (Bridgland 1994).

Critical to our understanding of both the Pleistocene and Holocene sediments in the estuary is the neotectonic history of the region. Progressive (isostatic) uplift of south-east England during the Pleistocene (Maddy 1997; Westaway et al 2002; 2006) is attested to by the presence of terraces along the valley sides beneath which fluvial sediments are preserved (Gibbard 1985; 1994; Bridgland 1994, see Fig 5). The degree of effect of isostasy on Holocene sequences is debatable (Devoy 1979; 1982; Bingley et al 1999; Sidell 2003; Shennan et al 2012) although evidence from the area suggests to some that subsidence characterised much of the last c 12,000 years (Churchill 1965; Devoy 1979; 1982; Greensmith and Tucker 1980; Kelsey 1972; Shennan 1983; 1987; 1989a; 1989b; Long 1995).

Pleistocene Geology and Geomorphology

The recent geological development of the area and the establishment of the modern topography, including the Thames Estuary, have been a result of major drainage basin modifications during the Quaternary and in particular events during the last 500,000 years. The

Plate 1 Aerial view of the Thames Estuary, Swanscombe prior to construction of HS1

early Middle Pleistocene course of the River Thames has been identified far to the north of the modern channel where drainage occurred through the Vale of St Albans and into eastern Essex (Gibbard 1977; 1985) prior to its diversion during the Anglian cold stage. During this time the River Medway drained across the present-day mouth of the Thames northwards to converge with the ancestral Thames in eastern Essex (Bridgland 1983; 1994; 1999; 2003). The creation of the modern Thames Valley downstream of Reading and the deposition of the sedimentary record preserved in the London area today commenced with the advance of the Anglian ice and the blocking of the Vale of St Albans c 423–478ka BP.

Deposition of sediments in the modern Thames Valley began in the Late Anglian stage (Table 1) and continued intermittently throughout the later Middle and Upper Pleistocene (Gibbard 1985; 1994; Bridgland 1994). These bodies of sediment including sands, gravels and silts (remnants of former Thames floodplains) were subsequently incised by fluvial activity during periods of lowered sea-level and uplift to create terraces (Bridgland 2006). The extent of the modern floodplain was primarily defined by fluvial downcutting prior to the Last Glacial Maximum. At this time, erosion of the valley base appears to have been accompanied by erosion of both bedrock and older fluvial sediments along the valley sides. The most recent episodes of gravel deposition, responsible for the formation of the valley bottom gravels (or Shepperton Gravels) form the template onto which most of the alluvial and estuarine sedimentation occurred during the Holocene. These deposits have been traced by Gibbard (1994) as a spread of variable thickness downstream into the HS1 area and are commonly thought to belong to the very Late Devensian period (c 12ka–17ka BP).

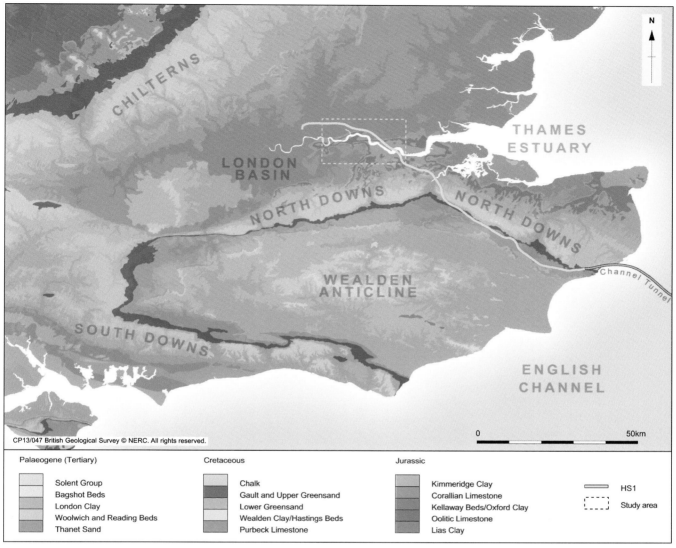

Palaeogene (Tertiary)	Cretaceous	Jurassic	
Solent Group	Chalk	Kimmeridge Clay	HS1
Bagshot Beds	Gault and Upper Greensand	Corallian Limestone	
London Clay	Lower Greensand	Kellaway Beds/Oxford Clay	Study area
Woolwich and Reading Beds	Wealden Clay/Hastings Beds	Oolitic Limestone	
Thanet Sand	Purbeck Limestone	Lias Clay	

Figure 4 Regional bedrock geology for south-east England

Table 1 The Quaternary sequence in the lower reaches of the Thames (from Bridgland 1995)

Terrace Formation	Members	Climate	Age	$\delta^{18}O$ Stage
Tilbury	Tilbury Alluvial Deposits	Warm	Holocene	1
Shepperton	Shepperton Gravel	Cold	Devensian	2
East Tilbury Marshes	East Tilbury Marshes Upper Gravel	Cold	Devensian	5d-2
	Trafalgar Square deposits	Warm	Ipswichian	5e
	East Tilbury Marshes Lower Gravel	Cold	Late Saalian	6
Mucking	Mucking Upper Gravel	Cold	Late Saalian	6
	Aveley Sands and Silts	Warm	Intra-Saalian Interglacial	7
	Mucking Lower Gravel	Cold	Intra-Saalian	8
Corbets Tey	Corbets Tey Upper Gravel	Cold	Intra-Saalian	8
	Purfleet Silts and Sands	Warm	Intra-Saalian Interglacial	9
	Corbets Tey Lower Gravel	Cold	Late Anglian?	10
Orsett Heath	Orsett Heath Upper Gravel	Cold	Late Anglian?	10
	Swanscombe interglacial deposits	Warm	Hoxnian?	11
	Orsett Heath Lower Gravel	Cold	Anglian	12
Black Park	Not presently recognised	Cold	Anglian	12
Lowestoft	Hornchurch Till	Cold (full glacial)	Anglian (Lowestoft Stadial)	12

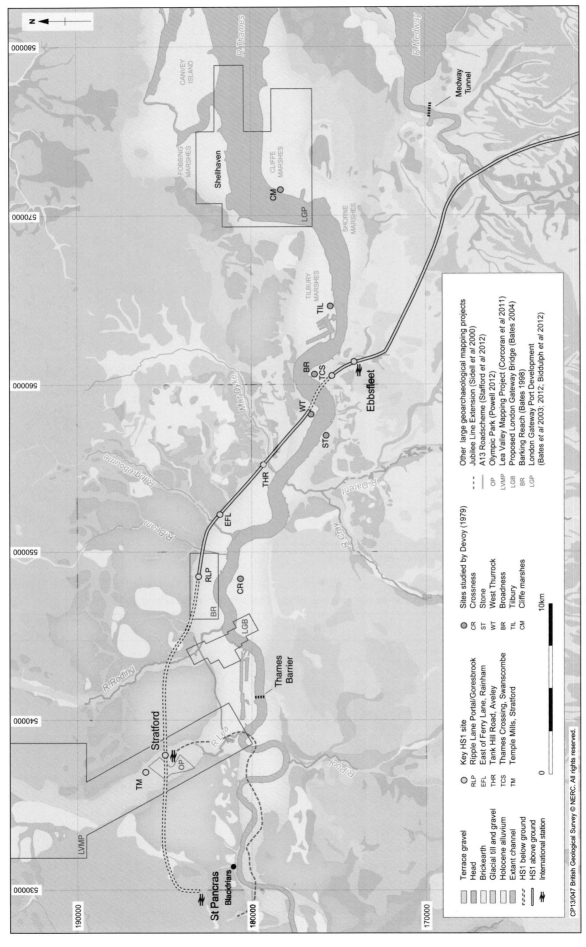

Figure 5 Quaternary geology of the Thames alluvial corridor showing the distribution of the main Pleistocene and Holocene deposits

This template, on which Holocene sediments were deposited, was created by fluvial activity under cold climate conditions during the Late Pleistocene (c 12ka–15ka BP). Contemporary global sea-level during these phases was perhaps between 25m and 125m lower than at the present time (eg, Yokoyama *et al* 2000 estimate a level of 120m below present during the Last Glacial Maximum at *c* 26.5ka to 20 ka BP, see also Clark *et al* 2012), rising through the Late Devensian period and into the Holocene. Sedimentary environments characterising this phase were dominated by those in which gravel and sand were the principal sediments deposited. Gibbard considers that the gravels of the Lower Thames were deposited under conditions that closely approximate to those of the River Donjek, Yukon (ie, the Donjek depositional model proposed by Miall 1977; 1996; Gibbard 1994) accumulating in a braided river environment (Fig 6) (Pl 2).

Of particular importance, both in terms of correlation, as well as determining the location of individual sand and gravel bodies in a given area, is the gradient exhibited by these terraces and their underlying sediment sequences. In all cases these sand and gravel bodies are known to dip downstream and individual terraces appear at lower elevation closer to the mouth of the modern estuary. The consequence of this dip is that older, higher terraces (and their underlying deposits) are likely to disappear beneath the floodplain in a downstream direction. For example, the East Tilbury Marshes Gravel lies beneath the floodplain downstream of Stone Marshes and boreholes for the Dartford Tunnel clearly indicate a wedge of sand and gravel buried beneath Holocene alluvium on the south bank of the Thames (Gibbard 1994).

Pleistocene sediments in the area are known to be relatively rich in Palaeolithic artefacts (flint tools) (Wymer 1968; 1999) although there appears to be a tendency towards declining numbers of artefacts in those deposits of younger age occurring at lower elevations in the landscape (Ashton and Lewis 2002) and very little material (if any) has ever been recovered from the sub-alluvial gravel (Shepperton Gravel). Palaeontological material (Bridgland *et al* 2004; Bridgland and Schreve 2004) may also be present in the Pleistocene deposits. A wide range of evidence has been recovered from these deposits including large and small mammals as well as plant, insect and molluscan material (Bridgland 1994). These have been used successfully to reconstruct local environments of deposition, regionally applicable climate signals and sea-level histories.

Holocene Geology and Geomorphology

Holocene sediments form a wedge thickening downstream to reach a maximum thickness of 35m east of the study area at Canvey Island (Marsland 1986). The Holocene deposits bury the complex composite Late Pleistocene surface underlain by Late Devensian gravels (Shepperton Gravels) in places but by older Pleistocene

Plate 2   Braided river environment Alaska, perhaps similar to the Lower Thames c 15ka BP

sediments (in all probability the East Tilbury Marshes Gravel) elsewhere. Between these two bodies of sediment colluvial and solifluction deposits may mantle the bedrock surface. Finally bedrock may well directly underlie the alluvium locally (Figs 7 and 8).

The nature of the sediments (Fig 7) burying the bedrock or pre-Holocene deposits have, with one exception, only been described superficially or treated on a site by site basis. No floodplain-wide survey has been conducted and consequently our knowledge of these sequences and their temporal evolution remains patchy. It is also recognised that sequences tend to be considered in a relatively simplified way where a generally useful model (such as that developed by Devoy (1977; 1979) or Long *et al* (2000)) is extrapolated by others across the full floodplain from channel margins to floodplain margins sometimes without detailed consideration of the likely complexity in environments across space. For example the presence of major tributaries, areas of impeded drainage or topographic features are all likely to modify the broad estuary based model at the localised scale.

An early account of the alluvium, in particular the buried sub-fossil forest now know to be present through much of the floodplain, was made at Blackwall by Pepys when he wrote in his diary entry on 22 September 1665:

… that in digging his late Docke, he did 12 foot under ground find perfect trees over-covered with earth. Nut trees, with the branches and the very nuts upon them; some of whose nuts he

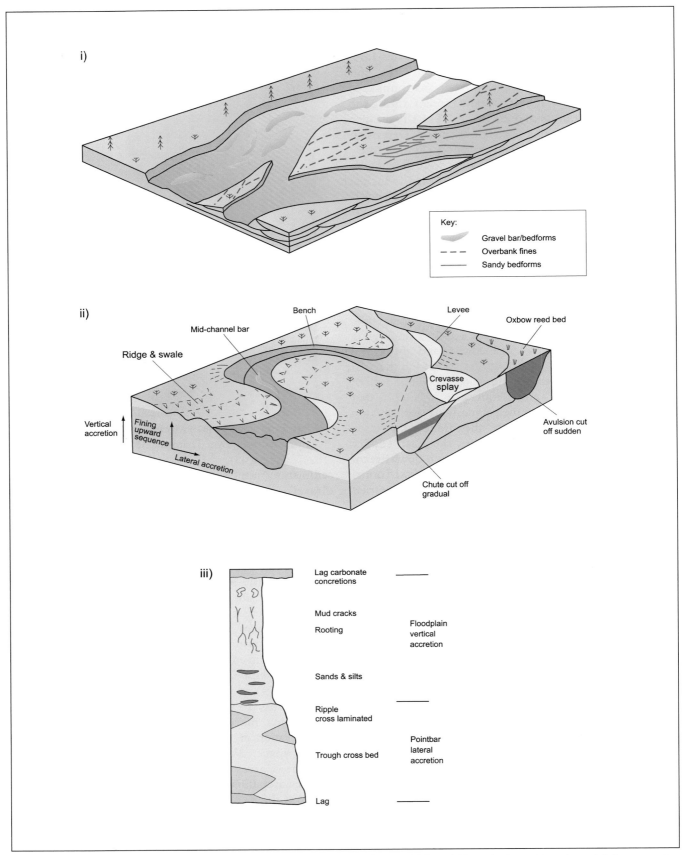

Figure 6 Models for explaining sediment sequences in the Lower Thames Valley: i) Donjek depositional model (low stand phase dominated by braided channel environments within active floodplain) (from Miall 1996); ii) Meandering river model (high stand phase characterised by single channel and stable floodplain) (from Brown 1997); iii) Stratigraphic column through meandering floodplain sequence (from Walker and Catt 1984)

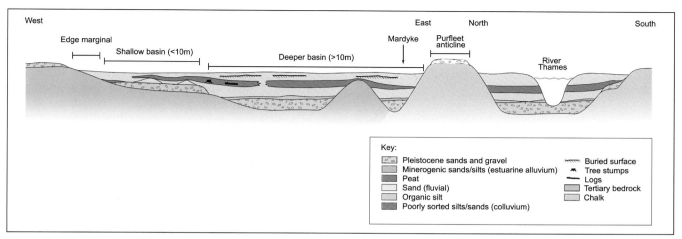

Figure 7 Schematic profile of sediments in the Thames Estuary along the route corridor. Note the distribution of at least two stratigraphically separated sets of buried gravels, the thinning of Holocene alluvium upstream and the intermittent distribution of peats and buried soils within the profile

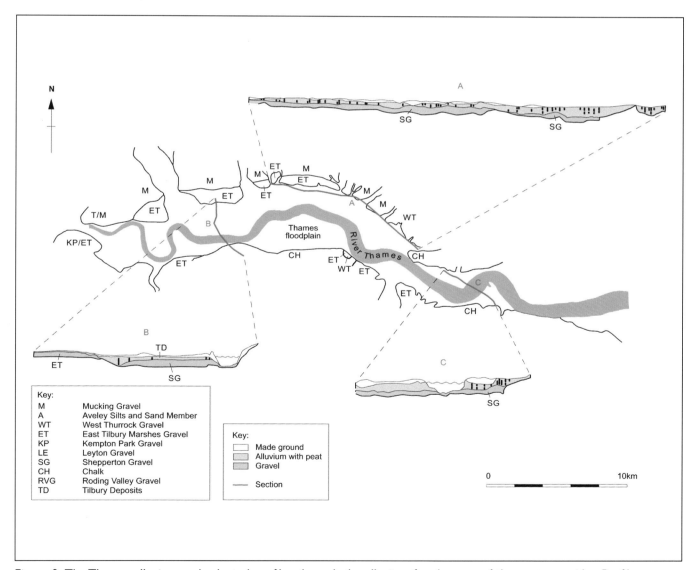

Figure 8 The Thames alluvium and selected profiles through the alluvium for the area of the route corridor. Profiles were generated from borehole information held by the Geotechnical Management Unit (GMU) for the project and the illustrations were constructed at an early stage of the project to enable regional patterns of sediment distribution to be understood within the context of the rail corridor

showed us. Their shells black with age, and their kernell, upon opening, decayed, but their shell perfectly hard as ever. And a yew tree he showed us (upon which, he says, the very ivy was taken up whole about it), which upon cutting with an addes [adze], we found to be rather harder than the living tree usually is.

Additional detail was given by Rev. Derham in 1712 when peat was discovered following a breach of the river in Dagenham and Havering Marshes (Whitaker 1889). Here he describes:

… the trees were all, as far as I could perceive, of one sort, except only one, which was manifestly a large Oak, with the greatest part of its Bark on, and some of its Heads and Roots. The rest of the Trees the Country People … take to be Yew: And so did I myself imagine them to be, from the hardness, toughness, and weight of the Wood.

He goes on to state:

I could see all along the Shores vast Numbers of the Stumps of those Subterraneous trees, remaining in the very same posture in which they grew, with their Roots running some down, some branching and spreading about in the Earth… Some of those Stumps I thought had signs of the axe.

Following this, descriptions have been provided by Lyell (1832), Spurrell (1885a; 1889), Whitaker (1889), Dewey and Bromehead (1921), Bromehead (1925), Dewey *et al* (1924), Dines and Edmunds (1925) and Churchill (1965). However, within the Thames Estuary, the most influential publications on the floodplain are those of Devoy (1977; 1979; 1980; 1982), based on work undertaken during the early 1970s, in which borehole stratigraphies were integrated with biostratigraphic studies to infer successive phases of marine transgressions and regressions. In this scheme peats were indicative of relative falls in sea-level (regressive phases) while clay-silt, minerogenic units were indicative of relative rises of sea-level (transgressive phases).

The work of Devoy typified geomorphological research work in the area at a time when attempts were being undertaken to establish regionally applicable relative sea-level curves, calibrate long term tectonic movements and establish biostratigraphic schemes (Churchill 1965; Devoy 1979; 1982; Greensmith and Tucker 1980; Kelsey 1972; Shennan 1983; 1987; 1989a; 1989b; Long 1995; Long and Shennan 1993; Long and Roberts 1997). Long term trends in sea-level indicate a progressive rise in sea-level datums following the sea-level minimum at the Glacial Maximum at *c* 26.5ka to 20ka (Clark *et al* 2012) to *c* 7ka BP (Late Mesolithic), minor fluctuations occurred within a slowed overall trend of rising levels (Shennan *et al* 2012). These sea-level changes have accompanied climatic change as a consequence of deglaciation and the development of the present climatic regime. However, these regional scale surveys cannot define local environments of deposition

or examine spatial heterogeneity in the floodplain during sequence development for the individual sites in question here. More recently a simplified model for floodplain development has been presented by Long *et al* (2000). A similar model was presented by Bates and Whittaker (2004) that examined the likely impact of these changes on human activity.

In contrast to these regional studies the last 20 years has seen a number of more detailed, site-specific investigations undertaken in association with archaeological investigations. These investigations have often been developer-led projects in which recording of alluvial sequences has taken place in conjunction with archaeological excavations. Larger projects include observations along the Jubilee Line Extension (Sidell *et al* 2000), the A13 (Stafford *et al* 2012), the Barking Reach area (Bates 1998; Bates and Bates 2000; Bates and Whittaker 2004), the Lea Valley Mapping Project (Corcoran *et al* 2011), the Olympic Park in the Lea Valley (Powell 2012) and the London Gateway Port Development at Shellhaven, Essex (Bates *et al* 2012; Biddulph *et al* 2012) (locations for these projects are shown in Fig 5). There are numerous individual site reports and some published journal articles (eg, Carew *et al* 2009; Crockett *et al* 2002; Sidell 2003; Sidell *et al* 1997; Sidell *et al* 2002; Wilkinson *et al* 2000). In the majority of cases these are restricted to the London end of the HS1 corridor, or the margins rather than the deeper parts of the floodplain.

Generally, the earliest elements of the sedimentary stack accumulating on the topographic template include fluvial sediments associated with the earliest, pre-transgressive phases of the Holocene record or the inner margin of the estuarine wedge in the lower reaches of the Thames Estuary (Fig 9) (this zone can be expected to migrate up and down stream in relation to changes in relative sea-level rates). Where the sediments form the earliest, pre-transgressive elements of the Holocene stack they will rest unconformably on the Late Pleistocene gravels of the Shepperton Gravel or the incised bedrock surface. Sediments associated with the fluvial elements of the stack are likely to relate to the meandering system type of Walker and Cant (1984) consisting of active channel, point bar, natural levees, floodplain and abandoned channel cut-off environments (Fig 6). Sediment types range from gravels to clayey-silts and peats. Predictable relationships exist between environments of deposition and sediment types across space and up-profile as illustrated in Figure 6. Typically these sediments are thin and intermittently preserved across the region. In addition to the fluvial sediments localised pockets of peat have been shown to be present across the region forming from the Late Glacial period onwards in hollows on the gravel surface (eg, at Bramcote Green in south London (Thomas and Rackham 1996)).

By contrast the estuarine elements of the stratigraphic stack, associated with brackish and marine waters in the estuarine funnel, are thick and well developed. The estuary has been classified as a tide

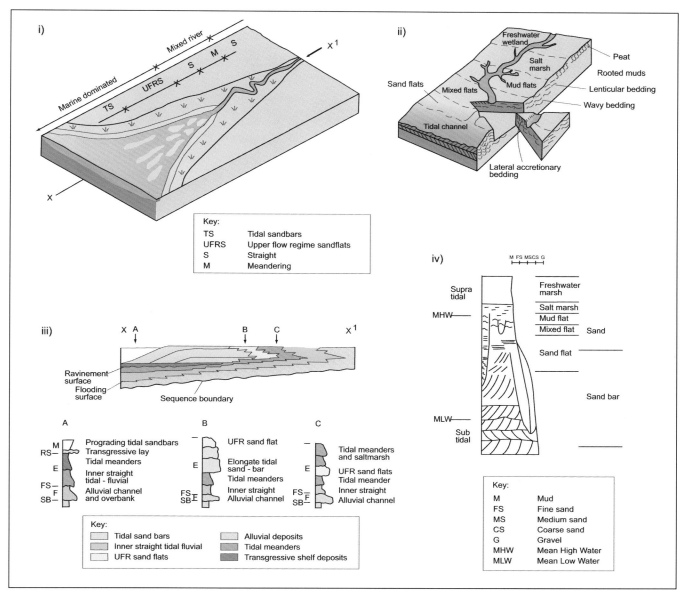

Figure 9 Models for estuarine contexts within the Lower Thames: i) tide dominated estuary model (from Dalrymple *et al* 1992); ii) saltmarsh zonation and cross-section (from Dalrymple 1992); iii) idealised cross-section through a tide dominated estuary (from Dalrymple *et al* 1992); iv) stratigraphic stack through an idealised saltmarsh (from Dalrymple 1992)

dominated estuary within which tidal sandbar (sub-tidal), upper flow regime sand flat (inter-tidal), straight (inter-tidal) and meandering (supra-tidal) segments can be found (*sensu* Dalrymple *et al* 1992) (Fig 9). Additional sub-division of the saltmarsh zones may also be undertaken into sub-tidal, inter-tidal and supra-tidal zones (Fig 9). Interbedded with the estuarine sediments are peats, often up to 3m in thickness, that are indicative of the phases of estuary contraction and the spread of freshwater wetlands and alder carr vegetation across the floodplain. These include the fossil forests of the Erith foreshore (Pl 3).

One particular aspect of much of the work that has been undertaken in the floodplain area has been the focus on the prehistoric landscapes and developments prior to Roman occupation. Where consideration is given to Roman and post-Roman activity (Sidell 2003) nearly all sites considered belong within the confines of the modern City of London, the Westminster area or Southwark, with little or no evidence from the floodplain area downstream. Thus although considerable interest in the Roman city and nature of the river (in particular the tidal head) has been shown since the 1970s (Milne *et al* 1983; Brigham 1990) this has not been translated into study and publication of contemporary sequences within the marshlands themselves. This is despite the well known occurrences of Roman activity at places such as Crossness (Spurrell 1885a). This is similarly true for Saxon and medieval periods, further hindered by notable gaps in the record for this period in East London (eg, Sidell *et al* 2000, 124), caused in part by scour. Consequently, we know little of marshland development within the area including the impact of sea wall constructions and changes associated with the floodplain consequent on human use of the area for cattle grazing, etc.

Plate 3 Fossil forest at Erith, Bexley

A Framework for Floodplain Development

On the basis of work undertaken in the 1980s and 1990s a model linking process geomorphology, sea-level change and patterns of sedimentation for the sub-floodplain estuarine sector of the Thames across the Late Pleistocene/Holocene period was developed (Table 2). This model incorporated some elements from other on-going research projects, but at the time the HS1 work was being carried out these works were not fully complete or published (eg, Bridgland 2000; Long *et al* 2000; Sidell *et al* 2000; Sidell 2003). The key elements of the model used in the HS1 investigations were:

- Accretion of the sand and gravel sequences associated with the East Tilbury Marshes Gravel occurred during MIS 6 through 5e (the last interglacial, Ipswichian) to MIS 3. Accretion of the sequences therefore happened during both cold climate and temperate events, and represent a variety of different depositional environments from braided to meandering river channels and estuarine situations;

- Down cutting and erosion occurred during or prior to the Last Glacial Maximum, resulting in terracing of the East Tilbury Marshes Gravel. This episode will have included solifluction events and remobilisation of sediments on the margins of the terraces;

- Accretion of the Shepperton Gravel during MIS 2 occurred under braided channel conditions;

- Infilling of hollows and cut-off channels on the Shepperton Gravel surface with organic sediments occurred during the Late Glacial period and Early Holocene. River behaviour shifts towards anastomosing channel patterns with stable channels;

- Establishment of meandering channel forms occurred in the Early Holocene with the development of wetland at lower elevations and at the downstream end of valleys, consequent with a backup of channels resulting from sea-level rise and the approaching freshwater/brackish water interface;

- Flooding of the deeper parts of the estuary by marine waters after *c* 6400 cal BC (7500 ^{14}C BP) and estuary expansion. Upstream in freshwater sector sand bar deposition occurred within stable channels;

- Estuary contraction and the spread of wetlands occurred, with peat accumulating after *c* 5000 cal BC (*c* 6000 ^{14}C BP);

- Estuary expansion occurred after *c* 1300–1200 cal BC (*c* 3000 ^{14}C BP) and re-establishment of estuarine conditions throughout much of study area.

This model is to a degree applicable across the study area where elements of all events can be seen or extrapolated from surface and subsurface data. However, localised erosion and sedimentation (perhaps associated with Thames tributary channels) are likely to

Table 2 Quaternary stages and geological events in the Lower Thames Valley

OI STAGE	EPOCH	STAGE	PERIOD	FLANDRIAN CHRONOZONES	GODWIN ZONES	CULTURAL PERIODS	CALENDAR YEARS BC/AD	^{14}C YEARS BP	UPSTREAM	DOWNSTREAM	ESTUARINE CHANGE
1	Holocene	Flandrian	sub-Atlantic	Fl III	VIIc	Post-medieval / medieval / Saxon & Danish / Roman / Iron Age	AD 1000 / 0 / 1000 BC	1000 / 2000 / 3000	Estuarine alluvium	Estuarine alluvium	Estuary expansion
			sub-Boreal	Fl II	VIIb	Bronze Age / Neolithic	2000 / 3000 / 4000	4000 / 5000	Peat accumulation in freshwater wetland	Estuarine alluvium	Estuary contraction
			Atlantic		VIIa	Mesolithic	5000 / 6000	6000 / 7000	Sand bar deposition	F/W wetland	Estuary flooding
			Boreal	Fl Ic	VIc / VIb / VIa / V / IV		7000 / 8000 / 9000	8000	Stable channel / meandering river		Channel and landscape stability
			pre-Boreal	Fl Ib / Fl Ia	III		10,000	9000 / 10,000	Anastomosing channel (f/w)	Terracing	Floodplain accretion
2	Pleistocene	Devensian	Loch Lomond Stadial (Younger Dryas)		II	Upper Palaeolithic	11,000 / 12,000	11,000 / 12,000	Braided channel (f/w) (Shepperton Gravel)		Erosion/incision
			Windermere Insterstadial (Bølling-Allerød)		I		25,000		Down cutting erosion		
3			Dimlington Stadial (Pleniglacial)								
4							50,000		Floodplain accretion and stabilisation (East Tilbury Marshes Gravel)		Floodplain accretion
5		Ipswichian				Middle Palaeolithic	70,000 / 110,000				
6		Saalian					125,000				

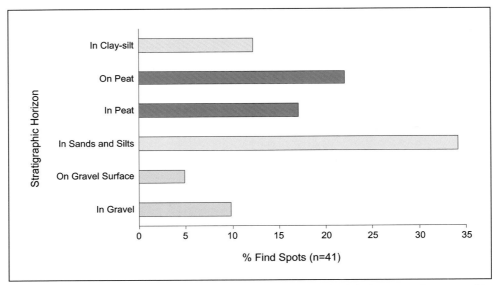

Figure 10 Distribution of all find spots in Thames alluvium by lithology type/stratigraphic position (from Bates 1998)

have influenced sequence development at the site specific level and consequently this model should be treated as applicable primarily at the scale of the floodplain. Additionally, timing of events in the model will vary depending on local geographic position. Thus upstream movement of the tidal head will occur through time resulting in a progressively more recent onset of brackish conditions in the river from Swanscombe Marsh to Ripple Lane. The converse would be expected in a downstream direction during relative sea-level fall when progressively later dates would be recorded for the transition downstream towards Swanscombe Marsh.

Archaeology

Prior to this volume, there was no integrated survey/summary bringing together all observations within the area of interest. However, as part of the HS1 project a summary review of published data was undertaken (to 1996) in order to try to understand the context of find spots. Previous workers, and indeed those responsible for designing many of the developer-funded projects in the region, have often held the assumption that prehistoric archaeological finds are mainly related to the peat stratigraphies or shallow islands within the alluvial tract. In order to test these assumptions archive

information was examined for all archaeological find spots (regardless of age/type, etc) to assess their stratigraphic context. This data (total number of useable records = 41) indicates that the largest number of find spots from the Lower Thames have no clear stratigraphic data attached to them. Of those find spots with stratigraphic data it is evident that artefacts have been recovered from a range of deposits including peat, clay-silt, sands and silts and on the gravel surface. Figure 10 illustrates the distribution of find spots by context type. The results of this study show that only 17% of all find spots occur within peat and that 22% of finds occur resting on peat, contrary to generally held expectations that artefacts and sites are associated principally with peat. Artefacts have clearly been recovered from a wide variety of sedimentary contexts not only peats. Significantly 34% of finds derive from sands and silts.

This information is restricted in that only for a few well investigated sites are the stratigraphic contexts of the finds clear in terms of environments of deposition. This information does, however, indicate that artefacts should be expected in most of the major sediment types likely to be encountered beneath the floodplain surface. Clearly the nature of the artefact assemblage, the degree of post-depositional modification and the preservation status of the artefact associations will vary depending on the nature of the sediment matrix from which the artefacts are recovered.

Part II
Strategies and Methods

Chapter 4

A Regional Research Design

The Regional Research Design

Developing a regional research design applicable to the whole HS1 route corridor from Folkestone to London was difficult due to the linear nature of the development area, cutting a transect across a series of landscape zones. Thus, rather than sampling discrete areas of the landscape, the route corridor samples a range of different geomorphological zones in which the characteristics of the associated archaeology was likely to vary considerably. The alluvial corridor that is the focus of the present study occupied a single major landscape zone of the Greater Thames Estuary. This zone has a distinctive historical character, landscape and natural history that has evolved over the last 450,000 years since the inception of the modern drainage patterns. This broad zone does, however, contain a range of local geomorphological zones each displaying a series of unique characteristics.

As part of the developing strategy for HS1 five key lines of enquiry were outlined for investigation early in the scheme (URS 1997):

- The natural landscape, its geomorphology, vegetation and climate;
- The modification of the landscape into humanly-occupied spaces;
- The manipulation and consumption by humans of natural resources;
- The organisation of landscape into social and political units;
- Ritual and ceremonial use of landscapes.

Encompassing these thematic issues are the broad time periods used to divide the research activity within the Thames Basin (defined in URS 1997):

A Hunter-foragers 400,000–4500 BC;
B Early agriculturalists: 4500–2000 BC (although this start date has since been revised to around 4000 for the area of the scheme);
C Farming communities: 2000–100 BC;
D Towns and their rural landscapes: 100 BC–AD 1700;
E The recent landscape AD 1700–1945.

Beyond these broad categories a series of research objectives were defined within the framework that are applicable to the current study including:

- Defining the nature of contemporary geomorphology and environment and its natural changes through time (periods A, B above);
- Defining the range of human activity and where it took place, particularly through the study of palaeoeconomy (periods A, B);
- Ascertaining the effect of climate and environmental changes on human lifeways and adaptive strategies (period A);
- Determining the nature and effect of clearance for agricultural activity in the landscape (period B);
- Defining the ritual and economic landscapes and their relationships (period B);
- Determining the spatial organisation of the landscape in terms of settlement location in relation to fields, pasture, woodland, enclosed areas and ways of moving between these (period C);
- Considering environmental change resulting from landscape organisation and re-organisation and the impact of population increase and concentration (periods C, D).
- Considering the environmental impact of industrialisation and urban development (periods C, D).

In addition to these broad areas of research, outlined prior to development of major project investigation strategies, belated consideration was also given to the technical issues associated with undertaking a project of this magnitude across a broad swathe of land including areas of deeply buried sediments. Although road (eg, Timby *et al* 2007; Brown 2008; Powell *et al* 2008) and pipeline schemes (eg, Coleman *et al* 2006; Gdaniec *et al* 2007) are now common in the UK, typically many of these have been developed across areas in which shallow stratigraphies have not impeded evaluation and excavation strategies even where they traverse areas of alluvium (Gdaniec *et al* 2007). This is not the case with the Thames alluvial corridor where sequence depths prohibit conventional approaches to the archaeological assessment. Consequently, the key aims of this report are based around the technical issues of the project linked to specific research objectives on an opportunistic basis. The objective is to document the strategy developed and used and the results obtained from the investigation, rather than a conventional historical narrative of landscape change and human activity.

A Strategy for Investigation

Strategies for investigating alluvial sequences and their contained archaeology in the Lower Thames area have developed in a piecemeal fashion in the past based on opportunistic findings made during the last 200 years. Additionally, approaches have also been influenced by findings from beyond the Thames in similar alluvial/estuarine wetland contexts elsewhere in the UK and beyond.

Thames-side archaeological discoveries made in the last 20 years (Meddens 1996; Meddens and Beasley 1990; Bates and Williamson 1995; Thomas and Rackham 1996; Bennell 1998; Sidell *et al* 2000; 2002; Crockett *et al* 2002; Haughey 2007; Wilkinson and Sidell 2007; Carew *et al* 2009; Stafford *et al* 2012) have primarily derived from developer-funded excavations associated with redevelopment of the floodplain for housing or commercial premises following its abandonment by shipping and other related industries and activities. Closely associated, and indeed driving assumptions made regarding the nature of the buried sedimentary sequences, have been Quaternary studies that have traditionally focused on the buried peat sequences (Devoy 1977; 1979; 1982) (Fig 8). The commonly held view was developed that while the peat sequences were indicative of semi-terrestrial, increasingly dry contexts, the minerogenic sediments burying the peats were indicative of considerably wetter conditions associated with inter-tidal and sub-tidal contexts. These have combined to produce a perception amongst some that archaeological remains within the floodplain are intermittently associated with peats and that, with the exception of boats and associated structures, the minerogenic sequences have little or no archaeological potential. That such assumptions are misplaced was demonstrated in the developing strategy for the HS1 investigations in 1999 (Fig 10), where the survey of known finds clearly illustrated that archaeological material derives from a number of different sedimentary bodies not simply the peat.

The strategy developed for this project recognised the historical association between the buried sediments and archaeology, but significantly considered that a greater complexity probably existed in the past, particularly with reference to the minerogenic sediments and their associated environments of deposition. It was also recognised that significant quantities of information were available in geotechnical archives (Barham and

Bates 1994) and that such information, if used in conjunction with an informed model for sequence development of the floodplain, could provide a key for understanding the sub-surface distribution of archaeological remains.

Developing the Strategy through the Project Lifetime

The key to developing a successful strategy (Fig 11) to investigate the buried sequences of the floodplain of the river was dependant on developing a strategy that was able to identify locations at which archaeological risk (ie, the likelihood of discovering archaeological material) was high, as well as being flexible enough to cope with changing engineering constraints and new opportunities for investigation through the lifetime of the project. Additionally, in a project with a field duration of some 10 years or more from start to finish, the impact of new technologies on the range of possibilities for investigation also needed to be taken into account. Developing such a strategy therefore involved both the implementation of approaches on a site by site basis, as well as developing a standardised, route-wide approach to investigation.

Initial work involved a route-wide assessment of resource in order to provide an alluvial predictive model from the route corridor (Chap 6). Desk-based study of extant data sources, particularly records held by national geoscience bodies (Culshaw 2005), as well as local authorities provided substantial quantities of data from previous geotechnical investigations. A very considerable body of data was also available from the geotechnical investigations associated with the design and build of the route. All data sources were held within an archive record office developed through the lifetime of the project (Geotechnical Management Unit). Coupled with this was an important body of data published on both the sedimentary sequences (and their associated biological remains) and the archaeological material for the area. These data sources formed the basis on which the project strategy was conceived (Barham and Bates 1994) and implemented (Barham and Bates 1995). The approach therefore sought to define stratigraphic sedimentary facies and chronostratigraphic 'envelopes' within which human activity is likely to have occurred, when the sediments were exposed as a land surface, and where such remains are more likely to have remained well-preserved after sealing by later sedimentation. Where such predicted 'envelopes' could be identified, and overlapped with zones of impact from HS1, they were considered to be of key importance.

With these general points in mind the approach adopted sought to ensure:

- The methodology was flexible and capable of being implemented at any point on soft ground on the HS1 route;

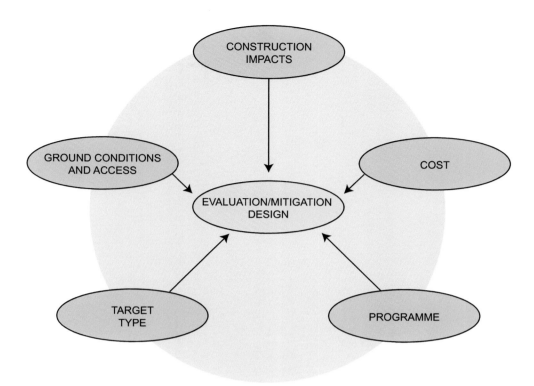

Figure 11   Factors involved in considering appropriate strategies for site investigations within the HS1 alluvial corridor

- The methodology and results could integrate with and be refined/tested by further geotechnical investigations, archaeological purposive investigations or observations/recording made prior to, or during, scheme construction;
- The methodology specifically aimed to exclude zones of low or very low archaeological potential and define with extra precision zones of moderate or high archaeological potential within a probabilistic model utilising a facies-based approach to the deposits of concern to the HS1 scheme;
- The methods used maximised information gain, minimised costs, and specifically targeted information unavailable at the start of the project (as required for evaluative purposes);
- Data generated was capable of being verified/disproved by subsequent supplementary or purposive field investigations and/or mitigation measures.

The implementation of this desk-based strategy resulted in a detailed, route-wide, assessment of the nature, distribution, age and archaeological potential of the alluvial sequences (URN and URS 1999) (Chap 6). The subsequent design of the field programme was therefore influenced by this survey of extant data as well as project specific aims and objectives (informed by the regional research agenda, URS 1997). An important

element of the project design also included detailed consideration of the engineering.

Following the route-wide assessment and the identification of areas of higher archaeological potential, site evaluation was undertaken in certain locations (eg, Thames River Crossing and Ebbsfleet, Chaps 9 and 10). This work was undertaken at specific sites in order to refine local alluvial predictive models and provide information on likely depths for sensitive archaeological horizons. A two-step approach to field investigation was instigated commencing with field trials for the techniques proposed (in order to clarify their suitability as well as to obtain preliminary data sets). The result of this stage of work was to enhance the predictive model and provide a first order sub-surface lithological model for the site area. Subsequent work(s) then followed depending on the nature of the geomorphological context, perceived complexity of sequences, as well as the engineering impact. The precise schedule and timings of works (ie, geophysical survey, borehole drilling, test pitting, trenching and excavation) varied between sites and was dependant on a number of factors including programme schedules.

The design of the programme relied on a mixed method approach to investigation combining a variety of data sources together in different combinations depending on geological, archaeological and practical (finance/accessibility) constraints.

Chapter 5

Project Concepts

A Geoarchaeological Framework for the Route Corridor

In order to identify evidence of human activity in areas of thickly stratified sediments and, indeed, to attach significance to the discovery of signals pertaining to human activity during evaluation, a consideration of the nature of the archaeological signals likely to be present in such areas was fundamental to designing the project. In conjunction with an understanding of the nature of the signals is the need to understand the landscape setting and local geomorphology of an area within which human activity of different kinds is more or less likely. For this reason a geoarchaeological model specific to the alluvial corridor was required. Thus the following factors were considered as basic elements within such a model:

- The nature of the archaeological signal;
- The relationship between archaeological signals/sites and sediments (sedimentary facies);
- The concept of palaeolandsurfaces and their identification within the alluvial corridor.

Furthermore approaches to modelling these sequences and the buried surfaces required consideration in order to place the evidence within a palaeogeographical context. These issues are considered below.

The Archaeological Signal

Within urban contexts, where houses, streets, etc are well defined, a site can be clearly isolated and defined, and the presence of such features in the archaeological record identified through clearly visible layers (such as within boreholes or trenches) Within the rural context, where activity is more dispersed, site definition is often less apparent. This is particularly the case for prehistoric sites where evidence of occupation or activity may be ephemeral and difficult to discern even during excavation. Alternatively the structure of the archaeological record may be based on size of archaeological occurrence (Table 3) (eg, see Fokkens 1998). Here occurrences are sub-divided into four classes: points, scatters, groups and systems. Within this four-fold sub-division all likely activity occurrences can be accommodated. It is clear that the different scales of archaeological 'site' will have different properties and their visibility in the landscape and within sedimentary units will vary. Their visibility to differing survey techniques will also vary. Archaeological sites can also be classified on the basis of site function and position in the landscape (Tables 4 and 5). These criteria can be combined and used within the framework of reconstructed landscapes for the range of environments expected to be present within the Lower Thames during much of the Holocene.

Additionally, a further class of archaeological signal in the landscape can be defined: archaeological proxy records. They are indirect records of human activity where activity results in changes in biotic, sedimentological or geochemical conditions within the area surrounding the human activity. For example pollen records showing evidence of woodland clearance and agriculture (Birks *et al* 1988), enhanced phosphate levels in sediment (Lippi 1988) and the results of deforestation and the resulting soil erosion/deposition (Bell and Boardman 1992) are indicative of human activity at varying distances from the point of sampling. However, results from these proxy records, unlike direct physical remains of human activity, are usually only recognisable following costly and time consuming laboratory investigation.

It should be noted that definition of the archaeological resource/signal is likely to depend on the objectives of the investigation project. The signals

Table 3 Size classification of archaeological sites (adapted from Bates 1998)

Unit size	Archaeological characteristics	Examples	Site terminology
<1m	Single artefact/dense scatters	Knapping episode	Point
1–10m	Artefact scatters/single structure/faunal residue scatters	Tent/hut, butchery site	Scatter
10–100m	Groups of scatters, structures	Settlements	Group
>100m	Associations of structural elements, routeways, field systems	Landscape systems	System

Table 4   Site types, site sizes, descriptions and locations within the landscape for the main types of archaeological sites expected in the area

Site	Site size	Site description	Site location	Site type
Find Spot	<1m	Single artefact lost or placed within a 'natural context'	Any point in landscape	Point
Production episode	1–10m	Single knapping episode, tool production point, etc	Anywhere in landscape but often in proximity to raw material source or source of material to be processed	Scatter
Processing episode	1–10m	Single exploitation episode eg, carcass butchery	Anywhere in landscape but often in proximity to water source, channel, etc	Scatter
Boat	1–10m or 10–100m	Hull or dug-out ranging from canoe to large merchant and warships	Within or adjacent to channels on mudflats	Scatter
Trackway	10–100m	Wooden trackway or lithic causeway	Within or on peat units in floodplain environment	Group
Revetment	1–10m, 10–100m	Wooden or stone construction at waters edge	Channel marginal situation	Group
Settlement/ Ritual	10–100m, >100m	Cluster of artefacts, structures including houses/huts, routeways and revetments	Gravel islands, channel margins, 'upland zones'. Floodplain surface, channel edge, shallow lake	Group

considered of archaeological relevance will therefore vary between projects. Additionally, the sampling strategies and methods of investigation employed to detect that signal will also vary and will depend on the 'site' target type/size and the methods at the disposal of the project team.

In this study an underlying principle of the methodology used considers the landscape to be the template on which human activity occurred and that the landscape forms the basic archaeological resource. While it is a useful exercise to consider the types of sites (points) that may form the focus of archaeological attention, one should remember that human activity is not simply restricted to sites but that humans use the whole landscape and that, therefore, the archaeological site is spatially continuous (Foley 1981; Pollard 1998). Identification and consideration of the landscape properties are, therefore, of prime importance.

Sedimentary Facies and Archaeological Sites

The nature of archaeological signatures has been described previously (Chap 3, *Archaeology*) and links have been implied between the nature of the archaeological signal and the location in the landscape of the archaeological remains (Table 4). This suggests that an association between sedimentary characteristics of these zones (ie, sedimentary facies) and their contained archaeology may be determined (Table 6). Defining the relationships between sedimentary facies and the nature of contained archaeological record can therefore:

1.   Provide predictive information on the likely types/focus of occupation/activity within a stratigraphic stack; and
2.   Provide predictive information on the likely taphonomic status (and history) of any material present within that stack.

Table 5   Site type and size classification of archaeological sites

Site	<1m	1–10m	10–100m	>100m
Find Spot	✓			
Production episode	✓	✓		
Processing episode	✓	✓		
Boat		✓		
Trackway		✓	✓	
Revetment		✓	✓	
Settlement/ritual			✓	✓

The factors defining the facies within the sedimentary stack are a function of the location of the space occupied by the sediments (ie, the accommodation space) in the environment and the interaction of a range of factors within that accommodation space (Fig 12). These characteristics, related to the nature of the environment of deposition, can therefore be linked to site types known to habitually occur in such environments. Additionally, the nature of the environments of deposition will influence the preservational status of those deposits, ie, whether or not artefacts, etc remain *in situ* after loss/discard.

In order to illustrate the principle involved the following example is provided:

Locations associated with animal capture/ discovery and subsequent butchery are often in water edge situations, on the slip off slopes on the inside bend of meanders or on floodplain flats. Many archaeological examples of such sites are known, for example, the tool production and butchery areas at the Uxbridge Late Glacial site (Lewis 1991; Lewis and Rackham 2011). Sediments within such areas exhibit grain sizes

Table 6 Environments of deposition, sediment characteristics and archaeological status

Environment zone	Environment of deposition	Dominant grain sizes	Stratigraphic characteristics	Organic content	Archaeological status
Deep gravel bed braided river (Donjek type) (based on Miall 1996)	Gravel bar (GB)	Gravel	Massive, matrix supported gravel (Gm) becoming horizontally crude bedded with planar cross-bedded (Gp) and trough cross-bedded (Gt) gravels	Low – rare reworked bones and shells	Mostly reworked
	Sandy bed (SB)	Sand and gravel	Solitary or grouped trough cross-beds (St) and planar cross-beds (Sp), ripple cross laminae (Sr), horizontal cross laminae (Sh), low-angle cross-beds (Sl) and broad, shallow scours (Ss)	Low – rare reworked bones and shells	Mostly reworked
	Floodplain floor (FF)	Sand, silt, clay	Massive with desiccation cracks (Fm) and fine laminated with very small ripples (Fl)		Larger elements may be *in situ*, smaller elements may be reworked
Meandering River (based on Walker and Cant 1984)	Active channel	Coarse gravels	Indistinct bedding but imbircation of pebbles and cobbles is common (Gh, Gt, Gp) – deposits are thin and discontinuous	Low – occasional waterlogged plan remains	Mostly reworked
	Point bars	Sands fine upwards along bar to silts	Large-scale trough cross-bedded coarse sands (St) in lower part of the bar to small-scale trough cross-beds higher on the bar, cross-beds show dip in downstream direction. Plane bed parallel laminae (Sh) may also be present	Low – occasional waterlogged plant remains and isolated faunal elements	Mostly reworked
	Natural levees	Fine sands and silts	Ripple and horizontally stratified units (Fl) overlain by laminates formed on the concave or steep-bank side of the meander loop adjacent to channel. Deposits are thickest and coarsest nearest to channel	Low to moderate and may include organic plant material	Larger elements may be *in situ*, smaller elements may be reworked
	Floodplains	Fine sands, silts and clays, peat	Fine laminations and ripple structures (Fl) to massive with desiccation cracks (Fm)	Considerable plant debris, faunal remains and showing considerable signs of bioturbation	Larger elements may be *in situ*, smaller elements may be reworked
	Abandoned cut-offs	Fine silt and clay, peat	Commonly well laminated with small ripples (Fl) to massive (Fsm) with desiccation cracks (Fm)	Plant remains, molluscs and other faunal elements common	Larger elements may be *in situ*, smaller elements may be reworked
Tide Dominated Estuary (based on Dalrymple et al 1992)	Elongated tidal sand bar zone (Marine dominated zone)	Sand	Cross bedded sand bars seaward of the tidal-energy maximum	Faunal remains and extensive bioturbation	Mostly reworked
	Upper flow regime sand flats (Marine dominated zone)	Sand	Braided channel patterns becoming confined to a single channel headwards	Faunal remains and extensive bioturbation	Mostly reworked, occasional *in situ* elements
	Straight-meandering-Straight (mixed zone)	Sands and silts	Bank attached bars and some mid-channel bars, meanders exhibit symmetrical point bars	Faunal remains may be extensive with common bioturbation	Mostly reworked but local *in situ* material possible
Saltmarsh	Supratidal zone	Silts and clays	Fine laminated beds	Bioturbation common, plant remains present becoming peat in places	Larger elements may be *in situ*, smaller elements may be reworked
	Intertidal zone	Sands, silts	Small-scale ripple cross-stratification and dune bedforms in channels, lenticular, wavy and flaser bedding common. Alternating thin sand and silt beds change higher up to silt with thin sand beds		Mostly reworked but some *in situ*
	Subtidal zone	Sands	Lateral accretion in tidal channels and point bars characterised by dunes and internal cross-bedding showing bimodal directions of forset dip. Mud drapes also present		Mostly reworked

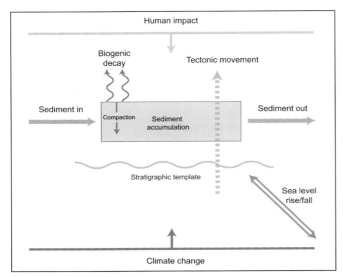

Figure 12 Schematic to show major factors controlling sediment accumulation patterns in a depositional basin

from gravels to fine silts that can be used to identify facies types associated with these situations in field sections or borehole data. This information can be used to indicate the presence of contexts within which evidence of past human activity may be found. Consideration of the grain size relative to the size/status of any contained artefacts will provide information on any potential for reworking within the deposit. For example gravel substrates, deposited under high-energy conditions, indicate a high likelihood that any contained artefacts will be reworked. Artefacts such as axes, contained within finer grained sediments, are less likely to have been reworked (Brown 1997), as supported by the often fresh condition of these, indicating a lack of rolling and transportation. Table 7 describes the properties of the major identified geomorphological zones within the Thames Estuary and their likely archaeological status.

Buried Surfaces and the Archaeological Record

The recognition of buried surfaces (used here to refer to presently buried former landsurfaces) is of critical importance not only within archaeology but also within geology and geomorphology. The identification of buried surfaces within stratigraphic sequences has been used to divide up stratigraphies into packages of sediments (contexts) considered to display genetically and temporally related features. The surfaces identified may be the result of changes in the nature of sedimentation, breaks or hiatuses in sedimentation or represent phases of erosion. The identification of buried surfaces within the stratigraphic stack can be considered as an element of a greater set of attributes within the stack that can be used to reconstruct the landscape (Widdowson 1997). Typically integration of a range of geological and geomorphological data within a conceptual model containing palaeosurface information is often the objective of geoarchaeologists tasked within placing the archaeological site/area of investigation within a (pre)historical context.

Within the stratigraphic stacks key zones of considerable archaeological importance are those indicating the presence of former landsurfaces. The inundation or burial of landsurfaces on which human activity has taken place can result in the sudden, *in situ* burial of human and animal remains. Amongst the best known examples of buried landsurfaces are those buried by the volcanic eruption of Vesuvius in AD 79 (Jashemski 1979) or the eruption of the volcano responsible for the deposition of the Laacher See pumice in the Neuweid Basin in the Central Rhineland (Street 1986; Ikinger 1990; Baales and Street 1996), another example is the well known buried surface at Boxgrove in Sussex (Roberts and Parfitt 1999). Other less spectacular landsurfaces are commonly found in the archaeological record and provide archaeologists with important time-slice views of the past (Brown and Keogh 1992a; 1992b).

Table 7 Main identified zones within the Thames Estuary and the likelihood of archaeological occurrences

Environment of deposition	Find spot	Production episode	Processing episode	Boat	Trackway	Revetment	Settlement/ ritual
Gravel bar	✓	✓	✓	✓	x	x	x
Sandy bed	✓✓	✓	✓	✓	x	✓	x
Floodplain floor	✓✓✓	✓✓	✓✓	✓	✓✓	✓	✓✓
Active channel	✓	✓	✓	✓	x	✓	x
Point bars	✓	✓	✓	✓	x	✓	x
Natural levees	✓✓	✓✓✓	✓✓	✓✓	✓✓	✓	✓✓
Floodplains	✓✓✓	✓✓	✓✓	✓	✓✓	✓	✓✓
Abandoned cut-offs	✓✓✓	✓✓	✓✓	✓✓	✓✓	✓	x
Supratidal zone	✓✓	✓✓	✓✓	✓✓	✓	✓	✓✓
Intertidal zone	✓	✓	✓✓	✓✓	x	x	x
Subtidal zone	✓	x	x	✓✓	x	x	x

x Not present   ✓ Low likelihood of occurrence   ✓✓ Moderate likelihood of occurrence   ✓✓✓ High likelihood of occurrence

Identifying and determining the lateral distribution of buried palaeolandsurfaces is of critical importance in the archaeological evaluation of an area. These features represent positions within the stack at which *in situ* assemblages of material may occur in the context of the landscape in which they were used. They may be identified by a series of features that can be used singly or in combination to determine the presence of a buried landsurface:

- In the absence of a clearly defined erosional contact, sudden changes in lithology within a core profile (Pl 4) either seen as a sudden change in sediment types or shifts in properties such as loss-on-ignition and total phosphates (Barham 1995);
- The presence of a palaeosol;
- The presence of zones of weathering, rooting horizons or enhancement of magnetic susceptibility signals (Allen 1987; Barham 1995) (Pl 4);
- The presence of major bedding planes.

The presence of these features may imply the location of a landsurface. However, in order to determine the significance of these features their lateral extent needs to be determined through the identification and correlation of these features within a number of boreholes. This is most easily achieved using the principles of facies analysis and the construction of a sub-surface stratigraphical model (Bates 1998). For example extensive buried landsurfaces have been identified and mapped in Pleistocene sediments on the West Sussex Coastal Plain (Bates *et al* 1997; 2000b).

Modelling Buried Surfaces

At an early stage in the development of the project it was realised that considerable importance would be attached to the use of borehole and other forms of geotechnical data for which there was abundant information from both ground investigations associated with the project and previous works associated with construction on the floodplain. Consequently, the rationale for the use of such point specific data (boreholes and test pit information) needed clarification in order to understand how it would contribute to sub-surface modelling to allow the geometry and topography of these sub-surface sediment bodies to be described and its limitations (Chew 1995). Building confidence in these models was crucial because we were unlikely to have a complete knowledge of the systems either across space or through time (Bowden 2004) and the conclusions from such work were likely to have far reaching impacts on works programming and costs.

Today it is increasingly common to visualise these bodies using geological modelling systems which allow the construction of integrated 3D models that provide the user (and reader) with pictorial images of the sub-surface (Culshaw 2005). The 3D geological

Plate 4 Thin section of landsurface beneath peat, Slade Green Relief Road, Bexley (width *c* 80mm)

models consist of a structural framework of 2D surfaces representing stratigraphic boundaries, chronostratigraphic horizons, etc that aim to produce a 3-dimensional representation of sub-surface deposits allowing the researcher the opportunity to investigate the relationships between deposits and the ability to predict sequence occurrence away from known data positions (Jones 1992). Images produced from the models implies a robustness with respect to the 'hardness' of the surfaces being created as well as the reliability of the relationship between data points when, in fact, our understanding of these surfaces and correlations are based upon often inadequate sampling intervals (of boreholes) and interpretations of sequences based on the application of facies models to the stratigraphies coupled with the surface expression of the associated sediment bodies.

One of the major outcomes of sub-surface modelling are the 2D/3D surfaces that may be used (where appropriate) to reconstruct palaeogeographies for areas of the landscape for which surface sediment expression bears little or no relationship to those buried at depth. Within the framework of archaeological investigations associated with development/destruction of sites such an approach has considerable practical use due to its ability to enable the user to identify buried landsurfaces and reconstruct local or regional palaeogeographies through a multi-disciplinary palaeoenvironmental investigation that allows a sequence of palaeogeographic maps to be

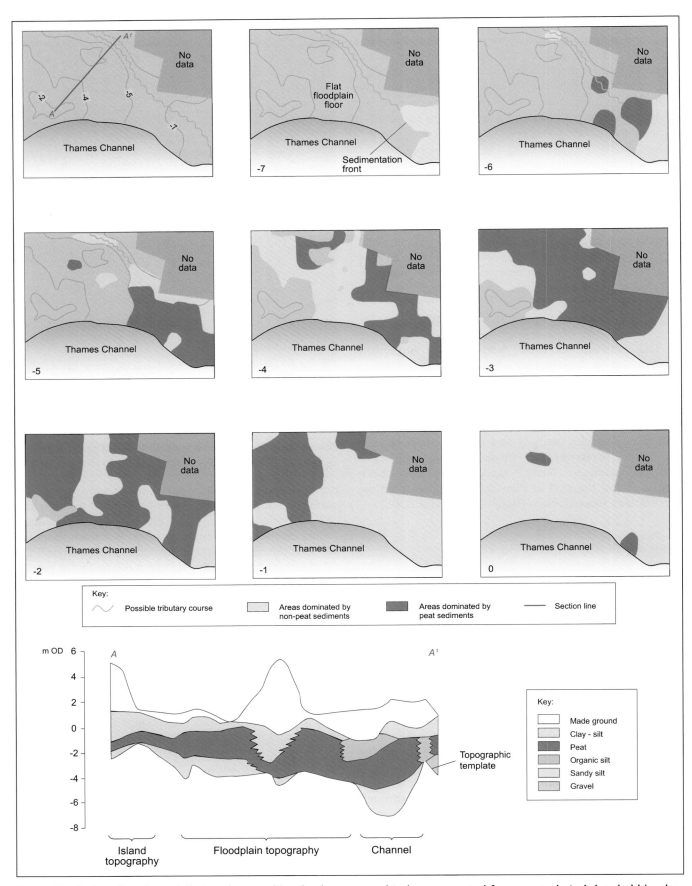

Figure 13 Barking Reach modelled surfaces and local palaeogeographical maps created from geotechnical data held by the GMU (from Bates 1998)

constructed. Examining these maps with knowledge of the preferred loci of human activity allows those locations at which such evidence may exist to be identified (Deeben *et al* 1997; Bates *et al* 2000b; Corcoran *et al* 2011). Other studies have a more geological objective (Chen *et al* 1996; Berendsen and Stouthamer 2001; Culshaw 2005; Bertrand and Baeteman 2005).

In the course of many archaeologically orientated projects correctly predicting the distribution of certain sub-surface deposits with a high archaeological potential has considerable financial implications for the developers. Unexpected archaeological finds may cost construction projects tens of thousands of pounds per day in project down-time while excavation proceeds and consequently the need to 'best guess' the archaeological significance of sites is paramount. However, it has been found that to achieve the goals of sub-surface modelling applying only borehole based surveys is often an inadequate response in many situations. This is particularly the case where approaches need to be flexible and vary from site to site depending on the geological conditions as well as project budgets and practical limitations imposed by ground conditions and the site infrastructure. Additionally, extra information may often be required from areas of the site between sample (borehole) locations and consequently it has been necessary to use not only boreholes but other approaches such as Cone Penetration Testing (CPT) as well as surface and sub-surface geophysics to meet the requirements at individual sites and fill in gaps between boreholes.

Similar arguments have been made by those involved in geotechnical studies associated with engineering construction activities (Lenham *et al* 2005; Culshaw 2005). Characterisation of the ground conditions in order to determine appropriate construction methods generally occurs in the initial stages of project development and may involve a range of techniques including borehole, CPT and geophysical techniques. However, it is recognised (Zhu *et al* 2003) that ground behaviour cannot be established and forecasted with 100% accuracy and that, in order to minimise uncertainties of ground conditions, careful consideration should be given to understanding the limitations of the information sources and the ways in which the information is combined to formulate models and interpretations. The limitations of a typical ground investigation survey are discussed in detail by Salvany *et al* (2004).

In many cases an integrated approach to archaeological investigation using a range of geological, geomorphological and palaeoenvironmental perspectives derived from direct and indirect observations of sub-surface stratigraphies is desirable prior to developing a conceptual model containing palaeosurface information. In some cases this information can be then used to place the archaeological site/area of investigation within a (pre)historical context as well as defining areas in which evidence of *in situ*

activity by past human groups/environments may occur. In individual cases the mixed method approach needs to be structured in order to address the needs of the site/problem and an important element of the investigation is the clear articulation and discussion of the methodologies used. In particular, the limitations of the sampling approaches and the impact that that approach may have on the interpretation derived from the investigation (ie, the confidence limits that may be placed on the conclusions of the investigation that relate to the location of sample points and correlations made between sample points) need to be articulated in order for confidence to be placed in the conclusions drawn. Discussion of this kind is rarely seen in the published literature however, this is of particular importance where complex frameworks for site and sequence correlations may be based on individual classes of data (eg, small mammals, etc).

An example of a modelled surface is shown in Figure 13 from the Barking Reach area (taken from Bates 1998; the location of the study is shown on Fig 5).

Palaeogeography and the Archaeological Record

The contextualisation of archaeological remains within the physical landscape, contemporary with human occupation, remains a key objective of many site and regional based archaeological projects. The study of palaeogeography entails the reconstruction of patterns of the earth's surface at a given time and through time. In particular it focuses on the ancient sedimentary environments and the contemporary ecological conditions. Such investigations can fix the location of shorelines, position of rivers and source areas of raw material (ie, for human use).

Reconstructing palaeolandscapes for key periods in the (pre)historic past is important to enable sense to be made of current distributions of archaeological materials, to make predictions regarding the likely distribution of remains prior to investigation and to contextualise the materials recovered from the fieldwork phase of a project. In such cases consideration needs to be given to understanding the evidence contained in the stratigraphic record pertinent to landscape reconstructions. It may be tempting to suggest that in the absence of direct archaeological evidence from a given area a verdict of no archaeological interest is deduced. However, if one accepts Foley's (1981) argument of spatially continuous use of the landscape then areas devoid of apparent archaeological remains become an integral part of the broader archaeological picture and therefore require investigation.

The processes involved in palaeogeographic reconstruction include all aspects of palaeo-environmental studies contributing to the palaeo-environmental reconstruction. When palaeogeographical reconstructions are formulated within the context of an archaeological project the question of the scale of investigation needs to be considered. Both the spatial and temporal scale of the reconstructions requires consideration and need to be framed in relationship to the nature of the archaeological question.

Successful uses of palaeogeographical reconstruction in archaeological studies have been undertaken in Greece (Kraft *et al* 1987; Sturdy *et al* 1997), the North Sea area (Verart 1996; Coles 1998; Gaffney *et al* 2007) and the Netherlands (Fokkens 1998). Within areas of deeply stratified sediments, for example, in the lower reaches of river valleys, considerable problems exist when attempting to investigate the palaeogeography due to the difficulty of access to sediment sequences required to reconstruct palaeogeographies.

Limitations of Past Geoarchaeological Approaches to Alluvial sequences in the Lower Thames Area

Commonly, geoarchaeological investigation of the floodplain area of the Lower Thames is conducted on an opportunistic basis, where section recording has been undertaken and purposive geoarchaeological boreholes have been drilled, and where development has been considered to have a possible impact on the deeply buried sediments (eg, Barham and Bates 1995; Bates and Williamson 1995; MoLAS 1996). These have typically been restricted in spatial extent where the distribution of the investigation is dictated by the size and nature of the construction impact. In many cases these studies have described the lithostratigraphic sequence preserved at the site and assessed the nature of the contained biostratigraphic evidence. However, these investigations have not commonly been pursued to the analysis phase of investigation. Notable exceptions include work undertaken on the Jubilee Line Extension (Sidell *et al* 2000), Silvertown (Wilkinson *et al* 2000; Crockett *et al* 2002), along the A13 (Carew *et al* 2009; Stafford *et al* 2012), and most recently the Olympic Park in the Lower Lea Valley (Powell 2012). Additionally, facies classification of the identified sedimentary units has only been undertaken sporadically and no attempt has been made to integrate this information into a regional lithostratigraphy (the organisation of sediment units into sequences based on their lithological properties) for the Lower Thames area.

Allied to the opportunistic approach to site investigation has been the absence of a framework for investigation. Although now widely acknowledged to be over simplistic and possibly requiring major modification, the only model for floodplain

changes remains that of Devoy (1977; 1979) based on the biostratigraphic analysis of selected borehole sequences. This was latterly simplified by Long *et al* (2000) and site specific investigations undertaken by Sidell (2003).

The following limitations of the approach were noted during the early stages of HS1:

- The framework model available for the Thames floodplain is based on the biostratigraphic approach of Devoy (1977, 1979) that has been updated and modified by Long *et al* (2000). This has been shown to be too simplistic and may require reinterpretation (Haggart 1995);
- Current geoarchaeological investigation of the floodplain is opportunistic and sites for investigation are defined by the commercial development rather than archaeological or geoarchaeological criteria;
- Facies ascriptions of sedimentary units described in boreholes and sections are only rarely presented;
- Core material is often assessed for the widest range of contained data (both sedimentological and biostratigraphical) diluting the potential impact of target specific aims and objectives tied to research questions;
- It is relatively rare that analysis phase works are undertaken on recovered and assessed core material;
- No model describing possible 3-dimensional development which integrates lithostratigraphic units, defined facies bodies and contained biostratigraphic and archaeological data exists across the whole area;
- Process of change is rarely examined in detail. While the outcome of change is well known (peat to minerogenic sediments, alder carr to saltmarsh/mudflats) the nature and timing of the change have not commonly been examined in detail;
- There is a tendency to oversimplify the nature of the environment rather than looking at the probable true heterogeneity of the landscape at any one given time;
- The presence of a model for sequence development would provide valuable information regarding the potential importance of development sites and the aims and objectives of assessment works to be undertaken on core material removed from investigation sites.

Chapter 6

Desk-top Investigation

The Desk-top Assessment

The data sources available to geoarchaeologists investigating the alluvium of the Thames, or any major river valley, can be listed:

- Bedrock and drift (Quaternary) geological maps (supplied by the British Geological Survey – BGS);
- Borehole data acquired for geotechnical ground investigation purposes (held by the Geotechnical Management Unit – GMU);
- Geomorphological map data (held by the GMU);
- Remote sensing data (including air photographs);
- Sub-surface geophysical data;
- Historical Environment Record data and other published records (held by English Heritage/ County Planning Departments);
- Field map, sequence logging and section drawings and descriptions.

Baseline geological maps from the BGS were utilised to outline the study areas and define the nature of the sequences likely to be present beneath the surface of the floodplain. This information acts as the prime source of data in determining the focus of the investigation as well as a first order indication of the likely nature of the sub-surface conditions and potential associated archaeology. Allied to this, and providing detail on the specific nature of the alluvial stack at a given location, were the borehole data obtained for geotechnical ground investigation as part of the project and held by the GMU. This data was archived and supplemented by additional data throughout the life of the project (a good example of the complexity in data gathering throughout the project lifetime is the Ebbsfleet area – see Wenban-Smith *et al* forthcoming). One of the major difficulties faced during the project was keeping up to date with new information from ground investigations, particularly once construction commenced, as responsibility for ground investigation switched from the GMU to the individual contractors. Other forms of data such as the geomorphological map data and remote sensing data were of limited use on the alluvial sector reported here (more use was made of this data on Section 1 of the project within the Kent sector). Limited sub-surface geophysical data was available and the HER of limited use only.

A Geoarchaeological Model for the Study Area

In this project, the evolution of the Thames floodplain area was viewed through a series of stages corresponding to major changes in process through time (Fig 14). In order to evaluate the geoarchaeological potential of the route corridor, a model was constructed that attempts to define some of the principle changes taking place within the area during the Late Pleistocene/Holocene time frame. A number of key points are noted:

- Human activity patterns vary across the landscape;
- Settlement sites are typically restricted to contemporary dry ground away from wetland/ inundated areas;
- Ecotonal zones within the landscape are often areas of intense human activity due to the resource abundance. A major ecotonal boundary is recognised as that between dry and wet ground;
- Wetland activity by humans is often ephemeral and related to resource exploitation (eg, traps and trackways) with the exception of unusual sites such as ritual sites and platforms (Pl 5);
- Coarse flint gravels deposited under periglacial conditions (Pl 6) are likely to contain only reworked flint artefacts of Pleistocene date;

Plate 5 Trackway from excavations along the A13 DBFO Road Scheme at Woolwich Manor Way, Newham

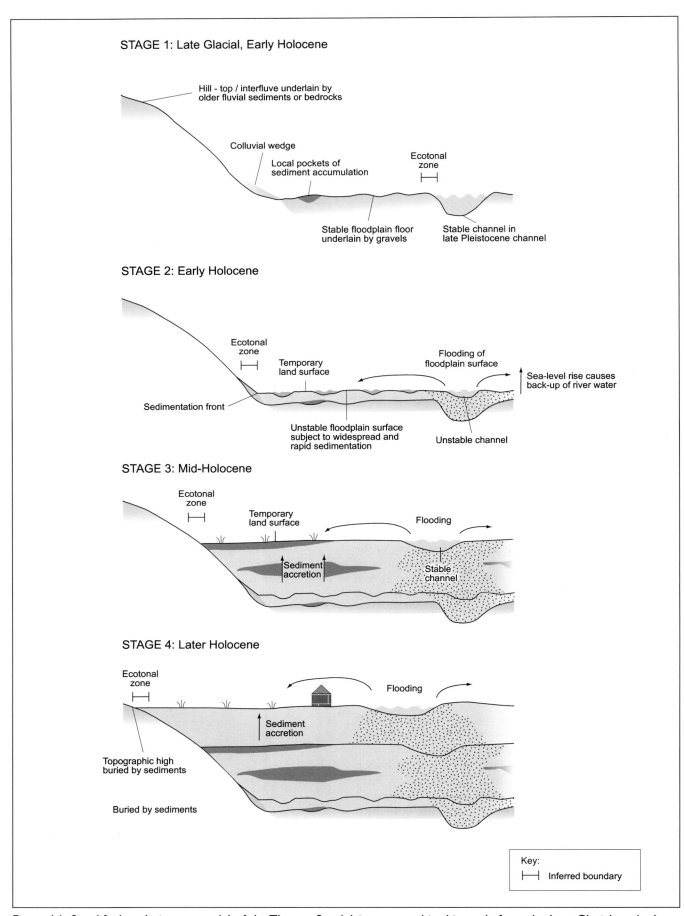

Figure 14 Simplified evolutionary model of the Thames floodplain area used in this study from the Late Glacial to the later Holocene (from Bates 1998)

- A major buried landsurface exists at the boundary between the coarse grained, cold climate periglacial deposits and the overlying Holocene sediments (Pl 7);
- Peat/organic silt accumulation occurs during times of wetland emergence with little or no minerogenic input (Pl 8);
- Minerogenic sediment deposition occurs during phases of relatively higher energy conditions including those driven by rising sea-level or within deeper water;
- Colluvial sediment wedges (colluvium consists of bodies of sediment located at the base of slopes through downslope movement caused by gravity) occur at the boundary between wetland and rising dry ground areas;
- Lithological units (typically used as the primary stratigraphic units in geoarchaeological evaluations) are likely to be time transgressive and careful consideration of the significance of the lithostratigraphic correlation should be undertaken.

These stages (modified from Bates 1998) were:

Stage 1a: Late Glacial

This phase, during sea-level low stand, is characterised by cold climate periglacial activity and coarse gravel/sand aggradation in the incised valley bottom. Within the area of investigation a deeply incised valley would have existed, flanked by higher ground, capped by older fluvial sediments from earlier episodes of sand and gravel aggradation. Exposed bedrock surfaces may also have existed on the valley sides. Areas of higher ground bedrock, possibly capped by older fluvial sediments, may also have existed within the floodplain area (Fig 14.1).

Sedimentation in the valley bottom would have been characterised by fluvially deposited coarse gravels and sands with soliflucted sands, gravels and silts at the margins of the floodplain blanketing the valley sides. These deposits would have consisted of bedrock mixed with older Pleistocene sediments and possibly aeolian inputs.

Stage 1b: Early Holocene

During this phase, following climatic amelioration, but prior to sea-level rise, the area would have been characterised by relict Late Glacial features (see above) with a stable channel within the old Late Glacial main channel. The floodplain of the river adjacent to the main channel would have stabilised with the development of the Holocene vegetation and probably formed a relatively dry ground area. Higher gravel areas existed as 'islands' of isolated older Thames gravels in the floodplain and on the valley sides (Fig 14.2).

A key ecotonal area probably existed adjacent to the main Thames channel and any floodplain tributaries. Higher ground would have provided additional landscape resources within different environments.

Plate 6 Cold stage gravels exposed during excavations at Liverpool Street Station, Central London, in the early 1990s

Plate 7 Buried surface at top of gravels, HS1 Swanscombe

Plate 8 Peat and clay-silt within alluvium, HS1 Swanscombe

Plate 9 Sand and gravel island within alluvium, Colne
floodplain, Longford, Heathrow

Stage 2: Early Holocene

During this stage sea-level rise begins to influence
sedimentation and fluvial dynamics within the valley
floor area. As sea-level rises channel stability decreases
and flooding of floodplain areas begins due to backing-
up of fluvial water behind the landward migrating
estuarine front. The floodplain surface becomes unstable
due to widespread flooding and rapid sedimentation.
Minerogenic sedimentation probably characterises this
phase, burying the former dry floodplain surface (Pl 7).

During this period the ecotonal zone between wet
and dry ground migrates inland and rises in datum
across the flooding surface. This boundary also
represents the position of the maximum landward
projection of the zone of wetland sedimentation on the
topographic template at any datum or time, and is called
the sedimentation front. Thus wetland environments
begin to expand at the expense of the dry ground areas.
Temporary landsurfaces may exist within the flooding
area but these are likely to be ephemeral and of local,
short duration, significance only. Dry ground areas
remain as 'islands' within the wetland and at the margin
of the wetland zone (Pl 9).

Stage 3: Middle Holocene

This phase is characterised by apparent fluctuating rates
of sea-level rise in which alterations between organic and
inorganic sedimentation dominate the area (Pl 8).
Temporary emergence of surfaces at or above flooding
level stimulate the growth of organic sediments and lead
to peat growth. Peat growth subsequently expands as
channel stability is regained after initial flooding.

The ecotonal zone between wetland and dryland
continues to move inland and topographic variation is
lost. During times of peat accumulation complex
boundaries between peat and non-peat wetland
ecosystems emerge within the wetland. Wetland now
dominates in the floodplain area as dry ground zones
shrink rapidly (Fig 14.3).

Stage 4: Later Holocene

This phase is characterised by the final submergence of
the former floodplain topography and the loss of much
of the floodplain diversity. Typically organic sediment
growth appears to cease after topographic elevation
is buried.

This model accounted for the patterns shown in
Figure 13 from the Barking Reach area at the scale of the
operational landscape and it is noted that this model
refers primarily to the process by which former
floodplain topography is inundated and lost. However,
locating the exact position of the dry ground/wet ground
interface is problematic at a site specific level because
this will shift seasonally as well as with changing local
topographic position (eg, in relation to the position of
active channels). Consequently, this was a best guess for
understanding landscape scale change within the region
but not a precise reflection of position at the site level. It
is also difficult to determine the relationship between
submergence of the floodplain topography and changes
within the wetland at some distance from the dry
ground/wet ground boundary. This is primarily a result
of problems in correlating between these two areas
caused by lateral facies variation and the problems of
autocompaction of the peat (Allen 1999).

Chronological Control

In order to determine the timing of on-set of
sedimentation onto the topographic template
radiocarbon age estimates (uncalibrated radiocarbon
years (^{14}C BP), this convention is used throughout the
volume and compared against calibrated (cal BC/AD)
dates where appropriate) were selected from situations
where organic deposits immediately overlie the
Pleistocene gravels or sands (ie, where minimal sediment
compaction is likely). All radiocarbon age estimates from
contexts where peats were present within stacks of
unconsolidated sediments were ignored (however, these
age estimates are clearly important for defining age
relationships within the sediment body).

The selected age estimates were plotted against depth
and regression curves fitted to the data (Fig 15; see
Bates 1998; Bates and Whittaker 2004 for detailed data).
Because of the selection of the data no compaction and
distortion of the data has occurred. Two distinct groups
of age estimates were identified consisting of an older
and younger group of age estimates where a steeper
curve was fitted to the older group. This data indicates
more rapid rates for the onset of sedimentation occurred
prior to *c* 5000 cal BC (*c* 6000 ^{14}C BP) with slower rates
thereafter (ie, within the later Mesolithic). The slowing
of the rate of onset of sedimentation occurred after
attaining datums of *c* -5.0m OD. This sub-division is a
function of rising sea-level and the infilling of the
accommodation space (ie, sedimentary basin space
defined by the shape of the topographic template).

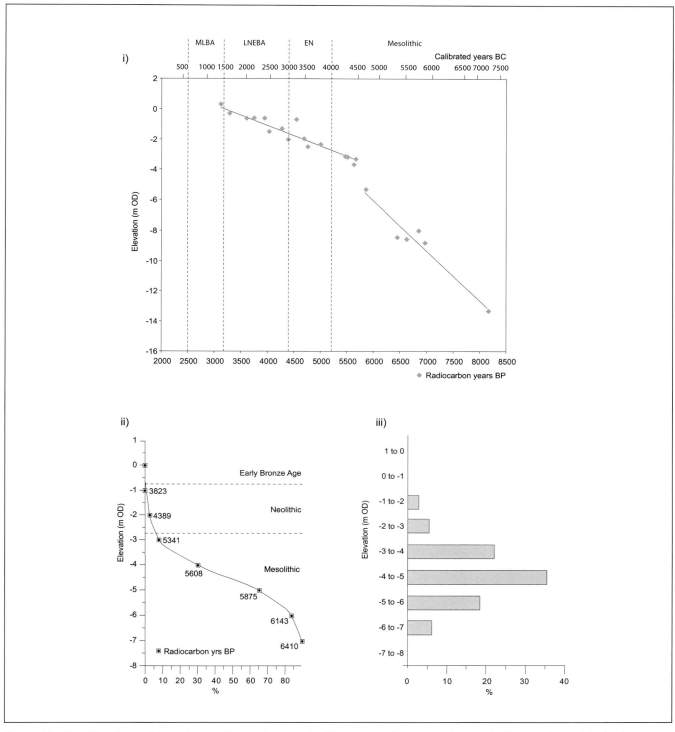

Figure 15 Time/depth model used to calibrate the speed of landscape change on the north Thames floodplain in the area of Barking Reach (from Bates 1998). i) Conventional radiocarbon age estimates (BP) plotted against depth for organic onto gravel situations for selected sites in Lower Thames including trend lines for regression used in calculation of predicated age/depths. This plot shows an initial steeper plot prior to 6000 BP for the phase of rising sea-level followed by a phase of reduced gradient following sea-level attaining maximum elevations. Calculation of the slope of regression lines for each part of the curve allows a time/depth model to be produced. ii) Plot showing the percentage of the gravel surface resting below selected datums. Predicted age estimates (see i above) for specific 1m intervals are shown. This information suggests that only c 800 radiocarbon years elapsed between the onset of sedimentation at -6m OD and sedimentation attaining datums of -3m OD. During this time c 75% of all former dry ground within the Barking Reach area disappeared. iii) Percentage of the gravel surface between successive 1m contour intervals in the Barking Reach area. This plot shows that the majority of the gravel surface rests between datums of -3m to -6m OD

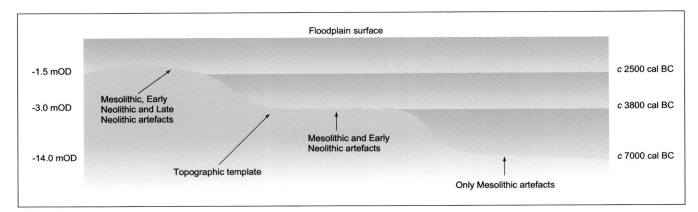

Figure 16 A model for temporal separation of artefact assemblages below floodplain surface based on elevation of the surface of the gravels

The data can be used to define a relationship between age and depth of a deposit at the sedimentation front (ie, the dry ground/wet ground contact on non-compressible substrates). Therefore the speed of inundation of the dry ground topography and the position of the dry ground/wet ground ecotone may be located either at a point on a cross section or spatially on topographic projections.

This relationship is illustrated in Figure 16 where the relationship between the inundation surface, time of inundation and archaeological potential are shown. This model was supported by previous finds from the margins of the Thames floodplain at sites such as Bronze Age Way, Erith (Bennell 1998) and Slade Green (Bates and Williamson 1995).

Subdivision of the Route Corridor

A representative stratigraphy of the route corridor was constructed after careful study of all data sources held by the Geotechnical Management Unit (GMU) at Rail Link Engineering (RLE). A selection of representative boreholes was used to construct the route corridor stratigraphy. The route corridor was divided at an early stage into a series of route windows (Figs 17, 19, 21, 23, 25, 27, 29 and 30), and linked to the distance from the St Pancras terminal end of the route corridor. These route windows were designated and defined by the GMU and provided the initial framework within which the geoarchaeological investigation for the route was conducted. Route windows 1 to 5 were excluded from this investigation at an early stage as it was recognised that they corresponded to areas of bored tunnel within the bedrock and fell outside the alluvial corridor recognised as the defining context for the geoarchaeological investigation. The following procedure was followed for the investigation of each of the route windows:

- A representative selection of borehole logs was selected from the length of each window. Typically 20 boreholes were selected per route window. It should be noted that the length of individual

route windows differs. This is modified slightly in the case of the Ebbsfleet Valley where greater complexity in the sedimentary architecture of the deposits was considered likely;

- The stratigraphy was plotted for each borehole and lithostratigraphic correlations were made between adjacent boreholes (Figs 18, 20, 22, 24, 26 and 28). For the Ebbsfleet Valley a fence diagram (Fig 31) illustrates the added complexity of the sequences;

- The stratigraphic profiles were examined in order to determine the position of the topographic template for the Early Holocene (ie, gravel/alluvium contact);

- The route corridor was subdivided into geoarchaeological zones based on the trend of the topographic template, the proximity of the route area to the higher (dry) ground at the edge of the alluvium, the nature of the sedimentary stack and dissimilarities in lithological continuity across space (Figs 17, 19, 21, 23, 25, 27, 29 and 30).

The stratigraphic profiles presented in Figures 18, 20, 22, 24, 26, 28 and 31 are summarised from the borehole information and were used to identify potential within individual windows. The stratigraphy is summarised in *Table 8*.

Window 6: 17.30–18.92km (East Roding Valley)

This section lies between route kilometres 17.30km and 18.92km (Figs 17 and 18). The route corridor lies close to the outcrop of the older, perched, Thames terrace gravels at the western end of the route corridor. Throughout much of this window the route corridor lies at least 200m from the edge of the floodplain and the higher ground underlain by Pleistocene sands and gravels of the East Tilbury Marshes Gravel.

Bedrock throughout this area of the route corridor consists of London Clay. The rockhead surface shows a distinct two-fold pattern with datums at around -5m OD between 17.3km and *c* 17.8km and below -8m OD throughout the remainder of the window. The upper surface of the gravel, ie, the Early Holocene topographic template, mirrors this two fold sub-division with surfaces

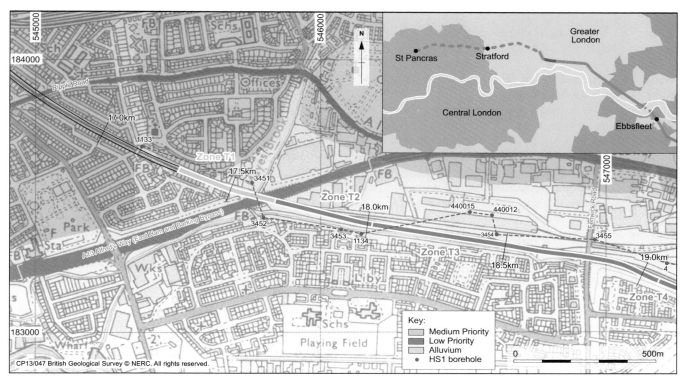

Figure 17 HS1 route corridor Window 6 (Zones T1–T3): location of boreholes

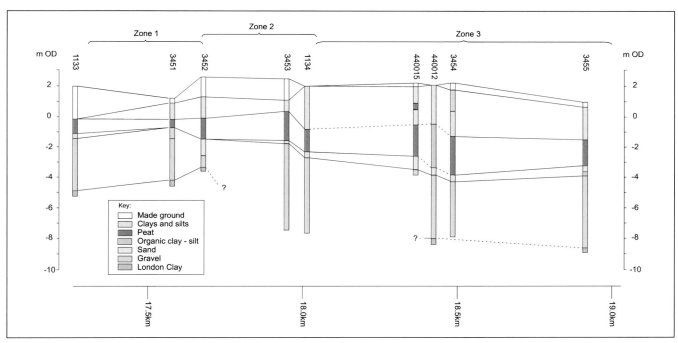

Figure 18 HS1 route corridor Window 6 (Zones T1–T3): lithological profile

at *c* -1.5m OD at the western end dropping to -4.0m OD at the eastern end.

Holocene sediments are dominated by a single major peat unit lying between datums of *c* -0.2m OD and extending to a maximum depth of -4.2m OD. This peat unit can be seen to thin out over the higher gravel towards the west where the peat directly overlies the gravel/sand sequence. Within the eastern part of the corridor peats overlie a thin basal clay-silt. Clay-silts cap much of the peat sequence and made ground is thickest towards the west. A single occurrence of a higher peat unit, extending upwards to *c* 0.5m OD is recorded in a borehole at 18.287km. Three geoarchaeological zones were defined in this area (*Table 8*).

Using the age estimates for onset of sedimentation on the topographic template initial flooding of the eastern end of the route corridor might have occurred during the Late Mesolithic by *c* 4500–4300 cal BC (*c* 5600 ^{14}C BP), with the western end of the route corridor remaining on the whole dry until *c* 2500 cal BC (*c* 4000 ^{14}C BP) at the end of the Late Neolithic period. Zone T2 may have formed an important ecotonal area during the period between 4500–2500 cal BC.

Window 7: 18.92–21.4km (East Roding Valley and West Dagenham Marshes)

This section lies between route kilometres 18.92km and 21.4km (Figs 19 and 20). The route corridor lies between 250m and 500m south of the boundary of the floodplain and the outcrop of higher, older Pleistocene sediments of the East Tilbury Marshes Gravel.

Bedrock consists of London Clay with Woolwich Beds appearing at c 21km. The rockhead surface shows a distinct two-fold pattern with datums at c -9m OD between 18.92km and 19.5km OD dropping to -10.0m/-12.0m OD throughout the remainder of the window. The upper surface of the gravel, ie, the Early Holocene topographic template appears to undulate between c -3.0m and c -6.0m OD.

Holocene sediments are dominated by a single major peat unit lying between datums of c 0.0m OD and extending to a maximum depth of c -5.0m OD. This peat unit overlies silts, clay-silts, sands or slightly gravelly units where the Pleistocene/Holocene contact lies below -4.0m OD. Peat directly overlies the Pleistocene gravel where the gravel surface extends upwards to -4.0m OD or less. The upper surface of the peat appears to undulate by over 2.0m in places, in particular higher upper surface peat datums are noted where peat directly overlies Pleistocene topographic highs and, to a greater degree, where the overlying sediments are at their thinnest, this feature is therefore probably an artefact of sediment autocompaction (see Allen 1999). Clay-silts cap much of the peat sequence and made ground is thickest towards the east. Five geoarchaeological zones were defined in this area (*Table 8*).

Using the age estimates for onset of sedimentation on the topographic template initial flooding of the lower parts of the route corridor, ie, in Zones T4 and T7, might have occurred by c 5000–4800 cal BC (c 6000 ^{14}C BP). Zone T5 would have remained generally dry until c 4300 cal BC (c 5500 ^{14}C BP), possibly as an island within the wetland zone. Two areas of floodplain tributary activity may exist at 19.325km and within Zone T7. However, no trace of channel activity exists within the overlying peat sequences at these points suggesting that the existence of these channels during the Holocene was of limited duration.

Window 8: 21.40–24.39km (Dagenham and Hornchurch Marshes)

This section lies between route kilometres 21.40km and 24.39km (Figs 21 and 22). The route corridor lies south of the outcrop of the higher, older Pleistocene sediments defining the edge of the alluvium. Two major valleys enter the floodplain from the north at c 22km and c 24km. Additionally, the route corridor appears to approach and possibly impact on the older Pleistocene deposits of the Mucking Gravel at c 23.5km.

Bedrock consists of Woolwich/Reading Beds or London Clay. The rockhead surface shows considerable variation in elevation along the window length and ranges from c -14.0m OD to -8.0m OD. The upper surface of the gravels shows similar variation in elevation between c -3.0m OD and -6.0m OD. Considerable internal variation exists within the gravel sequences suggesting the possible presence of some major channels.

Holocene sediments are dominated by a single major peat unit lying between -2.0m OD and -4.0m OD. The organic silts noted in places may be a local facies equivalent of the peat. Thin clay-silts, silts or sands exist in places below the peat. An upper complex of silts, sands and organic silts exists in the area. Made ground is extensively developed at the c 22km mark.

Six geoarchaeological zones were defined in this area (*Table 8*). Using the model outlined above it is likely that all areas of the window were submerged below the sedimentation front between c 4800–4300 cal BC (c 6000–5500 ^{14}C BP). Features in the Pleistocene gravel sequences indicate the possible position of two major infilled channels of Late Pleistocene age. A major zone of potential archaeological significance exists within Zone T12 coinciding with the location of Rainham Creek.

Window 9: 24.39km to 27.78km (Rainham, Wennington and Aveley Marshes)

This section lies between route kilometres 24.39km and 27.78km (Figs 23 and 24). The route corridor lies close to the Mucking and West Thurrock Gravel at the margin of the floodplain between 24.38km and 24.88km. Beyond this point the corridor lies to the south or east of the floodplain edge. Two valleys enter the floodplain at c 25.5km and 26.5km.

Bedrock consists of London Clay or Thanet Sand. The rockhead surface shows considerable variation in elevation along the window length and ranges from c -9.0m OD to -15.0m OD, with dips noted where two major valleys bisect the area The upper surface of the gravels shows similar variation in elevation with variations between -5.0m OD and -9.0m OD at the western end to datums of -12.0m OD in the east.

Holocene sediments are dominated by a single major peat unit centred between 2.0m OD and -5.0m OD. This peat unit may locally bifurcate into two or more sub-units. Thick clay-silts, silts, sands and organic units exist below the peat. An upper complex of silts, sands and organic silts exists in the area. Made ground is relatively thin through the length of the window. Three geoarchaeological zones were defined in this area (*Table 8*).

On the basis of the model proposed above it is suggested that initial inundation of the eastern end of the basin would have occurred c 6000 cal BC (c 7200 ^{14}C BP). The western part of the basin would have been inundated by c 6000–5500 cal BC (c 7000–6500 ^{14}C BP). Key floodplain marginal ecotones may be identified at the boundary between Zones T14 and T15 and the eastern part of Zone T14 may have acted as an important dry

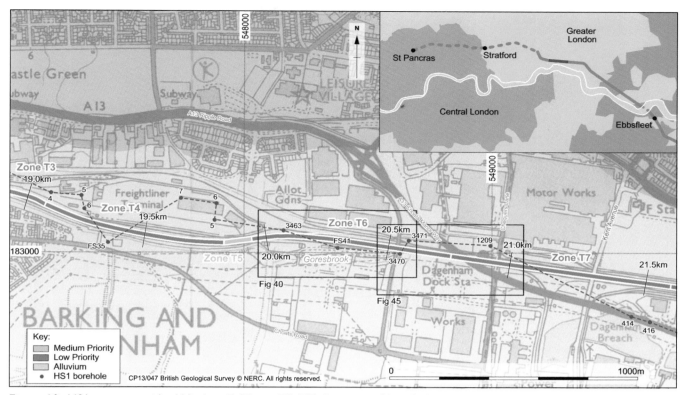

Figure 19 HS1 route corridor Window 7 (Zones T3–T7): location of boreholes

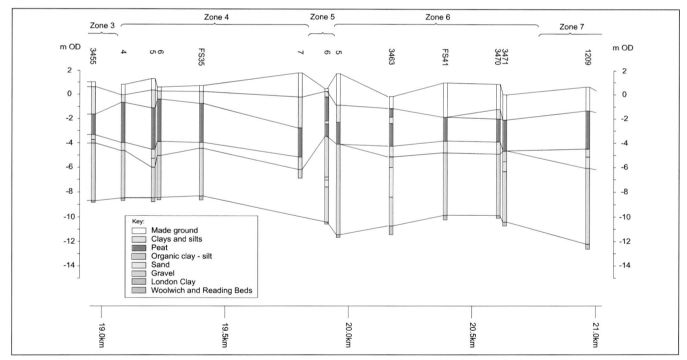

Figure 20 HS1 route corridor Window 7 (Zones T3–T7): lithological profile

ground zone as wetland inundation occurred in Zone T15. Similarly, the western end of Zone T14 may have formed a dry ground region during early infilling of Zone T13.

Window 10: 27.78–28.93km (Aveley Marsh and the Mar Dyke)

This section lies between route kilometres 27.78km and 28.93km (Figs 25 and 26). The route corridor lies across the mouth of the Mar Dyke.

Bedrock consists of Chalk. The rockhead surface shows considerable variation in elevation along the window length and ranges from *c* -5.0m OD at the western end, to -10.0m OD in the central area, climbing to *c* -1m OD at the eastern end, directly correlating with the mouth of Mar Dyke. Gravel is only present at the western end of the route corridor and in a Borehole 3503. Head deposits are noted either side of the Mar Dyke.

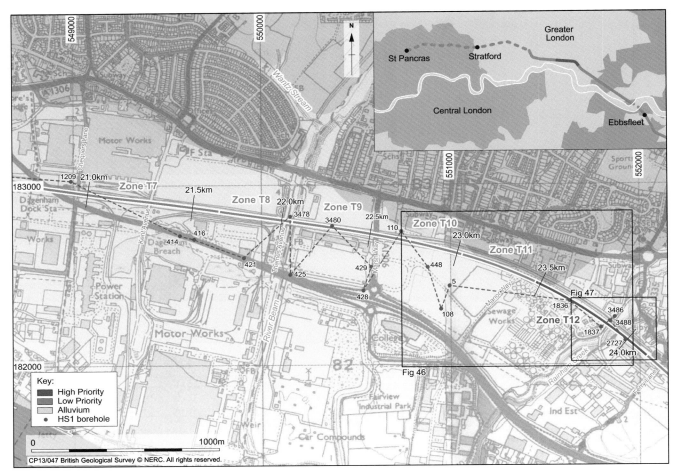

Figure 21 HS1 route corridor Window 8 (Zones T7–T13): location of boreholes

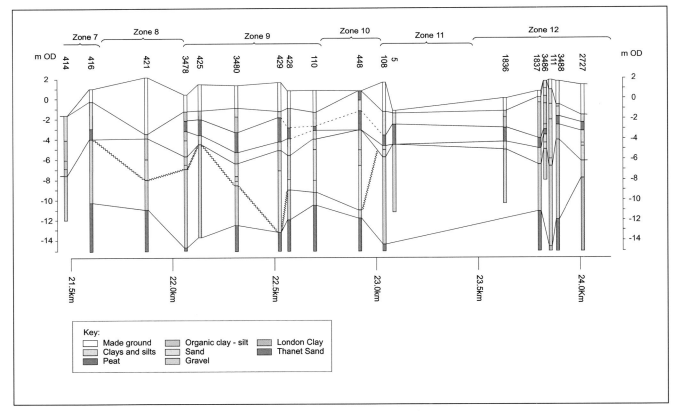

Figure 22 HS1 route corridor Window 8 (Zones T7–T13): lithological profile

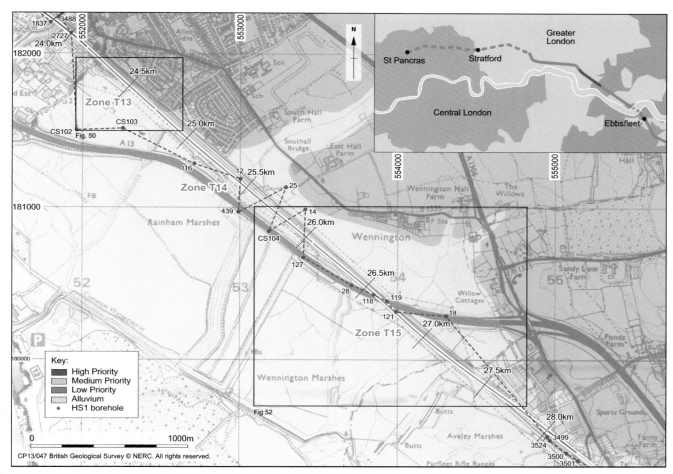

Figure 23 HS1 route corridor Window 9 (Zones T13–T15): location of boreholes

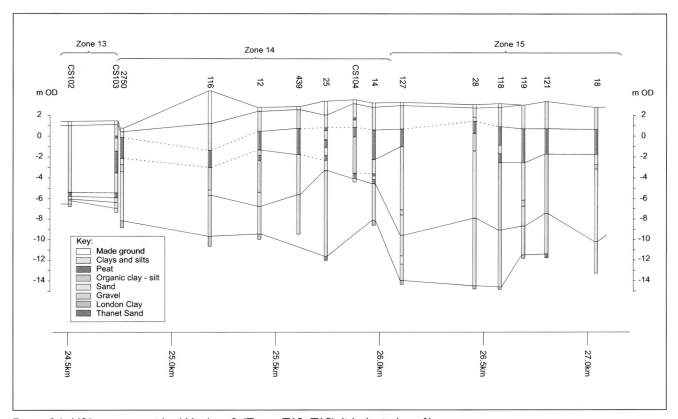

Figure 24 HS1 route corridor Window 9 (Zones T13–T15): lithological profile

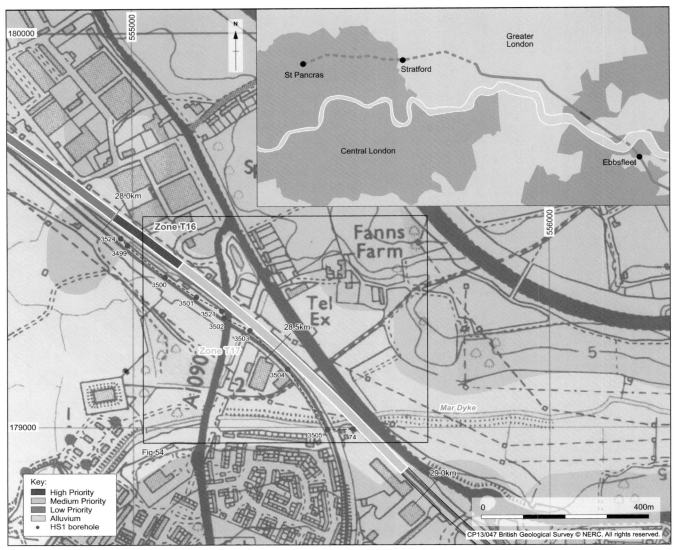

Figure 25 HS1 route corridor Window 10 (Zones T15–T17): location of boreholes

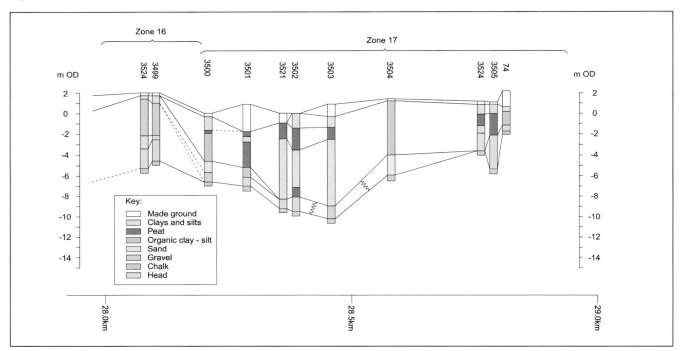

Figure 26 HS1 route corridor Window 10: (Zones T15–T17) lithological profile

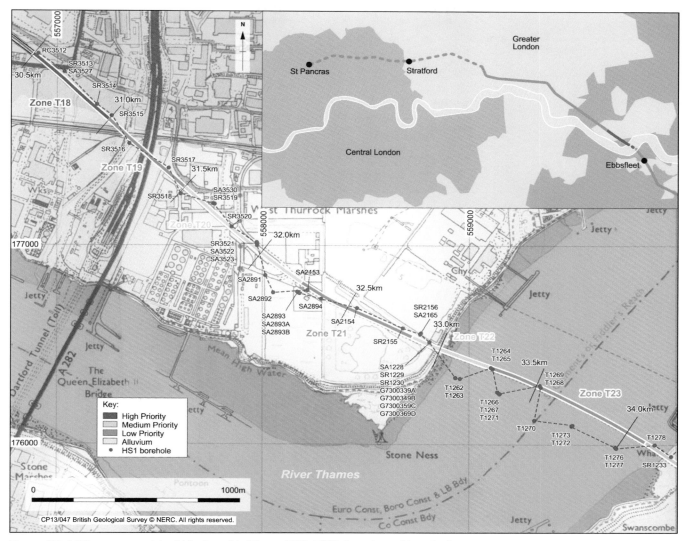

Figure 27 HS1 route corridor Window 11 (Zones T18–T23): location of boreholes

Holocene sediments are complex and include at least two peat units. Thick clay-silts, silts, sands and organic units exist above and below the peat. Made ground is relatively thin along the length of the window. Two geoarchaeological zones were defined in this area (*Table 8*).

The zones present here are complex and influenced strongly by the presence of a Thames tributary valley and remnant older Pleistocene sediments. Zone T16 probably formed an island or promontary within the floodplain remaining dry throughout much of the prehistoric past. Important ecotonal zones surround this area and these may have been a focus for dry ground activity within the rapidly expanding wetland area.

Within the Mar Dyke valley the steeply dipping topography of the Late Pleistocene landscape would have resulted in gradual ecotonal zone shifts through much of the prehistoric period. Dry ground zones around the wetland may have been the focus of considerable human activity.

Window 11: 30.50–33.15km (Thames Crossing)
This section lies between route kilometres 30.50km and 33.15km (Figs 27 and 28). The route corridor lies across

the width of the Thames floodplain on the north bank of the Thames.

Bedrock consists of Chalk. The rockhead surface shows some variation in elevation along the window length. Valley edge rockhead datums dip steeply southwards from 30.5km to 31.0km dropping from 9.0m OD to -15.0m OD. Within the main area of the window rockhead datums lie between -13.0m OD and -15.0m OD. The upper surface of the gravels is commonly about -10.0m OD. Holocene sediments are complex and include at least two peat units. Thick clay-silts, silts, sands and organic units exist above and below the peat. Made ground is relatively thin along the length of the window. Six geoarchaeological zones were defined in this area (*Table 8*).

Within this area inundation of the lower portions of the remaining exposed gravel surface would have taken place by about *c* 6000 cal BC (*c* 7200 ^{14}C BP). Within Zone T20 a major, possibly Early Holocene, channel has been noted within or cut into the top of the gravels. Areas associated with the edge of this channel may have considerable archaeological importance.

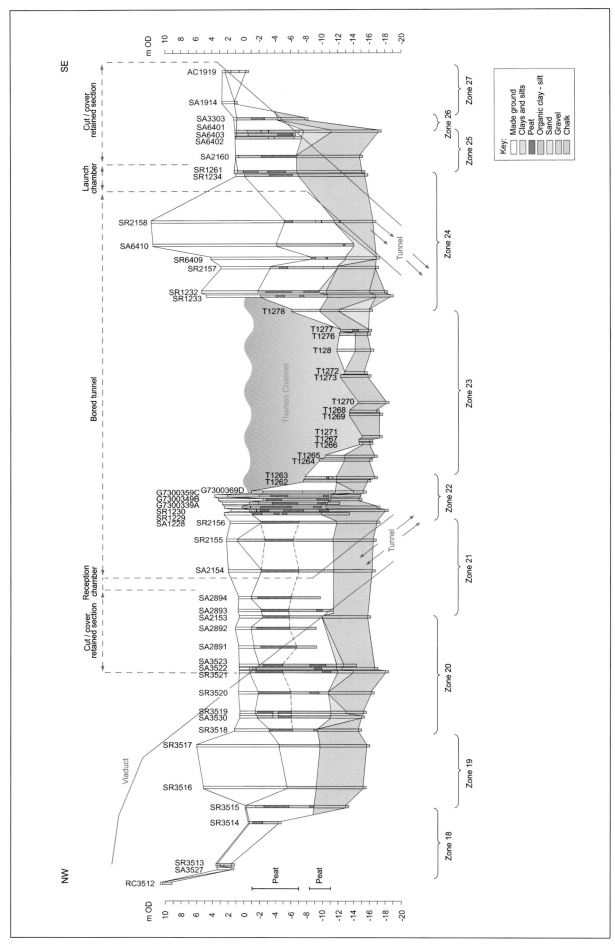

Figure 28 HSI route corridor Window 11 and 12 (Zones T18–T27): lithological profile

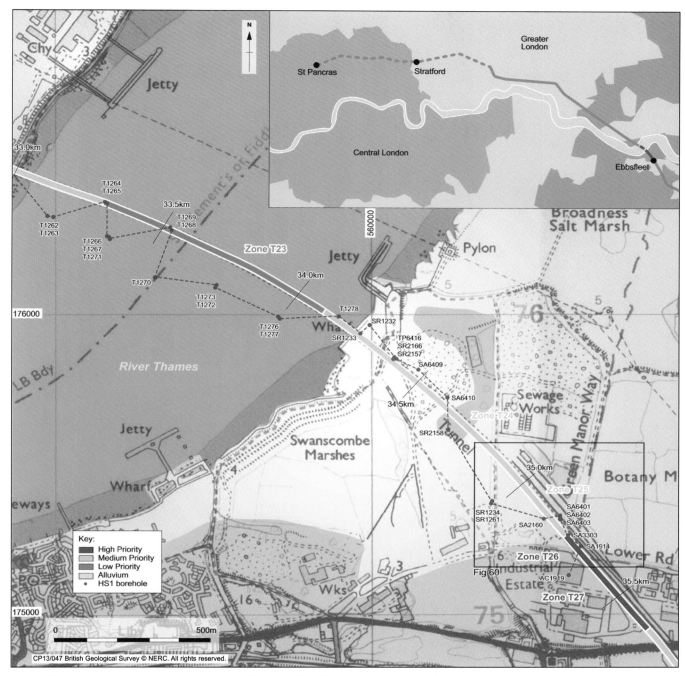

Figure 29 HS1 route corridor Window 12 (Zones T22–T27): location of boreholes

Window 12: 33.15–36.30km (Thames Crossing)

This section lies between route kilometres 33.15km and 36.30km (Figs 28 and 29). The route corridor lies across the width of the Thames floodplain.

Bedrock consists of Chalk. The rockhead surface shows considerable variation in elevation along the window length and ranges from depths of -17.0m OD at the northern end to 0.0m OD at the southern end. Gravel is present beneath much of the route corridor. Holocene sediments are complex and include at least two peat units. Thick clay-silts, silts, sands and organic units exist above and below the peat. Made ground is present along the length of the window.

Five geoarchaeological zones were defined in this area (*Table 8*).

This window is complex and illustrates rapidly changing nature of the preserved sediments between the modern channel and the floodplain edge. Important ecotonal zones are preserved within this region. Initial flooding of the region probably commenced by *c* 6000 cal BC (*c* 7200 ^{14}C BP). A step-like pattern to the Early Holocene topographic template with benches at *c* -7.5m OD, -4.5m OD and 0.0m OD suggest sequential flooding of the south bank may have provided suitable dry ground locations for occupation.

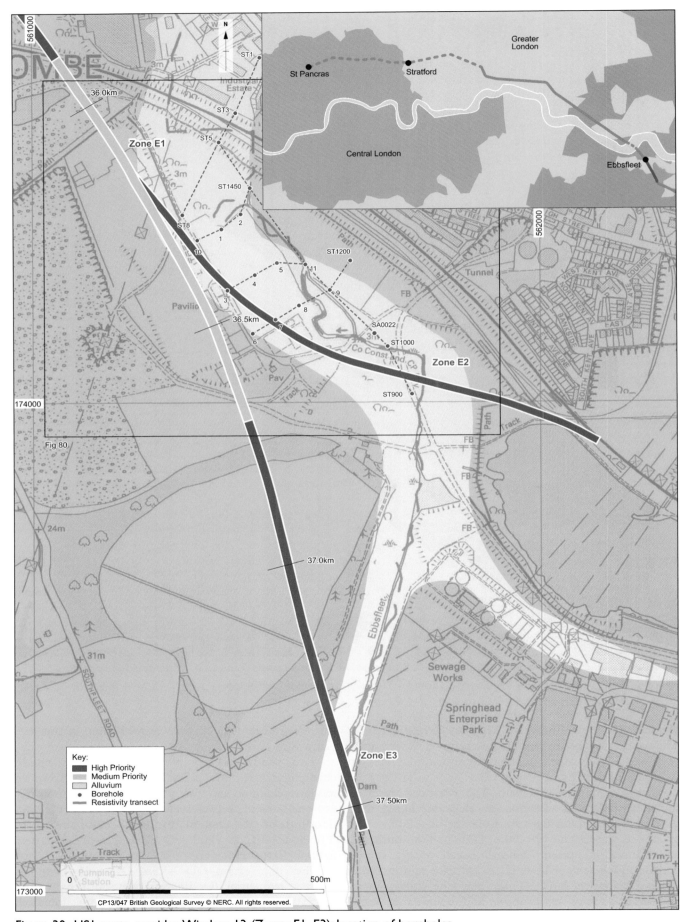

Figure 30 HS1 route corridor Window 13 (Zones E1–E3): location of boreholes

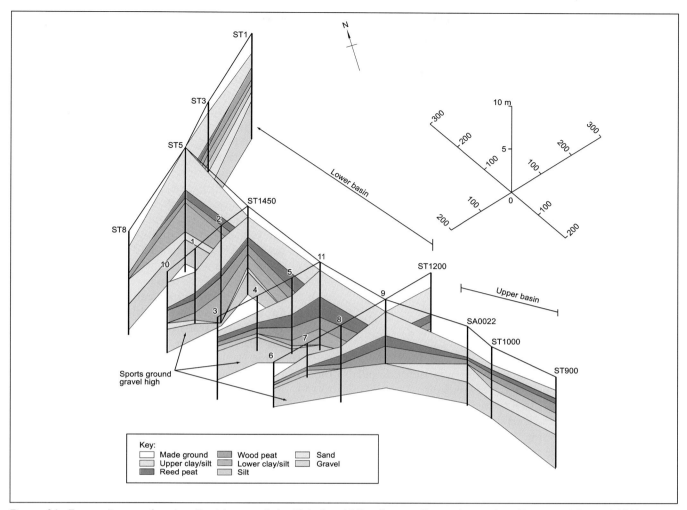

Figure 31 Fence diagram for the alluvial area of the Ebbsfleet Valley Sports Ground complex (Bates and Bates 2000)

Window 13: 35.90–37.55km (Ebbsfleet Valley)

This part of the route corridor lies within the south bank tributary known as the Ebbsfleet Valley (Fig 30). The valley is well known for the Pleistocene sands and gravels present on the valley sides (Wenban-Smith 1995; Oxford Archaeological Unit 1997). Less well known are the rich prehistoric archaeological remains associated with the alluvium in the valley bottom (Burchell 1938; Burchell and Piggott 1939; Sieveking 1960; Barham and Bates 1995; Oxford Archaeological Unit 1995; 1997; URL 1997). These previous works have demonstrated that complex stratigraphies exist in the valley base consisting of clay-silt and organic silts/peats (Fig 31). Towards the valley sides these units probably interdigitate with colluvial sediments derived from the valley margins. The unconsolidated Holocene sediments overlie basal sand and gravel units of probable Late Pleistocene age.

The route of HS1 through the valley consists of the main line running north-west to south-east (Fig 30) along the valley edge area (primarily impacting on the Pleistocene valley side sediments) prior to crossing the River Ebbsfleet 300m south of the sewage works. A major station complex was proposed for the site. A connection with the North Kent Line is made from the southern end of the station complex near South Kent

Avenue (Fig 30), crossing the main Ebbsfleet Valley to the east of the Roman building complex (URL 1997).

The Ebbsfleet Valley sedimentary sequence consists of a complex set of deposits showing variable 3-dimensional patterns (Fig 31). Archaeological material contained within these deposits reflects a wide variety of environments of deposition from dry land to tidal mudflats. Important assemblages of artefactual remains from the Neolithic and Roman periods exist in this area. Radiocarbon age estimates suggest initial infilling of the lower parts of the basin prior to *c* 5500 cal BC (*c* 6500 ^{14}C BP), with inundation of the gravel high by *c* 3000 cal BC (*c* 4400 ^{14}C BP).

A Route Specific Geoarchaeological Model for the Study Area

The investigation of the individual route windows defined adequately the nature of the succession in each area and the associated archaeological potential. Specifically it enabled a summarised profile to be drawn up (Fig 7) that illustrated the nature of the sequences along the route corridor. A number of individual features were noted:

- Across much of the western end of the route corridor a two-fold sub-division of the alluvial tract was noted with a shallow basin at the western end of the tract and a deeper basin at the eastern end of the tract;
- The sub-division into two areas indicated that the time depth of the fine grained sediments increased from west to east and the depth to topographic template also increased towards the east;
- A major rise in the topographic template was noted west of the Mar Dyke;
- A buried Pleistocene terrace was noted in the vicinity of the Thames crossing area (south);
- A major peat bed was noted throughout much of the route corridor, although its presence became intermittent towards the west;
- Basal organic sequences were present above the gravel surface across much of the eastern and Thames Crossing areas.

Status and Adequacy of the Data

The mapped status of the alluvium was definitionally relatively poor for a variety of reasons. The BGS mapping is reliable only to a spatial precision of c ±50m for edge boundaries. For certain sectors of the route the GMU provided mapping at greater spatial precision. However, the spacing of boreholes is not designed to establish edges to alluvial units and therefore edge definition to better than ±50m (and perhaps even 100m) is unlikely.

It should be remembered that surface 'edge' boundaries mapped for alluvium may shift spatially by 10–100m on gently dipping bed contacts when traced sub-surface, for example, Holocene alluvial overlapping Pleistocene gravels. Surface mapping may be a poor spatial indicator of subsurface deposits, even in shallow superficial sediments. In addition the urbanised and industrial character of the landscape makes mapping boundaries difficult without extensive ground investigation surveys. The borehole data held in the GMU and that subsequently gathered as part of the HS1 project have, however, allowed a refinement to be made in terms of defining edges and boundaries of the alluvium. However, even on completion of the project, the distribution of data along the route corridor remained uneven and skewed to areas of major engineering structures rather than targeting areas of potential archaeological interest.

Methodologies for Field Investigation

Borehole Investigation

Information from boreholes is often available in geotechnical reports (Clayton *et al* 1995) undertaken for a range of site investigation purposes and can provide information suitable for deriving predictions relevant to understanding the 3-D geometry of the buried sediment bodies. It should be remembered, however, that the distribution of borehole data across a given site (as well as the methods and techniques used) is typically dependent on the geological conditions, the type of structure and construction design, and methods to be employed (Bell 1993). Additionally, because such data collection is driven by commercial requirements, it may have only restricted predictive value in geological terms. In such situations, preliminary models derived from engineering boreholes may be usefully supplemented by 'purposive boreholes' during a second phase of drilling investigation.

A range of equipment is available for investigation of sub-surface contexts from unpowered manually driven devices such as Hiller borers and Russian (D-section) corers, which retrieve variably undisturbed sediment cores from soft sediments, to powered mechanical corers with a number of interchangeable coring heads (eg, Eijkelkamp system); small portable drill rigs, including the Terrier 2000 self-propelled drill rig with a windowless liner sampling system; wireline percussive drilling; sonic drilling; and multi-purpose rigs such as the Comacchio system (Bates *et al* 2000a; Clayton *et al* 1995). Selection of appropriate drilling equipment varies dependant on a number of factors including costs, site ground conditions, nature of the overburden, the type of sediment likely to be encountered in the sub-surface and the nature of the samples required for analysis.

Applications of coring and augering methods in archaeology include tracing the lateral extent of near-surface sites as part of cultural resource evaluations (Stein 1991), investigation of deposit depth and composition prior to excavation on middens, mounds and tells (eg, Reed *et al* 1968), the coring of rockshelter deposits (Bailey and Thomas 1987), assisting in reconstructing off-site palaeo-environments (Barham 1999) and understanding the development of urban areas (Densem and Doidge 1979; Ammerman 2000). Coring has also been deployed to assist in mapping archaeologically significant facies environments beneath urban areas, such as tufas in the Lower Dour, Kent (Bates and Barham 1993), and to stratigraphically link excavated sequences into adjacent palaeolandforms and landsurfaces (eg, Barham and Bates 1994). In Europe, coring coupled to excavation trenching, has been used in the study of agricultural systems buried beneath alluvium (Martín-Consuegra *et al* 1998).

Non-archaeological uses include the construction of lithostratigraphic models of Quaternary-age sediment bodies, including Holocene alluvium members and formations (Bridgland 1988; Gibbard 1985; 1994), and the recovery of samples for biostratigraphic analysis, radiocarbon dating and palaeoecological reconstruction of floodplain environments (Devoy 1979). Good examples of the use of large datasets in the construction of sub-surface models include the work of Chen *et al* (1996) on the North China Plain, Berendsen and Stouthamer (2001) in the Rhine-Meuse delta region, Weerts *et al* (2005) in the Netherlands, Culshaw (2005) in Manchester and the Neath/Swansea area of south Wales.

Cone Penetration Testing

The cone penetrometer was developed in the Netherlands in 1934 (Vermeiden 1948) and has gained a wide acceptance within geotechnical engineering for determination of soil properties and stratigraphy. The method is based on the interpretation of the resistance of the tip of the cone rods and friction on the trailing sleeve as the cone is advanced into the ground. The technique is fast, economic and useful for sub-surface sediment characterisation and stratigraphic analysis. It is especially suited to fine-grained sediments (Table 9), however, caution must be given to interpretation of CPT data in coarse sand or gravel, with the latter often causing complete cone rejection.

A typical setup consists of a 20-tonne capacity hydraulic penetrometer mounted in a heavy tracked vehicle ballasted to produce a reaction weight of about 14 tonnes. A 7.5 or 5 tonne capacity electric cone may be selected such as the Fugro piezo-cone penetrometer. In this case the cone has a 60° apex at the tip, a 10 or 15cm² base area and a 150 or 200cm² sleeve surface area combined with pore water pressure element (and resistivity probe). The cones are vertically advanced at a standard rate of 2cm/sec for readings of tip resistance and sleeve friction. Both tip resistance and sleeve friction are related to sediment type and moisture content and the ratio of the tip resistance to the sleeve friction provides information that can be used to classify sediment type (see Chap 11, Fig 66). Pore pressure readings can also be taken during the cone drive. Resistivity of the sediment can be measured using an array of electrodes that record the bulk resistivity of the soil around and between the electrodes. Bulk resistivity represents the total electrical resistance contributed from all sources (grains, matrix material and water) and is a useful downhole check on surface measured ground resistance properties (see below). Output from the cone penetrometer includes curves of tip resistance, sleeve friction, pore content and electrical resistivity with depth.

Examples of the application of CPT data to Quaternary geological/palaeoenvironmental or archaeological projects are limited but it has been used to construct large-scale stratigraphic models of the Po Plain, Italy (Amorosi and Marchi 1999), to produce cross-section data (Howie *et al* 1998) and to locate the presence of buried structures under the Metropolitan Cathedral in Mexico City (Ovando-Shelley and Manzanilla 1997).

Table 9 Sediment classification based on CPT data (based on Clayton *et al* 1995) and approximate ranges of physical properties for some common materials (after Telford *et al* 1990; Reynolds 1997; and Guegiem and Palciauskas 1994)

Sediment type	Cone resistance	Friction ratio	Excess pore pressure	Density	Resistivity
Organic sediments/peat	Low	Very high	Low	1.1–2.4	10–300
Normally consolidated clay	Low	High	High	1.6–2.6	1–80
Sand	High	Low	Zero	1.7–2.3	80–500
Gravel	Very high – refusal	Low	Zero	1.7–2.4	80–500
Chalk	Very high – refusal			1.5–2.6	50–200

Table 10 Electrical properties of selected sediments

Material	Density Mg m^{-3}	P-velocity ms^{-1}	S-velocity ms^{-1}	Resistivity Ohm-m	Magnetic susceptibility
Clay	1.6–2.6	1000–2500	500–1500	1–100	
Silt	1.8–2.2	500–2500	250–1000	10–200	
Sand	1.7–2.3	200–2000	100–1500	50–500	
Peat	1.1–2.4	100–500	100–500	10–300	
Gravel	1.7–2.4	400–2500	200–1500	50–500	
Sandstone	1.6–2.7	1400–5000	800–3000	$10–10^8$	0–21,000
Chalk	1.5–2.6	2000–5000	800–3000	50–150	
Shale	1.7–3.2	2000–4500	800–2500	20–1000	60–18,600
Granite	2.5–2.8	4500–6500	1500–3000	$300–10^6$	10–50,000
Basalt	2.7–3.3	5500–6500	2000–3000	$10–10^7$	500–182,000

Electrical Geophysical Investigation Techniques

Electrical techniques are extensively used in near surface geophysical investigations and include both direct current (DC) resistivity methods and indirect electromagnetic (EM) methods. All electrical techniques induce electrical currents in the ground, which are used to measure the variation in ground conductivity or its inverse resistivity. Different materials (solid rock and drift deposits), and the fluids within them, show different responses to an applied electrical current. In general, sequences with high clay contents show higher conductivity as do saturated sequences, especially sequences where saline waters are present. Conversely sequences with low clay content, sands and gravel or bedrock, such as limestones and chalks, show low conductivity or high resistivity (Table 10). Direct current resistivity is one of the most common methods for field practice relying on directly placing an electrical current into the ground using two electrodes and measuring the response (the electrical potential) to that current over a set distance between two additional electrodes. By combining measurements made at a number of different electrode locations and separations it is possible to construct geo-electric pseudo-sections. These sections can then be interpreted as geologic sequences when correlated with borehole or CPT ground truth data. A number of commercial systems have been designed for the rapid acquisition of 2D pseudo-electrical resistivity sections, including the Lund System (Abem Ltd), Campus Instruments and SYSCAL (Iris Ltd) systems.

Electromagnetic techniques have been extensively developed and adapted over the last 15 years to map lateral and vertical changes in conductivity (Reynolds 1997). Two types of electromagnetic survey are currently practised: i) time domain electromagnetic (TDEM) surveys which are mainly used for depth soundings and more recently in advanced metal detectors, and ii) frequency domain electromagnetic (FDEM) surveys that are used predominantly for mapping lateral changes in conductivity. Both electromagnetic survey types rely on inducing electrical currents in the ground by creating an electromagnetic field in a coil of wire located at the surface. In FDEM, the secondary electric currents are recorded by an additional electrical coil located at the surface. FDEM has proved particularly successful in mapping near surface and surface changes in conductivity because at low electrical induction numbers the ratio of the secondary and primary magnetic fields is linearly proportional to the terrain conductivity (McNeill 1990). FDEM potentially represents one of the most useful geophysical techniques in archaeological investigations as changes in conductivity are often associated with differences between archaeologically significant lithological sequences (see Table 10) and also disturbed ground. Instrumentation exists to survey to a range of depths by using different source and receiver coil separations (see Table 11).

Both DC and EM approaches have been successfully used to map lithology, channel-belts and valley fills (Baines *et al* 2002), to study the palaeohydrography and subsurface geology of sites in the Nile Delta (Ibrahim *et al* 2002), and to map Holocene and Pleistocene sediments in the Medway Estuary (Bates *et al* 2007) and in Sussex (Lewis and Roberts 1998; Bates *et al* 2000; Bates and Bates 2000).

Designing the Survey Strategy

Developing a methodology for implementation within projects, either associated with archaeological investigation works or speculative ground investigation for Quaternary research, should be approached on a site by site basis. However, a number of elements may be combined together to facilitate investigation. Desk-based study of extant data sources, particularly records held by national geoscience bodies (Culshaw 2005) or local authorities, often provides substantial quantities of data from previous geotechnical investigations. Design of the field programme will be influenced by both the extant data sets and the project specific aims and objectives. Commonly, a two-step approach to field investigation is recommended, commencing with field trials for the techniques proposed, in order to clarify their suitability as well as to obtain preliminary data sets. This stage will allow appropriate techniques to be selected and provide a first order sub-surface model. The precise timings of works (eg, geophysical survey, borehole drilling) will be dependent on a number of factors, but typically geophysical surveys would be concluded prior to, or during, the final phase of ground truth drilling and sampling. Finally, recovery and laboratory logging of cores, coupled with assessment of the contained microfossils allows initial environments of deposition to be assigned to each sedimentary unit.

The successful design of a mixed method approach to investigation is dependent on the careful construction of the survey methodology, based on the consideration of a number of key geological and practical (finance/accessibility) factors. Key points to consider are:

1.   The nature of the geological/geomorphological system. While it is obvious that sequence complexity varies according to the geological systems and local geomorphological constraints, it is important to ensure that an adequate

Table 11 Approximate depth of investigation ranges for Geonics Ltd electromagnetic survey instruments

Instrument	EM-38	EM-31	EM-34	EM-34	EM-34
Coil Spacing	1m	3.7m	10m	20m	40m
Horizontal Dipole	0.75m	3m	7.7m	15m	30m
Vertical Dipole	1.5m	6m	15m	30m	60m

sampling interval (both vertically and laterally) is adopted that takes into account the likely levels of variation within the system being studied.

2. Field study size area. This is dependent on the perceived nature of the sediments/system being investigated and questions being asked, including the experience of the fieldworker. In commercially driven projects this may be defined by the construction area. However, that may, or may not, make geomorphological sense for understanding the regional context and the broader stratigraphic relationships of deposits.

3. Project aims and objectives and the goals of the project in terms of information required and models being tested. Sampling of a fluvial gravel body, for example, the Boyn Hill Member of the Lower Thames (Bridgland 1994; Gibbard 1994), for either contained archaeological material or gravel clast lithological analysis, requires radically different sampling types and frequency of interventions (many as opposed to one or two respectively).

4. Sequence recovery or sequence logging. The necessity to recover samples for characterisation or undisturbed testing will determine the type of borehole technique used. Sites where it is only necessarily to broadly categorise the underlying sediments and sub-surface topography could be investigated rapidly (and cost-effectively) through the application of geophysical techniques or CPT survey, coupled with occasional ground truth boreholes. If it is important to an individual project to look at the structure of the sediments and sample these for further assessment/analysis (eg, dating) then collection of sleeved borehole samples would be required.

5. Depth of sequences. The depth of burial of the features/deposits of interest is important as different techniques have different investigation ranges (equally applicable to drilling techniques as well as geophysical surveys). With all geophysical techniques the depth range is technique dependent, resulting in a "trade off" between the investigation depth and resolution of the technique with respect to the feature of interest. A technique that will look deep into the earth generally does so with lower resolution compared to a technique designed to investigate shallow depths. With boreholes it is often the case that sample recovery becomes poorer with depth.

6. Target size. An estimation of the target size is necessary prior to selecting appropriate techniques and survey parameters such as the spatial frequency of sampling. The target size should be considered in conjunction with the depth range for individual techniques.

7. Measurement/sampling station interval. This depends on the nature and complexity of the geological system, as well as (for geophysical investigations) the burial depth, target size and techniques selected. In the case of geophysical surveys these have traditionally been conducted along line profiles or on grids, therefore the station spacing along the lines must be calculated together with the line separation in order to not miss a particular target size. Determining locations for boreholes is, in part, dictated by the perceived complexity of the sub-surface geology as well as the nature of the evidence that is necessary to extract from the samples (ie, larger samples and at more frequent intervals will be necessary if project objectives are the recovery of evidence pertaining to human activity (rather than vegetation or water body reconstruction based on pollen or foraminifera respectively).

While many of these points are likely to be very familiar to readers they are rarely discussed in the literature. Considered discussion of the sampling strategies used, their strengths and weaknesses, and the limitations in the study, should form an essential part of the discussion of the project and write-up. Failure to inform the reader and consider such information will make it difficult to address the success or failure of a project. For example, the failure to locate certain deposits or certain classes of palaeoenvironmental data needs to be considered in the light of the methodologies used and systems from which the material came. The dangers of inadequate survey design have recently been discussed by Salvany *et al* (2004) in the Agrio River valley, Spain.

Part III
Field Investigation of the HS1 Corridor

Chapter 7

The Lea Valley

*by Catherine Barnett, Michael J Grant and Martin Bates
with contributions by Nigel Cameron, Phil Harding, David Smith,
Chris J Stevens, John Whittaker and Sarah F Wyles*

The area of the Lea Valley impacted on by HS1 includes both the Stratford Box and the Temple Mills Depot (Fig 5). The archaeological remains and site-related sedimentary sequences for the former have been reported separately (Valler and Crockett forthcoming; Barnett *et al* forthcoming). This area (Window 3) was not assessed in the original 1999 desk-top study (Chap 6), although individual geoarchaeological desk-top studies were carried out for both sites prior to field investigations (Table 12). The sites lie between 5m and 6m OD, a topography created in part by the character of Holocene deposits in the Lea Valley and enhanced by the creation of the modern railway shunting yards. To the east the ground rises to form the east side of the valley. Bedrock geology is mapped as the London Clay Formation, largely eroded in the valley bottom itself, overlying a sequence of Palaeocene deposits that are collectively referred to as the Lambeth Group (Woolwich and Reading Beds), which lie on Cretaceous Upper Chalk (British Geological Survey 1993). The Woolwich and Reading Beds include sandy elements (Upper Thanet Beds) and pebble beds (Upnor Formation).

The principal Quaternary deposits recorded in the area comprise the Lea Valley Gravel (Gibbard 1994; equivalent to the Shepperton Gravels of the Lower Thames), deposited during the infilling of the valley during the Middle to Late Devensian period (*c* 26,000–9,700 cal BC), and are known to contain Upper Palaeolithic flint artefacts (Bridgland 1993). These gravels are also known to contain occurrences of the 'Lea Valley Arctic Plant Beds' (Warren 1912; 1915), organic deposits containing a 'full glacial' plant assemblage (Reid 1949; Allison *et al* 1952), insect assemblage typical of arctic tundra (Coope and Tallon 1983), cold indicator and dwarfed specimens of molluscs (Warren 1912, 239) and 'steppe tundra' fauna (Lister and Sher 2001), which have been radiocarbon

dated to between 34,700 and 20,650 cal BC (see Powell 2012 for details). These have generally been recorded as lying towards the base of the Lea Valley Gravels at several locations in the Lower Lea Valley and adjacent tributary valleys, with local occurrences recorded at the former Temple Mills Pit by Warren (1912) and beneath the Olympic Park in a borehole by Corcoran and Swift (2004). Grant and Norcott (2012; see also Corcoran *et al* 2011) have suggested, based upon deposit modelling of the area, that the local deposits in the Stratford area might be associated with a tributary river (course of the present Phillibrook Stream) draining into the River Lea through the centre of the Temple Mills Depot footprint, although no evidence for these deposits was uncovered in the borehole survey across the site.

Softer unconsolidated sand, silt, clay and peat, which overlie the Lea Valley Gravel, represent Holocene fluvial activity within the floodplain of the River Lea. A number of palaeochannels that cut the earlier gravel are filled with these softer sediments. The likelihood of former land surfaces of Late Upper Palaeolithic, Mesolithic and Neolithic date preserved below and within these deposits is well-documented (eg, see Corcoran *et al* 2011).

Investigations of the Stratford Box site (Fig 32) are examined elsewhere (Valler and Crockett forthcoming; Barnett *et al* forthcoming) and are not the focus of study here. However, it should be noted that investigation of the borehole logs from the route corridor and the purposive drilling of a number of additional boreholes identified the presence of at least two bodies of gravel beneath the floodplain here (Fig 35, see below). No trace of the Lea Valley Arctic Beds was found and the main focus of attention was close to the active course of the Lea where some evidence of later prehistoric activity on the floodplain was recovered. Here we report on the findings at Temple Mills sheds located to the north.

Table 12 Summary of fieldwork events, Stratford Box and Temple Mills

Event name	Event code	Type	Interventions	Archaeological contractor
Stratford Box	ARC SBX00	Evaluation	3839-3844TT, 7BH (CP)	Wessex Archaeology
Stratford Box	ARC SBX00	Excavation		Wessex Archaeology
Stratford Box	ARC SBX00	Watching brief		Wessex Archaeology
Temple Mills Depot Boreholes	ARC TPD04	Evaluation	12BH	Wessex Archaeology
Temple Mills Depot Evaluation	ARC TPD04	Evaluation	4038TT–4044TT	Wessex Archaeology
Stratford Connection	ARC SCX04	Watching Brief		Wessex Archaeology

TT = trench   BH = borehole   (CP) = Cable percussion

Temple Mills

Construction Impacts

Development at Temple Mills Depot included the construction of a 400 x 100m service shed for Eurostar trains, a separate facility to allow replacement of bogies (wheeled chassis; generically referred to as the Bogie Drop), a storage warehouse and ancillary works including an office block (Fig 33). In addition, a new section of track following the east bank of the River Lea (the Stratford Box Connection) to connect the high-speed railway through Stratford Box (the below-ground housing for Stratford International station) with Temple Mills Depot was also constructed.

Key Archaeological Issues

Desk-top study of the area noted records of 17 imprecisely provenanced Neolithic axes in an area focused at the north-west end of the main Eurostar shed, while additional records indicated a possible, but poorly provenanced, Roman causeway towards the south-east end of the shed (Fig 33). From at least the 16th century the marsh was being drained by a network of open ditches and/or natural channels collectively known as the Stratford Back Rivers which are shown on 18th century maps as forming the boundaries of a patchwork of small pasture fields. Towards the end of the 19th century this (by then largely defunct) drainage system had been replaced by sewers and culverts, and most of the former ditches and channels had been lost from the visible landscape.

Roman settlement associated with roads and a cemetery was also noted, as well as Saxon river-side activity. The sites of several medieval buildings fall within the study area, including Ruckholt Manor, Chobham Manor, the Temple Mills watermill complex and St Mary the Virgin Church.

Post-medieval sites include places of worship and several other notable buildings including Leyton House, Leyton Grange, Ive Farm, Etloe House, the *White House* public house, medical facilities and structures relating to crossings over the River Lea. Several post-medieval industrial premises worthy of note were also recorded, including hop-drying sheds, calico printers and a silk mill. Twentieth century structures in the study area include the church of St Luke, two Second World War anti-aircraft sites, and most recently the Olympic Park.

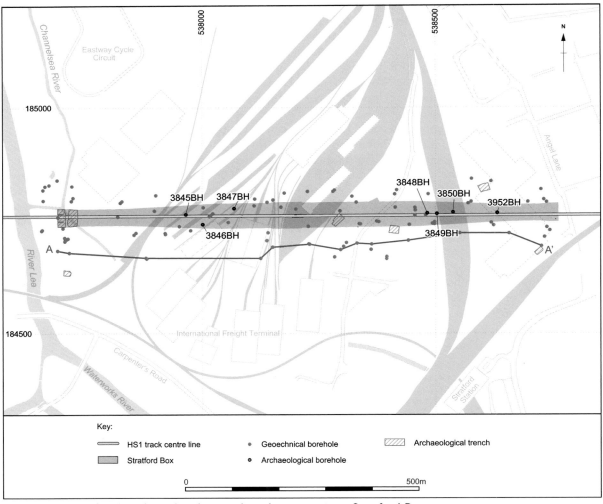

Figure 32 Plan of archaeological and geotechnical interventions, Stratford Box

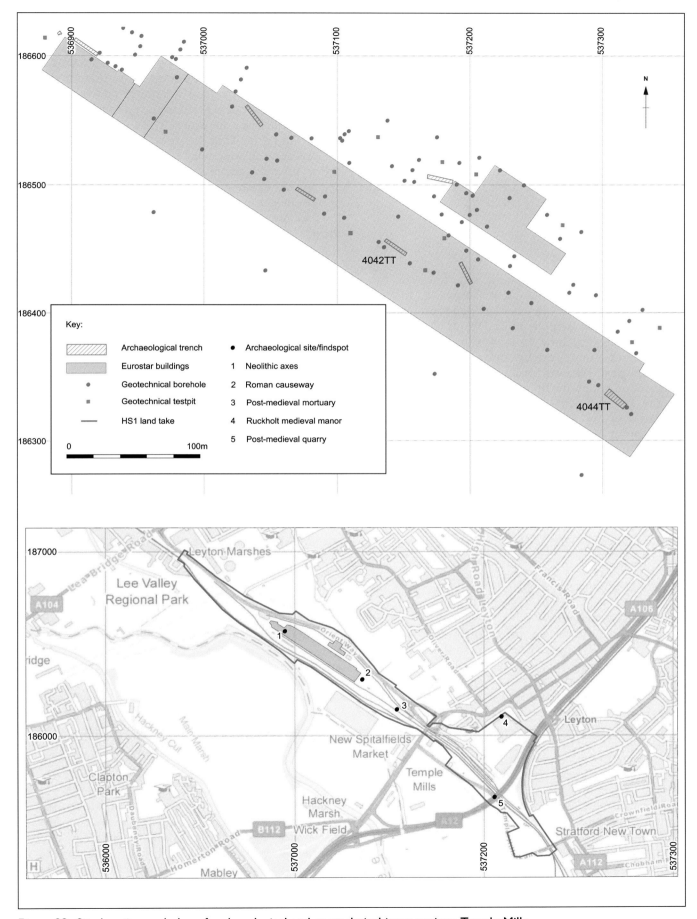

Figure 33 Site location and plan of archaeological and geotechnical interventions, Temple Mills

Strategy, Aims and Objectives

A mixed approach was used to the investigation of the Stratford Box/Temple Mills area that included borehole investigation as well as conventional trenching and excavations. The initial desk-top assessment of the route corridor only focused on the main Stratford Box site (at the time of production of the assessment it was unclear that development would be taking place at Temple Mills). Consequently, drilling initially focused on the box area, leading to a programme of targeted excavations within the box area. Excavation at Temple Mills followed later in the project.

Methodologies

An initial desk-top assessment was followed by a purposive borehole survey and a series of machine-excavated evaluation trenches on land proposed for redevelopment at Temple Mills Depot. Thereafter, an archaeological watching brief was maintained on all groundwork that might have impacted upon archaeological remains, including the Stratford Box Connection. Subsequent palaeoenvironmental analysis on the key sediment sequences at Temple Mills was carried out by Catherine Barnett (dating, wood, sediments), Michael Grant (pollen), Chris Stevens (waterlogged plant remains), David Smith (insects), John Whittaker (ostracods and foraminifera) and Sarah Wyles (molluscs). Diatom assessment was carried out by Nigel Cameron, though these were found to be generally absent in the two trench sequences investigated. Interpretation of the sedimentary sequences was carried out by Catherine Barnett and Martin Bates.

Results of the Investigations

Desk-top assessment

One hundred and eleven geotechnical logs of varying quality from previous surveys were examined to inform and model the sub-surface stratigraphy. Of these, 71 provided data that was of sufficient quality to be incorporated into a database. In addition, a further 12 purposive boreholes were drilled at locations across the proposed development area, their location designed to fill gaps within the geotechnical record and/or to provide clarification of ambiguous logs. These failed to uncover deep organic sediments that could be associated with the Lea Valley Arctic Beds.

The Lea Valley Gravel was found in all boreholes with a surface elevation of *c* 3m OD (Fig 34). The gravel was crossed, through the central part of the main shed footprint and to the west of the Bogie Drop, by a 1.5m deep palaeochannel, aligned approximately north–south that matched closely the course of a north to south flowing tributary stream of the River Lea shown on Rocque's Survey of London (1744–6). The gravel surface rose, with minor undulations, towards the north-

west end of the main shed footprint, while to the south-east, the eastern bank of the channel formed a ridge beyond which the gravel surfaces fell to the south-east into a second palaeochannel, possibly a former meander. The gravels were overlain by peat (up to 0.7m thick) and sediments rich in molluscs were identified at the base of the Holocene sequence within the palaeochannel and in the possible river meander. These deposits, and Lea Valley Gravel flanking the palaeochannels, were capped by Holocene alluvium/clay (Fig 36). Between 1.0m and 2.5m of madeground (average 1.8m) capped the sequences, much of which was railway ballast with a surface height of 6.0–6.5m OD.

Preliminary analysis of geotechnical logs within the vicinity of the site demonstrated that the site lay within a location containing river-side gravel ridges that was potentially favourable for prehistoric occupation from at least the Mesolithic period through to the Bronze Age or Early Iron Age.

Trench excavations

The location of the seven trenches (4038TT–4044TT), each aligned approximately NW–SE, along the long axis of the site are shown in Figures 33 and 34 and key profiles in Figure 36; an environment summary is given in Table 18.

Trench 4042TT

This trench (Fig 36) was one of two (also 4044TT, below) that were positioned specifically to evaluate the archaeological and environmental potential of the peat deposits recorded in the borehole logs, and obtain samples from them. The trench was located towards the eastern side of the palaeochannel and high-energy fluvial activity is indicated at the base of palaeochannel sequence by the presence of sands and gravels, probably reworked from the underlying Devensian gravel matrix.

Shelly silt (Late Glacial)

The overlying deposits were significantly finer grained suggesting deposition within the channel under a fluvial regime of decreasing energy. This sediment consisted of a fine shelly silt unit (context 420004) that produced a moderately sized assemblage of beetles (*Tables 13* and *14*; Fig 37). The assemblage is dominated by a range of water beetles and other taxa associated with watersides. The majority of the water beetles recovered are indicative of slow-flowing or stagnant pools of water. Examples of water beetles that favour this environment are *Hygrotus decoratus*, *Ochthebius minutus*, and the *Hydroporus*, *Agabus* and *Enochrus* species (Nilsson and Holmen 1995; Hansen 1986). Another typical indicator for this kind of environment is the 'reed beetle' *Donacia vulgaris*. This species is associated with a range of emergent waterside plants such as *Juncus* spp. (rushes), *Carex* spp. (sedges), *Sparganium* spp. (bur-reeds) and *Typha* spp. (bulrushes) (as are many of the *Notaris* species of weevil). Similarly the 'leaf beetle' *Prasocuris phellandri* is associated with waterside umbellifers (Apiaceae). A small number of species suggest that a faster flowing river or stream, with a gravelly or sandy bed, must have been also present in the river system. This is suggested by the

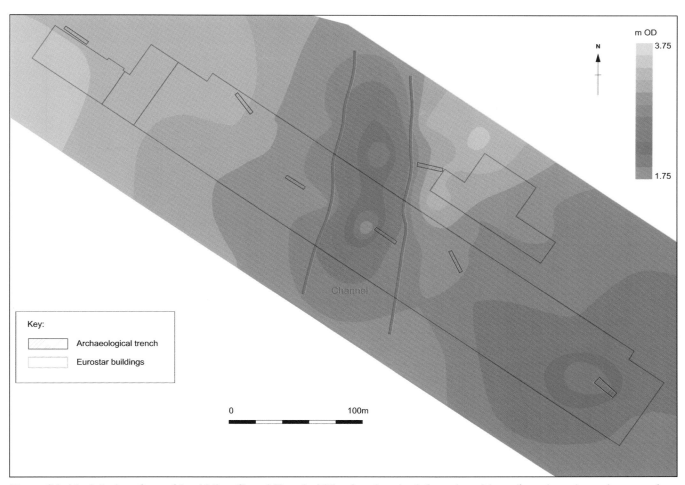

Figure 34 Modelled surface of Lea Valley Gravel, Temple Mills, showing the inferred position of a palaeochannel across the gravel surface

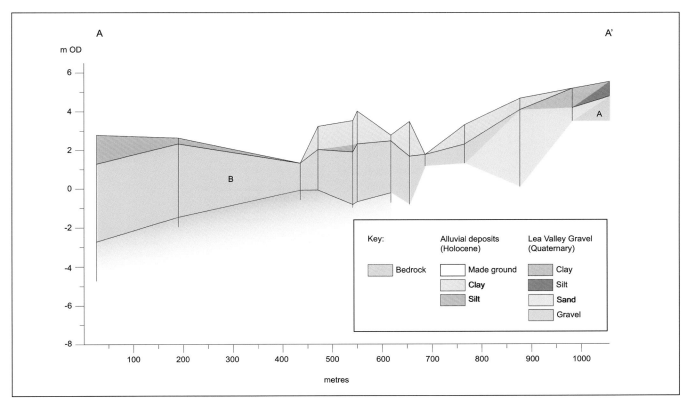

Figure 35 Borehole cross-section through Stratford Box

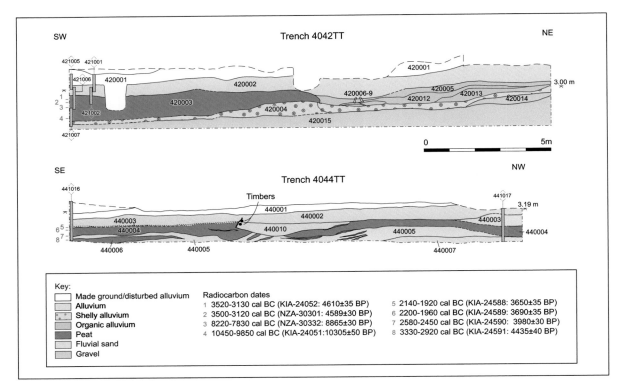

Figure 36 Cross-section through trenches 4042TT and 4044TT at Temple Mills

Table 18 Temple Mills palaeoenvironmental summary

4042TT	4044TT	¹⁴C years BP	Lithological summary	Palaeoenvironmental summary	Inferred human activity
420001	440001		Weathered clay-alluvium and made ground	Semi-stable landsurface with soil formation	17th and 18th century artefacts
	440002		Clay-silt and organic alluvium	Slow moving or stagnant water. Reduction of tree cover in local environment	Charred wetland plant remains indicate local burning activity on floodplain
	440003		Tufa sand and pellet gravel	Old land surface formed on fluvial gravels	Burnt flint on weathered surface possibly indicative of human activity in Early Bronze Age
	440004	3650±35 (KIA-24588) 3690±35 (KIA-24589) 3980±30 (KIA-24590)	Woody peat and peaty alluvium	Alder carr dominates local wetland	
	440005		Sand	Moderately fast flowing water close to channel edge	
	440006	4435±40 (KIA-24591)	Sandy-woody peat		
420002		*4610±35 (KIA-24052) *4589±30 (NZA-30301)	Clay-silt alluvium	Initial expansions of lime, ash and alder woodland	
420003		8865±30 (NZA-30332)	Peat	Expansion of mixed oak woodland	
		10305±40 (KIA-24051)		Fen developed locally with expansion of tree cover (pine)	Peak in micro-charcoal which may be the result of deliberate on-site burning
420004			Tufa sand and pellet gravel	The terrestrial environment was dominated by herbs with marshland in places. Locally channel conditions were characterised by slow-flowing or stagnant pools of water perhaps under cool conditions	
420015	440007		Sands and gravels	High energy braided channel environment under cold climate conditions	

* Dates suspected as being erroneous (too young)   TT = trench 'diving beetle' *Stictotarsus duodecimpustulatus*, the hydreanid *Hydraena riparia* and the 'riffle beetle' *Esolus parallelepipedus*, all of which are typical of this type of water condition (Nilsson and Holmen 1995; Hansen 1986). The occurrence of species that indicate the presence of areas of both fast and slow flowing water in the same insect fauna is not uncommon in the palaeoentomological record. This is particularly true where main river channels interact with a range of oxbow cut-offs, slow back channels and fen swamps in large multi-channelled river systems (ie, Osborne 1988; Greenwood and Smith 2005; Smith 1999; Smith and Howard 2004). Unfortunately, there were very few indicators for the nature of the landscape that surrounded the watersides at this time. The only species that is specifically indicative of surrounding vegetation is *Lochmaea suturalis*. This is the 'heather beetle' and, as the name suggests, it feeds on heather (*Calluna* spp./*Erica* spp.) in moorland and heathland. There are no indicators for the presence of woodland or scrubland in the area. However, none of the distinctive species associated with glacial climates in general, and the Late Glacial in particular, were recovered in these faunas (ie, Atkinson *et al* 1987; Coope 1977; Coope and Brophy 1972). This probably suggests that the material dates either from the Windermere interstadial or from some point in the Early Holocene.

Pollen from the shelly silt and the lower parts of overlying peat (PAZ TR4042-2, Fig 38) show an environment dominated by herbs, including Poaceae (grasses), Cyperaceae (sedges) and *Filipendula* (dropwort/meadowsweet). *Pinus sylvestris* (pine) and *Betula* (birch) are also present in low amounts, with some pollen grains of the latter probably derived from *Betula nana* (dwarf birch). *Juniperus communis* (Juniper), *Populus* (probably derived from *Populus tremula*, aspen) and *Salix* (willow) are also present and are typical of a Late Glacial assemblage. A number of typical Late Glacial pollen types are identified including *Helianthemum* (rock-rose) and *Polemonium caeruleum* (Jacob's ladder), along with an increase in *Filipendula* which is recorded within many contemporary dated sequences from along the Lea Valley (eg, Stratford Box, Barnett *et al* forthcoming; Enfield Lock, Chambers *et al* 1996; Innova Park, Ritchie *et al* 2008; Olympic Park, Powell 2012). The rise in *Filipendula* is often interpreted as indicating a response to rising temperatures after the end of the last glaciation (*cf* Barnett *et al* forthcoming), though it could be attributed to two different species of *Filipendula* likely to be present at this time – *Filipendula vulgaris* (dropwort), associated with steppe vegetation (Bell 1969; Godwin 1975, 183), or *Filipendula ulmaria* (meadowsweet), found in marshy habitats (suggested by the high values of Poaceae and Cyperaceae) and often associated with *P. caeruleum* (Godwin 1975).

The local wetland environment is also represented by *Typha latifolia* (bulrushes), *Sparganium emersum*-type (bur-reeds), *Potamogeton natans*-type (pondweed), *Myriophyllum*

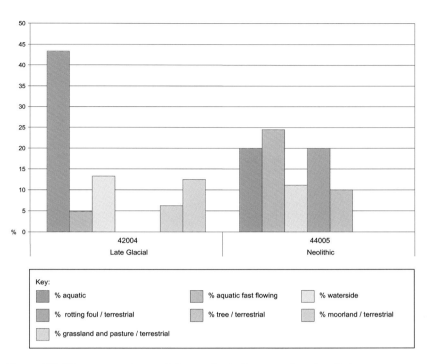

Figure 37 The proportions of the ecological groups for the Coleoptera from Temple Mills from Late Glacial and Neolithic contexts

verticillatum (whorled water-milfoil) and *Myriophyllum spicatum* (spiked water-milfoil), suggesting slow-moving water conditions. It is likely that *Ranunculus acris*-type (buttercup) is also associated with this environment. A number of large Poaceae grains are present within these basal samples, and are within the size range that is commonly associated with cereals. Similar contemporary deposits from the Holderness area, Yorkshire (Tweddle *et al* 2005), yielded pollen grains of a similar size, identified as belonging to Poaceae groups outlined by Küster (1988) of *Bromus hordeaceus*-type (soft brome), *Glyceria*-type (sweet-grass) and very occasionally *Cerealia*-type (cereals). The exact species/types identified here is uncertain (due to the pollen methodology applied at the time of analysis), though those distinguished in contemporary sequences from the adjacent Olympic Park were found to be predominantly *Glyceria*-type (Powell 2012).

Alnus glutinosa (common alder), *Quercus* (oak) and *Corylus avellana*-type (hazel) pollen are also present in low amounts, yet it is unclear whether they are derived from reworked material, long-distance transport or the existence of small localised stands. For *A. glutinosa* a local presence is supported by the presence of a single *Alnus* seed within these deposits which is thought to be contemporary and not derived from reworked material. It is not clear which species of *Alnus* the seed is derived from (or indeed the pollen), though it is most likely that this may be derived from *A. incana* (grey alder) rather than *A. glutinosa*, as the former is more likely to be associated with the contemporaneous climatic conditions. *Quercus* is not thought to be derived from local stands but more likely derived from reworked material (see below) or long distance transport. Godwin (1975, 279) notes that in a number of Late Glacial (Late Weichselian) pollen diagrams there is a low presence of *Quercus* that increases through the Early Holocene. He attributes this to long-distance transport, with

Thames Holocene

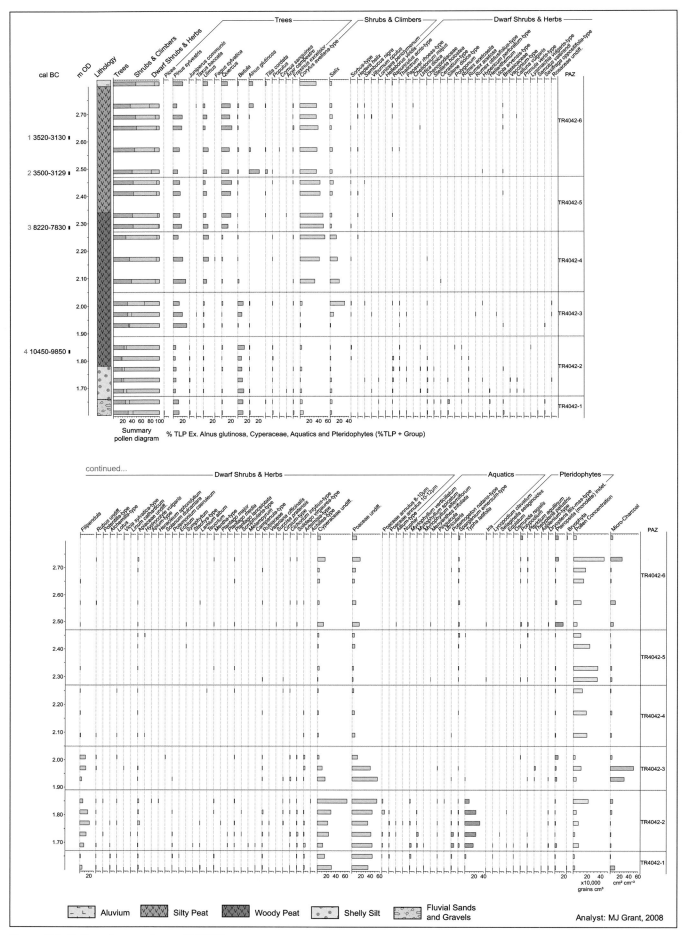

Figure 38 Pollen diagram from 4042TT

the slow increase in values representing expansion away from its glacial refuge. It is also possible that *C. avellana*-type pollen is derived from similar processes to *Quercus*. However, *C. avellana*-type also incorporates pollen derived from *Myrica gale* (bog myrtle), as it is often difficult to separate these two species (Edwards 1981) especially if they are poorly preserved. The earliest (albeit tentative) record of *M. gale* in the UK is from the Late Glacial (Skene *et al* 2000, 1090), with leaves of *Myrica gale* found locally at the Crown Wharf Ironworks site on the opposite side of the Lea Valley dating to *c* 9000–8000 cal BC (Stephenson 2008). The modern distributions of *M. gale* indicates an abundance in areas of swamp, often associated with *Phragmites australis* (common reed), *Cladium mariscus* (great fen sedge) and *Carex* sp. (Skene *et al* 2000, 1081), similar to the vegetation community represented in this sequence. It is therefore possible that small patches of *M. gale* may have existed at this time within the Lea Valley, accounting for the early low presence of *C. avellana*-type pollen.

The shelly silt also contained waterlogged plant remains (*Table 15*) of mainly aquatic species including *Chara oogliana* (stonewort), *Ranunculus* subg. *Batrachium* (water-crowfoot), *Ceratophyllum demersum* (hornwort), *Potamogeton* sp., *Schoenoplectrus lacustris* (bristle club-rush) and *Cirsium/Carduus* sp. (thistle), representing vegetation growing towards the waters' edge. *Chara* sp. are submerged aquatic algae found in still brackish or fresh bodies of calcareous water, such as ponds, lakes and ditches. As they thrive in low nutrient conditions they are often characteristic of the first colonisers of newly formed water bodies, and normally later displaced by vegetation as nutrient levels increase. Similarly *C. demersum* is more characteristic of pond, ditches or very slow flowing rivers.

The freshwater ostracod assemblage from the shelly silt is shown in *Table 16*. Eight species were recorded but the assemblages were very similar between samples. Ecologically, the ostracods seem to suggest a permanent pool with lots of vegetation. Although all the ostracod species live in Britain today, several are characterised by Meisch (2000) as cold stenothermal forms (species linked to permanently cold waters) – *Candona candida*, *Fabaeformiscandona protzi* and *Pseudocandona rostrata* – and make up the bulk of the fauna. Moreover, these species, together with *Eucypris pigra*, are northern European and Holarctic forms which are rare in southern Europe today. This could be construed, therefore, as supporting a cold climate during the end of the Late Glacial; although some other characteristic species thought to have become extinct at this time (eg, *Leucocythere batesi*, *Ilyocypris schwarzbachi*, *Limnocythere falcata* and *Amplocypris tonnensis*) are notably absent from the assemblage.

A single rich mollusc sample from context 420004 produced a freshwater dominated assemblage, with terrestrial elements only accounting for 1% of the total (*Table 17*). The freshwater snails are dominated by three species: *Valvata piscinalis*, *Gyraulus laevis* and *Gyraulus crista*. *V. piscinalis* favours larger bodies of slowly flowing or still water, with a preference for muddy or silty substrates, while *G. laevis* is found very locally in clean, quiet water usually among weeds. *G. crista* lives in most kinds of lowland aquatic habitats apart from those liable to dry up. The high number of opercula (mouth coverings) to shells of *Bithynia* spp. in this sample, a ratio of

13:1, may indicate that the context was laid down under fairly low energy fluvial conditions at this location. The occurrence of *Lymnaea truncatula*, *Succinea oblonga* and *Pupilla muscorum* in the assemblage is likely to indicate the local presence of poorly vegetated areas, such as bare mud in marshes. Although possibly intrusive from the overlying peat, a small number of shells (less than 2% of the assemblage) were identified as specimens of *Gyraulus albus*, *Planorbis carinatus* and *Bithynia leachii*, three species believed to be introduced in the Early Holocene period. These species would all be found in the slowly flowing, permanent, well vegetated aquatic environment generally indicated by the assemblage.

Peat

Subsequently, organic input increased and peat (context 420003) formed in shallow standing water in the deepest (central) part of the channel. This peat was exposed in trench 4042TT and, to a lesser extent, 4043TT. A carr/fen environment is indicated by large quantities of wood and some *Phragmites* within the peat, the latter suggesting emergent reed communities. A date of 10,450–9850 cal BC (KIA-24051, 10,305±50 BP), from the base of the silty clay peat in 4042TT indicates that peat formation began during the end of the Late Glacial. At the top of the sequence there are two upper radiocarbon dates of 3500–3120 cal BC (NZA-30301, 4589±30 BP) and 3520–3130 cal BC (KIA-24052, 4610±35 BP), derived from a twig fragment and *Phragmites australis* stem respectively. However this dating appears too young, especially when the pollen from the top of the sequence is compared to the contemporary pollen sequence in the base of Trench 4044TT. The problem of dating the top of these early sequences in the Lea Valley is also encountered at the nearby sites of Omega Works (Spurr 2006), Enfield Lock (Chambers *et al* 1996), and on the Olympic Park (Trench 71; Powell 2012) and it is probable that later intrusive material might be responsible for the dating issues encountered at these sites (see chapter 8 in Powell (2012) for details). Therefore the length of peat formation is unclear, though it can be assumed, based upon the pollen assemblage (emerging *Alnus glutinosa* and consistent presence of *Pinus sylvestris* at the top of the sequence), that it is only likely to extend up to *c* 7000–6000 cal BC. Raised gravel areas to the west, east and north, not subject to peat accumulation, may have been relatively dry at this time, allowing use and access to the fen and aquatic resources. However, no clear indication of an old (buried) land surface was been identified at the top of the sands and gravels and below the overlying alluvium during examination of the monoliths.

Pinus sylvestris pollen expands (obtaining values of greater than 20% TLP) at the start of PAZ TR4042–3 towards the base of the peat. An early expansion of *P. sylvestris* has been recorded in number of sequences from other lowland sites across southern Britain. Increases of *P. sylvestris* to values above 20% TLP occur at Bagshot, Surrey (Groves 2008), and Silvertown, London (Wilkinson *et al* 2000), at *c* 9550 cal BC, at Pannel Bridge, East Sussex (Waller 1993) prior to *c* 9550 cal BC and at Gatcombe Withy Bed, Isle of Wight (Scaife 1987) prior to 9450 cal BC. A threshold of 20% TLP is commonly applied to *P. sylvestris* to indicate local presence as the tree produces a large amount of pollen that is well dispersed (Bennett 1984).

However, the low sustained values of *P. sylvestris* in preceding levels may indicate small isolated stands rather than the pollen being derived purely from long-distance transport.

The increase in *Pinus sylvestris* coincides with a peak in micro-charcoal which may be the result of deliberate on-site burning, possibly to promote reed growth, as has been found in other lowland sites of a similar age (eg, Thatcham, Barnett 2009; Star Carr, Mellars and Dark 1998). At Star Carr, Mellars and Dark (1998, 231) suggest that the burning of reedswamp could have been undertaken to either improve the production of certain lakeside plants as a food resource, or alternatively is related to hunting strategies by attracting animals to graze on the new growths of reeds and other plants. The pollen assemblage contains a number of changes associated with this peak in micro-charcoal, including an increase in *Pteridium aquilinum* (bracken) with a temporary drop in *Filipendula* and *Betula* values, suggesting disturbance located along the wetland edge. The increase in *P. sylvestris* coinciding with the increase in micro-charcoal could suggest that fire may have played an important role during its expansion, as it is known to positively respond to a moderate-severity fire regime (Agee 1998), and could suggest a natural source of the burning rather than being purely of anthropogenic origin (eg, Grant *et al* 2009). The formation of an underlying mat of peat would have also made the local reed beds more susceptible to burning. The decrease in micro-charcoal coincides with an increase in *Betula*, *Filipendula* and *Salix*, but no recovery to high values of Cyperaceae and Poaceae. The local vegetation is now very different from that found previously, with *Salix* and *P. sylvestris* being more extensive within the floodplain environment, colonising dryland areas between the palaeochannels and also forming damp woodland upon the peat deposits within these channels.

At the base of PAZ TR4042–4 there is an expansion of *Ulmus* (elm) and *C. avellana*-type upon the local dryland. This is later followed by the expansion of *Quercus* that has been dated to 8220–7830 cal BC (NZA-30332, 8865±30 BP; base of PAZ TR4042–5). During this time the amount of *Salix* reduces, possibly with additional reductions caused by its distancing from the sample site. *Pinus sylvestris* still remains an important component, though does undergo some reduction in its abundance and/or distribution. The arrival of deciduous trees would have restricted the habitats available to *P. sylvestris*. However, *P. sylvestris* values show little change suggesting that it remains competitive, though it is likely that a large amount of this pollen is derived from *P. sylvestris* growing within or on the edge of the floodplain zone.

Upper alluvial deposits

Minerogenic input increased towards the top of the peat, with clay added by fluvial activity. A further increase in river activity is then indicated by the deposition of a thick amorphous gleyed alluvial clay unit across the site (contexts 420001/2). The raised gravel areas were also affected, showing the same alluvial unit, perhaps deposited directly by channel flow, although deposition by overbank sedimentation is not discounted. A wide, active river channel is, therefore, indicated with channel (and possible overbank) deposits extending across the area assessed. A broad N–S channel orientation, as identified during geotechnical investigation (Fig 34), is supported.

The channel is suggested to have formed a tributary of the River Lea.

Pollen from base of PAZ TR4042–6 records an initial expansion of *Alnus glutinosa*, *Tilia cordata* (small-leaved lime) and *Fraxinus excelsior* (ash). However, as stated above, the associated radiocarbon date (3500–3120 cal BC, NZA-30301, 4589±30 BP) is thought to be erroneous, especially as the neighbouring sequence from Stratford Box (Barnett *et al* forthcoming) shows the presence of *Tilia cordata* and dominance of *A. glutinosa* locally by 6000–5790 cal BC (NZA-32948, 7014±40 BP, *cf* Powell 2012). Typical dates for the expansion of these taxa at other sites across southern Britain are *c* 7500 to 5000 cal BC for *A. glutinosa* and *c* 6000 to 4000 cal BC) for *T. cordata* and *F. excelsior* (eg, Birks 1989).

The expansion of *A. glutinosa* coincides with a peak in micro-charcoal. The occurrence of fire is commonly associated with the expansion of *A. glutinosa* at a number of sites across the UK (eg, Smith 1970; Bennett *et al* 1990; Edwards 1990; Edwards and McDonald 1991; Grant *et al* 2009; Grant and Waller 2010), but it is still unclear whether this is a natural process or the result of anthropogenic activity. Fluctuations in *A. glutinosa* values prior to its successful establishment are common in sequences from southern Britain (eg, Pannel Bridge; Waller 1993), often interpreted as reflecting fluctuating ground water levels in addition to burning and disturbance factors. Changes in the ground water level are supported by increases in Cyperaceae, Poaceae, Pteropsida (monolete) indet. and *Sparganium emersum*-type suggesting wetter conditions. The increase in the minerogenic component of the silty peat unit towards its top would suggest that overbank flooding became increasingly common, allowing more rapid sediment deposition and incorporation into the peat. This is followed by the deposition of thick overlying amorphous gleyed alluvial clays, including deposition over raised gravel areas, and likely indicating extensive flooding.

At some UK sites the expansion of *Alnus glutinosa* occurs at the expense of *Pinus sylvestris* which Bennett (1984) suggests is due to *A. glutinosa* being more competitive than *P. sylvestris*, leading to the latter's demise. At this site, however, *P. sylvestris* continues to play an important role within the local vegetation with no clear sign of succession occurring, though in part this may be related to fluctuating water levels affecting the successful establishment of *A. glutinosa* on-site initially limiting competition. *P. sylvestris* values are greater than 20% TLP at several levels – though there is the possibility that some of the *P. sylvestris* pollen towards the top of the sequence in 4042TT may be derived from reworked sediments, as the amount of minerogenic sediment increases upwards. However, the taxa present within the pollen assemblage do not indicate a strong presence of reworked pollen, with pollen concentrations and preservation both good, so it is likely that the *P. sylvestris* is of a contemporary nature.

An immature (azonal) soil has been identified at the top of the palaeochannel sequence and in one profile (4038TT) was found to contain 17th/18th century pottery, brick and tile fragments, indicating relatively recent formation and use as a stable land surface. The soil was formed on alluvium, which itself showed indications of desiccation and terrestrialisation, notably extensive movement and redeposition of iron oxides through the profile. Disturbance by bioturbation below the soil was, however, apparently minor, with humified root voids in occasional recovered sequences, notably in the upper alluvial clay. In 4038TT, this soil (context 380002) was eroded/truncated by another unit of gleyed alluvial clay (context 380001), indicating formation or redirection of an existing river channel relatively recently.

Trench 4044TT
Interbedded sand and peat

A woody peat (context 440006) was identified interbedded with sand (context 440005) at the south end of 4044TT, palaeochannel sequence 2 (Fig 36). The base of the peat dated to 3330–2920 cal BC (KIA-24591, 4435±40 BP), slightly younger than the upper radiocarbon date from the top of the peat in 4042TT. The pollen assemblages are very different between these two assemblages further supporting the assertion of erroneous radiocarbon dates from the top of the sequence in 4042TT. The basal sandy peat sequence was overlain by a more extensive peat (context 440004).

The sand (context 440005) produced a rather small assemblage of insects (*Table 13*). The majority of these are not very helpful in terms of reconstructing the landscape. However, there are a few species present which provide limited evidence for water conditions and the surrounding environment. A range of species of Elmid 'riffle beetles' were recovered, which are typical of fast flowing waters, often flowing over clear sands and gravels. Taxa such as *Hydraena riparia*, *Macronychus quadrituberculatus* and the Oulimneus species are frequently recovered from these habitats (Hansen 1986; Holland 1972). *M. quadrituberculatus* appears to be particularly associated with larger fast flowing rivers in the archaeological record where gravel river beds and deep pools are present (Greenwood and Smith 2005; Smith and Howard 2004). Slow flowing areas of water, or still waters along river banks, are also suggested by the presence of the 'reed beetle' *Plateumaris braccata* which is associated with *Phragmites australis*. Finally, there is limited evidence from the insect fauna for the nature of the surrounding vegetation in the area at the time of the deposits formation. This is indicated by *Hylesinus crenatus* which is associated mainly with *Fraxinus excelsior* and *Phleophagus lignarius* which is found in the deadwood of a range of hardwood trees (Koch 1992). There are many earthworm granules in this context which signifies a local source of a more terrestrial nature.

A total of 1257 shells from a relatively wide range of species (24 taxa) were also retrieved from this context (*Table 17*). The terrestrial element only represented 2% of the total assemblage, with shells generally from species which favour shady grassy or marshy environments. There is an indication of some marshy areas, which may well have been liable to dry out at times, together with poorly vegetated areas on the channel margins. These environments would have been exploited by *Lymnaea truncatula*, *Anisus leucostoma* and the terrestrial species. The fresh water element of this assemblage is dominated by *Valvata piscinalis* and *Bithynia tentaculata*, with significant numbers of *Gyraulus crista*, *Valvata cristata* and *Bithynia leachii*. The occurrence of *Ancylus fluviatilis*, although only in small numbers, within this assemblage may indicate small patches of quick-flowing or even turbulent water, in the

vicinity of this area of the channel, such as scour along the channel edge. The ratio of 1:3.5 of opercula to shells of *Bithynia* spp. in this sample is again indicative of low energy fluvial conditions at this location, though perhaps slightly faster flowing than associated with sample 421003. The two dominating species thrive in large bodies of slowly-moving, well-oxygenated water with a preference for muddy or silty substrates with dense growths of aquatic plants, also suitable for the other significant mollusc species found.

The pollen sequence from 4044TT (Fig 39) contains much higher values for *Alnus glutinosa* than at the top of 4042TT, indicating that by the time the peat began to form it was well established and has probably formed alder carr woodland on-site. The dryland woodland is also better represented in 4044TT, with higher values for *Tilia cordata*, *Quercus* and *Fraxinus* excelsior, but lower for *Ulmus* and *Corylus avellana*-type.

While the sediments from 4044TT demonstrate significant fluvial activity there is little variation in the pollen assemblage during these phases. *Corlyus avellana*-type is found to be slightly higher during the main phase of peat accumulation (Zone TR4044–2) with reductions in Poaceae and Cyperaceae. There is also a reduction in *Polypodium*, Pteropsida (monolete) indet. and *Pinus sylvestris*, now a minor component of the local vegetation. This may suggest that the sediments in PAZ TR4044–1 contain some reworked pollen, as these taxa are more resistant to damage and are easier to recognise when corroded than other pollen types. Low pollen concentrations also help to support the suggestion of possible over-representation of damage resistant pollen and spores. There are occurrences of disturbance indicators such as *Plantago lanceolata* (ribwort plantain) and *Pteridium aquilinum* throughout PAZ TR4044–2, yet there are no distinct disturbance phases recorded within the dryland or wetland assemblages. Micro-charcoal values remain low supporting the suggestion of limited disturbance. The high *Alnus glutinosa* values, indicating the presence of alder carr, may account for the limited local disturbance. Although alder carr can provide useful resources, the vegetation is often of a closed nature with wet and boggy ground, hindering easy movement. The closed nature of the alder carr canopy would have also resulted in a certain amount of pollen and micro-charcoal filtration, reducing any observable disturbance signals from the dryland or the wetland–dryland edge.

The main peat body in the trench (context 440004) contained large fragments of apparently *in situ* mature wood of *Alnus glutinosa* (mainly twig and branch material) that clearly demonstrate the presence of alder carr in the immediate area. A bed of sand-sized tufa with occasional oncoliths (context 440003) rested on the peat at the northern end of the trench and suggests moving water for a time at least. This unit thinned considerably to the south where it was only 60mm thick. The occurrence of wood and a fire-cracked flint in this horizon suggests that the surface of this unit may have been exposed for some time as a land surface, which was used by local populations. The layer has been dated to 2140–1920 cal BC (KIA-24588, 3650±35 BP), of Early Bronze Age date, not uncommon for the peat units of Central London (Sidell *et al* 2000; Sidell *et al* 2002). A thin peat layer above indicates that the immediate area became marshy once again.

Thames Holocene

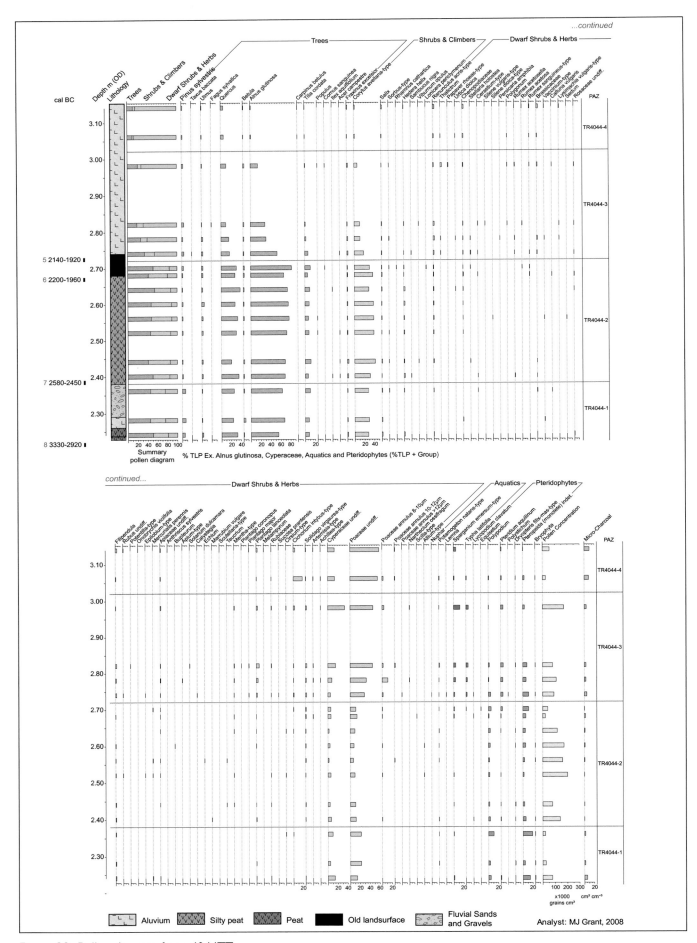

Figure 39 Pollen diagram from 4044TT

Upper alluvial deposits

Subsequent deposition of the massive alluvial silts and clays (context 440002) indicate a return to channel influenced sedimentation, the fine deposits indicative of a low energy regime and/or overbank sedimentation during flood events.

Only one species of ostracod, *Cypria opthalmica*, was noted in the upper part of the deposit. These were preserved as flexible organic valves, the calcium carbonate presumably having been decalcified. *C. ophtalmica* is remarkably tolerant to a wide range of environmental factors (Meisch 2000), including high organic pollution. It occurs in permanent and temporary, stagnant and flowing waters. Its occurrence in ponds and streams choked with leaf-litter is also well known. Its single occurrence may be an artefact, however, as other ostracod species, if present, may have been totally destroyed by the acidic nature of the water or sediments. The occurrence of ostracods in the upper part of context 440002 is mirrored by the occurrence of cladocerans (water-fleas), as indicated by the preservation of their organic-walled ephippia (egg-cases). Both ostracods and cladocerans have the same ecological requirement. Towards the middle part of the context testate amoebae belonging to one species of *Difflugia* have been noted. They live in all manner of moist and fresh water habitats from moss, soil, peat, to standing water (Ogden and Hedley 1980).

The main changes in the pollen diagram from 4044TT occur over the PAZ TR4044-3/4 boundary, associated with the buried surface at the top of the peat prior to its inundation by minerogenic alluvium. This transition of Early Bronze Age date contains a reduction in trees and the expansion of Cyperaceae, Poaceae, large Poaceae grains and aquatic pollen types. There are increases in *Plantago lanceolata* and *Pteridium aquilinum* that coincide with the reduction in tree pollen. This could suggest (along with the burnt flint from the landsurface) some human activity and disturbance upon the site during the Early Bronze Age. Human activity in the Lea Valley area is known to have been extensive during the Bronze Age (Corcoran *et al* 2011) and so human impact within the woodland is to be expected around the Temple Mills site. *Tilia cordata* is known to have been extensive across the Greater London area and existed as a major component until its demise during the Late Neolithic–Bronze Age (eg, Scaife 2000, 113–115; Rackham and Sidell 2000, 23; see Grant *et al* 2011), though a later Roman decline has been found at the Lodge Road site, Epping Forest (Grant and Dark 2006). This has often been attributed to human activity, supported by increases in *Cerealia*-type pollen grains and other anthropogenic indicators. However, Waller and Grant (2012) have demonstrated in the Lower Thames that these changes can be the result of wetland changes alone, with the apparent increases in *Cerealia*-type pollen grains actually derived from local wetland grasses that increase in abundance as the alder canopy reduces and the wetland makes a transition from alder carr to open marsh. Investigations on the Olympic Park (Powell 2012) also demonstrated that many of the large Poaceae grains attributed to cereals were derived from wetland grasses, increasing as the canopy opened. The only occurrences of *Cerealia*-type pollen grains found on the Olympic Park were directly associated with settlement sites on the floodplain edge. At the Temple Mills Depot the decline in *T. cordata* does coincide with the transition from organic (peat) to minerogenic sedimentation

and may indicate, as suggested above, that the clastic sediment deposition, lateral wetland expansion and transition in the wetland vegetation is responsible for the observed decline in *T. cordata* values.

The increasing Poaceae values are likely to be derived from vegetation within the floodplain, such as *Phragmites australis*, with Cyperaceae also growing along channel margins and cut-offs. The large Poaceae grains, as already stated, are most likely to be derived from wetland grasses such as *Glyceria* rather than cultivated cereals. The aquatic pollen present is indicative of slow-moving water and marshy conditions with *Typha latifolia*, *Sparganium emersum*-type and *Potamogeton natans*-type present. Although there is a sharp stratigraphic boundary between the old land surface and the overlying alluvium, the decline in *Tilia cordata* (and other trees and shrubs) occurs gradually (over multiple sample depths) suggesting that the wetland vegetation transition upon the floodplain is also gradual and that the sequence does not contain a large hiatus (though the development of an immature (azonal) soil does suggest that some form of stasis in sedimentation had occurred).

The decline in *Tilia cordata* recorded in 4044TT (Fig 39) can therefore only be interpreted as an apparent decline due to the changes in local processes rather than actually relating to its decline upon the dryland itself. A decline in *T. cordata* and other woodland taxa probably occurred around the site at this time due to dry land clearance but it is not possible to reliably identify this within the pollen sequence due to the dominance of the wetland pollen signals, particularly Poaceae and Cyperaceae. However, the opening up of the floodplain vegetation (transition towards open marsh) would have made this area more suitable for pastoral activity, as shown by the construction of timber structures (platforms and trackways) and evidence of animal husbandry along the Thames Estuary at this time (Meddens 1996; Meddens and Sidell 1995; Stafford *et al* 2012; Carew *et al* 2009).

Waterlogged plant macrofossils also indicate more open conditions in context 440002, including the presence of species of disturbed/open ground, including *Chenopodium album* (fat-hen), *Atriplex* (orache), *Ranunculus acris/repens/bulbosus* (buttercup), *Persicaria hydropiper* (water pepper), *Rumex* sp. (dock) and *Carex* sp. Indications of scrub are also present with fruits of *Alnus glutinosa*, *Rubus* sp. (bramble) and thorns of *Crataegus/Prunus* sp. (hawthorn/sloe).

Discussion

The palaeoenvironmental evidence from the two trenches at Temple Mills Depot provides a record of landscape and vegetation change dating from the Late Glacial through to the Bronze Age. Detailed analysis of the pollen record suggests a considerable chronological break between the two sequences, even though the radiocarbon dates could suggest closer continuity. Alternations between fluvial activity and peat formation dominate the record, with vegetation associated with channel activity present at the start, developing into alder carr as fluvial activity weakened (possibly through the channel becoming an abandoned cut-off) in this location. Channel flow shifted in this area of the floodplain prior to the development of open marshy conditions and increased overbank flooding. The evidence also indicates that through time the foci of deposition shifted across the floodplain and consequently infilling of channels may have occurred in one place prior to deposition commencing elsewhere. However, at the site level the Temple Mills Depot sequence seems to provide an intact record of the Late Glacial to Early Holocene transition, with the introduction and expansion of temperate woodland observable.

Among the key points identified are the following:

- The presence of Late Glacial/Early Holocene pollen of *Alnus* sp. coincides with the presence of a seed of *Alnus* sp. which is likely to be *in situ*. This suggests an early presence of *Alnus* in the landscape, and may indicate the local presence of *Alnus incana*. This adds to a growing amount of evidence that indicates the presence *Alnus* sp. in the British Isles at this time (eg, Waller 1993);

- Micro-charcoal analysis has identified that fire coincides with vegetation transitions in both trenches (Figs 38 and 39). It is possible that during the Early Mesolithic reedbeds were being burnt, either to improve plant yields or to attract game;

- The decline of *Tilia cordata* around Temple Mills during the Early Bronze Age, although occurring at the same date as other declines attributed to anthropogenic drivers, is related to changes in floodplain dynamics that affect the pollen load rather than an actual decline of woodland upon the dryland;

- The presence of Early Holocene insect faunas is significant because the archaeoentomology of London is particularly under-researched. Although a range of Roman, Saxon and medieval

deposits from Central London have produced insect faunas (ie, Smith 1997; 2002; 2006a; Smith and Chandler 2004) very few date from the earlier Holocene. This paucity is more significant because despite a range of investigations of Early Post-glacial deposits throughout the area of Greater London (ie, Chambers *et al* 1996; Lewis *et al* 1992; Sidell 2000; Sidell *et al* 2000; 2002; Thomas and Rackham 1996) none of these sites, except for a very small fauna from Bramcote Green (Thomas and Rackham 1996), Olympic Park (Powell 2012) and Runnymede Bridge (Robinson 2000a), has included any reports on any associated insect remains. This situation gives the possible Early Holocene insect fauna from Temples Mills some regional importance despite its deficiencies;

- Insect faunas of the later Holocene, particularly the Neolithic from the area that is now Greater London, are also under-researched. The only sites with proven Neolithic insect faunas in the Greater London area are at Runnymede Bridge, Surrey (Robinson 2000a), West Heath Spa, Hampstead (Girling 1989) and Altas Wharf, Isle of Dogs (Smith 1999) (though also see Elias *et al* 2009). Again, despite its limitations, the Neolithic insect faunas from Temple Mills are of some importance. Locally, the only other sites in the area that have produced insect faunas are that of the Anglo-Saxon deposits examined at Glover Drive, Edmonton (Smith 2006b) and the Olympic Park (Powell 2012).

- A picture of a dynamic and often unstable landscape has been presented. This mosaic environment offered rich wetland resources to local populations, with temporary stable landsurfaces becoming available and exploited during the Neolithic and Bronze Age.

Chapter 8

Dagenham and Hornchurch Marshes

with contributions by Nigel Cameron, Andrew Haggart, Elizabeth Huckerby, Richard Macphail, Mark Robinson, Rob Scaife, Wendy Smith, Lucy Verrill and John Whittaker

The East Roding Valley (Zones T1–T5)

The original 1999 study identified five geo-archaeological zones (Zones T1–T5) between 17.30km and 19.94km (Chap 6 *Window 6* (Fig 17) and *Window 7* (Fig 19)). Zones T1 (17.30–17.66km) and T5 (19.83–19.94km) were designated of medium archaeological priority due to relatively high elevations recorded in the surface of the Pleistocene gravels. The remaining zones were designated low priority. However, the route of HS1 runs deep underground within the London East Tunnel for the entire length of Zones T1 to T5 and construction impact on Holocene deposits was restricted to a single ventilation shaft at 17.785km in Zone T2. Although a watching brief carried out during construction recorded a sequence of Holocene alluvium and peat deposits overlying Pleistocene gravel, no detailed recording or sampling was carried out and no archaeological remains were observed.

West Dagenham Marshes (Zones T6–T7)

The route of HS1 exits the London East Tunnel at Ripple Lane, Dagenham (*c* 20.2km, Zone T6, Figs 19 and 40). From here it traverses the Thames floodplain on a piled slab eastwards across the Dagenham Marshes, approximately 450m north of the river and 200m south of the terrace edge. Prior to construction the area was level waste ground covered with scrub and rough grass, crossed by metalled tracks and railway lines to the north. Recent land-use has been predominantly industrial with much of the area artificially raised above the original floodplain surface, resulting in thick deposits of modern made ground sealing the natural alluvial sequence. The area immediately to the south of the HS1 corridor had previously been occupied by buildings associated with the Gas Works which were destroyed by bombing raids during the Second World War. In the post-war period an oil storage depot was built in its place.

Construction Impacts

Due to the thickness of made ground, construction impact on the natural alluvial sequence, apart from the piling, was restricted to works associated with the tunnel portal, advanced service diversions, and the diversion of

the Goresbrook stream to the south. The approach to the tunnel portal consisted of an *in situ* concrete box within a sheet pile cofferdam with an internal diameter of approximately 7m, truncating the alluvial sequence and underlying natural gravel. The service diversions consisted of a series of open cut trenches, within a combined easement of *c* 12–15m to an average depth of *c* 2m. Depth increased to approximately 3m east of Chequers Lane employing closed box shoring techniques. Two pipe-jacked crossings were excavated; beneath the HS1 line and LTS railway (20.6km) via existing caisson chambers, and cofferdam excavation at Chequers Lane (21.0km). The stream diversion, between 20.050km and 20.665km, comprised the excavation of a large open V-shaped cut, *c* 30m wide and *c* 4m deep (-2.4m OD) for approximately 470m, to the south and parallel to the line of HS1. At the eastern end the diversion carried on in a narrow concrete box beneath HS1 for a further *c* 170m.

Key Archaeological Issues

The 1999 study designated Zones T6 and T7 (Chap 6 *Window 7*; Fig 19) of low archaeological priority due to the low elevations in the surface of the Pleistocene gravels. It was predicted that initial inundation of the lower parts of the route corridor, that is in Zone T7, would have occurred during the Late Mesolithic period, by *c* 5000–4800 cal (*c* 6000 ^{14}C BP). It was also proposed an area of floodplain tributary activity may have existed within Zone T7, although no trace of channel activity existed within the overlying peat sequences at this point suggesting that the existence of these channels during the Holocene was of limited duration.

The earliest archaeological finds from the Dagenham area are of Palaeolithic date, including stone tools from the basal Mucking Gravel at Upton Park, Forest Gate, Manor Park and Little Ilford (Wymer 1999, map 10). Later prehistoric finds include the Dagenham Idol, an unusual carved wooden figurine, made from Scots Pine (*Pinus sylvestris*), found during the construction of the Ford Motor Works in 1922. Radiocarbon dating places it in the Late Neolithic to Early Bronze Age period, 2470–2030 cal BC (OxA-1721, 3800±70 BP; Coles 1990). A Late Bronze Age looped and socketed axe was also found to the south of Ripple Road (MoLAS 2000). Timber trackways have been found on a number of sites in East London in the former marshlands, leading down from the first gravel terrace onto the floodplain (Carew *et al* 2009; Meddens 1996; Meddens and Beasley 1990; Stafford *et al* 2012). The majority date to the Bronze Age, with the dates ranging from *c* 2100 cal BC at Woolwich Manor Way Area 1 (Stafford *et al* 2012) to *c* 1000 cal BC at the Tesco site, Barking (Meddens 1996), although a much earlier pair of trackways have been found to the south of the River Thames at Belmarsh West (Hart 2010), dated to *c* 3850 cal BC. Generally they are of timber construction, but also include a metalled causeway located 240m to the north of HS1 at the Hays Storage Depot (Divers 1996). The causeway was 4m wide and consisted of gravel, flint and sand laid over a thick bed of peat and sealed by alluvial clay. The gravel terraces of the Lower Thames are known to have been intensively settled in the Late Iron Age and Roman periods (Wilkinson *et al* 1988). There is significant evidence for settlement in the Barking area, including an Iron Age defended settlement at Uphall (Greenwood 1989; 2001). Barking and Dagenham both appear to have developed as local centres during the Anglo-Saxon period. Dagenham is first mentioned in AD 690 and an abbey of Benedictine nuns was founded at Barking in AD 666. Dagenham is known to have been an early medieval manor and by the 13th century the marshes, which were prone to frequent flooding, were used for fishing, fowling, reed growing and tanning. There are references to floods, marshland management and river defences throughout the medieval period, although more systematic reclamation was undertaken from the 16th and 17th centuries.

Methodologies

Prior to any fieldwork commencing, a desk-top geoarchaeological assessment of borehole records was carried out in the area to be effected by the construction of the Ripple Lane tunnel portal and the Goresbrook stream diversion. The purpose of the assessment was to examine the nature of the buried palaeotopography and characterise the patterns of sediment accumulation across the site, building on the data presented in the 1999 study. Ultimately the assessment aimed to predict the most likely location for the preservation of archaeological remains under threat from construction that could be targeted for evaluation trenching; 48 borehole and test pit records were examined from the HS1 archive (Fig 40). The lithological data was entered into geological modelling software (Rockworks 98) for correlation and analysis into key stratigraphical units.

Following the desk-top assessment three evaluation trenches were excavated to assess the impact of the Goresbrook stream diversion on any archaeological remains (Pl 10). No archaeological remains were identified during the evaluation. The archaeological mitigation strategy comprised a watching brief during construction along the entire length of the diversion. Watching briefs were also carried out during the advanced service diversions immediately to the north and east of the Goresbrook stream diversion, and during the construction of the tunnel portal. A summary of the fieldwork events is presented in Table 19.

Although no archaeological remains were encountered during either the evaluation or watching

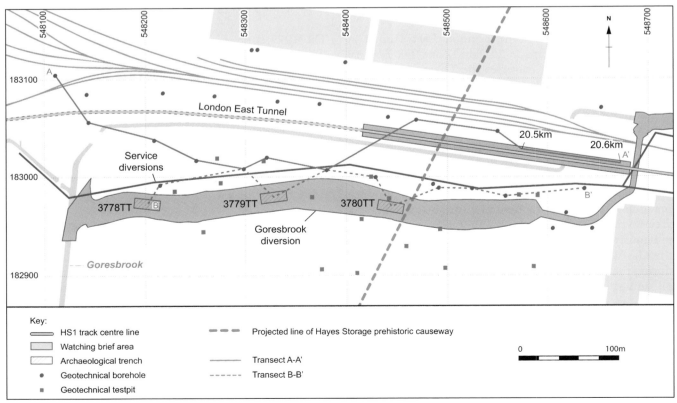

Figure 40 Plan of archaeological and geotechnical interventions, Ripple Lane Portal and Goresbrook

brief phases, a considerable number of palaeo-environmental samples were examined during the lifetime of the project that serve well in characterising the environments of deposition associated with the recorded sediment sequences. Interpretation of the sedimentary sequences was carried out by Elizabeth Stafford. The pollen assessments were carried out by Andrew Haggart (Goresbrook), Lucy Verrill and Elizabeth Huckerby (Ripple Lane Portal) and Rob Scaife (the service diversions), the waterlogged plant remains by Mark Robinson (Goresbrook and the service diversions) and Wendy Smith (Ripple Lane Portal), the diatoms by Andrew Haggart (Goresbrook) and Nigel Cameron (Ripple Lane Portal) and the ostracods and foraminifera for all phases of fieldwork by John Whittaker. Micromorphology (Richard Macphail) was also carried on horizons from the sequence at 20.5km thought to represent an early inundated landsurface (Appendix B, Pls 11A–E). Eight radiocarbon dates were obtained during the assessment and post-excavation stages in order to provide a basic chronological framework for the sediment sequences examined (Appendix A).

Results of the Investigations

Desk-top assessment

The desk-top assessment identified six major stratigraphic units. London Clay bedrock was only attained in some boreholes that penetrated beyond the full depth of the overlying Pleistocene fluvial gravels. Gravel was noted in all boreholes extending across the whole study area. Overlying the gravels was a finer grained sandy clay and sandy silt unit. This unit was not present across the entire site area but was typically missing from parts of the western-central areas. Locally it appeared to become sandier with depth. Directly overlying the gravels and silts was a major peat unit varying between 0.20m and 3.25m in thickness. Differences in the composition of the peat were noted with a zone of lower, woody peat, in places beneath an upper amorphous peat. Sealing the peat lay extensive deposits of minerogenic clay silts. Local variation in the nature of the alluvium was noted, for example, a peat unit was noted at the top of the sequence in a number of boreholes. Made ground capped the alluvial deposits varying between 0.5m and 3.6m in thickness with an average thickness of 2.50m.

Plate 10 Excavations at the Goresbrook diversion

The modelled topography of the gravel surface, that is, the pre-inundation surface of the Thames floodplain is illustrated in Figure 41a. A clearly elevated region is seen towards the western end of the site. This would have formed an island at some point after wetland expansion commenced over the gravel surface (Fig 41b). A low-lying area, probably representing a buried Thames tributary, exists to the east. The distribution of boreholes containing sand at the base of the alluvium is restricted to this area and it was suggested these sands may represent fluvial deposits associated with the infilling of the buried tributary channel. A second tributary may also have existed at the extreme western end of this area. The thickest sequences of alluvium (a combination of the upper silt clay, peat and sandy clay silt) lie within the areas of the possible buried channels. East to west transects of the main stratigraphic units are illustrated Figures 42 and 43. The gravel high is noted towards the western end of the corridor; the sandy clay silt unit can be seen to thin towards this high (Fig 42). On the basis of the projected gravel surface topography through this area the gravel lies on average between depths of -3.5m and -4.5m OD. It was predicted, utilising the modelled data from the Barking Reach area presented in the 1999 study, that the likely timing for onset of sedimentation onto the gravel surface along the line of the stream diversion would be during the Late Mesolithic period at *c* 4700–4000 cal BC (*c* 5800–5300 ^{14}C BP). It was suggested therefore that only Mesolithic artefacts could be expected on the surface of the gravels within this area; later prehistoric material would lie within the alluvial stack and would consist of material deposited in floodplain situations.

Table 19 Summary of fieldwork events, West Dagenham Marshes

Event name	Event code	Type	Zone	Interventions	Archaeological contractor
Goresbrook diversion	ARC GOR00	Evaluation	6	3778TT, 3779TT, 3780TT	Oxford Archaeology
Goresbrook diversion	ARC 32001	Watching brief	6		Oxford Archaeology
West Thames advanced utility diversions	ARC 36100	Watching brief	6–7		Oxford Archaeology
Ripple Lane tunnel portal	ARC 25001	Watching brief	6		Wessex Archaeology

TT = trench

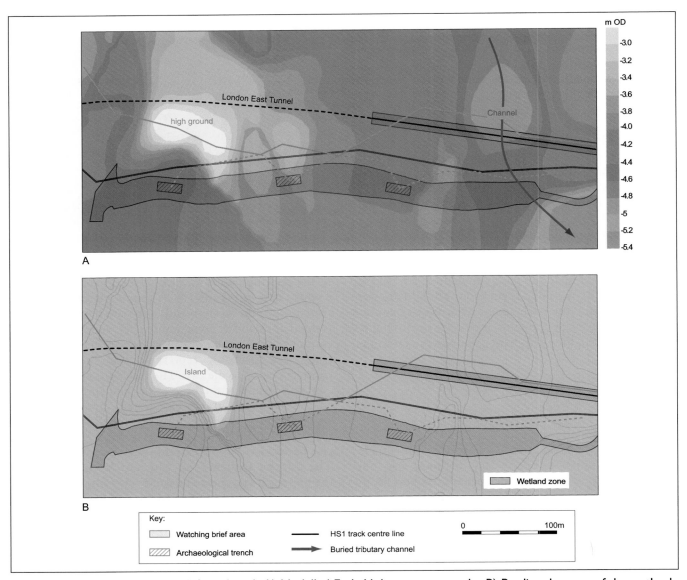

Figure 41 Ripple Lane Portal and Goresbrook: A) Modelled Early Holocene topography; B) Predicted extent of the wetlands at the beginning of the Neolithic (c -3.4m OD)

Trench excavations for the Goresbrook Stream diversion

Based on the results of the geoarchaeological modelling it was clear that construction of the Goresbrook diversion was unlikely to impact the Pleistocene fluvial gravels and the Early Holocene landsurface that lay deeply buried beneath substantial thicknesses of alluvium and peat (Fig 43). It would, however, remove the upper part of the peat profile and the upper silt clay alluvium. Three targeted evaluation trenches were excavated along the line of the diversion. Two trenches (3778TT and 3779TT) were sited adjacent to the gravel high. The trench at the eastern extent of the diversion (3780TT) was originally sited in the area marginal to the potential buried tributary and was targeted to coincide with the approximate alignment of the Hays Storage Depot prehistoric causeway. Due to practical restrictions, however, the trench had to be moved 45m to the west (Fig 40). The trenches were excavated in a stepped fashion to a maximum depth of 3.75m, with the base plans measuring 20 x 4m. No archaeological remains were encountered during the evaluation. The stratigraphy exposed was fairly consistent with the preliminary deposit modelling. As predicted only the upper three stratigraphic units; the made ground, silt clay alluvium and the upper part of the peat, were encountered and the investigation was therefore not able to test the modelled Early Holocene surface presented in the desk-top assessment. The watching brief carried out during construction similarly did not identify any archaeological remains to suggest that the Hayes trackway did cross the route. Palaeoenvironmental remains were assessed from the sequences in trenches 3778TT and 3780TT and one radiocarbon date was obtained from the top of the peat in 3780TT (Figs 43 and 44, Appendix A).

Trench 3778TT

In trench 3778TT a layer of undifferentiated mid-reddish-brown peat (context 7808) was encountered at

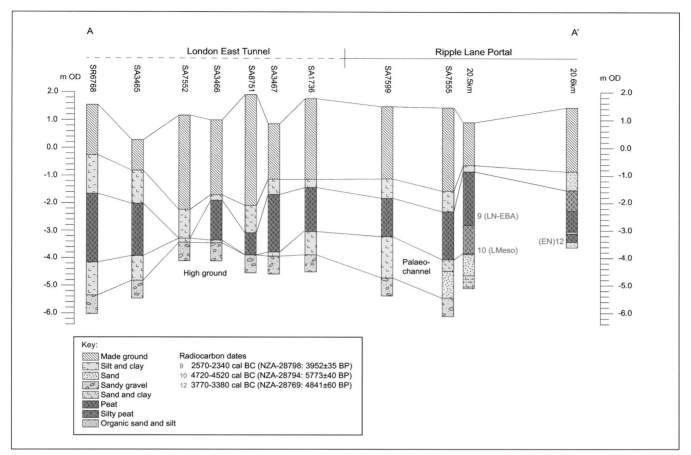

Figure 42 Transect A–A', Goresbrook and Ripple Lane Portal

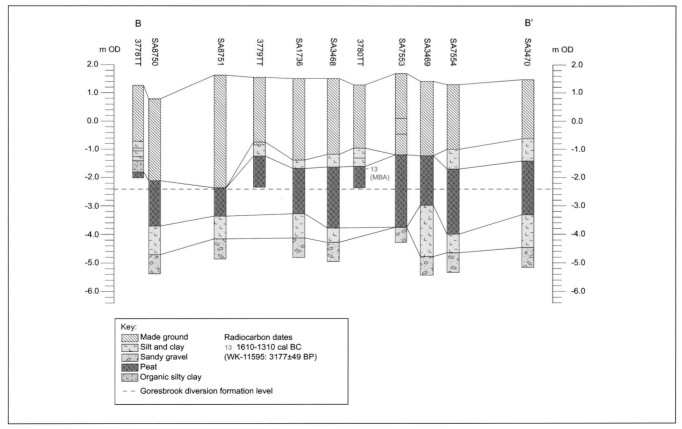

Figure 43 Transect B–B', Goresbrook and Ripple Lane Portal

the base of the excavation (Fig 44). The upper surface of the peat was at a uniform level of *c* -1.80m OD and was recorded to a maximum thickness of 0.50m but was not bottomed. Overlying the peat was a series of horizontally bedded silty clay alluvial deposits, all of which had been affected by discrete areas of modern disturbance. The lowermost deposit directly overlying the peat was a laminated organic grey silty clay up to 0.6m thick (context 7807). This was in turn overlain by a series of structureless yellowish-brown and light grey silty clays and silts (contexts 7806–7803). The sequence was capped by up to 2.25m of modern made ground comprising very mixed clay silts, clinker and building debris.

Peat

The pollen assemblage from the peat (*Table 20*) was dominated by fern spores, including the marsh fern *Thelypteris palustris*, along with an abundance of grasses and sedges. Tree pollen was low but included *Quercus* (oak), *Alnus glutinosa* (common alder), *Betula* (birch), *Ulmus* (elm) and *Pinus sylvestris* (pine). Waterlogged seeds (*Table 21*) included *Carex* sp. (sedges), *Berula erecta* (water parsnip) and *Hydrocotyle vulgaris* (marsh pennywort) suggesting open shallow-water fen conditions with few trees.

Organic clay

At the base of the overlying organic clay the pollen assemblages demonstrated a greater abundance of *Alnus* at 74% TLP. The plant remains also included seeds of *Alnus* as well as *Carex* sp. This suggests the fen at this location may have been succeeded by a brief period of swampy alder woodland. The diatoms, however, from the same level show an abundance of *Cyclotella striata*, a mesohalobous or marine-brackish form which is often abundant in estuaries in the spring plankton (Hendey 1964). The brackish presence is confirmed by the common occurrence of *Coscinodiscus eccentricus*, a polyhalobous form, and *Triceratum favus*, a polyhalobous benthic form often found in the plankton of the North Sea. A brackish saltmarsh component is also suggested with *Nitschia navicularis*, *Nitschia punctata*, *Diploneis didyma* and *Diploneis ovalis*. It seems likely therefore that the site was subject to periodic brackish water incursions, be they of minor inwash or more substantial nature.

Further up the profile the proportion of *Alnus* pollen rose slightly to 78% TLP and there were also small contributions from *Quercus*, *Ulmus*, *Pinus sylvestris* and *Fraxinus excelsior* (ash) which must have been occupying drier locations to landward. The diatoms from the same sample continued to suggest marine inundation with *Cyclotella striata* again abundant but also *Coscinodiscus* sp. including *C. eccentricus*. Other fully marine diatoms included *Grammatophora oceanica* var. *macilenta* and *Rhaphoneis amphiceros*, both of which are usually attached to marine substrates. There was still a brackish element with the common saltmarsh forms *Navicula peregrina*, *N. navicularis* and *Diploneis ovalis*.

There was a change in the pollen flora towards the top of context 7807; *Alnus* frequencies declined being replaced by pollen types suggesting a more open environment. This included Poaceae (grasses), Chenopodiaceae (goosefoots) and Plantaginaceae (plantains). The representation of the other trees such as *Quercus*, *Ulmus* and *Pinus sylvestris* rose, which

could be taken to suggest more successful transport into an open environment. The diatoms were less abundant, although *Cyclotella striata* was still the most common form. This sample also included examples of *Paralia sulcata*, *Triceratum favus*, *Hyalodiscus stelliger*, *Rhaphoneis amphiceros* and *Biddulphia biddulphiana*, confirming a fully marine presence. The presence of *Navicula navicularis* and *Scoliopleura tumida* suggests saltmarsh and sand flats may have existed in the vicinity. It is likely that the site at this point was undergoing a transition to becoming a vegetated saltmarsh.

Upper silts and clays

In the overlying minerogenic deposits of the pollen flora was similarly dominated by Poaceae, Chenopodiaceae and Plantaginaceae, including *Plantago maritima* (sea plantain). *Limonium* (sea lavender) was also present. The oxidised nature of the sediments and presence of Plantaginaceae in such high percentages could imply an open saltmarsh environment existed at the site, which was probably just below the contemporary mean high water spring (MHWS) at this time.

The diatom content was notably less abundant and more fragmentary in contexts 7804–7803. *Cyclotella striata* was still the dominant form with a range of other fully marine diatoms, this time including *Pseudopodosira westii* and *Grammatophora serpentina*. Slight grain size increases in these samples indicate a higher energy environment, perhaps slightly lower in the tidal frame. This may be supported by the pollen preservation, which shows higher counts for indeterminable broken and folded gains but this may equally represent increased sediment movement/load. Preservation of plant remains was also poorer in these upper deposits. The most numerous seeds were *Ranunculus sceleratus* (celery-leaved crowfoot), which occurs on nutrient-rich mud, perhaps indicating enrichment by grazing ungulates in the saltmarshes. The other seeds were either of plants which can occur in wet grassland, such as *Rumex* sp. (dock), *Potentilla* cf *repens* (creeping cinquefoil) and *Juncus* sp. (rush), or are weeds of disturbed habitats, such as *Carduus* sp. (thistle) and *Sonchus asper* (sowthistle).

Trench 3780TT

In trench 3780TT the lowermost deposit encountered was a layer of fibrous, reddish-brown peat (context 8004) which was excavated to a maximum thickness of 0.78m (Fig 44). The top of the peat, at -1.75m OD, was radiocarbon dated to the Middle Bronze Age, 1610–1310 cal BC (WK-11595, 3177±49 BP). The peat was overlain by two distinct layers of alluvium comprising 0.42m of dark grey silt clay (context 8003) and 0.5m of light yellow silty clay (context 8002). The sequence was capped by a 2.05m thick deposit of made ground (8001) comprising light grey silty clay, rubble, clinker and fragments of a metal container. Overall pollen concentration and preservation was poorer in this sequence, though this is greatly influenced by the high figure of indeterminable grains. No identifiable fragments of diatoms were preserved.

Peat

At the base of the sampled peat sequence *Alnus glutinosa* and *Corylus avellana*-type (hazel) pollen were the most abundant

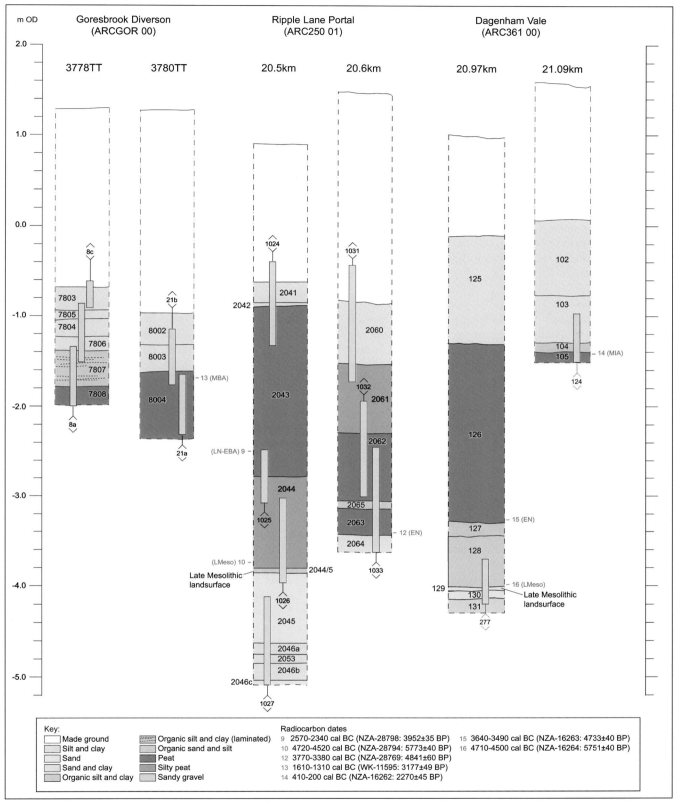

Figure 44 Sample profiles, Goresbrook, Ripple Lane and Dagenham Vale

taxa (*Table 20*). Other trees, including *Betula, Quercus* and *Ulmus*, showed a constant presence in all but the lowest level, while *Fagus sylvatica* (beech), *Fraxinus excelsior* and *Tilia cordata* (small-leaved lime) were sporadic in occurrence. With such a sparse pollen record it is difficult to be certain about environmental conditions, although the nature of the

stratigraphy suggests organic deposition predominated in an alder carr setting.

A major transition in the pollen spectrum occurred in the upper part of the peat with Poaceae and Cyperaceae (sedges) predominating. This suggests more open conditions now obtained as the site changed from alder carr to reedswamp. The presence of Chenopodiaceae and Plantaginaceae may be taken to suggest the proximity of saltmarsh to the site. The plant remains (*Table 21*) comprised emergent and shallow-water aquatic plants represented by seeds of *Carex* sp. accompanied by *Schoenoplectrus lacustris* (bristle club-rush) and *Potamogeton* sp. (pondweed). There were, however, seeds of plants likely to have been growing on peat that was above the water for most of the year, including *Lychnis flos-cuculi* (ragged robin), *Moehringia trinervia* (sandwort) and *Eupatorium cannabinum* (hemp agrimony). These can all grow in open fen woodland (carr) although no evidence was found of trees in the plant assemblage. The insects from the peat (*Table 22*) similarly suggest shallow-water reed fen with beetles of stagnant water, such as *Colymbetes fuscus* and *Plateumaris braccata* which feed on *Phragmites australis* (common reed), and *Thryogenes* sp. which feeds on reeds or sedges. Terrestrial insects included the dung beetle *Aphodius* sp., suggesting the nearby presence of domestic animals.

Upper silty clays

The pollen assemblages from overlying minerogenic deposits were dominated by Poaceae, Cyperaceae, Plantaginaceae and Chenopodiaceae, which given the context, suggests nearby intertidal saltmarsh. Charcoal concentrations were also extremely high in these levels suggesting nearby activity. The seed assemblage included species of wet, muddy, disturbed pasture, with *Ranunculus repens* (creeping buttercup), *R. sceleratus*, *Carduus* sp. and *Juncus* sp. The insects support this interpretation with *Longitarsus* sp. and *Apion* sp. feeding on grassland plants, *Hydrobius fuscipes* living in pools of stagnant water and *Aphodius* sp. feeding on the dung of domestic animals in pasture.

Watching brief on the Ripple Lane tunnel portal

Two sample profiles at 20.5km and 20.6km were assessed from the tunnel portal watching brief (Figs 42 and 44). Pollen was preserved in the sediments and provides some environmental information, although the results from the other specialisms were rather disappointing. Most of the samples contained iron oxide stained wood fragments or fragments of wood which appeared somewhat crystalline or mineralised. Only small quantities of waterlogged seeds were identified in two samples from the profile at 20.6km and only one sample produced diatom fragments, ostracods and foraminifera at the same location. Four radiocarbon dates were obtained from these sequences (Appendix A), although one from the top of the peat in the sequence at 20.6km (NZA-28710) produced an anomalous date suggesting modern contamination.

Chainage 20.5km
Basal sandy deposits

At 20.5km the basal deposits, between -5.1m and -3.82m OD, comprised a complex series of light yellowish-brown bedded sands, gravelly sands and sandy clays (contexts 2053, 2046 and 2045). These deposits may equate to the fill of the large channel feature identified during the desk-top assessment (shown in Fig 41a). The pollen assemblage from a sandy clay bed (context 2053) consisted of typical fen carr flora (*Table 23*). The most common taxa were undifferentiated fern spores and *Alnus glutinosa* with some *Salix* (willow), Cyperaceae and *Thelypteris palustris* (marsh fern). The pollen source area is likely to have been extremely localised as woodland and open-ground taxa representing dry ground away from the fen were very poorly represented. There was, however, a little evidence for the presence of mixed deciduous woodland on the drier ground away from the channel with *Quercus* and occasional grains of *Ulmus*, *Tilia*, *Fraxinus excelsior*, *Betula*, *Pinus sylvestris* and *Corylus avellana*-type. A single grain of *Taxus baccata* (yew) was also recorded from this level.

The overlying well-sorted sand (context 2045) is interpreted as water-lain, resulting from channel realignment. At the interface between the sand (context 2045) and overlying peat (context 2044) a thin deposit of organic sandy silt was noted. The pollen assemblage from this level suggested that the floodplain was vegetated by grasses with some alder carr, and that *Betula* and *Corylus*, with some *Tilia* and *Ulmus*, woodland or scrubland persisted. Thin-section analysis of the upper part of context 2045 (Appendix B, Pls 11A–C) revealed it to be composed of bioturbated sands and humic silts, with fine to very coarse woody roots. Fine amorphous organic matter occurred as highly humified microaggregates (excrement pellets; Pls 11A and 11B) along with rare traces of fine sand-size burnt flint and other minerals (Pl 11C). This once-bedded deposit probably formed as accreting colluvial sands and humic alluvial silts, with contemporary weathering and biological activity forming a semi-terrestrial acidic Ah/mor horizon topsoil (Babel 1975). The traces of burnt flint within the sediments suggests nearby occupation. Both Mesolithic and Bronze Age activity at West Heath, West Sussex, produced large amounts of sandy colluvium (Drewett 1989), while there may be a more direct analogue at Star Carr, North Yorkshire where Mesolithic activity is recorded along the interface between colluvial sandy soils and lake peat interface (Macphail 2006; Mellars and Dark 1998). In the immediate vicinity of HS1 attention is drawn to the recent excavations in the valley of the River Beam, Dagenham, which produced *in situ* Early and Late Mesolithic flint scatters on a sandy landsurface, sealed beneath peat and alluvium (Oxford Archaeology 2011), and on the south bank of the Thames at the B&Q site, Bermondsey; where Early Mesolithic activity was recorded along the shores of a palaeolake (Sidell *et al* 2002, 11–17).

Peat

The sand was overlain by a thick peat sequence at -3.82m OD, the bottom of which (context 2044) was radiocarbon dated to the Late Mesolithic at 4720–4520 cal BC (NZA-28794, 5773±40 BP). A second date was obtained from the peat at -2.49m OD producing at Late Neolithic to Early Bronze Age date of 2570–2340 cal BC (NZA-28798, 3952±35 BP). The peat can be divided into a lower brownish-black silty peat with abundant wood fragments (context 2044) and an upper darker, more humified and desiccated, peat (context 2043).

Thin section analysis of the lower part of the peat (Appendix B, Pls 11D–E) revealed the peat occurred above a sloping and irregular boundary, where there were initially bedded fine sands and silts and humified organic matter (mor humus). These beds included rare charcoal or charred organic

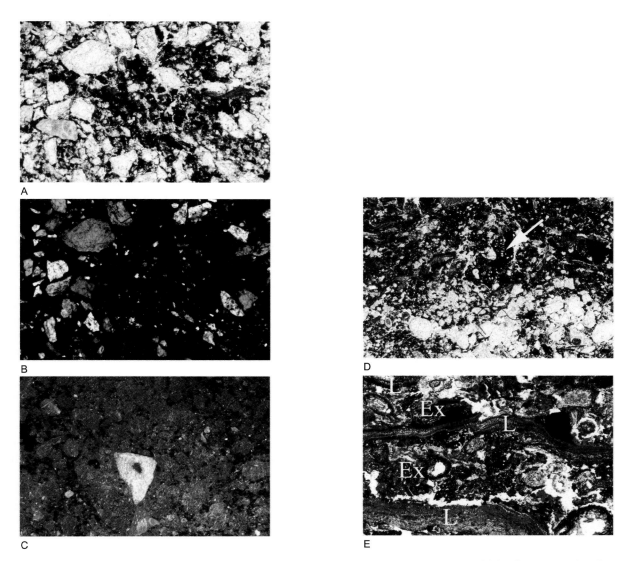

Plate 11 Microphotographs from 20.5km, Ripple Lane Portal. A) Monolith 1026(A), context 2045: Quartz sand and mor humus horizon-like micro-aggregates of amorphous organic matter. Plane polarised light (PPL), frame width is ~2.3mm. B)As A: Under cross polarised light (XPL), showing quartz sand and coarse silt associated with amorphous organic matter, probable relicts of original fine humic and coarse sandy bedding and possibly once a colluvial-wetland sedimentary interface. C) Monolith 1026(A), context 2045: Burnt flint as trace evidence of human impact locally. Oblique incident light (OIL), frame width is ~4.6mm. D) Monolith 1026(A), context 2044: Sand lens and an overlying peaty deposit containing a charcoal fragment (arrow) implying continuing occupation nearby; peats include both partially humified plant fragments and microaggregates of amorphous organic matter (see A. and B.). PPL, frame width is ~4.6mm. E) Monolith 1026(A), upper part of Context 2044: Layered plant remains (L), including leaves, and intercalated excrements (Ex) of soil mesofauna; a typical moder humus and common for woodlands. PPL, frame width is ~2.3mm

fragments (Pl 11D). Upwards, the peat was formed of layers of horizontal compact plant fragments and intercalated pellety amorphous organic matter (Pl 11E). These deposits probably indicate renewed colluviation, again possibly of anthropogenic origin as they contained charcoal within humic fine sands and silts. The layered organic sediments are not typical of peat (Dinç *et al* 1976; Fox 1985), but of a moder humus formed under presumed woodland (Babel 1975), which produced coarse woody roots both here and in context 2045. This is essentially a terrestrial soil feature and at this depth supports the early date for these contexts.

The pollen evidence from the peat indicated the expansion of alder carr on the floodplain with woodland of *Quercus*,

Corylus, Betula, Tilia and *Ulmus*, presumably on the drier ground. As the peat became more established, fen carr became reinstated with a ground cover, of *Thelypteris palustris* and Cyperaceae, that dominated the pollen assemblage. The identification of *Typha latifolia* (bulrush) and *Typha angustifolia* (lesser bulrush) at -3.23m OD in the silty peat (context 2044) suggests areas of reedswamp or slow moving rivers and ditches.

In context 2043 the decreasing quantity of silt in the peat is suggestive of declining allochthonous input, and stabilisation of the sedimentary environment. The pollen assemblage suggested a wet fen carr woodland of *Alnus glutinosa*, *Quercus* and *Betula*. The sustained levels of Cyperaceae pollen and the increase in *Osmunda regalis* (royal fern) spores indicate the persistence of fen or bog conditions, although the reduction in aquatic plant pollen and the absence of allochthonous mineral material indicate there was either a marked reduction in open water or an increase in shade from the surrounding canopy. The microscopic charcoal content appears to be highest in the more allochthonous deposits and therefore cannot be interpreted to reflect a local pattern of vegetation burning although this may have existed.

The peat grades upwards into a thin, 0.03m thick disturbed silty clay deposit at -0.88m OD and a substantial deposit of made ground to +0.9 m OD. Unfortunately environmental remains were not examined from the upper part of the peat and alluvium (upwards of -2.49m OD) due to sampling difficulties.

Chainage 20.6km

Basal silty clay and peat

At 20.6km the lowermost deposit encountered comprised a yellowish-brown silty clay alluvium (context 2064), overlain by a thick peat bed between -3.42m and -1.54m OD. The base of the peat was radiocarbon dated to the Early Neolithic at 3770–3380 cal BC (NZA-28769, 4841±60 BP). The lower part of the peat (contexts 2063 and 2062) was well humified and almost black with abundant small woody and bark inclusions. Between these two contexts, at -3.12m OD, the peat graded into a thin bed of dark organic sandy silt, 0.08m thick (context 2065). The upper part of the peat bed (context 2061), from -2.29m, was much siltier and contained large twigs and woody fragments.

The pollen data (*Table 24*) suggested a floodplain dominated by fen carr vegetation in much of the profile, from the lowermost silty clay deposit (context 2064) to around to the top of the woody peat (context 2062). *Alnus glutinosa* was the main taxon, with *Quercus* and a fern understorey. As the peat accumulated, allochthonous input declined and local taxa (principally *A. glutinosa*, Cyperaceae and ferns) dominated the pollen assemblage. The pollen from other taxa is probably under-represented in the pollen sum. From -2.66m OD upwards, reedswamp and then fen conditions began to develop, seen in the progressive peaks of Cyperaceae and *Thelypteris palustris*, and ultimately allogenic input increased as silt began to accumulate in the peat. Towards the top of the silty peat, *A. glutinosa* increased signalling that a wet fen carr woodland was again developing. The seed assemblage from the peat was very sparse comprising eroded seeds of *Betula* and *A. glutinosa*.

Upper silty clay

The peat was overlain by a unit of greyish yellow brown massive silty clay with iron mottling (context 2060) from -1.54m to -0.84m OD The pollen spectrum records a floodplain environment of fen carr with significant areas of grassland or open ground, suggested by the rich assemblage of herbaceous taxa. Two cereal-type pollen grains may indicate agriculture in the area and microscopic charcoal values were generally higher. Context 2060 produced a small diatom assemblage, although *Hantzschia amphioxys* was the only fragment identifiable to specific level. This is a freshwater diatom that is resistant to desiccation. It is a very common aerophilous diatom and therefore the presence of a single fragment is not

significant. Ostracods on the other hand were abundant and indicated brackish creeks and mudflats (*Table 25*). Unfortunately the date for the top of the peat produced an anomalous modern date (NZA-28710). However, brackish water ingress driven by marine incursion is likely to have occurred at a broadly similar period to that in the other adjacent sequences and comparisons of elevations and vegetation changes in the upper peat would perhaps suggest a later prehistoric date, assuming a lack of truncation.

Watching brief on the service diversions

Invariably the limited depth of excavation associated with the service diversions meant that only modern made ground deposits were exposed. Cofferdams excavated for the pipe-jacked crossing at Chequers Lane, however, were sufficiently deep to expose the full depth of the sequence to the surface of the Pleistocene gravels. Detailed recording and palaeoenvironmental sampling were undertaken from the lower part of the sedimentary sequence (below -3.10m OD) in the cofferdam immediately east of Chequers Lane at 20.97km. The upper part of the sequence was sampled (above -1.5m OD) during the pipeline main-lay 110m to the east at 21.09km (Figs 44 and 45). Three radiocarbon dates were obtained for these sequences (Appendix A).

Chainage 20.97km

At 20.97km fluvial gravel (context 131) was noted at -4.15m OD, overlain by a deposit of yellowish-brown medium sand (context 130). At the upper surface of the sand was a thin deposit of medium greyish-brown weathered sand (context 129). The weathered sand was sealed by a greenish-grey organic sandy silt (context 128) that became more clayey up-profile (context 127) to -3.3m OD. The interface of contexts 129 and 128 was radiocarbon dated at -3.88m OD to the Late Mesolithic, 4710–4500 cal BC (NZA-16264, 5751±40 BP). Above these deposits was a substantial layer of peat (context 126), that extended upwards to *c* -1.3m OD. The base of the peat was radiocarbon dated to the Early Neolithic, 3640–3490 cal BC (NZA-16263, 4733±40 BP). The peat was overlain by silty clay alluvium and a deposit of made ground to *c* 1.0m OD.

Basal sands

Preservation of environmental remains was poor in the basal sands although ephippia of cladocerans appear to indicate a freshwater environment.

Organic silt and peat

Macroscopic plant remains from the organic silt and lower part of the peat included abundant remains of *Alnus glutinosa* (*Table 26*). Seeds of herbaceous plants ranged from those of woodland floor, such as *Stellaria neglecta* (greater chickweed), through to those of fen woodland, such as *Scirpus sylvaticus* (wood club-rush), to those of shallow water such as *Oenanthe aquatica* gp. (water dropwort). Coleoptera (*Table 27*) included the *Chrysomela aenea* (alder leaf beetle), *Rhynchaenus testaceus* (a weevil which also feeds on alder leaves) and *Phymatodes alni* (wood-boring long-horn beetle), which is sometimes associated with dead alders. The insects also included species of decaying vegetation in fens, such as *Corylophus cassidoides* found in shallow pools of water and *Limnebius nitidus*, and species of aquatic plants, such as *Prasocuris phellandrii* which feeds on aquatic Umbelliferae, including *Oenanthe aquatica*. There was no evidence for environmental change in the sequence. The results suggest alder carr predominated, with areas of shallow water between higher areas of exposed peat.

The pollen evidence (*Table 28*) supports this interpretation with *Alnus* dominant. Cyperaceae with Poaceae were also important probably forming the understorey of the alder woodland. The terrestrial/dryland flora was dominated by trees and shrubs comprising largely *Quercus* and *Tilia* with some *Betula* and *Corylus avellana*-type suggesting adjacent mixed woodland, but *Quercus/Tilia* dominated on drier soil. There were few herbs and those which were present are most probably autochthonous elements.

Chainage 21.09km

At 21.09km the top of a peat horizon (context 105), exposed in the base of the pipe trench, was radiocarbon dated at -1.39m OD to the Middle Iron Age, 410–200 cal BC (NZA-16262, 2270±45 BP). The peat was overlain by organic silty clay (context 104) and silty clay alluvium (contexts 103 and 102) to -0.80m OD. The sequence was capped by deposits of made ground to +1.58m OD.

Peat and organic silty clay

Samples from the top of the peat produced some indicators of domestic animal grazing within the fen vegetation, such as seeds of *Potentilla anserina* (silverweed) (*Table 26*), and the scarabaeoid dung beetles *Geotrupes* sp. and *Aphodius* sp. (*Table 27*) There were some differences between the pollen spectra of the peat, the overlying organic silty clay and alluvium but these were not significant enough to warrant pollen zonation in the assessment study (*Table 28*). Trees were consistently 25–30% of TP (excluding *Alnus*) throughout the entire sediment profile.

Quercus was the most important with occasional *Betula, Pinus, Picea* (spruce), *Alnus, Tilia* and *Fraxinus. Corylus avellana*-type was the most important shrub. Herbs were also dominant throughout (60–70%), Poaceae dominated in the peat and organic silty clay (to 60%). Other taxa of importance in the organic silty clay include Chenopodiaceae and single grain of cereal-type pollen. Of the marsh and aquatic component *A. glutinosa* was at highest percentages in the peat and organic silty clay with Cyperaceae and, *Alisma*-type (water plantain) derived from a grass-sedge fen with alder surrounding the wetland margins.

Upper silty clays

Alnus glutinosa values declined in the minerogenic contexts in which *Typha angustifolia* became more important. Of note were the derived and redeposited pre-Quaternary palynomorphs in the mineral sediments. These are strongly indicative of the presence of other reworked Holocene pollen and spores. *Quercus* and *Corylus* remained as a more regional vegetation component. Expanding *Pinus* percentages reflect the propensity of its (saccate) pollen to float and its consequent frequent over-representation in fluvially derived sediments. Cereal-type pollen was present sporadically.

The autochthonous vegetation shows development from grass-sedge fen with near, fringing alder carr. This developed into wetter, poor fen with Cyperaceae. Prior to this, however, there is evidence (104) of freshwater with *Myriophyllum spicatum* (spiked water-milfoil). Increases in Chenopodiaceae and Hystrichospheres (dinoflagellates) suggest the possibility of saltmarsh habitats within the catchment. Seeds from the alluvial clays were sparse, but included *Callitriche* sp. (starwort), *Alisma* sp., *Mentha* sp. (mint) and *Juncus* spp. These results suggest the fen was replaced up the sequence by marsh with alluvial input.

Ostracods and foraminifera (*Table 29*) suggest some brackish/marine influence throughout, even though some freshwater/terrestrial components also occurred (washed in). The ostracod faunas were dominated by species living in

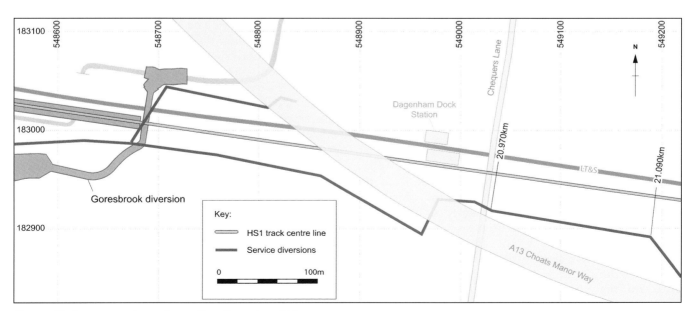

Figure 45 Location of sample profiles, Dagenham Vale

sheltered brackish creeks and intertidal mudflats. These are typified by *Cyprideis torosa*, *Leptocythere porcellanea*, *Loxoconcha elliptica* and *Cytherura gibba*, being common to abundant suggesting they are *in situ*. Conversely the freshwater species, usually *Candona* species, were quite rare. The foraminifera were also supportive of a brackish tidal mudflat environment (they were mostly small in size and consist of euryhaline species of *Ammonia*, *Elphidium* and *Haynesina germanica*). There were also quite a few fully marine species, possibly washed in by a tidal surge. However, two of the species (*Robertsonites tuberculatus* and *Elofsonella concinna*) are of special interest in that they do not live in southern Britain today, or even within the Holocene, being found in more northern climes today. It is suggested they may possibly be reworked from a Pleistocene deposit nearby.

Discussion

The dates and elevations for onset of organic accumulation above the sands and gravels at the tunnel portal site and Dagenham Vale are broadly similar occurring during the later Mesolithic period at *c* -4.0m OD, with peat accumulating during the Early Neolithic and Bronze Age. Overall the peats exposed appeared to be quite variable in character; reddish brown wood peats, silty peats and more humified black peats with abundant reed stems. The pollen work suggests the predominance of open fen and reedswamp with perhaps areas of alder carr to the edges. The variation between the profiles might suggest shifting local environments of fen and alder carr and this may be related to the topography and the presence of a major channel system in the vicinity. A higher silt component within the peat was probably a result of local flooding events. The radiocarbon dates and elevations for the top of the peats also showed variation and this is most likely related to truncation of the upper peat horizon by later alluviation, indicated by the contact between the peat and upper alluvial units being often very abrupt (see Waller *et al* 2006). The earliest date for change to minerogenic sedimentation was the Middle Bronze Age at the Goresbrook diversion (-1.75m OD, 3790TT) and the latest in the Dagenham Vale sequence occurring during the Middle Iron Age (-1.39m OD, 21.09km). The upper alluvium appeared to have formed in an environment of tidal creeks and mudflats although a significant freshwater signature was noted in a number of sequences probably related to inputs from streams from the gravel terrace.

Indirect evidence of Late Mesolithic or earlier human activity was identified during thin section analysis of the interface between the base of the peat and the underlying sands at 20.5km in the form of microcharcoal and burnt flint fragments. In addition there is evidence of colluvial inputs at this level in the sequences which may be of anthropogenic origin. Microcharcoal was also noted to occur within the peat sequences during the pollen assessments. Further east at 21.09km the upper part of the organic sequence, immediately prior to marine inundation was dated to the Middle Iron Age and here scarabaeoid dung beetles

Geotrupes sp. and *Aphodius* sp. are suggestive of fen vegetation such as rushes that was being grazed by domestic animals.

East Dagenham and Hornchurch Marshes (Zones T8–T12)

The route of HS1 continues on a piled slab alongside the existing London Tilbury & Southend railway line (LT&S) through the Ford Motor Works, immediately north of Dagenham Breach, crossing beneath existing road bridges at Kent Avenue and Thames Avenue (Fig 21). Exiting the Motor Works the railway continues eastwards through the Mudlands before skirting the northern edge of the Riverside Sewage Treatment Works (STW) (Fig 46). At 23.9km the railway traverses Rainham Creek (the Ingrebourne River) on a newly constructed viaduct before continuing eastwards towards Rainham Marsh. Prior to construction the land was occupied by factories and workshops associated with the Motor Works, concreted areas and patches of waste ground containing metalled trackways and railway sidings with ground levels averaging +1.40 to +2.00m OD. In the Mudlands the ground was covered by rough grass and scrub at +0.00–0.10m OD, rising to +0.70m OD at Manor Way and to +2.75m OD alongside the Riverside STW. At Rainham Creek modern flood defence bunds were located on either side of the watercourse.

Construction Impacts

The railway through this part of the route continued on a piled concrete slab. Aside from the piling, there was no direct impact on the underlying alluvium due to the thickness of the overlying made ground. The exception, however, was at Rainham Creek, where the railway passes over the watercourse on a newly constructed viaduct (Fig 47). The 454m three-span viaduct necessitated a minor diversion of the existing creek for a new road underpass. In addition to the main construction phase a series of advanced service diversions were carried out both to the north and south of the LT&S railway. A total of 2585m of open trenching was carried out, of which 595m employed box shoring edge support. The depth of excavation averaged 1.60 to 3.00m depending on the location of existing services. In total 835m of pipejacking was carried out via a series of deep caisson chambers and cofferdams to carry the services beneath existing railway lines and roads.

Key Archaeological Issues

The original 1999 study designated Zones T8–T11 (Chap 6 *Window 8*, Fig 21) of low archaeological priority. It was predicted that all areas were submerged below the sedimentation front during the Late

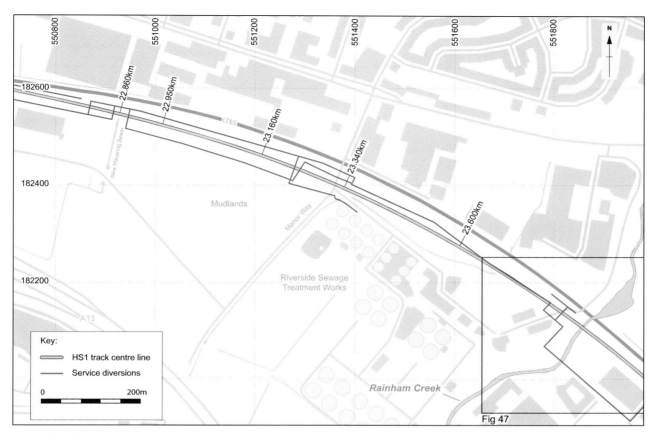

Figure 46 Plan of investigations from Mudlands Farm to Rainham Creek

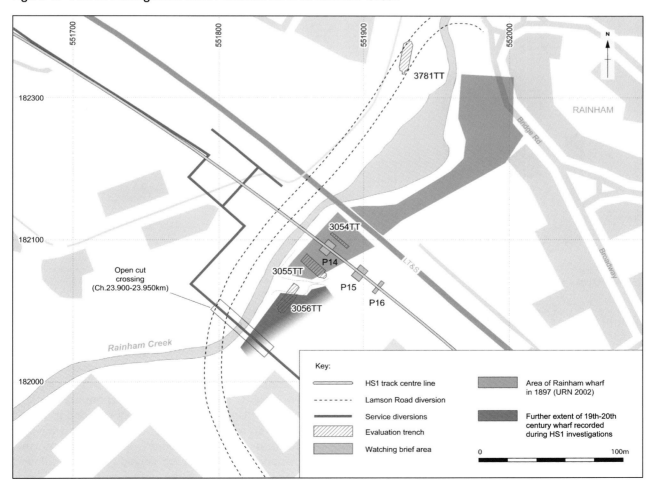

Figure 47 Detailed plan of investigations at Rainham Creek

Table 30 Summary of fieldwork events, East Dagenham and Hornchurch Marshes

Event name	Event code	Type	Zone	Interventions	Archaeological contractor
West Thames advanced utility diversions	ARC 36100	Watching Brief	8–12		Oxford Archaeology
Rainham Creek, Ferry Lane	ARC RAI00	Evaluation	12	3054TT, 3055TT, 3056TT, 3081TT	Essex County Council Field Archaeology Unit
Rainham Creek, Ferry Lane	ARC RAI00	Watching Brief	12		Essex County Council Field Archaeology Unit

TT = trench

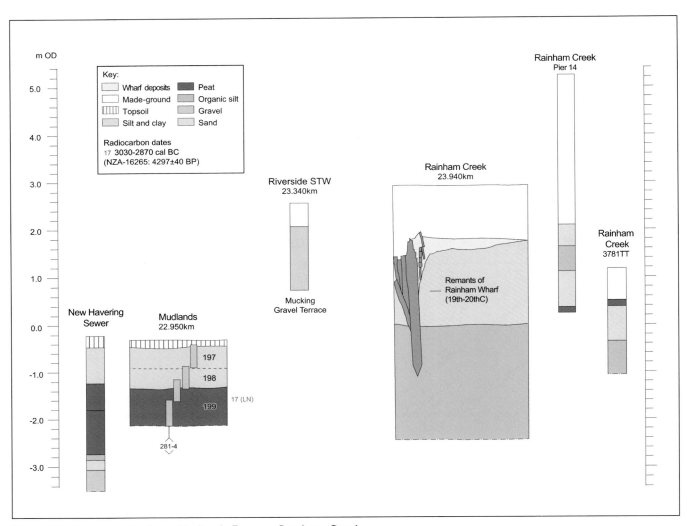

Figure 48 Cross-section from Mudlands Farm to Rainham Creek

Mesolithic at *c* 4800–4300 cal BC (*c* 6000 –5500 ^{14}C BP). Features in the Pleistocene gravel sequences indicated the possible position of two major infilled channels of Late Pleistocene age. A major zone of potential archaeological significance was thought to exist within Zone T12 (23.46–24.13km), corresponding with the Rainham Creek area.

Previous archaeological work has revealed archaeological remains associated with Rainham Creek. At Bridge Road, Rainham, Middle Bronze Age wooden structures were located on the bank of the creek: an insubstantial brushwood trackway constructed using coppiced alder and a small rectangular enclosure (Meddens and Beasley 1990, 244). Roman activity has also been confirmed by excavation in the vicinity. In both these periods the activity encountered probably represented the exploitation of the riverine and coastal environment as opposed to permanent settlement. Rainham village itself was probably founded in the Saxon period, although settlement appears to have been concentrated on the higher ridge to the north, the marshland and creek were probably being exploited for fishing, grazing and some arable cultivation. The creek was probably embanked in this period. It was anticipated that features associated with land reclamation and exploitation may have been present but were likely to have been disturbed by later activity. A post-medieval wharf is known to have existed from the 16th to 20th centuries, although it is possible the wharf was in existence in medieval period as sources mention shipments from London. The first documentary reference to a wharf is dated to 1526, and the location is shown on the Chapman and André map of 1777 in the northern part of the study area on the east bank of the creek. The wharf facilities were improved by Capt. John Harle in the early 18th century. He added granaries and warehouses, and dredged the channel. This wharf continued in use until the 1970s. The wharf to the south of the LT&S railway was built in 1872 by market gardener John Circuit and was last used in 1976 (URN 2002).

Methodologies

The investigation strategy for Zones T8–T12 comprised a pre-construction watching brief on the service diversions. The only archaeological remains identified comprised remnants of a wharf dated to the 19th to 20th century at Rainham Creek (see below). The area was the subject of three targeted evaluation trenches by Essex County Council Field Archaeology Unit (URN 2003) to assess the impact of the proposed road diversion and HS1, although no earlier structures were recorded (Fig 47). A watching brief was also maintained during the construction of the underpass, the viaduct and the Rainham Creek diversion. A summary of the fieldwork events is presented in Table 30. Sampling and assessment of palaeoenvironmental remains for this route section was limited, but did include a shallow profile at 22.950km in the Mudlands (Fig 46) along with a single date from the top of an exposed peat unit (Fig 48). Interpretation of the sedimentary sequences was carried out by Elizabeth Stafford. The palaeoenvironmental work was carried out by Rob Scaife (pollen), Mark Robinson (waterlogged plant remains and insects) and John Whittaker (ostracods and foraminifera).

Results of the Investigations

Watching brief on service diversions
Chainage 21.34–22.86km (The Ford Motor Works)
Due to the thickness of made ground in the area the service diversions rarely exposed more than 0.50m of the underlying alluvial sequences. Where excavation depth did increase, at road and rail crossings, visibility was often hampered due to the method of excavation and access restricted due to safety reasons (Pl 12). No open sections were available for detailed sampling during the excavations of the caisson chambers and cofferdams. The sediment sequences observed in the intermittent deeper excavations comprised very deep alluvial sequences, including a major peat bed, similar to that observed on the West Dagenham Marshes.

Plate 12 Pipeline excavations employing box shoring through the Ford Motor Works

Chainage 22.86–23.90km (The Mudlands and Riverside STW)
East of the Motor Works, in the area formerly occupied by Mudlands Farm (Fig 46), the route is situated at the very edge of the floodplain. Here Holocene alluvial deposits thin against an outcrop of the Mucking Gravel (Fig 21, Zone 11) which was observed during the service diversions (Fig 48). The surface of the gravels reached *c* 2.0m OD along the STW dropping to -3.05m OD beneath the New Havering Sewer (28.860km) in the west and towards Rainham Creek to the east. The gravel was overlain by Holocene alluvium at the eastern and western parts of the route section. A major peat unit, overlain by minerogenic alluvium, exists in these areas, with the surface of the peat averaging *c* -1.00m to -1.20m OD. The maximum thickness of peat observed was *c* 1.60m at the New Havering Sewer (28.860km). No Holocene alluvium existed in the central part of the route section between 23.160km and 23.600km. Here Pleistocene gravel was directly overlain by modern disturbed ground. Along the entire section of the route the diversions ran through a heavily populated service corridor immediately south of the LT&S. Extensive areas of disturbance were frequently noted in the pipeline main-lay and chamber excavations. This was particularly extensive alongside the Riverside STW. In the area immediately west of Manor Way a rapid drop in the elevation of the modern ground to +0.70m OD suggests that the deposits have been substantially truncated or levelled, possibly for construction

Plate 13 Timber revetment at Rainham Creek

purposes. If so, it was thought unlikely that any shallow archaeological features would have survived in this location. No archaeological remains were identified in this section of the route.

Palaeoenvironmental sampling was undertaken at 22.950km where the pipe trench measured *c* 1.8m in depth (Fig 48).

Peat

The gravels were not reached at 22.950km and therefore the Holocene sequence was not bottomed, the basal deposit encountered in the pipe trench comprised a dark brownish-black peat (context 199) between -2.17m and -1.31m OD. The lower part of the peat was very silty and contained abundant woody material but the upper *c* 0.20m was notably darker in colour and well humified. The top of the peat was radiocarbon dated to the Neolithic, 3030–2870 cal BC (NZA-16265, 4297±40 BP). As expected the pollen assessment suggested that the peat accumulated under a floodplain, alder carr environment. This is supported by the seed assemblage that included seeds and catkins of *A. glutinosa* (*Table 32*). The presence of *Lemna* sp. (duckweed) and *Oenanthe aquatica* gp. in the top of the peat however suggests the carr was followed by more open, and possibly wetter, conditions. The environment was freshwater with the basal peat containing decalcified freshwater ostracods (*Table 33*) and common cladoceran remains. *Quercus, Corylus* and *Fraxinus* grew in drier zones (*Table 31*), while nearby dry soils supported *Tilia* woodland, perhaps co-dominant with *Quercus*.

Upper silty clays

The peat was overlain by a bluish-grey silty clay alluvium (context 198) and a deposit of orangey-brown silty clay alluvium (context 197), capped by the modern topsoil to -0.34m OD. Towards the western end of the route section channel features were noted within the upper alluvium, truncating the top of the underlying peat. Seeds were absent

from the alluvial clay, apart from *Juncus* spp. The arboreal pollen remained relatively stable, aside from some reduction in *Quercus*, until a drop in tree and shrub types and rise in Poaceae in context 197, indicating a more open environment. There were some indications of saltmarsh/halophytic taxa (Chenopodiaceae) but also strong representation of freshwater reedswamp including *Littorella* (shoreweed), *Typha angustifolia*-type, *Iris* (iris) and Cyperaceae. *Potamogeton*-type may be from pond weed or sea arrow grass (*Triglochin maritima*). Ostracods and formainifera were only present in context 197 indicating a tidal mudflat and creek environment.

Chainage 23.90–23.95km (Rainham Creek)

The advanced service diversions in this area included an open cut crossing of Rainham Creek (Fig 47). The trench measured 50m long and 6.0m wide and was excavated to a depth of -2.6m OD. Edge support involved stepping and battering the sides of the trench and this, together with high water levels, despite de-watering, significantly reduced visibility of the deposits. At the time of the watching brief the ground was covered with rough grass. Modern flood defence bunds were located on either side of the creek and ground levels averaged +2.00 to +3.00m OD. Deposits consisted of modern made ground extending down to +1.62m OD, overlying minerogenic bluish-grey silty clay to -0.15m OD. Mid-brownish-grey organic silty clay with reeds and brushwood fragments extended to -2.20m OD, becoming more organic down profile to the base of excavations at -2.60m OD.

On the western bank of the creek the remnants of a 19th–20th century timber revetment was identified (Fig 48). The structure was overlain by modern dumped deposits and cut into the underlying minerogenic alluvium. The top of this structure was truncated at +1.64m OD. Artefactual material from associated deposits suggested a 19th–20th century date.

Trench excavations at Rainham Creek

The evaluation trenches (3054TT, 3055TT, 3056TT) were targeted specifically to investigate the area for earlier waterfront structures (Fig 47). Although substantial timber revetments were recorded in two of the trenches, flanking a buried tributary channel, all proved to be of 19th–20th century date (URN 2003, Pl 13). The evaluation trenches were relatively shallow (*c* 2.50m deep) and did not penetrate the underlying alluvial deposits to any great depth. The watching brief on the pile caps for the bridge piers recorded a substantial thickness of deposits similar to those described during the pipeline watching brief, although peat was encountered at the base of the excavations on Pier 14 (Fig 48).

Chapter 9

Rainham and Wennington Marshes

with contributions by Hugo Anderson-Whymark, Edward Biddulph, Paul Blinkhorn,
Emma-Jayne Evans, Richard Macphail, Mark Robinson, Rob Scaife and John Whittaker

Rainham and Wennington Marshes (Zones T13–T15)

East of Rainham Creek the rail corridor briefly skirts the terrace edge before continuing across the Rainham and Wennington Marshes, passing beneath the A13 flyover at approximately 26.5km (Fig 23). Prior to construction the land either side of Ferry Lane was occupied by warehouses with concrete areas and patches of waste ground. The marshes, however, comprised relatively open ground with rough grass and scrub, dissected by a network of extant drainage ditches. Ground levels averaged +2.60m OD in the west, dropping to +1.90m OD adjacent to Ferry Lane, and between +0.50m and +1.0m OD on the marshes.

Construction Impacts

The HS1 alignment across the marshes was designed to be as low as possible to minimise environmental impacts and construction whilst still maintaining stability across the soft ground. This involved a concrete slab 12m wide and 450mm thick supported by rows of four or five 600mm driven precast piles at 5m centres. Aside from the extensive piling, direct impact into the underlying alluvium on the marshes generally involved the removal of topsoil, although additional intrusive works included diversion of services and drainage ditches.

The service diversions comprised the excavation of a series of trenches in a combined easement to accommodate the Barking Power and Transco gas mains. Excavation was via open cut techniques with a total combined length of 2935m, 300m of which employed box shoring. The depth of excavation averaged 1.80–2.00m, increasing to 3.80m adjacent to Ferry Lane, and to a maximum of 3.50m where the diversions crossed existing drainage ditches. Two coffer chambers were excavated adjacent to Ferry Lane in order to carry the services beneath the road via a pipe-jacked crossing to a maximum depth of 6.0m. A further 375m of trench was excavated on Rainham Marsh in order to divert the Wennington Sewer. This excavation employed closed box shoring to a depth of 3.0m. The diversion of a series of existing drainage ditches from the HS1 corridor was also carried out between 24.83km and 25.70km. The ditches averaged 1.0m deep and 5.0m wide with the

edges sloping at an angle of 40°, reducing the width at the base to 1.50m.

Key Archaeological Issues

The 1999 study designated Zones T13–T15 (Chap 6 *Window 8* and *Window 9*; Fig 23) of low archaeological priority. Between 24.1km (east of Rainham Creek) and 24.9km (Rainham Marsh) the route corridor briefly traverses the edge of the Mucking and West Thurrock Gravel at the margin of the floodplain. Beyond 24.9km (Rainham and Wennington Marshes), however, the route lies to the south or west of the floodplain edge. Two valleys were identified entering the floodplain at *c* 25.5km and 26.5km, the latter corresponding to the former course of Wennington Creek which is known to have been navigable up until the later medieval period.

Examination of the borehole records suggested considerable variation in rockhead surface through Zones T13–T15. The upper surface of the gravels demonstrated similar variation. The Holocene floodplain sediments in the area are dominated by a major peat complex between *c* -2.0m OD and -5.0m OD, with thick clay-silts, silts, sands and organic units below the peat and an upper complex of silts, sands and organic silts. The thickness of modern deposits capping the sequence appeared to be relatively thin throughout these zones. It was predicted initial inundation at the eastern end of this route section at *c* 6000 cal BC (*c* 7200 ^{14}C BP), and the western end by *c* 6000–5500 cal BC (*c* 7000–6500 ^{14}C BP). Key floodplain marginal ecotones may have existed at the boundary between Zones T14 and T15 (*c* 26.0km), and the eastern part of Zone T14 may have acted as an important dry ground zone as wetland inundation occurred in Zone T15. Similarly the western end of Zone T14 (*c* 24.7km) may have formed a dry ground region during early infilling of Zone T13.

Methodologies

Initial fieldwork comprised an archaeological watching brief on the advanced utility diversions. Archaeological remains were identified in the base of a pipe trench

Table 34 Summary of fieldwork events, Rainham and Wennington Marshes

Event name	Event code	Type	Zone	Interventions	Archaeological contractor
West Thames advanced utility diversions	ARC 36100	Watching Brief	13–15		Oxford Archaeology
Rainham, Ferry Lane	ARC RFL02	Evaluation	13	4026TT	Oxford Archaeology
TW sewer diversion	ARC TAM01	Evaluation	14	3972TT	Oxford Archaeology
TW sewer diversion	ARC 31001	Watching Brief	14		Oxford Archaeology
Wennington Marsh	ARC WEN01	Evaluation	15	26501TT, 26502TT	Wessex Archaeology

TT = trench

located at the edge of the floodplain and the gravel terrace immediately east of Ferry Lane at 24.455km (Zone T13). This included a scatter of Early Neolithic worked and fire-cracked flint on a weathered sand horizon sealed beneath peat, and a concentration of Roman pottery and animal bone within the overlying alluvium (see below). Further east, beneath the A13 flyover at 26.54km (Zone T15), evidence of medieval activity comprised an assemblage of potsherds; animal bone and marine shell associated with a drainage ditch and buried soil dated from the 11th–13th centuries AD (see below). The watching brief was followed by a series of evaluation trenches targeted on archaeological remains. Unfortunately no further occupation evidence was identified, perhaps due to the very localised extent of the activity and the fact the trenches could not be placed in the exact locations where remains had originally been identified due to proximity of live services. A summary of the fieldwork events is included in Table 34.

A number of sample profiles were assessed for palaeoenvironmental remains from this route section. Interpretation of the sedimentary sequences was carried out by Elizabeth Stafford. The specialist assessments were carried out by Rob Scaife (pollen), Mark Robinson (charred and waterlogged plant remains and insects) and John Whittaker (ostracods and foraminifera). Subsequently detailed micromorphology (Richard Macphail) was carried out on three sequences containing *in situ* occupation horizons or buried soils (Appendix B, Pls 15A–C and 16A–G). This included deposits associated with the Early Neolithic flint scatter on Rainham Marsh and the medieval marsh soils on Wennington Marsh. A total of 10 radiocarbon dates were obtained during the assessment stage providing a broad chronological framework (Appendix A).

Results of the Investigations

A cross-section of the sequences recorded across the marshes is presented in Figure 49. The relatively shallow depth of excavation of the service diversions dictated that only the upper part of the alluvial sequence and the very top of the main peat unit were regularly observed during the watching brief (Pl 14). Deeper excavations were carried out at the road and drain crossings, although access for sampling purposes was restricted due to safety issues. Evaluation trench 3972TT at 24.755km was excavated to a depth of 4.5m and provided the opportunity to record and sample the main peat complex in greater detail, though the trench did not reach the underlying gravel deposits.

Watching brief and trench excavations on Rainham Marsh

24.455km (East of Ferry Lane)
Basal silty sand (Early Neolithic palaeosol)
In the base of a pipe trench at 24.455km (Figs 50 and 51) the lowermost deposit comprised silty sand (context 192). The upper 0.05m of this deposit appeared to be weathered greyish-brown, grading to light yellowish-brown down-profile. This weathered sand represents the remnants of a former landsurface and contained an *in situ* assemblage of worked

Plate 14 Open trench pipeline excavations on Rainham Marsh

and burnt flint of Early Neolithic date (see below, *The archaeological evidence*).

Unfortunately preservation of environmental remains was limited in the palaeosol; with only comminuted *Quercus* sp. (oak) charcoal fragments and waterlogged wood fragments recovered (*Table 35*). Thin-section analysis (Pls 15A–C) revealed context 192 to be a weakly humic palaeosol containing angular fragments of burned (rubefied, cracked and whitened/calcined) coarse and fine flint with coarse angular quartzite and rare 2mm size charcoal. The palaeosol was compact, and had a collapsed structure along with broad burrow or channel infills of coarse silt and fine charcoal and rare coarse roots (Pl 15A). The sharp boundary with the overlying silty peat (context 193b, Pl 15A) suggests rapid inundation and truncation of the palaeosol, causing loss of structure (loss of fines) associated with coarse silt inwash carrying fine detrital charcoal. The coarse quartzite and burnt flint are possibly relict of burnt midden occupations (as at Tank Hill Road, on Aveley Marsh; see Chap 10), and it is likely that these were once also associated with greater concentrations of charcoal than now present. There may be two reasons for this. First, the palaeosol may have been truncated during inundation, and second, gentle inundation and associated soil slaking tends to allow the liberation and lifting of light materials such as charcoal; this produced a widespread charcoal scatter at the Stumble Neolithic site on the Blackwater Estuary, while at the Mesolithic site at Goldcliff on the Severn much of the charcoal was found in the base of the estuarine silty clays that buried the site (Bell *et al* 2000; Macphail 1994; Macphail and Cruise 2000).

Peat

The palaeosol was sealed by a peat unit, *c* 0.3m thick (context 193a/b). The lowermost 0.05m of this deposit (context 193b) was very silty perhaps reflecting episodes of flooding and sedimentation prior to the accumulation of the main peat unit. The base of the main peat unit was radiocarbon dated to the Early Neolithic, 3520–3110 cal BC (NZA-16266, 4601±40 BP). Thin-section analysis revealed that the lower part of the peat contained trace amounts of fine burnt flint and charcoal, possibly picked up during inundation and concomitant localised reworking. It was coarsely layered, peat and minerogenic peat, with patches and fragments of humified peat and plant/woody fragments that had been mixed by both rooting and mesofauna activity. This implies fluctuating water tables and episodic exposure of the peat at this location.

The main peat unit (193a) produced large quantities of comminuted wood, although waterlogged seeds were restricted to *Urtica dioica* (stinging nettle). The pollen assemblage (*Table 36*) was typical of the Neolithic and Bronze Age of the region as a whole and at other sites examined in this study. *Quercus, Tilia* (lime) and *Corylus avellana* (hazel) woodland with *Fraxinus* (ash) were dominant, probably growing on drier soils above the floodplain, dense extensive alder carr grew locally. There were few herbs with only a small number of Poaceae (grasses) and Cyperaceae (sedges). Fern spores included monolete *Dryopteris*-type with *Pteridium aquilinum* (bracken) and *Polypodium vulgare* (common polypody).

A

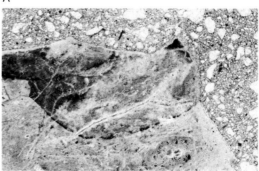

B

C

Plate 15 Microphotographs, 24.455km, East of Ferry Lane, Rainham Marsh. A) Monolith 256(B) thin section, contexts 192 and 193b: Palaeosol 192 contains coarse angular quartzite (Qtz) and burnt flint (BF); rubefied iron (~haematite) is poorly preserved because of iron depletion; relict root channels have been infilled with humic silt (Si) from ensuing minerogenic peat deposition (193b). Width is ~50mm. B) Monolith 256(B), context 192: Burnt flint in weakly humic palaeosol (see A.); note red colours and cracking. Plane polarised light (PPL), frame width is ~4.6mm. C) As B: Under oblique incident light (OIL), although in a gleyed environment, small amounts of relict iron staining still retain rubefied (haematite?) induced by heating

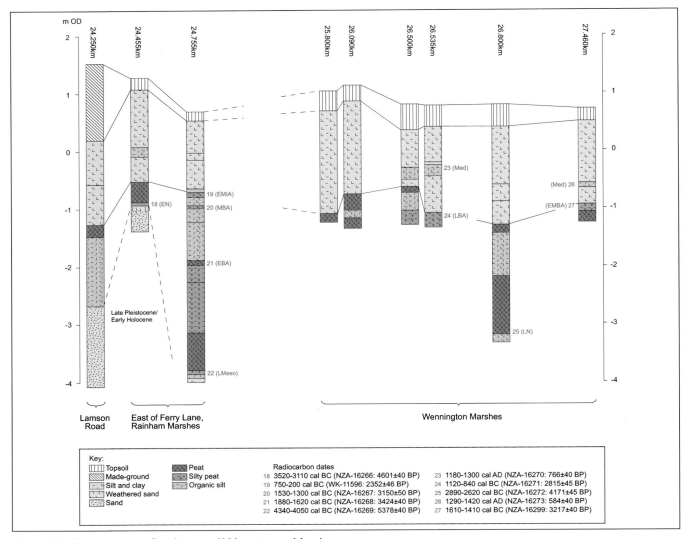

Figure 49 Cross-section, Rainham and Wennington Marshes

Upper silty clays (Roman channel deposits)

The peat was overlain by a bluish-grey silty clay alluvium (context 194), containing clasts of reworked peat, eroded from the underlying deposits, and occasional gravel clasts and lenses of coarse sand. The undulating and abrupt contact with the underlying peat suggests some truncation or erosion had occurred under relatively high-energy conditions, possibly indicating local channel activity. A concentration of Roman pottery and animal bone fragments (cattle, sheep/goat and horse) with butchery marks was recovered from this deposit, possibly inwashed deposits from a nearby settlement area. The condition of the pottery was poor, consistent with the effects of weathering and redeposition (see below; *The archaeological evidence*). Towards the eastern part of the trench bluish-grey silty clay interdigitated with layers of more organic silty clay that dipped northwards suggesting lower energy deposition. This was overlain by a homogeneous dark brownish-grey organic silty clay (context 195) that did not contain artefactual material. The waterlogged seed assemblages from contexts 194 and 195 were more productive. The plant species suggest nutrient rich mud and shallow water, with *Ranunculus sceleratus* (celery-leaved crowfoot), *Ranunculus* subgenus *batrachium* (crowfoot), *Apium nodiflorum* (fool's watercress), *Alisma* sp. (water plantain), *Carex* spp. (sedges) and *Eleocharis palustris*

(common spikerush). Some drier, nutrient rich habitats are also suggested with *Stellaria media* agg. (chickweed), *Chenopodium album* (fat hen), *Atriplex* sp. (orache), *Rubus* sp. (bramble) and *Rumex* sp. (docks). The pollen assemblage demonstrates the dominance of herbs indicating more open grass-sedge-reed fen or swamp. Poaceae was dominant but there was also a marked expansion of fen herbs; Cyperaceae and *Typha angustifolia/Sparganium*-type (lesser bulrush/bur-reed). Two grains of *Cerealia*-type pollen were also found and may suggest cultivation. However, as previously discussed (Chap 7, Trench 4042TT), the similarity of cereal pollen with some wild grasses such as *Glyceria* (sweet-grass) means that the evidence remains equivocal. Because cereal pollen is not widely dispersed it is likely that any cereal cultivation would have taken place in the vicinity of the site, perhaps on slightly higher and drier ground. However, there is also the possibility of water transport given the depositional environment.

There was some suggestion of marine or brackish water influences, with the halophytes *Plantago maritima*-type (sea plantain) and Chenopodiaceae (goosefoots). However, freshwater reedswamp and aquatic taxa were also present, along with algal *Pediastrum*, suggesting that these sediments were laid down in fresh water conditions with brackish water incursions. Fresh water conditions are also indicated by the

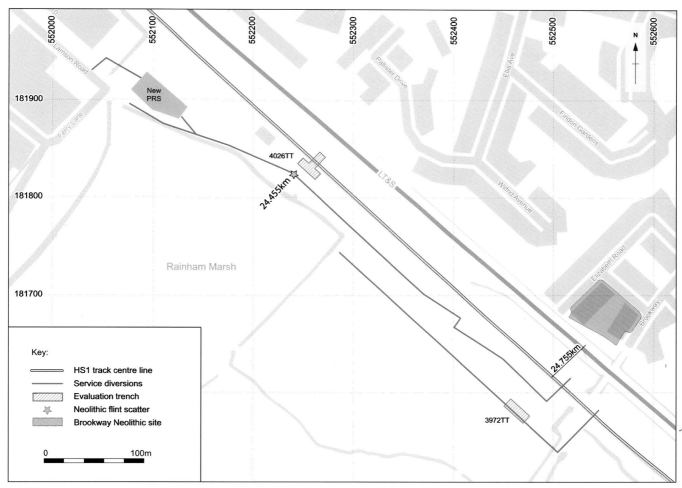

Figure 50 Plan of evaluation trenches and service diversions, East of Ferry Lane, Rainham Marsh

presence of Cladoceran (water fleas) valves and ephippia and partly decalcified freshwater ostracods (cf *Cypria opthalmica*) in context 195.

This sequence of deposits was sealed by further layers of sterile minerogenic alluvium that were not sampled. Context 166 comprised a grey and brown mottled silty clay, and context 392 a greyish-yellow-brown silty clay. The sequence was capped by the modern marsh topsoil (context 393) at *c* +1.20m OD.

Trench 3972TT

Evaluation trench 3972TT (Figs 50 and 51) was sited with the central alignment of the Rainham Sewer diversion, on a north-west to south-east alignment and was to coincide with the projected continuation of the prehistoric trackway previously identified at the Brookway settlement *c* 250m to the north-east. The trench was excavated to achieve a reduced base plan of *c* 15 x 4m to a depth of 4.50m; the maximum impact of the engineering works. The total excavation area on the surface was 25 x 12m. Safe trench support was achieved by stepping the edges of excavation.

Superficially the sediment sequence can be divided into three main units; a lower minerogenic alluvium, a thick organic complex and an upper minerogenic alluvium. Detailed on-site and off-site recording,

however, revealed much greater complexity (*Table 37*). Four radiocarbon dates were obtained from trench 3972TT; demonstrating accumulation of the peat and organic deposits spanned a considerable period of time from the Late Mesolithic to Iron Age. No archaeological remains were encountered; however the sampled sediment sequence provides a useful 'off-site' record for the artefactual material recovered from the sequence described at 24.455km above.

Lower clay silts

The lower minerogenic alluvial deposit (context 15), exposed in a sondage in the base of the trench, comprised a soft structureless mid-grey clay silt. Unfortunately environmental remains were poorly preserved in this deposit. The overlying more organic clay silt (context 14), at the interface with the overlying peat, was a little more productive with seeds of *Alnus glutinosa* (common alder) and *Corylus avellana* (*Table 38*). The marsh pollen taxa (*Table 39*) was similarly dominated by *A. glutinosa* suggesting locally an alder carr environment. Aquatic taxa were few but *Potamogeton*-type (pondweed) and *Myriophyllum spicatum* (spiked water-milfoil) were present demonstrating that a small proportion of these sediments were laid down in fluviatile/ overbank flow conditions. Of the tree pollen, *Quercus* and *Corylus avellana* were most abundant, with occasional *Tilia* (lime), *Ulmus* (elm) and *Fraxinus* (ash) which

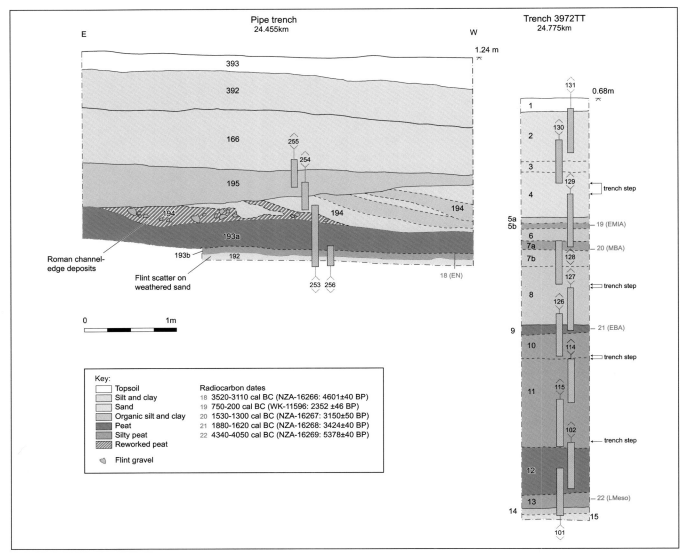

Figure 51 Sample profiles, East of Ferry Lane, Rainham Marsh

were probably growing on higher dry ground. There were few herbs with only occasional Poaceae, Apiaceae and single occurrences of other types.

Organic complex (lower)

The lower part of the organic complex (contexts 13–9) predominantly comprised alder carr wood peats between -3.86m and -1.87m OD. A thick unit of very silty peat (context 11) occurred between -2.55m and -3.12m OD which may indicate a period of localised flooding. Radiocarbon dating suggests these deposits accumulated between the Late Mesolithic and Early Bronze Age periods; context 13 was dated to 4340–4050 cal BC (NZA-16269, 5378±40 BP), and context 9 to 1880–1620 cal BC (NZA-16268, 3424±40 BP). The pollen assemblage from the peats was similar to that described above with locally dense alder carr which became more important and dominant on-site (contexts 12 and 13). Typically, there were traces of other fen carr elements such as *Frangula alnus* (alder buckthorn) and *Rhamnus catharticus* (buckthorn) and associated ground flora comprising *Lythrum salicaria* (purple loosestrife), *Typha angustifolia*-type and Cyperaceae. Spores of ferns were also important with

Dryopteris-type (monolete), *Polypodium vulgare* and *Osmunda regalis* (royal fern). There was a small peak in Cyperaceae just prior to the change from wood peat (context 12) to silty peat (context 11). The seed assemblage included *Cornus sanguinea* (dogwood), *Oenanthe aquatica* gp. (water dropwort), *U. dioica*, *Ranunculus* cf *repens* (creeping buttercup), *Carex* spp. and *Rubus* sp., along with *A. glutinosa* and *Quercus*. Occasional beetle remains (*Table 40*) included the small water beetle *Ochthebius* cf *minimus*, the alder leaf beetle *Agelastica alni* and the death watch beetle *Anobium* cf *punctatum*, along with freshwater Cladocerans.

Organic complex (upper)

Overall the upper part of the organic complex (contexts 8–5) between -1.87 and -0.70m OD had a much higher minerogenic component largely comprising organic silt clays suggesting wetter conditions with increased flooding and alluviation in a more open fen environment. Radiocarbon dating suggests these deposits accumulated up until the Early to Middle Iron Age. The change in lithology is mirrored by a significant change in the pollen assemblages. There was a reduction of both terrestrial woodland and the alder carr. The

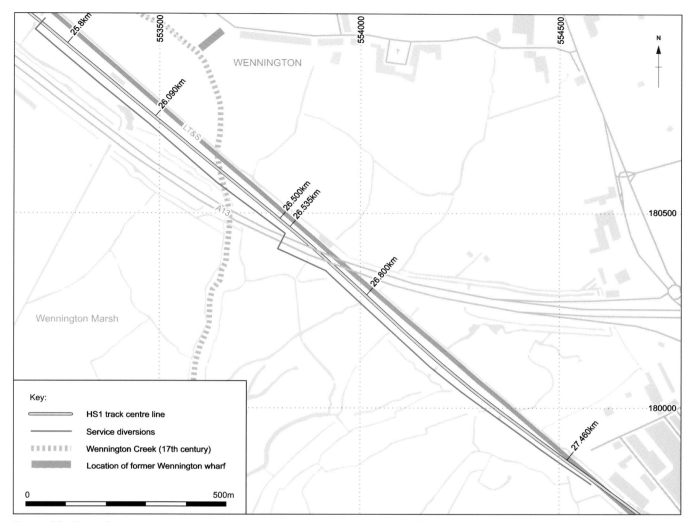

Figure 52 Plan of evaluation trenches and service diversions, Wennington Marsh

alder carr was replaced by grass-sedge-reed fen with alder still growing along its fringes but at further distance from the sample site. There was also an increase in the diversity of herb taxa, including both wetland/marsh taxa (eg, *Iris* (iris), *Typha latifolia* (bulrushes) and Cyperaceae), and dry-land herbaceous taxa. Poaceae attained high values along with Chenopodiaceae and *Plantago lanceolata* (ribwort plantain). Cereal-type pollen was also recorded, perhaps suggesting open land and cultivation in the catchment, although as discussed in the sequence above (24.455km) the identification of cereal-type pollen as opposed to some wild grasses remains problematic. Coleoptera from context 8 included *Helophorus* sp. (*brevipalpis* size), *Ochthebius* cf *minimus*, *Donacia* sp., *Plateumaris sericea*, *Prasocuris phellandrii*, *Apion* sp. and *Ceutorhynchus erysimi*. The seed assemblage was consistent with the development of an open fen environment and included *Ranunculus sceleratus*, *Polygonum hydropiper* (water-pepper) *Alisma* sp., *Sparganium erectum* (branched bur-reed) and *Juncus* spp. (rush). Of note was the presence of the ostracod *Cypria opthalmica* in context 8 (*Table 41*), along with opercula of the mollusc *Bithynia tentaculata* and Cladocerans, suggesting freshwater conditions prevailed at least in the lower part of the sequence. The expanding values of Chenopodiaceae pollen in the upper part however may be indicative of some episodic saline ingress.

Two thin peaty horizons were noted with the upper organic complex (contexts 7a and 5b) which show shifts to a wet terrestrial environment. Context 7a was dated at -0.93m OD to the Middle Bronze Age, 1530–1300 cal BC (NZA-16267, 3150± BP) and context 5b at -0.70m OD to the Early to Middle Iron Age, at 750–200 cal BC (WK-11596, 2352±46 BP). Brackish water incursion is indicated in the overlying organic silty clay layer (context 5a) by the occurrence of ostracods *Cyprideis torosa* and *Loxoconcha elliptica*.

Upper silty clays
Overlying the organic complex was a sequence of silty clay alluvial deposits (contexts 4–2). The principal tree and shrub pollen taxa remain as in the underlying deposits. Herbs were dominated by Poaceae, *Sinapis*-type (eg, mustard), Chenopodiaceae and Lactucoideae (charlocks), the latter peaking in context 2. The presence of *Armeria* (sea lavender and/or thrift) is a good indicator of saltmarsh. *Sinapis*-type, *Aster*-type and *Potamogeton* are also indicators of brackish water/saltmarsh when found in association with definite indicators such as *Armeria*. These deposits also produced a rich ostracod assemblage dominated by species living in sheltered brackish creeks and intertidal mudflats (typified by *Cyprideis torosa*, *Leptocythere porcellanea*, *L. elliptica* and *Cytherura gibba*) and being common to abundant, must be considered *in situ*,

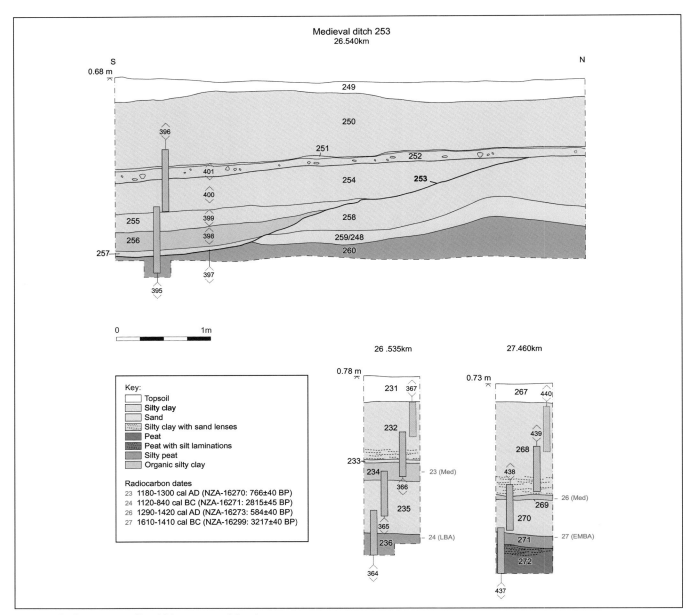

Figure 53 Sample profiles, Wennington Marsh

whereas the freshwater species (*Candona* spp. and *Limnocythere inopinata*) were quite rare. The foraminifera were also supportive of a brackish tidal mudflat environment; they were mostly small in size and consist of euryhaline species of *Ammonia*, *Elphidium* and *Haynesina germanica*.

Watching brief on Wennington Marsh

Chainage 26.535km
Peat

The pipe trench at 26.535km (Figs 52 and 53) was excavated to *c* 2.0m depth. The lowermost deposit exposed comprised 0.25m of silty peat (context 236) at -1.05 to -1.3 m OD. The top of the peat was radiocarbon dated to the Late Bronze Age at 1120–840 cal BC (NZA-16271, 2815±45 BP).

Waterlogged remains were very poorly preserved; limited to seeds of *Ranunculus* cf *repens* (*Table 42*). The relatively late date for the top of the peat is reflected in the character of the pollen

assemblage (*Table 43*). Trees and shrubs were low in abundance, but *Quercus*, *Corylus avellana*-type and *Alnus glutinosa* were present, with sporadic occurrences of *Betula*, *Tilia* and *Rhamnus catharticus* (buckthorn). Herbs were very abundant, particularly Poaceae along with Cyperaceae. Other taxa were from reedswamp and aquatic habitats with *Potamogeton*-type and *Typha angustifolia*-type. The peat also had high values of monolete *Dryopteris* spores (degraded cf *Thelypteris*) and *Pteridium aquilinum*. A single grain of cereal-type pollen was also present. Overall the pollen assemblage suggests the landscape, at least locally, was largely open. The depositional habitat was grass-sedge fen with some alder present, perhaps fringing wetter areas of the marsh.

Upper silty clays (medieval palaeosol)

The peat was overlain by a series of estuarine silty clay alluvial deposits at -1.05m and +0.43m. Context 235 comprised 0.58m of orangey-brown silty clay alluvium. Overlying this was context 234; a firm dark grey silty clay 0.21m thick (-0.26 to

-0.47m OD) that may represent an ephemeral dry period with increased soil formation. A single sherd of late 13th century pottery was recovered from this layer and charred cereal grain was radiocarbon dated to cal AD 1180–1300 (NZA-16270, 766±40 BP). Stratigraphically equivalent horizons directly south of the sample profile (contexts 239 and 240) in the west-facing section of the pipe trench provided further occupation evidence with pottery sherds of mid-12th century to late 13th century date along with fragments of marine shell; oysters, whelks and mussels (see below; *The archaeological evidence*).

Thin-section analysis of context 234 revealed fine, mostly parallel, laminations of silt, very fine sand and clay, 350–500μm thick (Appendix B, Pls 16A and 16B). The deposit became more massive and clayey upwards and contained much detrital, very fine charred and amorphous organic matter, which often retained a sub-horizontal orientation, along with earthworm granules (biogenic calcite; Pl 16C; Armour-Chelu and Andrews 1994; Bal 1982; Canti 1998). Lower energy deposition is suggested by thin to broad burrows which were characterised by clay clasts with organic matter. Vesicles, intercalations and clayey void coatings in burrows are indicative of general slaking, presumably associated with ensuing flooding. Inundation also probably led to inwash of fine sand down channels from the overlying deposit (context 233). Waterlogging and fluctuating water tables produced much weak iron (Fe) staining in the lower part of context 234 (see χ_{max} in Appendix B), with the more clayey massive upper part being more Fe depleted. Bulk analysis found a low organic content (3.85% LOI, Appendix B). Thus much of the dark colour is due to the presence of highly humified and fine charcoal (Babel 1975). There was, however, no evidence of phosphate enrichment associated with human activity and the magnetic susceptibility provided no evidence for burning. Caution, however, must be stressed with regard to the latter as gleyed deposits are not well suited to magnetic susceptibility analysis because of their generally low Fe content and the potentially unstable nature of Fe mineralogy. Although the exact sequence of events is difficult to fully elucidate, a putative ripened humic clay surface (first stage of weathering and soil formation; Bal 1982; Catt 1979) seems to have formed towards the top of context 234, and earthworms worked this material down profile. Local flooding/stream flow, perhaps associated with the nearby ditch at 26.540km (see below), may have eroded the top of context 234 and produced the overlying fine sandy sediments of context 233.

Thin section analysis revealed context 233 comprised a moderately to poorly sorted clayey sediment with coarse silt, and very fine to coarse sand. It included burnt coarse sand sized chert and much fine charred and amorphous organic matter fragments. It was also burrowed, rooted and both iron depleted and stained as in context 234, with a sharp but burrowed lower boundary (Pls 16D–16G). The sand was overlain by a further deposit of orangey-brown silty clay alluvium 0.64m thick (context 232) which was capped by the modern marsh topsoil to +0.78 m OD.

Unfortunately waterlogged remains were very poorly preserved in the alluvial sequence and were restricted to seeds of *Typha* sp. and *Juncus* sp. in layer 233. The pollen assemblages indicate an open environment similar to that from the top of the peat. Although a marked expansion of Chenopodiaceae which may be an indication of saltmarsh halophytic communities, freshwater marsh taxa also remained important. With the exception of context 234, the alluvium did contain rich faunas of brackish intertidal and creek-dwelling ostracods and foraminifera (*Table 44*), typified by the ostracod species *Cyprideis torosa*, *Leptocythere porcellanea*, *Loxoconcha elliptica*, *Leptocythere castanea* and *Cytherura gibba*, and foraminifera of *Ammonia*, *Elphidium* and *Haynesina germanica*. Fully marine ostracod species, probably washed in by a tidal surge, are represented by *Pontocythere elongata* in context 232. A minor freshwater/terrestrial component washed in from nearby coastal and floodplain pools and soils are represented by the ostracods *Candona* sp., *Heterocypris salina* and *Pseudocandona* sp.

Chainage 26.540km
The basic sequence at 26.540km was similar to that described at 26.535km above, but was located where the pipe trench dog-legged beneath the A13 flyover (Figs 52 and 53). The lowermost deposit exposed comprised a dark reddish-black well humified silty peat (context 260) at -1.05m to -1.3m OD. This was overlain by 0.20m of light greyish-yellow silty sand (context 259/248). The contact between the peat and the sand was very abrupt suggesting an erosional event. The sand contained a rich and diverse assemblage of foraminifera and ostracods (*Table 44*) similar to that described for the alluvium at 26.535km suggesting an estuarine environment with tidal creeks but with some freshwater input. The sand was overlain by a series of silty clay alluvial deposits and modern marsh topsoil to +0.68m OD.

Medieval ditch 253
In the east-facing section of the pipe trench, however, part of the profile of a large ditch or channel edge (feature 253) was exposed within the upper alluvium. Pottery recovered from the fills of this feature suggests it was broadly contemporary with the palaeosol (context 234) recorded at 26.535km. Feature 253 measured *c* 1.0m deep and was only partially exposed to a maximum width of *c* 4.3m at the top. The lowermost fill (context 257) comprised a firm mid-yellowish-brown silty clay. This was overlain by a dark grey organic silty clay (context 256) and a light yellowish-grey sandy silty clay (context 255). The upper fill (context 254) comprised a firm greenish-grey silty clay, sealed by a further deposit of bluish-grey silty clay with frequent flint gravel clasts (context 252). In addition to the pottery, a small assemblage of animal bone was recovered from feature 253 including cattle, sheep/goat, pig and a piece of deer antler, along with a quantity of charred cereal grain (see below; *The archaeological evidence*).

Waterlogged plant remains were largely absent apart from seeds of *Lemna* sp. (duckweed), *Alisma* sp. and *Typha* sp. (*Table 42*). The pollen evidence was similar to that described for the sample profile at 26.535km, with an overall low abundance of trees wth a general background presence of *Quercus* and *Corylus* (*Table 43*). The herb assemblages were diverse, coming from a range of habitats that may have included pastoral agriculture and arable cultivation (eg, *Plantago lanceolata* and cereal-type) as well as the autochthonous (on-site) vegetation.

A) Monolith 366 thin section, contexts 233 and 234: Very fine sandy context 233 over upper massive clayey context 234 and laminated silt and clay (see B.) in lower context 234. Width is ~50mm.
B) Monolith 366, lower Context 234: Composed of finely laminated silt and humic clay. Plane polarised light (PPL), frame width is ~4.6mm.
C) Monolith 366, upper context 234: Massive, clayey, with partially decalcified earthworm granule (biogenic calcite, arrow) in burrow in humic clay containing sparse silt. Crossed polarised light (XPL), frame width is ~4.6mm.
D) Monolith 366, contexts 234 and 233 interface: Burrowed boundary (arrows). PPL, frame width is ~4.6mm.
E) As D: Under XPL, showing humic clayey context 234 (with very low interference colours) and coarse silt and very fine sand in context 233.
F) Monolith 366, context 233: Partially iron-stained piece of burned chert (BCh) and partially decalcified, probable slug plate (biogenic calcite, BC). PPL, frame width is 2.3mm.
G) As F: Under oblique incident light (OIL), part-calcined and part-rubefied burnt chert (BCh) and biogenic calcite (BC); note other very fine rubefied mineral inclusions

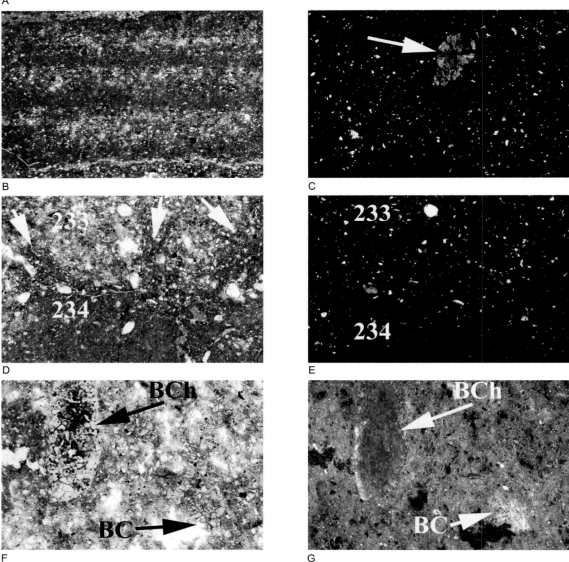

Plate 16 Microphotographs from 26.535km, Wennington Marsh

The latter is somewhat enigmatic because there is a strong representation of freshwater types in the on-site vegetation, especially Cyperaceae, but with high values of Chenopodiaceae which, with Hystrichopheres (dinoflaggellates) and *Aster*-type, may indicate saline conditions with development of saltmarsh. A notable peak of *Sinapis*-type may come from coastal/maritime taxa such as *Raphanus raphanistrum* (radish), *Cakile* (sea kale) or other coastal Brassicaceae. The ostracods and foraminifera provide the sediments with a strong brackish mudflat-and-creek signature throughout, with full tidal access (*Table 44*), although small numbers of cyprinid fish bones, vole teeth and frog/toad bones, suggest the possibility of small freshwater streams inputting here. The freshwater ostracods that were present are able to withstand low salinity.

Chainage 26.800km

At 26.800km (Figs 49 and 52) a deep sequence of deposits was exposed where the pipe trench crossed an extant drainage ditch. The lowermost deposit comprised a mid-grey organic silty clay alluvium between -3.35m and 3.20m OD (context 274). Overlying this was a thick peat bed (context 273) between -3.30m and -2.2m OD, sealed by a series of minerogenic alluvial deposits and modern marsh topsoil to +0.70m OD.

The base of the peat at -3.2m OD was radiocarbon dated to the Late Neolithic, 2890–2620 cal BC (NZA-16272, 4171±45 BP), suggesting the main period of peat formation occurred during the Late Neolithic and Bronze Age. Unfortunately only spot bulk samples were retrieved from the lower alluvium (context 274) and peat (context 273) due to safety issues when accessing the trench. The samples contained seeds and cones of *Alnus glutinosa* as well as *Quercus*, buds and seeds of *Rubus fruticosus* agg. (*Table 45*). The bark beetle *Dryocoetinus alni*, which is often associated with alder, was also present in context 274 along with the alder leaf beetle *Agelastica alni*, the water beetle *Ochthebius* cf *minimus* and *Stenus* sp. (*Table 46*). The pollen assemblage (*Table 47*) from both contexts 274 and 273 contained high numbers of trees and shrubs; *Quercus*, *Corylus avellana*-type and *Tilia*. *Alnus* was important forming freshwater alder carr woodland.

Chainage 27.460km

The pipe trench at 27.460km (Figs 52 and 53) was excavated to 2.1m. The lowermost deposit exposed comprised 0.30m of firm dark reddish-brown wood peat (context 272) with discontinuous laminations of blue silty clay and shell fragments at -1.36 to -1.06m OD. This was overlain by a further deposit of dark brownish-black fibrous silty peat (context 271) with frequent woody fragments (-1.06 to -0.92m OD). The top of the peat (context 271) was radiocarbon dated to the Early to Middle Bronze Age at 1610–1410 cal BC (NZA-16299, 3217±40 BP).

Peat

Environmental remains from the peat suggest mixed fen woodland and included buds of *Populus* sp. (poplar), nuts of *Corylus avellana* and seeds of *Rubus fruticosus* agg., *Urtica dioica*

and *Carex* spp. (*Table 45*), along with the water beetle *Ochthebius* cf *minimus* (*Table 46*). The pollen assemblage contained high values of *Alnus* and, with Cyperaceae and occasional aquatics (eg, cf *Callitriche*), show that an alder carr woodland was responsible for the peat accumulation (*Table 47*). There were numerous monolete spores of *Dryopteris*-type and also present was *Thelypteris palustris*. Herb diversity was smaller than in the overlying mineral sediments, although Poaceae has a basal peak. The importance of *Quercus*, with some *Fraxinus*, may also be attributed to growth in drier areas of this carr woodland. Woodland dominated by *Quercus*, *Tilia*, *Corylus* and *Fraxinus* was present in the catchment. *Tilia* was an important constituent of the woodland and, given its poor pollen representation (Andersen 1970; 1973), was possibly dominant or co-dominant with *Quercus* on the better drained soils.

Upper silty clays (medieval palaeosol)

Similar to other profiles on Wennington Marsh the peat was sealed by a series of estuarine alluvial deposits; initially an orangey-brown silty clay alluvium (context 270). The pollen assemblages at this level showed much reduced quantities of tree (especially *Tilia*) and shrub pollen and *Alnus* in the marsh category. Conversely, there were higher quantities of herbaceous-types with Poaceae dominant with greater diversity including peaks of *Sinapis*-type and *Cerealia*-type. Cyperaceae replaced *Alnus* as the dominant marsh taxon. There was some indication of tidal ingress with the brackish water ostracod *Cyprideis torosa* and the foraminifera *Ammonia limnetes* (*Table 48*).

Overlying this was a thin deposit of dark greyish-brown silty clay (context 269). Similar to context 234 at 26.535km (see above), this is interpreted as an ephemeral dry phase which saw increased soil formation. Sediment from the upper part of this context was radiocarbon dated to the medieval period, cal AD 1290–1420 (NZA-16273, 584±40 BP).

Thin-section analysis of context 269 (monolith 438, Fig 53; Appendix B) revealed a lower unit composed of heterogeneous humic clays with silt and a little sand (Pl 17A–D). Blackened, humified and charred organic matter inclusions were unoriented. The deposit was characterised by burrows and channels, an angular blocky structure, iron staining, and trace amounts of pyrite and gypsum. This lower unit may be interpreted as a ripened, once-laminated peaty or humic clay sediment. The uppermost 5mm of context 269 comprised a dark reddish brown layered humified peat with small biochannels containing very thin organic excrements (Pls 17A and 17F). It was not burrowed and the horizontal orientation of the plant fragments was preserved. Overall this probably records a renewed rise in water table which resulted in laminated peat formation. This peat, in turn, was affected by minor ripening (eg, humification and bio-chamber fills of organic excrements; Dinç *et al* 1976; Schoute 1987), again indicating fluctuating water tables. Bulk analysis revealed context 269 to have relatively high organic matter content and organic phosphate values were also higher. There was, however, no evidence of phosphate-enrichment beyond that which might be anticipated as a result of phosphate concentration through nutrient natural cycling and no signs of magnetic susceptibility enhancement.

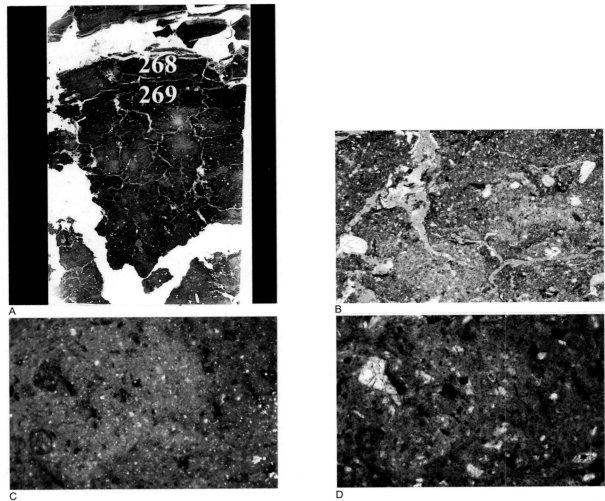

Plate 17 Microphotographs from 27.460km, Wennington Marsh. A) Monolith 438 thin section, contexts 268 and 269: Very fine sandy laminated context 268, over very dark reddish uppermost context 269 (partially humified peat). Peat formed over humic clays (lower context 269) that have undergone sediment ripening and angular blocky structure formation; minor post-depositional cracking has also affected the peat. Width is ~50mm. B) Monolith 438, lower context 269: Burrowed and homogenised humic silty clay, with curved planar void development (angular blocky structures). Plane polarised light (PPL), frame width is ~4.6mm. C) Detail of B: Under oblique incident light (OIL), showing biomixing of dark brown humic and pale poorly humic, clayey silts. Frame width is ~2.3 mm. D) As C: Showing presence of humic clay, coarse silt and very fine sand. PPL

The environmental remains suggest grassland, possibly pasture, was dominant on-site during this period. Waterlogged seeds included *Potentilla anserina* (silverweed) and some seeds of *Juncus* sp. Tree pollen values were low in samples from layer 269. Pollen in the upper horizon had better preservation than the lower and had high values of Poaceae along with some Lactucoideae and Cyperaceae. The lower horizon had typical differential preservation of pollen in favour of the more robust pollen taxon, Lactucoideae. No ostracods or foraminifera were preserved in this deposit but fragments of Cladocerans may tentatively suggest freshwater conditions.

Thin section analysis of the overlying deposit (context 268) revealed it to be composed of multiple thin (2–4mm) laminations of very fine sand and humic clay; the latter was also characterised by high concentrations of blackened and charred fine organic matter (Pls 17E, 17G and 17H). The evidence indicates renewed alluviation/flooding events. Arboreal pollen recovered in this layer compared to below with

increases in *Ulmus, Quercus, Corylus avellana*-type and *Alnus*. Herbs showed an expansion of Chenopodiaceae, which along with Aster-type and large (non-cereal) Poaceae may suggest marine/brackish water influence. The sequence was capped by the modern marsh topsoil to 0.73m OD. The ostracod and foraminifera assemblages were similar to others from the upper alluvium on Wennington Marsh suggesting a strong tidal influence.

The Archaeological Evidence

Early Neolithic
During the watching brief at 24.455km (Fig 50), on Rainham Marsh, an Early Neolithic *in situ* flint knapping scatter was identified in the base of the pipe trench within the sandy palaeosol (context 192) sealed by peat (see 24.455km above for detailed description of the

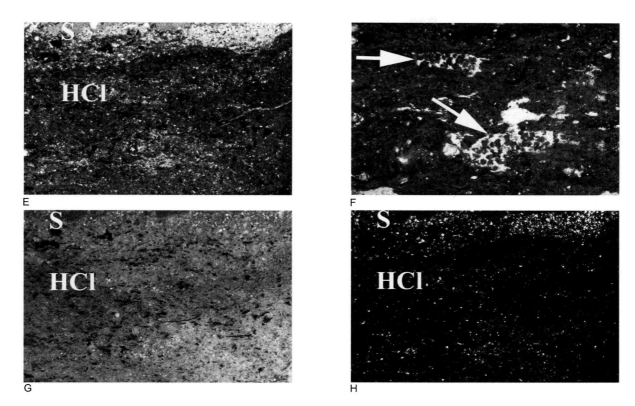

Plate 17 continued: E) Monolith 438, context 268: Junction between humic clay (HCl) and very fine sand (S) laminae. PPL, frame width is ~4.6 mm. F) Monolith 438, upper 5mm of context 269: Dark reddish brown humified peat colours and bio-channels containing very thin organic excrements of mesofauna (arrows); no coarse burrows were observed. PPL, frame width is 2.3mm. G) As E: under OIL; note very abundant sub-horizontally oriented detrital, blackened and charred organic matter in the humic clay (HCl) layer. Reddish staining on right hand side is due to iron impregnation. H) As E: Under cross polarised light (XPL); note occurrence of very fine sand- (S) size quartz

sedimentary sequence). The majority of the assemblage was recovered from the upper 0.10m of context 192, exposed over a 2m² area. A total of 65 worked flints were examined by Hugo Anderson-Whymark, which included 31 chips from sieving of bulk samples (*Table 49*). The 30 flakes were generally of narrow proportions (10 blade-like pieces) and many exhibited platform-edge abrasion. The flakes were struck using both hard and soft hammer percussors. Side and distal trimming flakes were present within the assemblage, indicating that cores were prepared on site. A fragment of a face rejuvenation flake was also present. A refitting exercise located a knapping refit between two blade-like flakes. Both flakes possessed a distinctive olive green cortex. Several flakes, although not refitting, appeared to be of the same flint. The presence of a refit and several possibly related flints indicates the material recovered may have formed part of an *in situ* knapping scatter. A single, platform flake core and two small, crude multi-platform flake cores were also present. Platform edge abrasion was apparent on two of the cores. Scars present on the side of a blade-like flake indicate that it was struck from a well-prepared blade core, although none were present in the assemblage. The reduction strategies employed on the majority of the assemblage, despite being relatively careful, exhibiting platform edge abrasion and face rejuvenation, appear to be aimed at the

production of flakes and blade-like flakes rather than blades and bladelets. A Neolithic date for the scatter would seem most appropriate and the radiocarbon date on the base of the peat sealing the flint scatter would seem to support this. The only diagnostic artefact recovered is a very fresh microlith of Late Mesolithic geometric form (Type 7a1, Jacobi 1978, 17).

The sedimentary and environmental evidence indicates that this activity is likely to have occurred on a slightly raised area of higher drier ground at the edge of the gravel terrace and an area of wetland alder carr that extended onto the floodplain. Oak, hazel and lime woodland, with some ash and elm, probably grew on the terrace. No other archaeological features were identified and the scatter probably represents a short-lived activity area, perhaps associated with more permanent settlement on the higher ground of the gravel terrace. At the Brookway site to the north-east evidence of Neolithic occupation was identified crossing from a dry gravel outcrop into the marsh. The artefact assemblage included pottery of the Plain Bowl tradition and some Mildenhall style wares, along with a large amount of flint knapping debris (MoLAS 2000). Neolithic features also included pits, post-holes, a gravel surface and a hearth. Some post-holes appeared to from part of a structure. At Launders Lane, further to the north, a ritual monument in the form of a ring ditch 15m in diameter was found associated with a central pit, Mildenhall pottery and worked flint (Meddens 1996, 325; MoLAS 2000, 68–9).

Later prehistoric

No archaeological remains were identified from the Bronze Age or Iron Age. The sedimentary and environmental evidence indicates fresh water alder carr continued to dominate the low-lying floodplain during the later Neolithic and Early Bronze Age with mixed oak woodland on the drier ground. The upper part of the peat/organic profiles examined on Rainham and Wennington Marsh frequently demonstrated a general trend to more open environments from the Middle Bronze Age with the development of freshwater grass-sedge-reed fen or swamp. The high minerogenic content of much of these deposits suggests increased episodes of flooding and alluviation were occurring. This was probably a result of rising water tables as a consequence of an increase in the rate of sea-level rise; a prelude to more widespread estuarine inundation.

The area around Rainham is rich in archaeology of this period. Major occupation appears to have been largely confined to the dry ground of the gravel terraces, as evidenced by the distribution of cropmarks, findspots and potential settlement sites. However, there is increasing evidence to suggest that activity extended onto the floodplain, in the form of seasonal activity. Increased wetness during the later periods may have instigated the widespread building of timber trackways to maintain access to the marsh. At Bridge Road, Rainham, wooden structures were located on the bank of Rainham Creek along the northern edge of a gravel rise, forming an insubstantial brushwood trackway constructed using coppiced alder. A small rectangular enclosure was identified adjacent to the trackway. Two radiocarbon dates from the trackway – 1430–1010 cal BC (Beta-58377, 3000±80 BP) and 1730–1270 cal BC (Beta-58378, 3210±90 BP) – place it in the Middle to Late Bronze Age (Meddens and Beasley 1990, 244).

Roman

Archaeological remains dating to the Roman period were recorded within the upper alluvium at 24.455km on Rainham Marsh (Fig 50). This comprised an assemblage of pottery and animal bone associated with a channel edge within an open environment of grass-sedge-reed fen or swamp. It is likely that the artefact assemblage represents in-washed deposits from a nearby area of activity at the floodplain edge. During the excavations at Brookway activity dating to this period was identified on the gravel terrace, including a field boundary and drainage ditch (MoLAS 2000). Ditches identified in a watching brief for the Horndon-Barking pipeline on Rainham Marsh were also thought to be of Roman date (Birbeck and Barnes 1995).

The pottery, assessed by Edward Biddulph, comprised 47 sherds, weighing 123g, and was recovered from channel deposit 194 (*Table 50*). The condition of the pottery was poor, with sherds being small and abraded, probably as a result of weathering and redeposition. Shell-tempered ware formed the largest proportion with smaller quantities of sand-tempered grey ware and grog-tempered ware. A single sherd of fine 'Upchurch'-type oxidised ware was also present and a rim sherd, possibly from a beaker, was present in grog-tempered ware. The oxidised and shell-tempered wares are characteristic of North Kent products, although local manufacture cannot be ruled out for the grey ware and grog-tempered ware. The pottery can be assigned to the late 1st century AD although, given the condition of the material and the possibility of it being entirely residual, final deposition may have occurred in the early 2nd century AD. The context also yielded two sherds of handmade, flint-tempered ware. This tends to date to the Iron Age, but is not necessarily out of place within a later 1st century assemblage.

The small animal bone assemblage, examined by Emma-Jayne Evans, comprised six bones of cattle, sheep/goat and horse. Butchery marks were noted on a cattle mandible and a sheep/goat 1st phalanx, which was also charred black, indicating that animals were processed, probably for consumption and/or marrow extraction. Fusion data suggests that at least one sheep/goat died before reaching 1½ years old.

Medieval

Medieval activity was recorded on Wennington Marsh, directly beneath the A13 flyover at 25.540–26.535km. This comprised an artefact-rich occupation soil and drainage ditch identified within the upper minerogenic alluvial deposits.

The pottery assemblage, examined by Paul Blinkhorn, consisted of 78 sherds with a total weight of 678g. The range of ware types present indicate that there was medieval activity at the site from around the time of the Norman Conquest until the mid-late 13th century, with perhaps another phase during the 16th century. The small size of the assemblage does however mean that it is possible that the medieval activity continued up until that time. Some of the pottery types are common in London, and where appropriate, the Museum of London fabric codes have been used (Vince 1985, 38). These include Shelly Limestone ware (SHEL), early medieval Sand and Shell ware (EMSS), London ware (LOND), Kingston-type ware (KING) and Mill Green ware (MG). Three other wares were also noted, and appear likely to be the products of kilns in Essex or south Suffolk. These include Sandy Coarseware (SANDY), a Micaceous Coarseware (MICA) and Red Earthenwares (RE). The pottery occurrence by number and weight of sherds per context by fabric type is shown in *Table 51*. Each date should be regarded as *terminus post quem*.

The small animal bone assemblage, assessed by Emma-Jayne Evans, comprised three bones, one each of cattle, sheep/goat and pig, along with a piece of red deer antler. With the exception of the antler, all exhibited butchery marks and fusion data suggests that the pig remains belonged to an individual that died before reaching two years of age. Fusion data, along with the presence of butchery marks, may suggest that pigs were kept for meat. As pigs can produce large litters outside the usual seasonal cycles followed by cattle and sheep, a plentiful supply of pork is always available; therefore pigs are usually killed prior to full maturation (Dobney *et al* 1996). However, the age at death of one individual may not be representative of the population as a whole. Carnivore gnawing was noted on a sheep/goat tibia, indicating that the bone was exposed on the surface before its final deposition.

The charred grain from feature 253, examined by Mark Robinson, included free-threshing *Triticum* sp. (rivet or bread wheat), hulled *Hordeum* sp. (hulled barley) and *Avena* sp. (oats) (*Table 52*). Arable weed seeds, such as *Galium aparine* (goosegrass) and *Anthemis cotula* (stinking mayweed) were also present. This assemblage is typical of Saxon or medieval crop-processing activity.

The concentrations of artefactual material at this location indicates there may have been a settlement nearby that was either seasonal or on higher ground. The site is approximately 500m to the south-east of the village of Wennington and originally lay within the ancient parish. The parishes probably formed out of early medieval Manors recorded in *Domesday Book*. The exact location of the Manors is uncertain but it is likely that historic centres of settlement grew up around them. Several early pre-Conquest charters mention land at Wennington given to Westminster Abbey, including a burh (fortified settlement/house) mentioned in a charter dated to *c* AD 1042–4 (*VCH Essex* vii, 182). At the time of the *Domesday* Survey the manor comprised 2½ hides and was in the possession of St Peter's, Westminster. The location of the village on the very edge of the marsh, close to a navigable creek inland, suggests that it may have originated as an early sea-borne settlement (*ibid*, 180). The size of the later parish of Wennington is far larger than the 2½ hides recorded in *Domesday Book*, suggesting that most of the marshland at that time of the *Domesday* recording was marsh and probably used to graze the sheep that are recorded for the manor (*ibid*, 185). During the medieval period it is probable that each of the Manors at Rainham, Wennington and Aveley owned a part of the coastal marsh, or at least had access to it for grazing or other seasonal activities (Oxford Archaeological Unit 2001).

The deposits at 26.535km and 26.540km are in the vicinity of the former Wennington Creek, which is thought to have run roughly north-east to the village of Wennington (Fig 52). Documentary sources suggest that this watercourse was navigable up until the late medieval period, after which it silted up (Oxford Archaeological Unit 2001, 11). The occupation soil may represent a phase of intentional land reclamation. By the end of the 12th century there are documentary references to 'inning' (ie, reclamation) of Wennington Marsh: in 1198 nineteen acres of 'New Land' is mentioned, in the early 13th century 'New marsh' and 'Old marsh' are distinguished and in 1563 the parish had 331 acres of 'inned' marsh (*VCH Essex* vii, 185). Reclamation took the form of the construction of channels around parcels of land. Marsh embankment at Wennington Creek, for which the earthworks are still extant to the south and east of the route corridor, began to be constructed in the 12th century. The purpose of reclamation of 'waste' (marginal land) would have been primarily economic, providing good-quality grazing for livestock and fertile land for crops. Investigations on Canvey Island *c* 20km to the east revealed remains of a series of medieval midden (rubbish) deposits and hearths dated from the 12th to 15th centuries which probably represent temporary settlement by shepherds (Wymer and Brown 1995 quoted in Green 1999, 18). It has been suggested, taking into account the position of Wennington Creek and cartographic sources, that the oldest (medieval) part of the reclaimed marsh occupied the north-eastern area shown on an estate map of 1619 (*VCH Essex* vii 185 in Oxford Archaeological Unit 2001), coinciding with the location of occupation deposits identified during the watching brief.

The occupation horizon at Wennington Marsh is overlain by additional minerogenic silt-clays, in some cases laminated with sand. If land reclamation was being carried out at this location it appears to have been initially unsuccessful and may have been temporarily abandoned. In the 13th century commissions were granted for the review and repair of the marsh defences in the region and serious flooding on Rainham marsh led to that community's taxpayers, together with those of neighbouring Wennington and Aveley, to petition for relief from a subsidy in 1452 on the grounds of their losses to the Thames (*VCH Essex* 7, 134–8 in Galloway and Potts 2007, 10).

Chapter 10
Aveley Marsh

with contributions by Catherine Barnett, Nigel Cameron, John Crowther, Matt Leivers, Richard Macphail, Wendy Smith, Lucy Verrill and John Whittaker

Aveley Marsh (Zones T16–17)

The HS1 route continues eastwards across Aveley Marsh where it skirts the edge of the gravel terrace and floodplain before crossing the Mar Dyke; a major tributary of the Thames (Fig 25). At the time of the investigations rough grass and scrub covered most of the route corridor. Ground levels averaged +0.30m OD, increasing to +1.30m OD eastwards.

Construction Impacts

The railway through this part of the route continued on a piled concrete slab and, aside from the piling, there was no direct impact on the underlying alluvium. The exception, however, was at the very eastern extent of Aveley Marsh where Tank Hill Road had to be diverted on a newly constructed bridge over the HS1 line. Prior to this a series of advanced service diversions were carried out on both sides of the railway. This comprised a total of 690m of open trenching to an average depth of 1.80–2.00m. Pipe-jacking was carried out via a series of deep caisson chambers and cofferdams to carry the services beneath existing railway lines and roads. A new Pressure Reduction Station (PRS) was also constructed immediately west of Tank Hill Road (Fig 54).

Key Archaeological Issues

The 1999 study designated Zones T16 and T17 (Chap 6 *Window 10*; Fig 25) of high and medium archaeological priority respectively. The sediment sequences here are complex and influenced strongly by the close proximity to the gravel terraces and the presence of the Mar Dyke tributary valley. The bedrock geology comprises Chalk overlain by Pleistocene gravel and head deposits. The Holocene sediments comprise peat and organic units intercalated with clay-silts, silts and sands.

The Pleistocene deposits in Zone T16 (28.0–28.2km) reached a maximum of c +1.0m OD, probably forming a promontory within the floodplain. This area probably remained dry throughout much of the prehistoric period and as such may have provided a focus for human activity. Within the Mar Dyke Valley the steeply dipping topography of the Late Pleistocene landscape would have resulted in gradual ecotonal zone shifts and dry ground zones around the wetland may similarly have been the focus of considerable activity.

Methodologies

Initial fieldwork comprised an archaeological watching brief on the advanced utility diversions (Fig 54). Small assemblages of worked flint were retrieved in the base of the pipe trench excavations at the edge of the topographic high in Zone T16 (28.135km) and either side of Tank Hill Road during the construction of the new PRS (c 28.380–28.425km). The flint was consistently located on the surface of a weathered sand horizon directly overlying Pleistocene deposits outcropping at higher elevations along the floodplain edge and sealed beneath shallow deposits of Holocene peat and alluvium. The watching brief was followed by a series of evaluation trenches located immediately west of Tank Hill Road in order to assess the impact of the piers for the new Tank Hill Road bridge. Following the

Table 53 Summary of fieldwork events, Aveley Marshes

Event name	Event code	Type	Zone	Interventions	Archaeological contractor
West Thames advanced utility diversions	ARC 36100	Watching brief	16–17		Oxford Archaeology
Tank Hill Road	ARC PFC01	Evaluation/ excavation	17	3963TT, 3964TT, 3983TT, 3984TT, 3985TT, 3986TT, 3987TT, 3988TT, 3993TP–3998TP	Wessex Archaeology
Tank Hill Road	ARC 310T02	Watching brief	17		Wessex Archaeology

TP = testpit   TT = trench

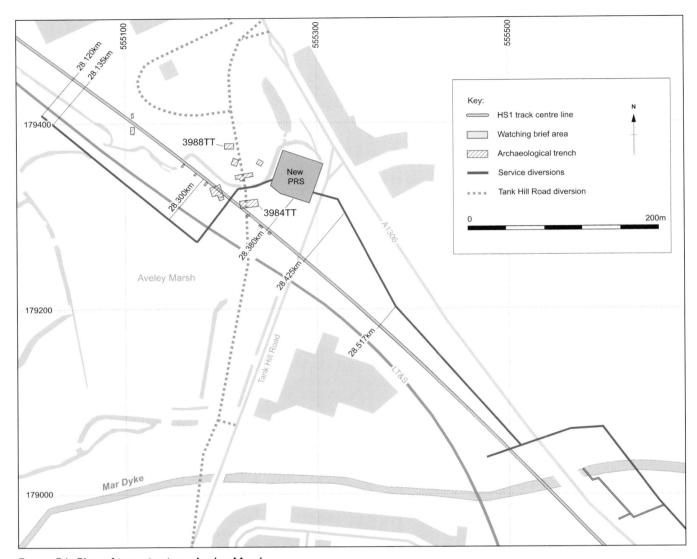

Figure 54 Plan of investigations, Aveley Marsh

identification of dense artefact scatters of mainly Late Mesolithic data, but flint of Late Upper Palaeolithic to the Early Bronze Age date was also recovered, the area was the subject of detailed excavation (Leivers *et al* 2007). A summary of the fieldwork events is included in Table 53.

Post-excavation work included the detailed analysis of a number of sample profiles in order to characterise the environments of deposition associated with the sediments and the artefactual evidence. Unfortunately it was only possible to sample the shallower sequences exposed during the watching brief. No detailed sampling was undertaken on the deeper floodplain sequences to the south of the HS1 corridor on Aveley Marsh and adjacent to the current Mar Dyke channel due to access and safety restrictions during the excavation of the caisson chambers. Interpretation of the sedimentary sequences recorded during the pipeline watching brief was carried out by Elizabeth Stafford. Palaeo-environmental work in the pipe trench at 28.517km was carried out by Lucy Verrill (pollen), Wendy Smith (waterlogged plant remains), John Whittaker (ostracods and foraminifera) and Nigel Cameron (diatoms). Five

radiocarbon dates were obtained from the sequence providing a broad chronological framework. The excavation sequence associated with the flint scatters at Tank Hill Road was interpreted by Catherine Barnett (sediments), Richard Macphail (micromorphology) and John Crowther (soil chemistry). The archaeological and environmental sequences from Aveley Marsh and Tank Hill Road have been published in detail elsewhere (Leivers *et al* 2007). The following sections provide a summary of the results.

Results of the Investigations

Watching brief on service diversions

During the advanced service diversions Pleistocene fluvial gravels were frequently exposed in the base of the excavations in the western part of the route section between 28.120km and 28.300km (south of the HS1 centre line), overlain by Holocene peat and silty clays. A topographic high was noted to the west where the surface of the gravels was noted at *c* -0.8m OD, overlain by sandy deposits to -0.15m OD (Fig 55). This

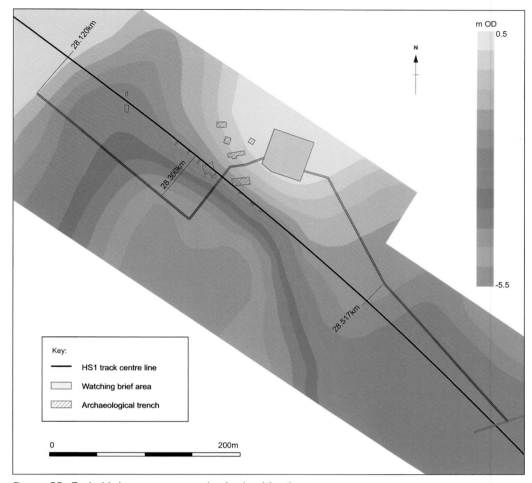

Figure 55 Early Holocene topography, Aveley Marsh

corresponds with the promontory identified during the 1999 study (Zone T16). The surface of the sands, where exposed, appeared to be 'weathered', producing occasional pieces of worked flint, and was interpreted as the remnant of a former dry landsurface probably dating from the Early to mid-Holocene. The surface dropped rapidly in elevation eastwards towards the Mar Dyke, with a corresponding thickening of the overlying peat and silty clay deposits. To the north of the HS1 centre line, either side of Tank Hill Road, the alluvial deposits thinned against the rise of the gravel terrace. Variable deposits, consisting of greenish grey clay and chalky gravel, were identified in the base of the excavations, overlying Chalk bedrock. These were interpreted as Pleistocene solifluction deposits, eroded from the higher ground. Overlying this, a discontinuous fine sandy deposit of varying thickness was noted, sealed by a thin layer of peat and silty clay alluvium. The sequence was capped by 0.30–1.0m of modern made ground at this location. The upper part of the sandy deposit, again, appeared weathered and produced a small assemblage of worked flint.

Chainage 28.517km

Palaeoenvironmental sampling was undertaken in the pipe trench located on the floodplain of the Mar Dyke at 28.517km. This was considered a useful 'off-site'

sequence for the activity located on the higher ground around Tank Hill Road where the sequences were comparatively shallow and vertically conflated. Unfortunately the depth of recoverable sediments at 28.517km was insufficient to sample from layers contemporary with the earliest occupation of the site (if they existed) and only covered the later phases of occupation at Tank Hill Road. This was due to access and safety restrictions.

Lower clay silt and peat

At the base of the exposed sequence lay a minerogenic alluvial deposit of slightly sandy clayey silt (context 379), probably deposited by moderate to low energy over-bank flooding from an adjacent channel (Fig 56). This deposit became more organic up profile grading rapidly into dark reddish-brown silt, approaching the interface with the overlying peat complex at -1.93m OD. A radiocarbon date of 2480–2290 cal BC (NZA-27528, 3909±30 BP) suggests accumulation of peat at this location commenced in the Late Neolithic–Early Bronze Age (Appendix A; Barnett 2007, 33). The basal part of the peat (context 378), between -1.93 and -1.65m OD, comprised a mottled dark brown to black well humified slightly silty peat with abundant twigs, larger wood fragments and bark.

The diatom flora from the basal alluvium and peat (Fig 57) was composed mainly of freshwater species associated with shallow-water habitats (eg, *Anomoeoneis sphaerophora, Amphora*

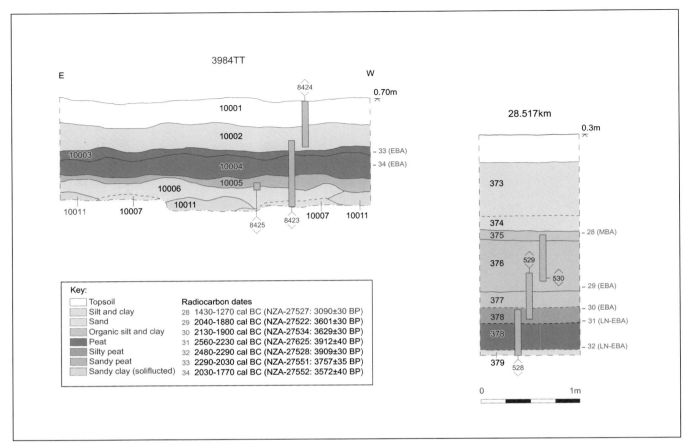

Figure 56 Sample profiles, Aveley Marsh

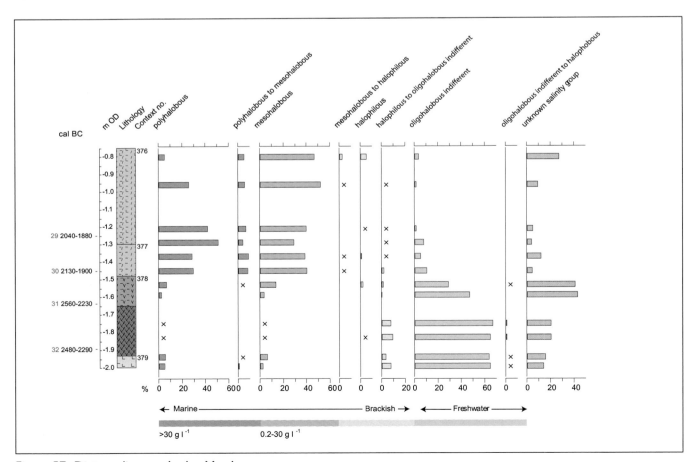

Figure 57 Diatom diagram, Aveley Marsh

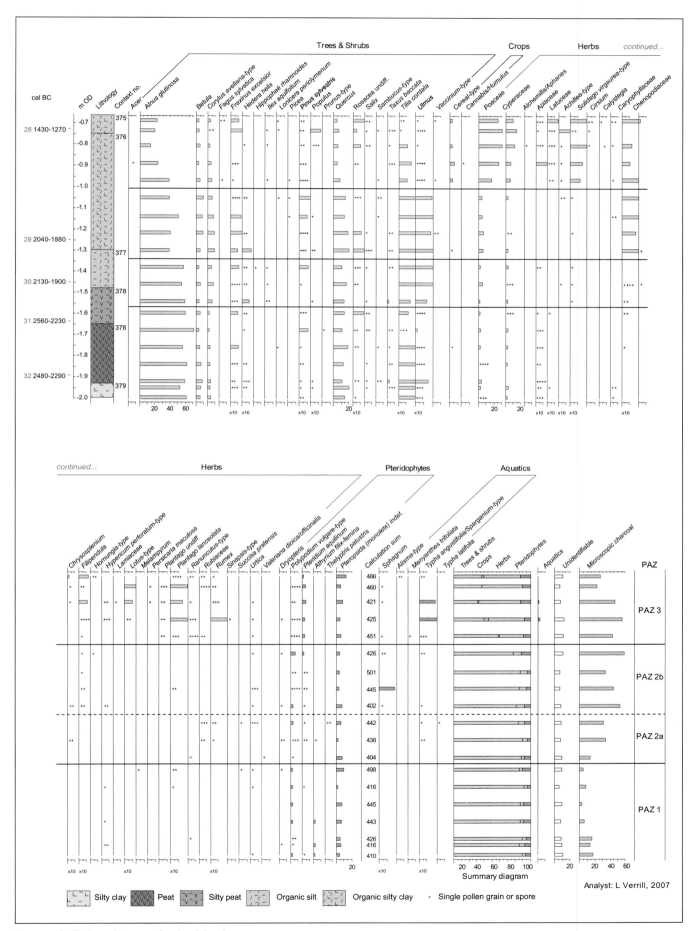

Figure 58 Pollen diagram, Aveley Marsh

libyca, *Gomphonema angustatum*, *Gyrosigma acuminatum*, *Sellaphora pupula* and *Pinnularia major/nobilis*; Cameron 2007, 35–6). The plant and pollen data indicates that the local landscape was dominated by floodplain alder carr, with the dryland component consisting of a mixed deciduous woodland. The peat contained frequent seeds and catkins of *Alnus glutinosa* (common alder) and occasional seeds of *Ranunculus* (buttercup), *Rubus* (bramble), *Solanum* sp. (nightshades) and cf *Scirpus sylvaticus* (wood club-rush) (*Table 54*). The pollen assemblages (Fig 58) are characterised by a high representation of *Alnus* followed by *Quercus* (oak) and *Betula* (birch), with lower values of *Corylus* (hazel) and *Tilia* (lime), *Ulmus* (elm) and *Betula* (birch). The non-arboreal component of the assemblage comprised low percentages (<5%) of Poaceae (grasses), Cyperaceae (sedges) and monolete spores (ferns). There was no evidence from the pollen of crop cultivation or vegetation clearance. A short-lived decline in *Tilia* was noted at -1.67m OD, followed immediately by a resurgence. If this is a true temporary decline (rather than a relative change to an increase in alder), it might be argued that an episode of coppicing or pollarding took place. Although microscopic charcoal values temporarily increase at the same point, which could indicate clearance by fire, only one other arboreal pollen type, *Quercus*, declines at the same time, and there is no corresponding increase in open-ground pollen taxa.

Organic silts and clays

Above -1.65m OD the peat became increasingly silty and less woody, grading into an organic silt at -1.48m OD (context 377) and an organic clay silt unit at -1.29m OD (context 376). Radiocarbon dating suggest these silty deposits began to accumulate from the Late Neolithic to Early Bronze Age at 2560–2230 cal BC (NZA-27625, 3912±40 BP). The increasing silt content suggests consistent low-energy flooding which may have been seasonal, transporting sediment from an adjacent channel. Diatoms suggest increasing marine influence during this period. Initially freshwater conditions continued, but in the organic silt (context 377) the percentage of freshwater diatoms began to decrease and marine taxa gradually increased (eg, *Paralia sulcata*, *Cymatosira belgica*, *Podosira stelligera*, *Rhaphoneis* spp., *Actinoptychus undulatus* and *Thalassiosira decipiens*). Brackish water species at the more saline end of the scale also increased (eg, *Cyclotella striata*, *Diploneis didyma*, *Nitzschia compressa*, *Nitzschia granulata* and *Nitschia navicularis*). Towards the top of context 376 preservation was poorer although the decline of some species suggested that, although salinity at the site remained high, the transport of allochthonous marine species to the sediments appears to have declined (Cameron 2007, 35–6).

The seed assemblage was similar to that described above but with the addition of *Taxus baccata* (yew), *Caltha palustris* (marsh-marigold), *Persicaria hydropiper* (water pepper), *Iris pseudacorus* (yellow iris) and *Mentha* sp. (mint), although seeds were absent from the upper part of context 376. The pollen spectrum initially sees a decline in *Alnus* from context 377 upwards which then levels out until the top of the sequence where it declines again. Although the proportion of open ground expanded only very slightly, the presence of Chenopodiaceae (goosefoots) may reflect the estuarine location rather than the alternative ruderal habitat usually

interpreted from this family (eg, Behre 1981). The pollen data for the upper part of context 376 showed much greater reductions in most arboreal pollen taxa and in expansion of grasses. Mixed agricultural activity may be suggested, with disturbed ground indicated by the presence of *Plantago lanceolata* (ribwort plantain), *Rumex* sp. (docks) and *Taraxacum*-type (dandelion). Poaceae and *Filipendula ulmaria* (meadowsweet) are likely to represent both the wetland environment and areas of open grassland. Cereal-type pollen is consistently present, however, as previously discussed (Chap 7, Trench 4042TT), the similarity of cereal pollen with some wild grasses such as *Glyceria* (sweet-grass) means that the evidence remains somewhat equivocal. Subsequent work on this sequence (Waller and Grant 2012) has indicated these cereal-type grains, found highest in PAZ-3, were derived from wetland grasses (notably *Glyceria*-type) and not cereals.

Between -0.75 and -0.65m OD a slow-down in accumulation is indicated by the deposition of a thin unit of brownish-black organic silty clay (context 375) suggesting lower energy deposition, perhaps as a result of slight channel shift away from this location. Radiocarbon dating suggests a Middle Bronze Age date of 1430–1270 cal BC (NZA-27527, 3090±30 BP).

Upper silty clays

Above -0.65m OD there was an abrupt change in lithology to inorganic structureless minerogenic silty clay probably representing a significant ingress of tidal waters during the Middle or later Bronze Age. Unfortunately no environmental data was retrieved from the upper alluvium due to sampling problems.

Excavations at Tank Hill Road

Detailed recording of the sediment sequence at Tank Hill Road (Barnett and Macphail 2007, 5–6) revealed a basal clean soft white fine–medium sand (Trench 3984TT, context group (gp) 10007) part of/derived from the underlying Pleistocene fluvial sands and gravels (Fig 56). At the top of the sand was a dirty slightly humic grey sand (context gp 10006) representing a weathered dry landsurface in which a series of dense flint scatters were recovered. This was overlain by 0.10m of highly humic sandy peat (context gp 10005). The pollen assemblage from the upper portion of the buried soil contained high numbers of degraded *Tilia* pollen, which as a robust pollen grain has become over represented in the poor preservational environment of the soil profile (Keatinge 1982; 1983). At this time, there is evidence of alder carr close by and *Quercus*, *Ulmus* and *Corylus* were present (Scaife 2007, 29–32).

Thin-section analysis (Pl 18) in 3984TT (Kubiena 8425) indicated that the weathered sand (context gp 10006) was composed of poorly humic, coarse silt to fine sands with common coarse stones including flint (Barnett and Macphail 2007, 5–6). Trace amounts of fine charcoal and the presence of likely burned stones are indicative of an anthropogenic input, consistent with the presence of artefacts. This soil horizon was highly

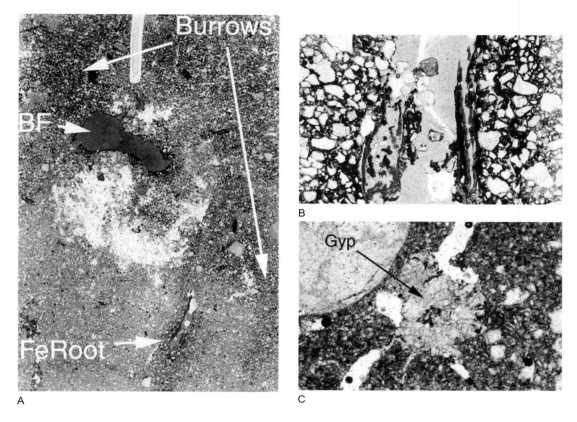

Plate 18 Microphotographs from hearth, 3985TT, Tank Hill Road. A) Kubiena 8535 thin section: The base of the hearth deposit that includes burnt flint (BF) is burrow-mixed into the subsoil sands (natural); note iron stained root traces (FeRoot). Frame width is ~50mm. B) Kubiena 8535: Iron-replaced root and associated void iron hypocoating in the 'natural' under the hearth. Plane polarised light (PPL), frame width is ~4.6 mm. C) Kubiena 8535: Detail of gypsum ($CaSO_4$); some dissolution is apparent around crystal margins. PPL, frame width is ~2.3mm

compact and the lack of void space is best explained by wetting and structural collapse caused by later inundation, peat formation and alluviation. Analysis of the overlying sandy peat indicated it was composed of once-laminated fine sands and wood peat. The peaty material included lignified remains of wood and amorphous peat burrowed by mesofauna which produced abundant organic excrements. A new shallow acid peaty gleyed soil profile was therefore superimposed over the previous stable sandy landsurface. The grey colouration of the weathered sand is, in part, attributable to humic colloids washed down and clear evidence for bioturbation exists. An eluviated soil (Ea) horizon was discerned in 3988TT on higher ground to the north-east of the site. Elsewhere, this layer was not fully developed, although a highly leached B horizon developed, with the acidic nature of the peaty layer and the open loose sands underlying it enabling groundwater leaching. The greater degree of development shown in 3988TT indicates it was dry and exposed to soil forming processes for longer than the rest of the site, which may explain the greater concentration of later prehistoric artefacts in that area. The sands across the site show evidence of being heavily rooted, the voids traceable to the overlying peaty soil and filled with gypsum crystals (in 3984TT) and humic material translocated from it, the voids also coated with iron oxides. As a consequence,

any artefactual and environmental remains in the upper sands and indeed new material deposited in/on the peaty soil surface were subject to vertical movement through rooting and worm sorting.

Following the formation of the sandy peat, the continued spread of wet marsh conditions led to the accumulation of up to 0.25m of terrestrial fen peat (context gp 10004), which buried the soil profile and effectively sealed it although rooting continued to have an effect. Radiocarbon dating suggests peat accumulation commenced during the Late Neolithic to Early Bronze Age, from as early as 2400–2140 cal BC (NZA-27553, 3809±30 BP from the higher part of the site in 3988TT; Barnett 2007, 29). A gradual transition with desiccated iron-stained peat at the top (context gp 10003) to the stiff sticky clay alluvium (context gp 10002) that forms the upper portion of the sedimentary sequence indicates gradual inundation of the terrestrial peat, with no truncation of its upper surface observed. The deposition of up to 0.35m of fine overbank alluvium occurred under high water level/flood conditions. The trigger for these events may in part have been internal such as a shift in channel position but also relates to a wider change in the Thames Estuary with estuary expansion (Long *et al* 2000), the increase in brackish/marine influence clearly demonstrated by the diatom assemblage reported for the off-site sequence at 28.517km.

Plate 19 Excavation of the flint scatters at Tank Hill Road

The Archaeological Evidence

Immediately west of Tank Hill Road, large spreads of Late Mesolithic struck flint were identified associated with the weathered sand horizon, along with concentrations of burnt flint probably marking the locations of hearths. A limited amount of Late Upper Palaeolithic flintwork, Early Neolithic struck flint and pottery and Late Neolithic–Early Bronze Age flintwork also occurred within the same sand layers, sealed by peats and alluvium.

As previously stated the findings from Tank Hill Road are reported in detail elsewhere (Leivers *et al* 2007). In summary, although the material was vertically conflated, the horizontal distributions were only blurred,

and technologically distinct elements could be identified. The main area of Mesolithic flint working concentrated around a very dense concentration of burnt flint in and overlying a shallow cut filled with burnt sand, the only feature identified other than later tree-throw hollows. Soil micromorphological analysis (Barnett and Macphail 2007, 6–7) revealed the hearth (3985TT, Kubiena 8535) cut a poorly humic well sorted sand (with coarse silt), the parent material/subsoil of group 10006 (Fig 56), and of probable river terrace origin (Hucklesbrook soil association; Jarvis *et al* 1984). The layer was marked by post-depositional rooting and secondary iron deposition, with iron impregnation of soil channel margins (hypocoatings) typical of a drowned soil (Bouma *et al* 1990; Macphail 1994) (Pl 18A–B). The base of the hearth fill comprised burrowed sands with fine charcoal-rich silt inwash (Pl 18C) and burnt flint, and was strongly leached. The main part of the fill consisted of fine sands with charcoal and relict burned small stones, was strongly burrowed, with some burrows infilled with silt and charcoal, implying biological working of this probable 'combustion zone', a common phenomenon affecting hearths (Goldberg and Macphail 2006a; 2006b, 167–8; Goldberg and Macphail 2012). A rare and enigmatic infill feature of dark iron-stained clay is unlikely to be related to general clay inwash that can develop during inundation, or result from inundation-induced soil slaking (eg, Macphail 1994; Macphail and Crowther 2004; Macphail and Cruise 2000) since only one example is present. This may be a relict trace of clay movement caused by the release of potassium in ash-rich deposits and commonly recorded in pits containing burned residues (Courty and Fedoroff 1982; Slager and

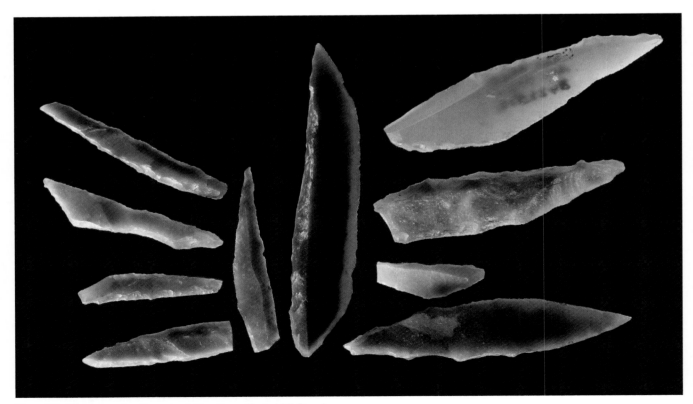

Plate 20 Photograph of worked flint from Tank Hill Road

Van der Wetering 1977). The hearth, as with the soil recorded in 3984TT, was sealed below a wood peat with post-depositional rooting and iron staining.

The retouched tools (Pls 19 and 20) were dominated by microliths, seemingly manufactured around the hearth. Other manufacturing areas were identified to the west (tranchet axe manufacture and maintenance); evidence for later leaf-shaped and barbed and tanged arrowhead manufacture was concentrated to the north.

The Late Mesolithic material probably represents repeated human utilisation of a gravel island or promontory overlooking the floodplain; an ideal location for the exploitation of a range of both wetland and dryland resources. There was, however, an absence of evidence for structural and faunal remains at the site which to a certain extent precludes detailed discussion of the nature of the activities carried out.

Summary

The environmental evidence indicates that during early occupation, Tank Hill Road was an open sandy island or promontory of the terrace edge. This became increasingly wooded with oak, elm and hazel (Leivers and Barnett 2007, 36–41). Wet marsh conditions progressively spread, with peat formation on the floodplain from the later Neolithic to Early Bronze Age.

Peat growth soon affected the floodplain edge occupation site, with the encroachment of fen communities and alder carr onto the sand island. The differing degrees of soil maturity across the site indicate this spread was diachronous, with higher drier areas persisting to the north-east of the site, enabling continued access or occupation.

The peat would have formed a succession of semi-stable terrestrial land surfaces, which, although waterlogged, would have allowed continued access to the nearby riverine resources at least seasonally, although the growth of dense alder carr would have impeded this access. The spread of stable, though waterlogged, terrestrial surfaces represented by the peat in the Early Bronze Age would have caused a change in the opportunities offered to local groups. On the one hand the ephemeral exploitation of the rich fen habitats for food is likely to have increased but the spread of peat over once dry sand islands would have forced occupation back from the floodplain margins onto higher ground.

Gradual inundation of the peat occurred, at first dominated by fresh water conditions, with repeated high water conditions leaving a deposit of fine overbank sedimentation. The pollen and diatom evidence suggest that influence of saline water increased from the Middle Bronze Age and into the Iron Age, reflecting wider changes in base level throughout the Thames Valley.

Chapter 11

The Thames River Crossing

with contributions by Hugo Anderson-Whymark, Alistair J Barclay, Richard Bates, Nigel Cameron, John Crowther, Jessica M Grimm, Richard Macphail, Lorraine Mepham, Sylvia Peglar, David Smith, Wendy Smith, Lucy Verrill and John Whittaker

The Thames River Crossing (Zones T18–27)

Construction Impacts

Construction impacts on the southern side of the river at Swanscombe (Figs 28 and 29) consisted of the excavation of a 450m long box (including a tunnel boring machine (TBM) launch chamber) (Pl 21) taking the railway through the Holocene floodplain deposits and underlying Pleistocene river gravel sediments into the underlying Chalk. Construction of the passage beneath the river was by bored tunnel through the Chalk. An excavated box was also constructed on the north side of the river at Thurrock to receive the TBM along with a new viaduct carrying HS1 over the A282 (Figs 27 and 28). The main archaeological investigation focused on the southern side of the river, where impact was likely to be considerable, in particular near to the floodplain edge where evidence of human activity was considered most likely. Full details of all investigations are listed in Table 55.

Key Archaeological Issues

Early in the project construction through the southern crossing area was considered likely to impact on a broad transect of Holocene sediments across a substantial portion of the floodplain (Chap 6, *Window 12*). The 1999 model designated Zones T25–T27 medium to high priority areas (Figs 28 and 29) The projected length of the construction impact offered the opportunity to investigate a broad slice of floodplain sediments (through a full sequence of Holocene deposits) from floodplain edge nearly 0.5km into the floodplain. Evidence from elsewhere in the region (Bates and Whittaker 2004) suggested that such sequences might contain archaeological remains, particularly towards the edge of the floodplain and in dry ground situations marginal to the wetland. Construction impacts in the northern crossing area at Thurrock were more limited with HS1 continuing westwards on a purpose built viaduct after exiting the Thames Tunnel. The northern portal in Zones T20–21 was considered in the 1999 model to be of medium to low priority (Chap 6, *Window 11*; Figs 27 and 28).

Strategy, Aims and Objectives

Following the route-wide desk-top assessment (Chap 6, *Windows 11* and *12*) a three stage investigation was undertaken within the study area. An initial programme of works (Stage 1) was developed in Swanscombe Marshes (Figs 59 and 60) in order to determine the nature and distribution of the main sediment bodies present and, in particular, to locate the precise position within the route corridor of any topographic highs, adjacent to the wetland, on which evidence for human activity may exist. These objectives were addressed using a combination of geophysics and intrusive borehole/cone penetration methods (Fig 60). Following this stage of works an area of high archaeological potential was identified at the south eastern end of the works area where a purposive archaeological excavation (Stage 2) was undertaken at the appropriate location on the line of the route. This was achieved through the excavation of a cofferdam (3880TT) to ascertain the nature of any human activity associated with the gravel high (Fig 60). A final phase of works (Stage 3) was a watching brief during construction on the full area of excavation for the route tunnel approaches.

Table 55 Summary of fieldwork events, Thames River Crossing

Event name	Event code	Type	Zone	Interventions	Archaeological contractor
Archaeological boreholes at Thames Crossing	ARC TMS00	Evaluation	20	Geophysical survey 2BH(CP), 7BH(MOS), 5BH(RES), 11BH(PIEZ)	Wessex Archaeology
Thames Crossing	ARC TMS01	Excavation	25	3880TT	Wessex Archaeology
Thames Crossing	ARC 32001	Watching brief	25		Wessex Archaeology

BH = borehole   (CP) = Cable percussion   (MOS) = Mostap   (RES) = Resistivity   (PIEZ) = Piezocone   TT = trench

Plate 21 View of construction of cut and cover tunnel boring machine launch chamber, Swanscombe

Methodologies

Initial desk-top investigation (Chap 6, *Window 12*) was undertaken using extant geotechnical data from boreholes, cone penetration tests and the published literature. The results of the desk-top investigation were a detailed cross-section illustration (Fig 28) that provided an impetus for the field investigations of Stage 1. The desk-top investigation identified that a wedge of Holocene alluvium thinned towards the valley margins

and buried a sequence of one or more bodies of Pleistocene sediment. These bodies of sand and gravel, coupled with the bedrock surface topography, defined the topographic template on which human activity occurred. However, insufficient data existed to adequately map this surface and predict foci of human activity. Because of sequence depths (5–10m of Holocene deposits) trial trenching in advance of construction activity, following standard archaeological practice, was both impractical and costly. Furthermore excavation during the construction window would be an expensive exercise that also ran the risk of causing major delays following unexpected discoveries. Consequently Stage 1 involved a mixed method approach in order to attempt to define precisely areas of high archaeological potential and/or interesting palaeoenvironmental sequences and, therefore, focus excavation attention (Stage 2) to limited areas of the construction footprint. Those areas identified as of high archaeological potential could then be examined either in advance, in targeted trenching exercises, or excavated during planned time slots within the overall construction timetable (Bates *et al* 2007).

Field investigation in Stage 1 (Fig 60) involved geophysical survey, purposive cone penetration tests (CPT) and boreholes. This work was undertaken by Martin and Richard Bates (see Bates *et al* 2007). The electromagnetic survey was conducted using the Geonics EM–31 and EM–34 terrain conductivity instruments across the full width of the route corridor and an Abem Lund electrical resistivity instrument along the line of the route. The initial geophysical survey was conducted in order to investigate the sub-surface electrical properties of the deposits and provide more localised targets for CPT and borehole sample recovery.

Following the non-invasive geophysical survey, targets for sub-surface investigation were noted and ground investigation techniques were employed to rapidly characterise sedimentary properties of the deposits (using CPT) and recover sediment samples (shell and auger boreholes and Mostap boreholes) (Fig 60). The principal considerations in selecting techniques involved the need to recover sample material for characterisation and dating as well as the need to cover large areas of the site to recover proxy information on sub-surface sediment types. The CPT survey was used to inform the location of Mostap

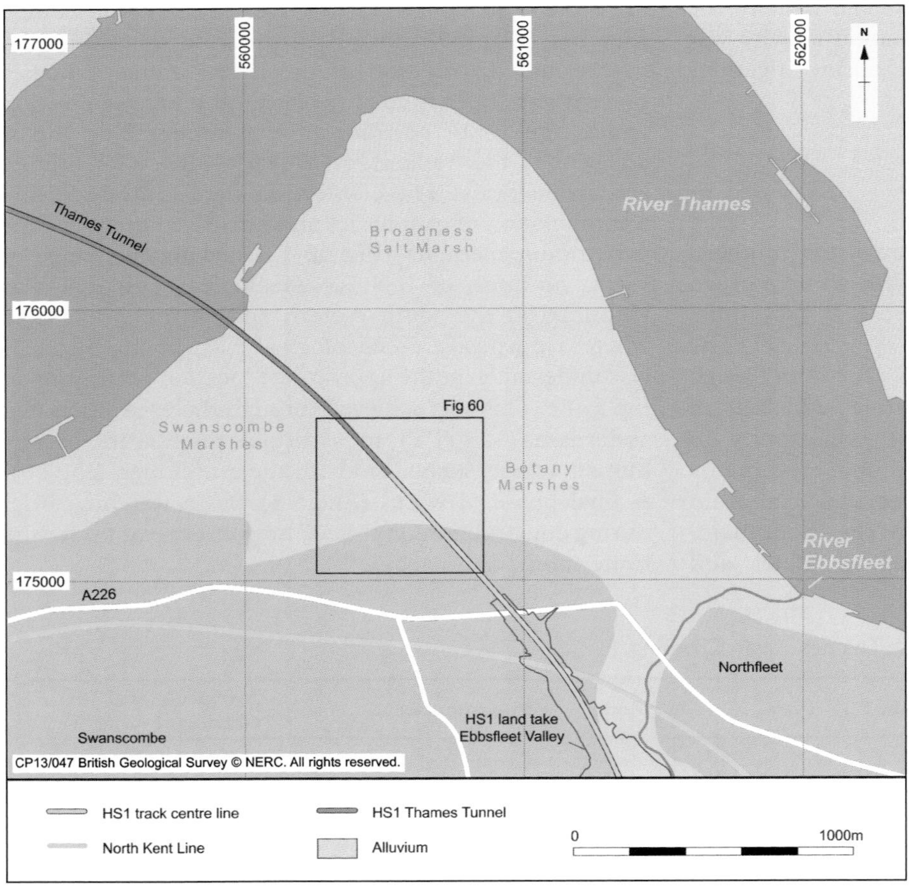

Map legend:
- HS1 track centre line
- North Kent Line
- HS1 Thames Tunnel
- Alluvium

0   1000m

Figure 59 Site location plan showing Thames River Crossing (south bank) for HS1, area of cut/tunnel and edge of alluvium

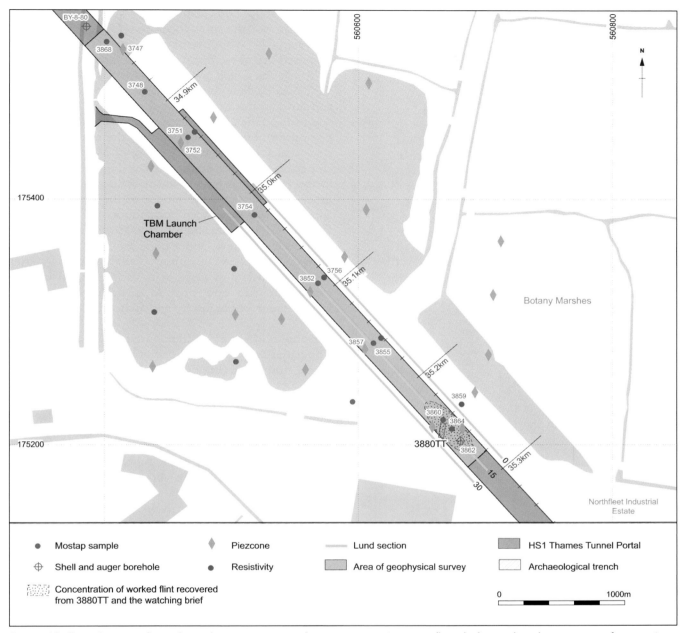

Figure 60 Distribution of geophysical survey areas and cone penetration tests/boreholes undertaken as part of purposive geoarchaeological investigations in Stage 1 Thames River Crossing (south bank) works

cores in order to obtain samples for palaeo-environmental analysis and absolute dating. The use of shell and auger boreholes at either end of the sample transect was governed by the need to penetrate the underlying gravels (which CPT/Mostap cores cannot) and record the level of the Chalk rockhead. Consequently a combination of sampling techniques was used to recover 1.5m continuous cores through the soft sediments (Mostap cores), 0.45m cores through the soft sediments and bulk samples from the underlying gravels (shell and auger cores). The intensity of survey points and transects and the number of sample locations was limited to an extent by cost implications and access constraints, but the final sampling resolution (in this case beyond the construction footprint in order to adequately understand the sub-surface stratigraphy;

Fig 60) was predicted to be adequate to enable a detailed reconstruction of the buried stratigraphy and to identify the sub-surface location of the key topographic locations for archaeological activity.

Confirmation of the nature of the stratigraphic sequences within the study area was subsequently possible through direct observation of the deposits during trench excavation (Stage 2) and the watching brief (Stage 3). For the Stage 2 response, a single, sheet piled, trench (3880TT) was sited and excavated by mechanical excavator through the alluvium (Pl 22). Finally a watching brief was undertaken on the full length of the excavated box.

Post-excavation work included the analysis of a number of sample profiles for palaeoenvironmental remains in order to characterise the environments of

Plate 22 Cofferdam excavation 3880TT, Swanscombe

Plate 23 Basal sands and gravels observed during watching brief excavations of the main TBM launch chamber, Swanscombe

deposition associated with the sediments and the artefactual evidence. Interpretation of the sedimentary sequences was carried out by Martin Bates and Elizabeth Stafford. The palaeoenvironmental work was carried out by Sylvia Peglar and Lucy Verrill (pollen), David Smith (insects), Wendy Smith (waterlogged plant remains), John Whittaker (ostracods and foraminifera), Nigel Cameron (diatoms), Richard Macphail and John Crowther (micromorphology and soil chemistry). A chronological framework for the analysis was provided by 15 radiocarbon dates (Appendix A).

Results of the Investigations

Geophysical survey, cone penetration tests and borehole ground-truthing

The results of both electromagnetic surveys (Figs 61 and 62) indicated lower conductivity at the south-east end of the section (shown as darker shades on the figures). This decrease in conductivity is consistent with the expected rise towards the surface of the Chalk bedrock surface as it rises steeply southwards beneath the site from approximately 20m depth to less than 4m depth. Furthermore, the pseudo-section (Figs 63 and 64) indicated two possible steps in the gravel profile and it is proposed that these might represent terraces.

Above the Chalk, a gravel layer was identified on the CPT data by cone refusal (base of logged data) (Figs 65 and 66) and this was correlated with a small increase in resistivity on the 2D geoelectric pseudo-section data (Figs 63 and 64). Direct observations of the sediment bodies were achieved through the drilling of Mostap and shell and auger boreholes across the site (Fig 66B). Examples of the typical logs are shown in Figures 67 and 68. In order to understand the nature of the sequences, and compare results between techniques, the information from the CPT testing and Mostap/shell and auger drilling have been combined and a number of key stratigraphic units identified within the study area (*Table 56*). Many of these units can be traced laterally across the site and provide a framework for the interpretation of site history and archaeological potential.

Borehole 'off-site' sequence history

The pattern of sediment distribution across the majority of the study area (Fig 66C) is clearly illustrated by the boreholes presented in Figures 67 and 68 in which a complex of intercalated peat and clay-silt units overlie coarser sands and gravels (Pl 7 and 8). The underlying sand/gravel (III/IV, *Table 56*) is clearly seen in the CPT data (Fig 66A) where cone refusal has taken place (Pl 23). In the majority of the boreholes two distinctive peat units are clearly seen above the basal sand/gravel unit (Fig 66B). This is also reflected in the CPT data that shows the peats through the presence of two peaks in the friction ratio below the high associated with the modern ground surface (Fig 66A). The main peat unit (VIII), occurring between depths of -3m and -6m OD towards the northern end of the box, rises in the southerly direction. In places this peat can be seen to be divided into two units by an intervening clay-silt unit (seen in the borehole samples, eg, BH3751, Fig 68). The lower peat or organic silt (-9m rising to -7m OD southwards before disappearing) is less marked. Both organic units are overlain by clay-silts.

Examination of palaeoenvironmental remains was primarily carried out from the deep sequence of sediments in borehole BH3751 (Fig 68). Diatoms, waterlogged plant remains and insects were present in a number of the samples initially assessed, however the abundance, quality of preservation and species diversity was low and the samples were not subject to detailed analysis. The results of the assessment of these remains do provide information on the environments of deposition and have therefore been presented along with the better preserved pollen, ostracod and foraminiferal evidence for completeness. Eleven radiocarbon dates were obtained from borehole BH3751 (Appendix A) providing a chronological framework. Additional detailed analysis of ostracods and foraminifera along with soil micromorphology was also carried out on the lower clay silts in borehole BH3748 (Fig 67).

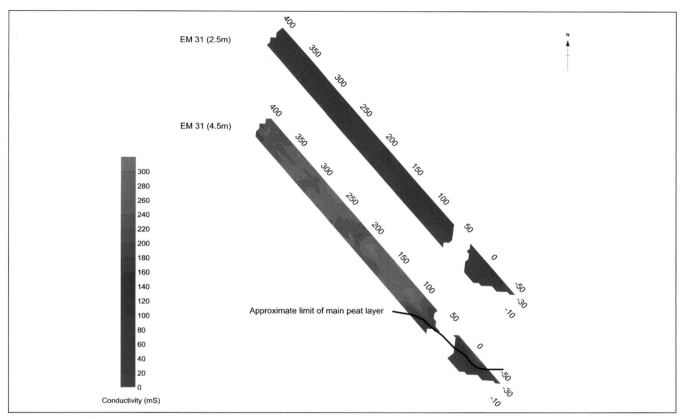

Figure 61 EM Conductivity maps from EM-31 orientated in line with route corridor in Swanscombe Marsh showing gradients in electrical conductivity at depths of 2.5m and 4.5m below ground surface. Red colours indicate high conductivity, blue colours low conductivity. At 2.5m depth sediments are typically of low conductivity indicative of likely over-consolidated near surface sediments. At 4.5m depth conductive sediments mapped across much of the route corridor with low conductivity mapped at the southern end. This southern zone probably marks the extent of bedrock or sand and gravel at depths in excess of 4m below ground surface

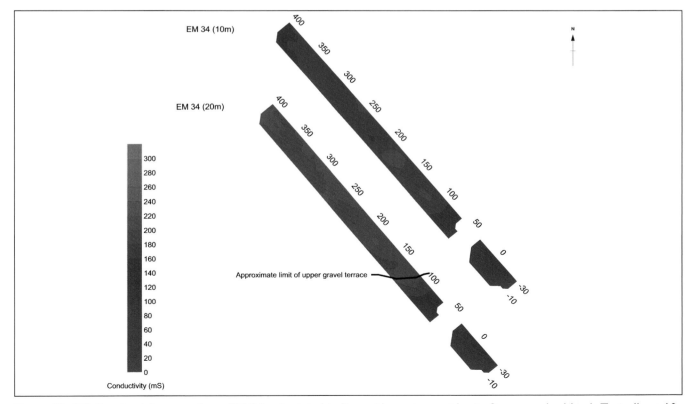

Figure 62 EM Conductivity maps from EM-34 orientated in line with route corridor in Swanscombe Marsh. Typically at 10 and 20m depths relatively low conductivity values are associated with bedrock presence

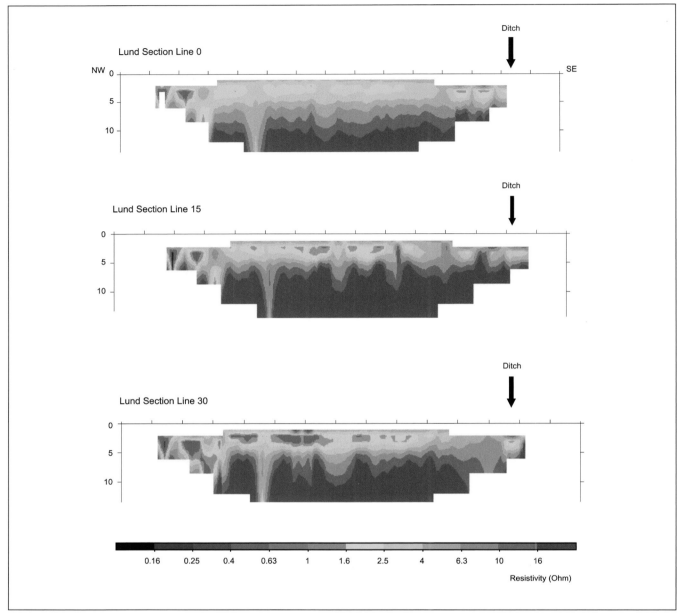

Figure 63 LUND electrical resistivity profiles along line of route corridor. Yellow/green colours represent low resistances (higher conductivities) associated with the Holocene alluvium. Red colours are areas of high resistance (low conductivity) associated with bedrock Chalk or gravel

Basal gravels

The Holocene sediments are underlain by sands and gravels below -8m OD throughout much of the northern area of investigation (as evidenced in the shell and auger boreholes at the northern end of the box). This sand and gravel was not investigated in detail but is likely to correlate with the Shepperton Member of the Lower Thames and was probably deposited after 15ka BP (Gibbard 1994). The sediments to the south, within the area of the archaeological excavation, will be considered later (see below).

Lower peat and organic silts

The onset of sedimentation above the gravels is characterised by the accumulation of organic material. Examination of the remains from borehole BH3751 (Fig 68) indicate that this sediment and the minerogenic material immediately above it

contained occasional diatoms (*Table 57*) and plant remains (*Table 58*). Initial assessment of the organic silt at the base of the sequence produced a pollen spectra which is almost entirely composed of *Pteridium* (bracken) spores. The overlying peat contained some *Alnus glutinosa* (common alder) pollen, with lesser amounts of indeterminate ferns but in general the counts were low and this part of the sequence was not analysed in detail. The plant assemblages, however, showed an abundance of *A. glutinosa*, some *Scripus sylvaticus* (wood club-rush) and Cyperaceae (sedge). In the same interval diatoms are either absent or rare. Only two fresh water, non-planktonic, diatom species (*Meridion circulare* and *Gomphonema olivaceum*) were recorded, the latter with optimal growth in fresh water of slightly elevated conductivity and the former associated with flowing, fresh waters. Radiocarbon dating (Fig 68 and Appendix A) indicates that the basal organic silt began

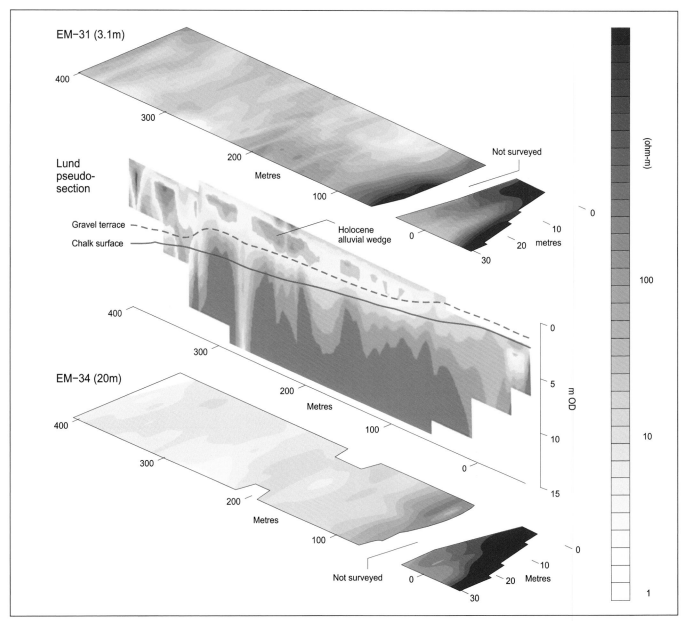

Figure 64 Combined EM Conductivity maps and LUND electrical resistivity survey in route corridor. Top EM-31 surface geophysics, middle LUND pseudosection, base EM-34 surface geophysics (Bates *et al* 2007). Data used to interpret the geometry of the Holocene alluvial wedge, gravel and bedrock surfaces

accumulating around 6610–6430 cal BC (NZA-27599, 7669±50 BP) with the onset of peat accumulation around 5900–5730 cal BC (KIA-14479, 6935±35 BP). A date for the top of the peat of 5470–5220 cal BC (NZA-27603, 6357±35 BP) provides a maximum age for the start of minerogenic sedimentation.

Lower clay silts

Minerogenic clay-silts dominated between -8.43m and -5.05m OD in BH3751 (Fig 68). Low numbers of brackish water, benthic diatoms (eg, *Campylodiscus echeneis*, *Nitschia navicularis*) and marine plankton (*Paralia sulcata*) occur at -8.43m OD. Although the number of diatoms present is low, these species indicate that the sediments formed under estuarine conditions. The first brackish foraminifera occur at -7.93m to -7.98m OD (Table 59). Thereafter, the interval up

to and including -6.03m to -6.08m OD contains a mixture of saltmarsh agglutinating foraminifera and tidal mudflat-living calcareous foraminifera (mainly small *Ammonia* spp.) which occur in very large numbers. Murray (2006, 66–67) points out that the typical high- to mid-marsh species are *Jadammina macrescens* and *Trochammina inflata* and these occur as dominant or subsidiary taxa. Other species confined to marshes include *Haplophragmoides wilberti* and *Tiphotrocha comprimata*, and to these indigenous species we can add *Arenoparrella mexicana*, which are quite rare in the European context. Species found on the seaward side of marshes and on adjacent intertidal and shallow subtidal areas include the calcareous *Ammonia* group, which are particularly common in sediments with >80% mud/silt (*ibid*, 67).

These sediments also contain numbers of discernable diatoms (>75 microns), which is of interest as foraminifera not

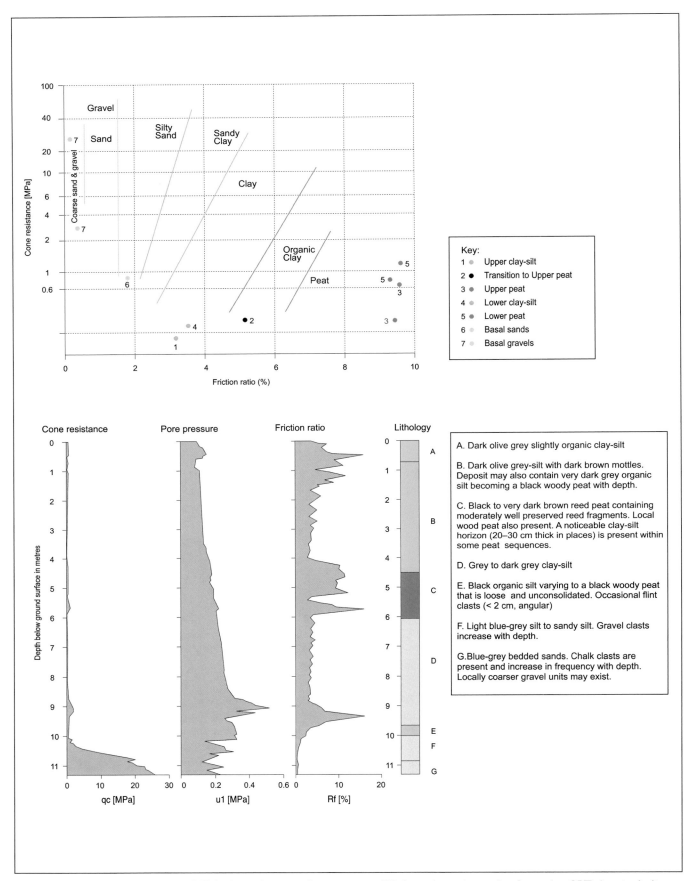

Figure 65 Top: Cone resistance (MPa) plotted against friction ratio (%) for selected samples from the CPT data including recognised zonations of differing sediment types. Base: Cone resistance, pore pressure and friction ratio plotted against lithology from representative profile at Thames River Crossing (Bates *et al* 2007)

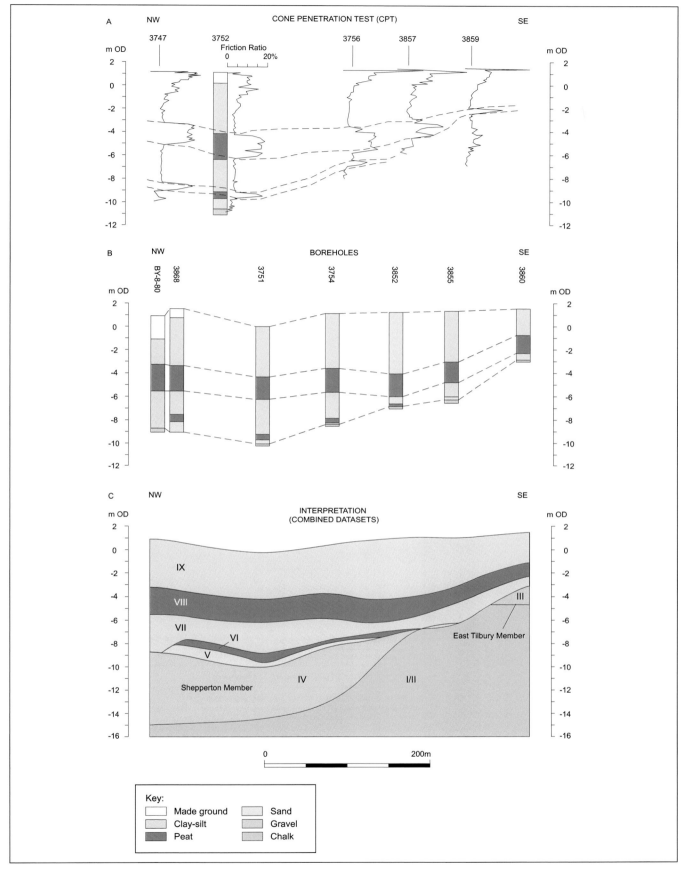

Figure 66 A) Cone penetration test (CPT) results from selected test locations B) Lithology of selected boreholes
C) Interpreted lithostratigraphic section based on CPT and borehole information (Bates *et al* 2007)

Thames Holocene

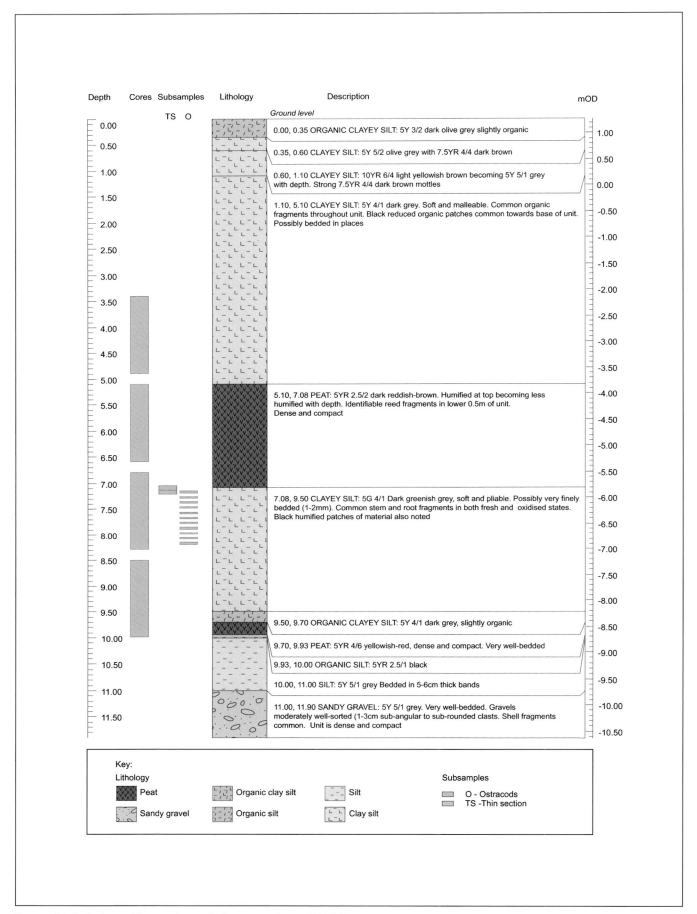

Figure 67 Lithological log and sample locations from BH3748

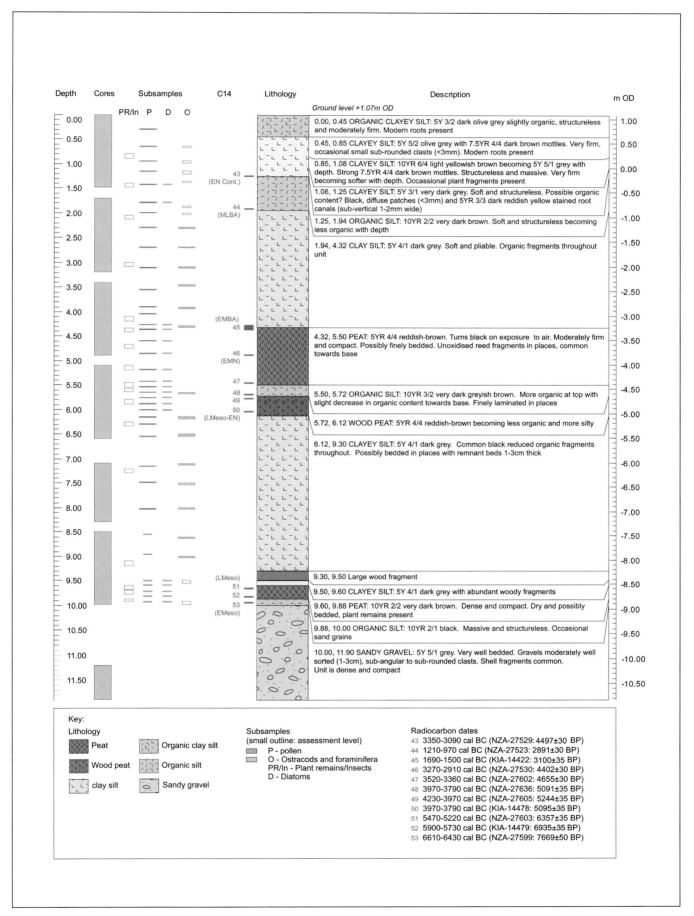

Figure 68 Lithological log and sample locations from BH3751

Thames Holocene

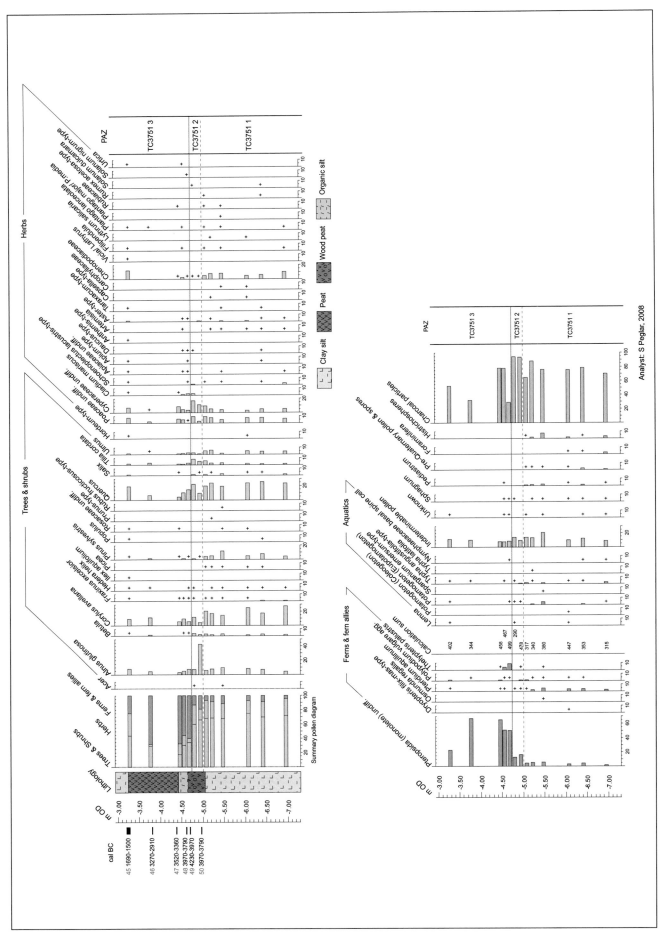

Figure 69   Pollen diagram from BH3751

only harbour symbiotic diatoms within their shells, but also ingest them for food. The two together in large numbers indicates, therefore, a healthy *in situ* mudflat fauna. Brackish creek and mudflat ostracods are much rarer but occur between -6.98m and -6.03m OD. Both foraminifera and ostracods are totally absent in the interval -5.48m to -5.08m OD immediately below the main peat unit.

Evidence from the pollen profile (PAZ TC3751 1, Fig 69) suggests the pollen assemblages are dominated by about 70% tree and shrub pollen (AP), mainly of *Quercus* (oak), *Ulmus* (elm), *Tilia* (lime) and *Corylus* (hazel), but also with some *Pinus* (pine). Some Poaceae (grasses) and Cyperaceae (sedges) pollen is present, but other herbaceous and fern taxa are quite rare apart from Chenopodiaceae (goosefoots) which is characteristic ofsaltmarshes. Aquatic taxa and the remains of the green alga *Pediastrum*, which grow in freshwater, are also present. The remains of hystrichospheres, restricted to brackish/salt water, were also found, but could possibly be reworked from earlier sediments. The assemblages therefore suggest that both fresh and brackish water sediments are represented within the zone, being of estuarine origin, with saltmarsh and reedswamp vegetation growing close by on the floodplain. On higher, drier ground regionally, mixed deciduous woodland with *Quercus, Ulmus, Tilia* and *Corylus* was growing. There is no evidence for any human impact locally during this zone although charcoal particle values are quite high, but these may originate from some distance.

A close sampling interval for ostracods and foraminifera was undertaken on sediments immediately below the main peat in BH3748 (Fig 67; *Table 60*). Here, 11 samples (10cm thick at 5cm interval) were examined between -6.93m and -5.88m OD. Below -6.43m OD the sediments were deposited in saltmarsh and tidal mudflats with full tidal access. Between -6.43m and -6.18m OD mid–high saltmarsh, a period of accretion and undoubtedly the onset of the sea-level regression was recorded. The three samples immediately below the peat at -5.88m to -6.13m OD were entirely devoid of foraminifera.

Thin section analysis of the upper part of the minerogenic silts at -5.93m to -5.83m OD (Fig 67; Appendix B) show that the sediments are composed of laminated (1–2mm thick) humic clays, with sparse coarse silt, and are characterised by very abundant and generally horizontally oriented detrital plant fragments; their character suggests a mudflat situation (Pl 24 A–C). There are also very abundant coarse roots producing sediment disruption and working. The sediment features minor iron staining, probable carbonate concentrations, and occasional fine gypsum crystal formation throughout. By contrast the basal parts of the main peat unit at -5.79m to -5.77m OD consist of horizontally layered monocotyledonous plant fragments in a humic clayey matrix with very sparse silt (Pls 24D–E). The sediment shows iron staining, probable carbonate concentrations, and occasional fine gypsum crystal formation throughout. Laminated *in situ* formed peat becomes dominant upwards (Pls 24D–E). The boundary between this peat and the underlying minerogenic sediments is subtle but sharp and differs by featuring greater amounts of horizontally layered plant fragments and less mineral material (Pls 24A–C). There is no evidence of sediment ripening/soil formation in the underlying minerogenic sediments (Pls 24A–C) although the presence of the sharp boundary between the two units does suggest a degree of disconformity between them and the presence perhaps of a short lived hiatus in sequence accumulation.

The main peat bed

The nature of the main peat varies across the site. The principal feature of the peat is the intermittent presence of a two-fold sub-division into a thin lower peat (below -4.63m OD in borehole 3751) and a thicker upper peat (starting at -4.43m OD), with an intervening silt horizon. The lower part of the peat did not appear to contain diatoms except for a fragment cf *Cyclotella striata* (an estuarine planktonic species) at -4.81m OD and a number of chrysophyte stomatotcysts from the sample at -4.95m OD. The majority of chrysophytes are associated with fresh water; although there are also brackish water taxa. The chrysophyte taxa here are all of indeterminate type. As in the examples found here, chrysophyte stomatocysts are usually heavily silicified and it is common to find them in sediments subject to drying out where they are less susceptible to complete dissolution than less robust silica algae remains.

A major change in pollen spectra is noted at the transition from the clayey silts to wood peat (PAZ TC3751 1/2 boundary). *Ulmus* values drop sharply at the base of the peat, possibly signifying the 'elm decline', a synchronous event generally dated to about 5500–5000 BP throughout northwest Europe. Sediment from 0.06m above the PAZ TC3751 1/2 boundary gave a radiocarbon determination of 3970–3790 cal BC (KIA-14478, 5095±35 BP). The pollen assemblages are dominated by *Alnus* and *Quercus* pollen, together with fern spores (Pteropsida (monolete) undiff.). High values of *Alnus*, with Cyperaceae (including *Schoenoplectrus lacustris*-type (bristle club-rush)) and *Cladium mariscus* (great fen sedge) support an interpretation of alder woodland on the floodplain. *Tilia* pollen has its highest values during this PAZ and suggests that *Tilia* dominated mixed woodland was growing on drier higher land in the area. There is no evidence of any marine influence during this PAZ and Chenopodiaceae pollen values, often characteristic of saltmarshes, are almost absent. Age estimates for the accumulation of the lower part of the peat between 3970–3790 cal BC (KIA-14478, 5095±35 BP) and 4230–3970 cal BC (NZA-27605, 5245±33 BP) have been obtained from this sequence. A change in pollen spectra occurs at -4.75m OD. Fern spores completely dominate the assemblages, suppressing all other pollen taxa. The ferns include the marsh fern *Thelypteris palustris* and suggest that the local vegetation was fern-rich fen/marsh at this time. *Tilia* values decrease at the PAZ TC3751 2/3 boundary. This may be the so-called 'lime decline' which is thought to be human induced, but it could also be that the land on which the *Tilia* was growing was inundated by water which *Tilia* could not tolerate.

The clay-silt horizon separating the lower from the upper parts of this peat unit suggests that a phase of channelling, flooding or temporary submergence may have occurred. At -4.57m and -4.47m OD within this horizon a few poorly preserved diatoms indicative of estuarine conditions, including benthic brackish water taxa such as *Nitzschia navicularis, Diploneis didyma, Campylodiscus echeneis* and *Nitzschia granulate* have been recorded. The planktonic marine diatom *Podosira*

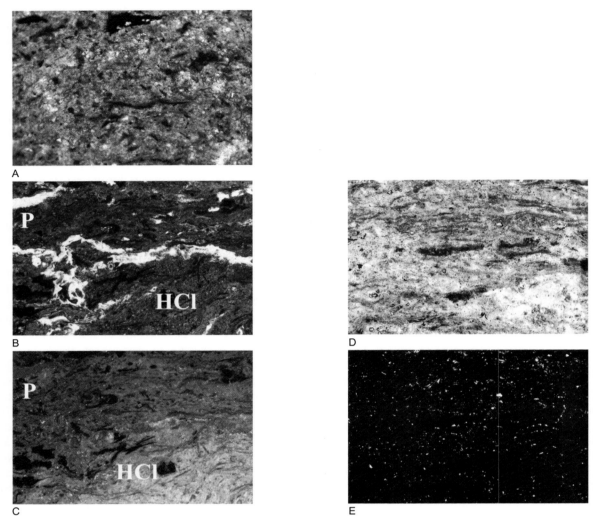

Plate 24 Photomicrographs from Borehole 3748, Swanscombe. A) Borehole BH3748(B): Detail of humic clays, with sub-horizontally oriented humifying (brown staining) detrital organic matter (size-range and staining also infers moderately local origin). Plane polarised light (PPL), frame width is ~0.92mm. B) Borehole BH3748(A): Junction between humic clay (HCl) and overlying peat. PPL, frame width is ~4.6mm. C) As B: Under oblique incident light (OIL), showing more humic clay (HCl) with sub-horizontally oriented detrital organic matter, and overlying peat (P), which is richer in organic fragments and less clay-rich; note absence of any biological working or ripening features between the two sediments. D) Borehole BH 3748(A): Detail of laminated peat. PPL, frame width is ~0.92mm. E) As D: Under cross polarised light (XPL); note sparse and 'laminated' silt content

stelligera is present at -4.47m OD. Agglutinating foraminifera of mid- to high saltmarsh situations have also been recorded within this clay-silt horizon.

The upper part of the peat at -4.35m OD contained only the fresh water diatom species *Meridion circulare* associated with flowing water. Diatoms were absent from the samples taken at -4.11m and -3.78m OD. A single fragment tentatively identified as the marine planktonic diatom *Thalassionema nitzschiodes* was found in the sample at -3.53m OD towards the top of the upper peat. However, this diatom has a robust, heavily silicified valve and its presence may reflect preferential preservation. At the top of the upper peat at -3.29m OD, near the transition into the overlying clay-silt, marine (*Rhaphoneis surirella, Rhaphoneis* spp.) and estuarine (*Cyclotella striata*) plankton diatoms and a single valve of the freshwater diatom *Achnanthes minutissima* occurred. Samples from -4.13m to -4.03m OD and -4.58m and -4.5m OD both produced single

individuals of the 'reed beetle' *Plateumaris braccata* (*Table 61*) which is usually associated with *Phragmites australis* (common reed) (Koch 1992). The sample from -4.13m to -4.03m OD also contained several individuals of the small 'water beetle' *Chaetarthria seminulum* which often is held to be typical of stagnant and still waters (Hansen 1986). This information therefore confirms the presence of fresh water peats becoming influenced by encroaching brackish conditions up-profile. The sediments change from wood peat at the base to an organic silt with reed fragments suggesting that the water level had risen.

Few subsamples within the upper part of the peat, PAZ TC37513, had a sufficiently high concentration of pollen and spores for full analysis. The two sub-samples that were countable were dominated by fern spores. There is an increase in Chenopodiaceae pollen at the top of the PAZ perhaps marking an increase in marine influence with the growth of saltmarsh, but fresh water aquatic pollen taxa are also present. Regionally

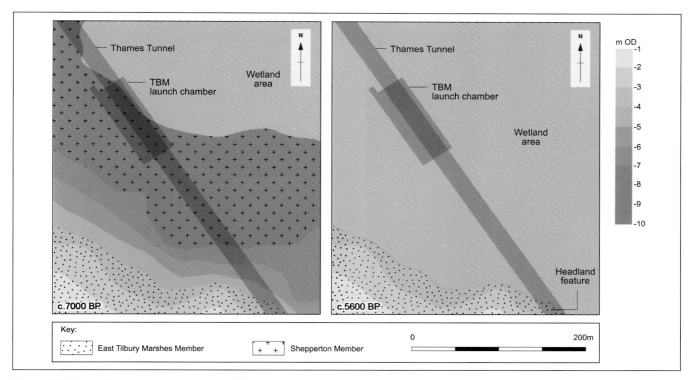

Figure 70 Early Holocene topography of the route corridor beneath Swanscombe Marsh based on borehole, CPT and geophysical survey data showing position of the headland feature (Bates *et al* 2007)

some mixed deciduous woodland with *Quercus* and *Corylus* continued. Age estimates date the start of peat formation above the clay-silt horizon to 3520–3360 cal BC (NZA-27602, 4665±30 BP), while the top of the peat is dated to 1690–1500 cal BC (KIA-14422, 3310±35 BP).

The upper clay silts

The minerogenic sediments above the main peat at -3.27m to -1.21m OD contain ostracods and foraminifera indicative of mid–low saltmarsh, tidal flats and creeks (*Table 59*). Within this sequence diatoms are well preserved and the assemblages are relatively diverse with a moderately high number of valves. The assemblage represents estuarine conditions with a component of mesohalobous benthic diatoms (eg, *Nitzschia Granulata* and *N. navicularis*) along with brackish and marine plankton (eg, *Cyclotella striata* and *Paralia sulcata*).

Above -1.21m OD, the lithology changes and ostracods and foraminifera were absent. This appears to be a real disappearance rather than a problem due to decalcification of the sediment as agglutinating foraminifera of mid–high saltmarsh, such as *Jadammina macrescens*, have a shell of mineral grains stuck together with an organic cement on an organic template. Even in the most reducing environments they occur, often in a collapsed state, but they can still be found, albeit with difficulty within the organic debris. In spite of a careful search they do not occur above -1.21m OD and this interval might be taken to indicate a shift to a fresh water environment. The two uppermost diatom samples examined, lying between -0.72m and -0.35m OD are taken from an organic silt. The diatom assemblages are well preserved and contain a mixed assemblage ranging from freshwater to marine species. However, the marine component is of planktonic species eg, *Paraliasulcata* and *Rhaphoneis* spp. and is

allochthonous, whilst the brackish (and smaller freshwater) part of the assemblage is of probable autochthonous diatoms. Notable amongst the mesohalobous diatoms here are the high numbers of *Diploneis interrupta*, a brackish water aerophile that when it occurs in large numbers is often, although not exclusively, associated with the supra-tidal zone, for example pool habitats in saltmarshes (Vos and de Wolf 1993). The occurrence of substantial numbers of oligohalobous indifferent diatoms such as *Navicula rhyncocephala* is also consistent with an upper shore habitat. However, the diatom preservation here is good and this is unusual for saltmarsh depositional environments.

Headland sequence history

Of particular significance from the archaeological perspective was the identification at the southern end of the route corridor of a topographic high or headland feature. This headland was identified by rises in the gravel surface and sufficient data was available for an attempt to be made to model the shape of this feature (Fig 70). This promontory was considered a likely location for human activity predating the period of submergence of the landscape beneath the ever encroaching alluvial envelope. On the basis of previous work in the Thames (Bates and Whittaker 2004) the higher parts of this headland will have been flooded during the late Mesolithic *c* 4500–4300 cal BC (ie, [14]C 5600 BP). Changes to the modelled topography consequent with flooding are postulated in Figure 71. To investigate this situation a purposive cofferdam (3880TT) was sited and excavated in advance of construction (Pl 22). This was followed by a watching brief during construction.

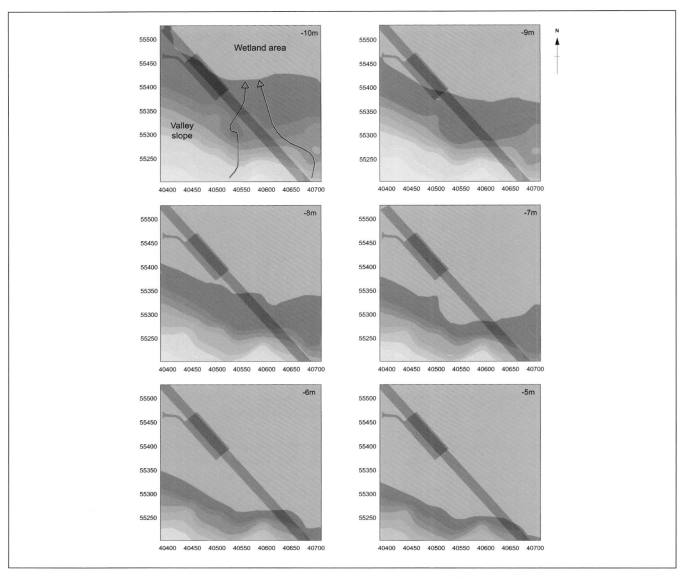

Figure 71 Topographic reconstruction of the site showing successive 'drowning' of landscape during rising water levels at successive 1m intervals (-10m to -5m OD)

Table 62 Excavated stratigraphy, 3880TT

Context	Description	Finds / Interpretation	General WB context
388001	Mid-orangey brown clayey silt. Contained frequent root holes	Alluvium	1
388002	Mid-grey clayey silt. Contained occasional root holes	Alluvium. Occasional struck flint, one sherd Late Bronze Age pottery	1
388003	Mid-grey clayey silt	Alluvium. Occasional struck flint	1
388004	Dark greyish brown peat	Occasional worked flint. Much increased in density in lowest 100mm. Animal bone	2 (upper) 10 and 11 (lower)
388006	Mid-greenish grey (clayey) sandy silt containing occasional roots and branches. (Surface slopes down steeply to the NE, possible channel truncation)	Remnant alluvial deposit. Frequent worked and burnt flint on the surface and in the top 100mm but little below. One sherd pottery and one frag possible ground stone tool	3
388005	Mid-grey and white speckled mix of silty clay and chalk. Contains occasional broken flint becomes paler and chalkier with depth	Degraded upper part of chalk bedrock	–

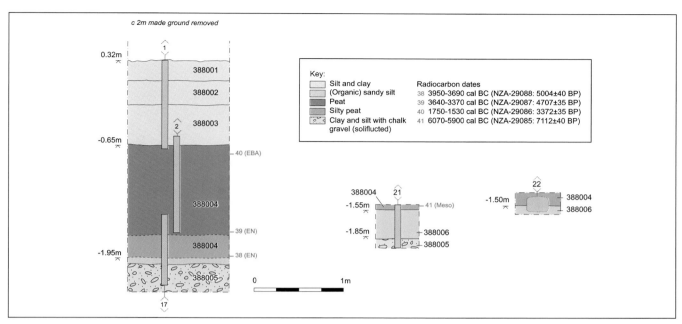

Figure 72 Sections through excavated sequences in 3880TT

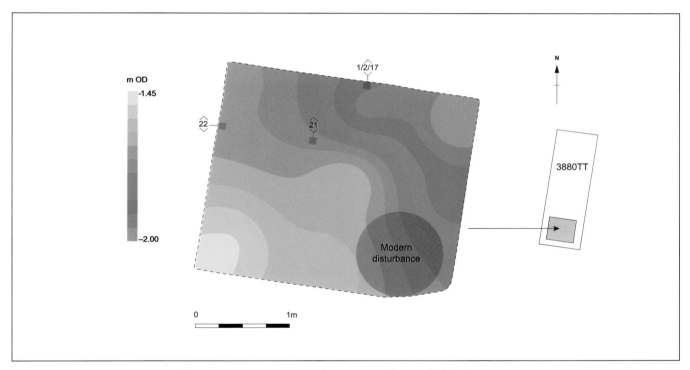

Figure 73 Modelled surfaced of context 6 and location of sample profiles in 3380TT

Borehole data (*Table 56*) indicated that the main peat (VIII) thinned out and rested on the gravel high (Fig 66) potentially sealing any artefacts. This provided a target depth for excavation. Once the cofferdam was completed it was decided that mechanical excavation would remove the bulk of the minerogenic and organic sediment but it should cease some 20cm above the base of the peat. Hand excavation followed to expose the peat base and the contact with the underlying clastic sediments. The excavated stratigraphy (Table 62) produced a significant number of artefacts associated with a disturbed landsurface beneath the peat confirming the predictions

made on the basis of the various phases of ground investigation (the lowermost peat (VI) and overlying clay-silt (VII) is missing in this part of the site). As a result of this strategy being adopted minimal risk to development was taken and the works were scheduled into a complex construction programme from an early stage. An additional check on the broad patterns of sediment accumulation was possible through careful monitoring of the deposits excavated during the construction of the cut and cover works associated with the railway (Pl 21). These observations confirmed the patterns identified from the borehole/CPT and geophysical surveys.

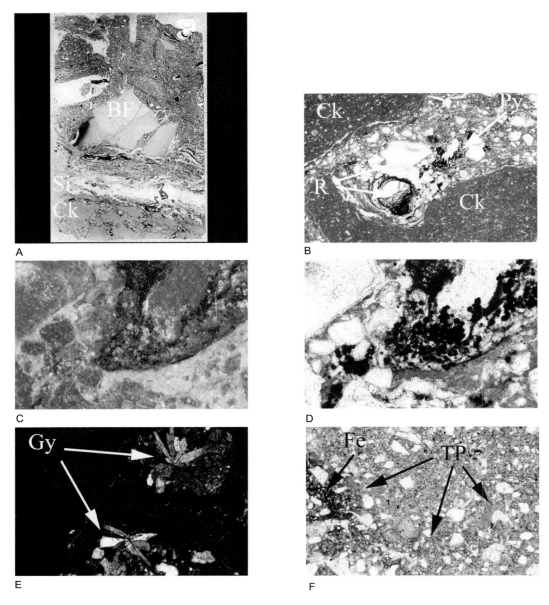

Plate 25 Photomicrographs from 3880TT, Swanscombe. A) Monolith 17(B) thin section, contexts 388005 and 388006: Late Glacial chalky (Ck) and silty clay (Si) beds, below a palaeosol containing coarse burned flint (BF). Frame width is ~50mm B) Monolith 17(B), context 388005: Late Glacial chalk clast (Ck) slurry (soliflual) deposit, with post-depositional rooting (R) and associated pyrite formation (Py; see C and D). Plane polarised light (PPL), frame width is ~4.6mm. C) As B: Detail of pyrite framboids associated with the decay of organic matter under waterlogged conditions. PPL, frame width is ~0.92mm. D) As C: Under oblique incident light (OIL); note typical 'brassy' colour of pyrite. E) Monolith 21(C), context 388005: secondary calcium sulphate (gypsum, Gy). Cross polarised light (XPL), frame width is ~2.3mm. F) Monolith 21(C), context 388005: Textural pedofeatures (TP), intercalations and void coatings and infills associated with structural collapse; later rooting associated with secondary ferruginous hypocoatings (Fe). PPL, frame width is ~4.6mm

Stratigraphy and palaeoenvironment from 3880TT
A rectangular cofferdam, 12m by 4m in plan (3880TT, Fig 60), was constructed and the uppermost 2m of material inside the cofferdam was removed without archaeological supervision. This included more than a metre of hardcore makeup that had been deposited across the whole site area to form a suitable working surface for heavy plant. From a depth of 2m the deposits were then mechanically excavated under constant archaeological supervision. Running sections through the sediment sequence were maintained and sampling

was undertaken of each 1m profile before removal. A sequence of clay-silts and peat was removed in this way.

Hand excavation commenced when the base of the peat was shown to lie not far beneath the existing level of excavation. Worked flint was recovered from the lowest 100mm of the peat, from the surface and through the top 100mm of the underlying sandy silt. The sedimentary sequence within the excavated area consisted of seven main units (Table 62). The sampled sequences and locations within the cofferdam are illustrated in Figures 72 and 73.

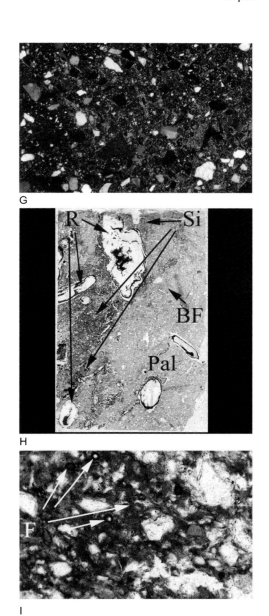

Plate 25 continued: G) As F: XPL, showing moderately well oriented (~birefringent) textural pedofeatures. H) Monolith 21(C) thin section: 'Sandy' palaeosol (Pal) contains burned flint (BF), markedly affected by post-inundation rooting (R) and associated inwash of humic and peaty silts and clays. Width is ~50mm. I) Monolith 21(B), context 388006: Detail of peaty infill of root channel (from context 388004 above) that contains much fungal material (F). PPL, frame width is 0.92mm

Basal chalky solifluction deposits

The basal unit consisted of a mixture of silt and chalk that appeared to become less chalky up-profile (context 388005). It contained the occasional piece of flint (occasionally frost-shattered) but no humanly worked material. Thin-section analysis (monolith 17, Fig 72; Appendix B) showed that the upper part of this unit was composed of 10mm of finely bedded silts and silty clay over more than 2mm of weakly bedded chalk gravel (Pls 25A and B). These chalk clasts are set in a calcareous silt and sand loam matrix, which also records in-washed yellow clay from above. Secondary features

include rooting and localised pyrite (Pls 25B–D) and traces of nodular carbonate formation, possibly including $NaCO_3$ and not simply $CaCO_3$. In monolith 21 (Fig 72; Appendix B) context 388005 is again a gravel-rich deposit, but here it is ironstone- and flint-rich, with only traces of the original calcareous matrix mixed with silty clay. Secondary gypsum is associated with root traces (Pl 25E). In general biological material was absent from this deposit although a single sample did produce a small amount of pollen including tree and open-ground taxa as well as a high microscopic charcoal particle count (although this is likely to be intrusive). The deposit appears to be a chalk- and silt-rich solifluction deposit that resembles chalky head deposits found at other HS1 sites such as White Horse Stone, Kent (Macphail and Crowther 2004) and Holywell Combe, Folkestone (Preece and Bridgland 1998). Subsequently, these deposits were rooted and anaerobic breakdown of organic matter is associated with pyrite formation (Kooistra 1978; Miedema *et al* 1974; Wiltshire *et al* 1994).

Lower (clayey) sandy silt

Overlying the solifluction deposits was a greenish-grey clayey and sandy silt unit (context 388006). The surface of this deposit appeared eroded and was steeply sloping. A number of pieces of worked flint and burnt flint were recovered from the top 100mm of this deposit. Artefacts were also recorded on the surface of the deposit at the interface with the overlying peat, along with an assemblage of animal bone (see below; *The archaeological evidence*).

Thin section analysis (monolith 17, Fig 72; Appendix B) revealed this deposit, just below the interface with the peat, to be a massive, poorly mixed humic silt and medium sand containing numerous coarse burnt flints (Pl 25A), and trace amounts of charcoal. The micromorphology appears to record a short-lived episode of weak biological working and alteration related to inundation, and associated rooting by semi-aquatic plants, which transformed the 'soil' through slaking and related structural collapse. Upwards this context becomes increasingly humic, with very abundant coarse roots and mixing the fabric. Secondary nodular carbonate formation along root channels probably reflects periodically fluctuating water tables and the calcareous nature of the underlying Late Glacial deposits. Stratigraphically this deposit in monolith 17 is correlated with similar sediment in monolith 21. However it should be noted that this correlation was not observed directly in the field and radiocarbon dates from the peat above this deposit in both monoliths exhibit very different ages, perhaps reflecting erosion of 388006 within monolith 17 by local channel activity (Fig 72; Appendix A).

As in monolith 17, thin section analysis of monolith 21 revealed this 388006 to be a massive, partially mixed silt and medium sandy loam, dominated by textural pedofeatures (intercalations and void infills; Pls 25F and 25G) caused by structural collapse, mixing and 'bedding'. Secondary features include roots and rare gypsum (Kooistra 1978), and many ferruginous (Pl 25F) and carbonate impregnations, with some finely dusty clay void coatings associated with rooting. In the upper part of this unit down-profile clay movement and slickenside-like fabric features relate to rooting and structural collapse higher up. The fabric features indicate *in situ*

Thames Holocene

Figure 74 Pollen diagram from 3880TT

thixotrophic (water saturated) conditions. Iron and calcium carbonate impregnation is again linked to rooting into calcareous gravels below, and ensuing oxygenation (iron movement) because of root penetration and water table fluctuations. This deposit, at the interface with the overlying peat, is markedly affected by root mixing with humic silt and silty clay rich in plant tissues and fungal material (Pl 25I), possibly related to fleshy semi-aquatic rooting. Rare charcoal and possible fine burned mineral is evidence of local burning, possibly related to resource use or occupation.

The pollen (monolith 17, Fig 74; PAZ TC3880–1) contained quite high values of obligate aquatic taxa (eg, *Callitriche* (starwort), *Potamogeton* (pondweed) and *Typha angustifolia*-type (lesser bulrush) typical of freshwater, suggesting that open areas of reedswamp were present. The pollen assemblage (bottom two samples) contain about 50% tree and shrub pollen (arboreal pollen; AP) and 50% herb pollen (non-arboreal pollen; NAP) and fern spores. The NAP is dominated by Poaceae and *Plantago lanceolata* (ribwort plantain) together with many other herbs characteristic of grassland/pastures (eg, *Taraxacum*-type (dandelion), *Trifolium*-type (clover), *Potentilla*-type (cinquefoil) and *Ranunculus acris*-type (buttercup)). Also present are cereal-type grains including possibly barley (*Hordeum*-type) and pollen taxa characteristic of weeds of arable crops or open ground. The AP, with pollen of *Quercus*, *Tilia* and *Corylus*, is evidence for mixed deciduous woodland growing on the dryland, with *Alnus* growing on the wetland. Also present are pollen of shrubs and trees which may be characteristic of woodland edge (though some are also found naturally occurring in alder carr): Rosaceae undiff. (rose), *Prunus*-type (sloe/cherry), *Rubus fruticosus*-type (blackberry), *Rhamnus cathartica* (buckthorn) and *Viburnum opulus* (guelder rose). These assemblages indicate that mixed deciduous woodland was present regionally possibly with small patches of cleared and thinned woodland used for pasturing and growing cereals quite close to the site.

The main peat and upper clay silts

The peat (context 388004) was approximately 1.4m thick and the base of this unit has been dated to the Early Neolithic, 3950–3690 cal BC (NZA-29088, 5004±40 BP) in monolith 17 (Fig 72). Here, peat composition varies; between -1.95m and -1.73m OD it is silty peat while between -1.73m and -0.74m OD it contains abundant woody fragments and roots. The top of the peat in this location (monolith 2) has been dated to the Early Bronze Age, 1750–1530 cal BC (NZA-29086, 3372±35 BP). Occasional pieces of struck or burnt flint were recorded throughout this unit (see below; *The archaeological evidence*) along with an assemblage of animal bone, although the frequency was much greater within the lowest 100mm of the peat.

The pollen assemblage (PAZ TC3880–2) is dominated by *Alnus* with *Quercus*, *Corylus*, *Tilia* and ferns. NAP are at lower values than in PAZ TC3880–1, particularly towards the top of the zone. These results would indicate that alder fen carr with an understory of ferns was growing on the site at this time, with the loss of the woodland openings which were used for pasture and cereal growth in PAZ TC3880–1. Further evidence of alder carr growing on the site is provided by clumps of *Alnus*, *Salix* and Cyperaceae pollen which would have been broken up if they had travelled some distance. The development of the alder carr may have been in response to dropping water levels associated with estuary contraction and relative lower sea-levels, allowing alder carr to grow on areas that were previously reedswamp. Raised values of *Betula* (birch) at the base of the zone may give further evidence of abandonment of the openings in the woodland as *Betula* is often the first colonising shrub/tree of abandoned cleared ground. Charcoal values are also down on those of PAZ TC3880–1 suggesting less human impact on the local environment. Mixed deciduous woodland with *Tilia*, *Quercus* and *Corylus* was growing on drier ground away from the site. It is possible that there is a hiatus towards the top of the main peat unit, at the PAZ TC3880–2/3 boundary. Pollen assemblages between the two zones are very different. The top of the peat at -0.74m and -0.64m OD is recorded as dried out peat whereas -0.64m to 0.12m OD are silty clays (contexts 388003–1). The dried out peat could suggest that some of the sediment could have been eroded away, particularly as the site became waterlogged and the silty clay was then laid down. At the PAZ TC3880–2/3 boundary there is a drop in *Tilia* values and this may represent the 'lime decline'. It is here dated to 1750–1530 cal BC (NZA-29086, 3372±35 BP), in the Early to Middle Bronze Age, which is found to occur in many wetland sequences at this time (see Grant *et al* 2011) including those listed in this study (see Chap 10) and often associated with human activity (though see Waller and Grant 2012).

NAP values are much higher in PAZ TC3880–3, particularly grasses, with concomitant drops in AP values. Charcoal values also rise. There is evidence of marshes/fens (Cyperaceae), but also of pastures and, in the overlying silty clays, cereal growth. These changes may be indicative of increased human impact around the site, probably on the higher drier ground, with some clearance of woodland for agriculture. Obligate aquatic pollen values rise and remains of the green algae *Pediastrum* and *Botryococcus* indicate the presence of fresh water, but Chenopodiaceae pollen values also rise, a taxon characteristic of saltmarsh, suggesting that saltmarshes may have been present not far away at this time. The pollen assemblages may suggest fluctuating fresh and saline conditions such as found under tidal conditions and that saltmarsh may have been gradually approaching the site throughout the zone. There is evidence for reworking of sediment during this zone with the recording of pre-Quaternary pollen and spores, and the very variable preservation of the pollen.

The uppermost sediments consisted of a series of stratified clay-silts. The top layer (388001)had been partly oxidised to a pale brown colour. Diatoms were present in both 388002 and 388003 and in both cases samples produced brackish and marine diatom species (*Table 63*). Halophilous species occur in the sample from context 388003. However, these halophiles, *Navicula cincta* and *N. mutica*, are also tolerant of desiccation (aerophilous diatoms) and occur in habitats such as ephemeral pools and on the banks of water bodies. From the evaluation counts, it appears that allochthonous marine planktonic diatoms are more common in the sample from context 388003 than in the sample from context 388002 (eg, *Paralia sulcata*, *Cymatosira belgica* and *Rhaphoneis* spp.). In the sample from context 388002 mesohalobous, benthic or epipelic (mud-

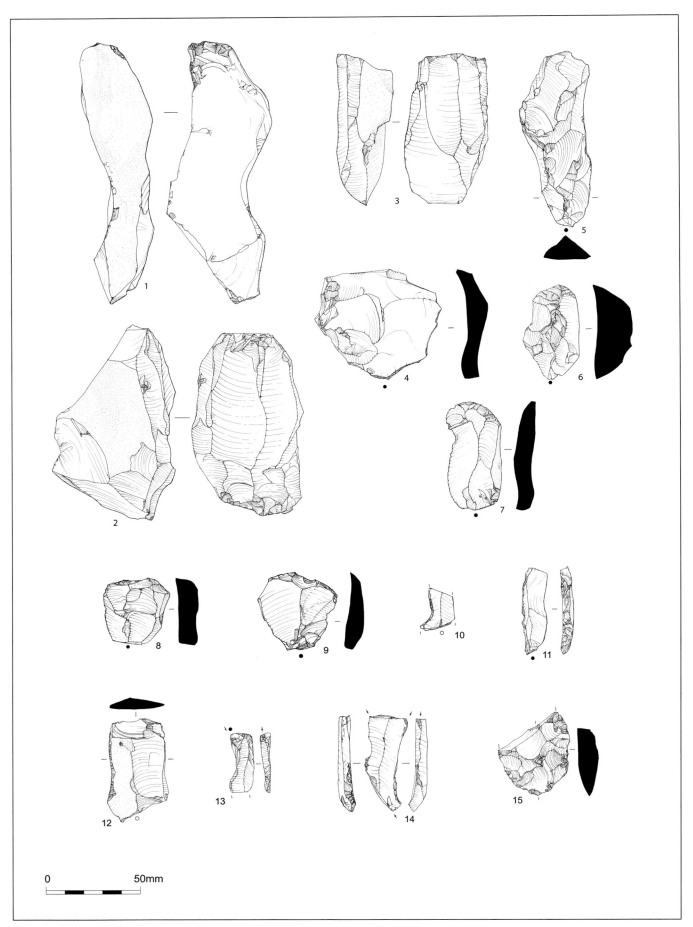

Figure 75 Worked flint from the Thames Crossing at Swanscombe

surface) diatoms such as *Nitzschia navicularis, N. granulata, Diploneis interrupta* and *D. smithii* (a polyhalobous to mesohalobous species) appear to be more common. Both samples contain *Cyclotella striata*, a planktonic diatom typical of the estuaries in general.

Summary

The evidence from the excavated sequence indicates that the site was located on a small area of high ground projecting from the valley side into the floodplain of the river. This finger of land was defined by a sequence of solifluction lobes that had undergone reworking and local mobilisation on the slope after initial deposition. Subsequently fluvial erosion of the sediment resulted in the trimming and incision noted to the north and east by presumed local stream activity. These minor channels were subsequently infilled by peaty-silt and eventually by a thick deposit of peat. Finally mudflat conditions developed across the site.

The Archaeological Evidence

The artefactual material recovered from both the coffer excavation (3880TT) and the watching brief included a small assemblage of pottery along with animal bone, with a large assemblage of worked flint, analysed by Hugo Anderson-Whymark (*Tables 64–71*). In total the assemblage comprises 521 worked flints and 302 fragments (7541g) of burnt unworked flint, the majority recovered from either the base of the main peat unit (388004) or the upper part of the underlying sandy silt alluvial deposits (context 388006) and the equivalent watching brief contexts (see *Table 64* and Fig 75).

Catalogue of illustrated flint from the Thames Crossing at Swanscombe
(Fig 75)
1. Bruised flint? A thermally fractured piece of flint exhibiting two areas of edge-damage along one side and further damage at one end. The edge-damage is consistent with heavy use, but is less prominent than on bruised blades in known long blade assemblages. A Late Upper Palaeolithic date is possible, but equally this flint may be contemporary with the Upper Palaeolithic flint it is associated with (ARC TMS00, 388006).
2. Prismatic bi-polar blade core. Note the one dominant platform for blade removal and the minimally prepared back of the core. Abandoned due to an internal thermal flaw. 343g. Upper Palaeolithic (ARC TMS00, 3 88006, SF74).
3. Single-platform blade core. Plain platform with platform-edge abrasion. Note the minimally prepared rear of the core. 112 g. Upper Palaeolithic (Chainage 35.250km).
4. Platform rejuvenation tablet. Plunging removal from a blade core with platform-edge abrasion. Note the presence of more than one removal on the platform surface. Upper Palaeolithic (Chainage 35.250km).
5. Crested blade. Upper Palaeolithic (Chainage 35.250km).
6. End scraper manufactured on a small plunging uni-facially crested flake. Upper Palaeolithic (ARC TMS00, 388006, SF107).
7. End scraper on a flake. Burnt. Upper Palaeolithic. (Chainage 35.250km).
8. End scraper on a flake. Upper Palaeolithic (Chainage 35.250km).
9. End scraper on a flake. Upper Palaeolithic (Chainage 35.250km).
10. Edge retouched flake. Slight abrupt concave edge retouch along the right-hand side of a blade-like flake. Proximal and distal breaks. Upper Palaeolithic (Chainage 35.250km).
11. Curved backed blade. Distal end intentionally broken. Upper Palaeolithic (ARC TMS00, 388006, SS196).
12. Edge-retouched blade-like flake. Straight semi-abrupt edge-retouch along left hand side of a side trimming flake (ARC TMS00, 388006, SS196).
13. Burin on a platform edge. Note retouch after the burin removal. Upper Palaeolithic (residual, Chainage 35.250km).
14. Burin. Two burin on truncation removals and one dihedral burin removal. Note additional edge retouch after the burin removals had been made. Upper Palaeolithic (residual, Chainage 35.250km).
15. Laurel leaf. Tip broken. Early Neolithic (Chainage 35.250km)

The vast majority of the flint assemblage from the watching brief was recovered close to 3880TT excavation (*c* 35.245–*c* 35.260km, *Table 65*, Fig 60). The flints from the sandy silt are in pristine condition and may have been preserved *in situ*, although no distinct concentrations or scatters were observed. Many of the flints from the overlying peat are technologically similar to those recovered from the sandy silt and are likely to have been reworked from there.

Two distinct groups of flints were identified; Upper Palaeolithic and Neolithic. The raw material exploited was relatively consistent across the excavation areas and between the two periods; it was exclusively flint procured in the form of reasonably-sized derived nodules. The cortical surface of nodules either exhibited a thin 1–2mm chalky crust or was entirely abraded. The cortex was generally white to grey in colour and the flint was dark grey with variable degrees of lighter grey mottling. The flint was of good flaking quality, but contained occasional large thermal flaws which hindered knapping. Thermal faults were more prominent in this raw material than among the large nodules exploited at Springhead. The original size of the nodules is indicated by three refitting flints from the watching brief (35.250km) that were struck from a nodule in excess of 150mm long.

The flint was generally in pristine condition, due to preservation within peat and alluvial deposits. The flint from the upper part of the peat and alluvial deposits in the watching brief (contexts 1 and 2) and the unstratified flints generally exhibited moderate post-

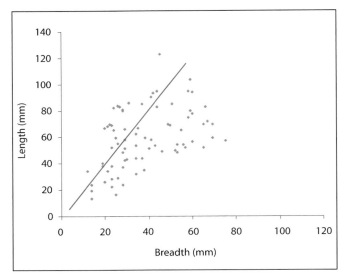

Figure 76 The length to breadth ratio of flakes from 388006 and 3

depositional edge-damage suggesting redeposition. Several Upper Palaeolithic flints were present in the lower levels of the peat deposits exhibited slight edge-damage. This indicates that these flints were probably reworked from the lower alluvial deposits. The distribution of these flints was comparable to the scatter in the underlying deposits and indicates limited horizontal movement.

The majority of the flint exhibited no surface cortication. A small number exhibited a slight mottled bluish/white surface cortication and others bore a dark surface staining typical of flints recovered from peat. A significant proportion of the flint assemblage was burnt (18%), notably six of ten end scrapers. A large proportion of the assemblage was also broken (47.7%); this total includes numerous breaks resulting from burning.

Upper Palaeolithic worked flint

The Upper Palaeolithic flint assemblage was recovered over an area 53m in length from 35.220km to 35.273km and extends laterally beyond the limits of the tunnel portal. A small number of flints from the excavation were three dimensionally recorded and demonstrate a spread with no distinct artefact concentrations. The distribution of flint from the watching brief was referenced to specific chainages (Table 65). These demonstrate a concentration of flint around 35.250km. The flint from the lower part of the peat also follows this distribution pattern and it appears that Upper Palaeolithic artefacts from the sandy silts have been reworked into the base of the peat. A limited number of Neolithic flints, considered below, were also present in this deposit. Due to the presence of Palaeolithic and Neolithic flints in peat, a technological attribute analysis was only undertaken on securely sealed Palaeolithic flints from the sandy silt (contexts 388006 and 3, 35.250km). The assemblage is considered below in relation to debitage and retouched tools.

Debitage

A complete reduction sequence, from core preparation to abandonment, is present in the Upper Palaeolithic assemblage. A large proportion of the flints from context 3 (35.250km) exhibit a distinctive chalky cortex and appear to derive from the reduction of a large flint nodule. The early stages of core reduction are well represented in the assemblage. Core preparation flakes form 9.1% of the flake assemblage and 56% of the assemblage exhibit some of the cortical surface (Tables 66 and 67); 9% of flakes also exhibit cortical butts (Table 69). Knapping refits were identified between three large trimming flakes removed early in the reduction sequence (35.250km). In addition, 22% of flakes exhibit cortex along one or both sides and 13% of flakes exhibit cortex at the distal end. The majority of these flakes result from the preparation of cores, rather than their final reduction.

The cores appear to have been well dressed, with much of the cortex removed from the front of the core before blade production commenced. The back of the core is generally minimally prepared and frequently exhibits some cortex. Seven crested flakes and blades were present in the assemblage. Three short crested flakes were detached from dressed nodules to prepare platforms; one of these was retouched into an end scraper (Fig 75, 6). Blade production was then initiated by the removal of a crested blade. Four uni-facially crested blades are present in the assemblage. The longest crested blade is broken, but measures 93mm in length, and two complete examples measure 80mm and 84mm respectively. These crested blades provide a good indication of the size of blade produced. Once blade production had commenced, the platforms were maintained and extended by the removal of large core tablets (Fig 75, 4); three tablets were recovered from context 3. Only two small face rejuvenation flakes were present indicating that few minor adaptations were made to cores during blade reduction. Two single-platform blade cores, two bi-polar blade cores (Fig 75, 2 and 3) and one unclassifiable blade core were recovered from contexts 388006 and 3; an additional three bi-polar cores from contexts 388804 and 11 also appear to date from the Upper Palaeolithic. One of the single-platform blade cores is pyramidal in form, whilst the other single-platform blade core and bipolar cores are prismatic. The 'other' blade core has been extensively worked, with flakes removed late in the reduction sequence, but prior to this it appears to have been a prismatic single platform blade core. In all cases, the bi-polar blade cores exhibit a primary platform, from which the majority of blades are detached, with the second platform used to modify and correct the angle of the core's face. The single-platform blade cores were abandoned at 112g and 117g, whilst the bi-polar cores were abandoned between 84g and 343g (average 227g). The final blade removals measure 50mm–76mm. In addition to the blade cores, a single-platform flake core, a multi-platform blade core and two tested nodules were recovered from contexts 388006 and 3. These cores show limited preparation and may represent the production of flakes for adaptation into scrapers.

The technological attributes of 208 complete and broken flakes from contexts 388006 and 3 (35.250km) were recorded and the 75 complete flakes were measured (Fig 76). The average flake in the assemblage measures 59mm long by 38mm wide and 12mm thick. Blades, flakes with a 2:1 or higher length to breadth ratio, represent 32% of the flake debitage, a total comparable with the blade industries of the Mesolithic (Ford 1987). This total may, however, be exaggerated as few small flakes are present in the assemblage as the flint was hand collected and no sieving was undertaken. The 24 complete blades in the assemblage measure 34–125mm in length and have average dimensions of 72mm by 28mm by 9mm thick. The 125mm blade is the only example over 100mm and falls within the size range of Late Upper Palaeolithic long blade industries. There are, however, no specific attributes to suggest this blade is not contemporary with the rest of the assemblage. The range of butt types supports the observations made from the cores (*Table 69*). The majority of flakes exhibited plain butts (67%), having been struck from platforms created by tablet removals. A further 9% of flakes exhibited more than one removal on the platform. Punctiform and linear butts (8.9% and 5.9% respectively) are not infrequent and result from the hammer being struck close to the edge of the core and removing only a minimal area of the platform. These removals are commonly associated with platform edge abrasion. Facetting was present on nine flakes (6.7% of the flake assemblage). The faceting on three of these flints reflects the removal of rejuvenation tablets, and one results from the removal of a blade across the platform. The other five examples result from the abrasion of the platform as well as the platform face. No *en éperon* butts, typical of Creswellian industries, were recorded. Platform-edge abrasion was recorded on 66% of flakes. The abrasion was particularly prominent and frequently took the form of large clusters of step fractured removals up to 10mm long. Large blades tended to exhibit the heaviest edge-abrasion and the edges of some platforms were bevelled. The termination of the flakes examined (*Table 70*) indicate the majority were successful. Feathered terminations are most frequent (56%), with roughly equal proportions of plunging and hinged removals (20% and 18% respectively). Only 4% of flakes resulted in step fractures.

Core reduction appears to have employed both hard and soft hammer percussors (*Table 71*). 41% of flakes exhibited developed hertizan cones typical percussion using hard hammer, such as stone, whilst 26% of flakes exhibited more diffuse bulbs typical of percussion with a soft hammer, such as antler (Onhuma and Bergman 1982). The pattern of hammer use is not entirely consistent, but cortical trimming flakes were more commonly removed using hard hammer percussion, whilst blades were generally removed using a soft hammer.

Retouch

The lower alluvial silts (388006 and 3) yielded three burins, nine end scrapers, four notched flakes, two edge retouched flakes and a curved backed blade; three burin spalls were also recovered. In total, retouched tools represent 7.7% of the flint assemblage recovered (excluding chips). In addition, two burins, two burin spalls and a distally truncated retouched flake were retrieved from the Neolithic deposits (388004 and 11); these may be considered as residual Upper Palaeolithic flints. The five burins are all manufactured on blades; three have one removal, one has two removals and the other had three removals. Two of the removals were dihedral, one of which was struck towards a notch. Three burins were struck on breaks, a further two were struck from the platform edge and one on a straight distal truncation (Fig 75, 13 and 14). The burin on a straight truncation was notched after the flake was removed, two other burins also bore additional edge retouch.

The nine scrapers were all manufactured on flakes. In all cases retouch was confined to the distal end of the flake and was gently curving, although occasional irregularities in the retouch were noted (Fig 75, 7–9). The retouch was generally semi-abrupt, but one scraper exhibited abrupt retouch. The scrapers were all either recovered in the excavation or at 35.250km of the watching brief. It is notable that five scrapers were burnt, breaking four of the examples. Burning is more prevalent among the scrapers than other tools or in the assemblage as a whole. This may indicate that the scrapers were used for a task undertaken close to a fire, or involving the use of fire. The task or location of the task ultimately resulted in the deliberate or accidental burning of these tools.

The four notched flints in the assemblage include one small 8mm notch in the side of a flake and a broad 21mm by 5mm deep notch in a broken blade (Fig 75, 10). Two flakes exhibited two adjacent notches. On one flake these were semi-circular and measured 5mm and 6mm wide respectively and on the other the notches measured 13mm and 5mm. It is unclear if it was the notches that were intended for use or the point created between the two. The location of the these paired notches on the side of the flakes indicate that any use would have to have been in a transverse, rather than rotary, movement; this may suggest a graving function. The two edge-retouched flakes include one blade-like flake with semi-abrupt edge retouch along the left hand side (Fig 75, 12) and a limited area of retouch on a broken flake that was used as a scraper.

The most diagnostic artefact is a curve-backed point with a distal truncation (Fig 75, 11). The blade exhibits heavy slightly curving abrupt retouch along the right hand side. This retouch has been struck from the ventral surface with the exception of one removal from the dorsal. The distal end was removed by a blow to the

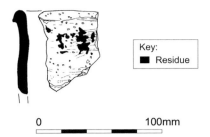

Key:
■ Residue

0   100mm

Figure 77 Early Neolithic, Plain Bowl. Rolled rim and neck sherd from a closed vessel of necked hemispherical form

dorsal surface. Comparable tools are present in many Final Upper Palaeolithic assemblages including Hengistbury Head, Dorset (Barton 1992, fig. 4.23) and Pixie's Hole, Devon among other sites (Barton and Roberts 1996).

In addition to the formally retouched tools, several flakes and blades bore edge damage consistent with use. This use-damage usually took the form of micro-flaking along the edge of artefacts but, in a few examples, was more prominent and suggested contact with hard materials. One thermally fractured piece of irregular waste measuring 125mm exhibited two areas of edge-damage along the long side of the artefact and a further area on one end (Fig 75, 1). This damage consists of clusters of scalar and step fractures extending up to 5mm into the surface of the artefact. This damage may plausibly be considered as bruising; a use-damage characteristic of Late Upper Palaeolithic long blade industries. The edge-damage on this artefact is, however, notably less prominent than the damage on bruised blades and flakes in known long blade assemblages, for example, at Springhead. Moreover, as the damage is on a thermally fractured flint, there are no technological attributes to consider if this flint belongs to the current industry or a later long blade industry. The question of the date of this flint must remain open, but, on reflection, it is probable that this artefact is contemporary with the current assemblage. It is possible the damage on the artefact results from working a hard material, such as antler, as has been proposed for the bruising on long blades (Barton 1986).

Neolithic worked flint
The Neolithic peat deposit (context 388004 and 11) yielded 221 flints and 74 pieces (3043g) of burnt unworked flint. As discussed above, many of the flints in these contexts have been reworked from the underlying alluvial silts and date from the Upper Palaeolithic. Several diagnostic Neolithic flints are, however, present and some of the debitage is also Neolithic. This is particularly apparent among the cores as, with the exception of the three Upper Palaeolithic bi-polar blade cores, considered above, the six cores in the peat exhibit a distinctly different reduction strategy to the Upper Palaeolithic material. The cores are all aimed at the production of flakes and blade-like flakes. Flakes have been struck from a single platform on two cores, whilst

three cores exhibit multiple platforms. The multi-platform cores exhibit *ad hoc* working with the cores being rotated as flaking creates new surfaces that can be used as platforms. A small discoidal core, weighing 44g, was also recovered. These reduction techniques are characteristic of the Neolithic and the discoidal core is most characteristic of the later Neolithic.

The diagnostic Neolithic artefacts include a reworked fragment of a partly polished implement, a broken laurel leaf and a mis-shaped arrowhead. A serrated flake and a backed knife are also probably Neolithic. The polished implement (context 11, 35.250km) is fragmentary, but originally measured by 30mm wide by in excess of 33mm long and 13mm thick. The form of the implement is unclear, but one side was flat and the surface was only was partly polished; this may suggest an adze-like implement. An axe thinning flake may represent a further flake struck from the surface of this tool. The laurel leaf (context 11, Fig 75, 15) dates from the Early Neolithic and may be considered contemporary with the sherd of Plain Bowl pottery (Fig 77; see below). It is not possible to classify the mis-shaped arrowhead to any particular form and only a broad Neolithic/Early Bronze Age date can be suggested.

Due to the presence of residual flints, the Neolithic assemblage is difficult to characterise. The assemblage, however, includes several Neolithic tools, perhaps indicating a broad range of activities. A refitting exercise proved unsuccessful and it seems likely that only limited knapping, as suggested by the presence of cores, was undertaken at this location. The presence of a sherd of Early Neolithic pottery, various bones of cattle and sheep/goat, along with piece of worked red deer antler (see below), may suggest this was the location of short term habitation and associated activities. The discoidal core represents debitage from a technology more typical of the later Neolithic. It is possible that this core occurred higher in the peat sequence and is of later date that the other artefacts, but this cannot be confirmed as the precise location of the artefact was not recorded.

Prehistoric pottery
Eleven sherds of handmade prehistoric pottery were recovered during the watching brief (*Tables 72* and *73*). The assemblage was examined by Alistair Barclay and Lorraine Mepham. The condition of the pottery sherds is fair to poor, but most sherds are only moderately abraded (mean sherd weight overall 13.3g). Nine plain sherds are from the basal part of the main peat unit (watching brief context 11). This includes a rolled rim in a flint-tempered fabric (FA1/EN), identifiable as deriving from an Early Neolithic Plain Bowl of slightly necked hemispherical form (Fig 77). Some of the other plain body sherds could be from the same or similar vessels. Charred residue on the outer neck of the rim sherds and on the interior surfaces of two of the body sherds indicate use as cooking pots. A second rolled rim sherd in a leached shelly fabric (S1/EN) could be from a similar type of vessel. The remaining sherds (including

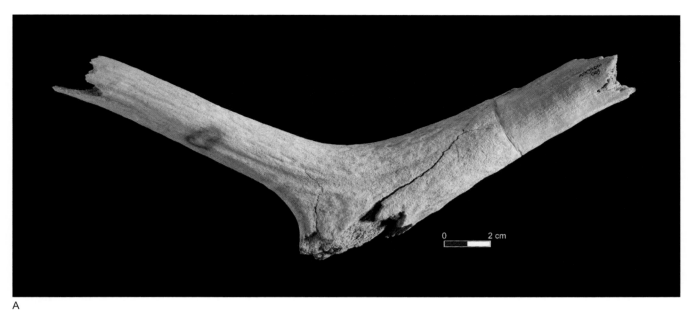

A

B

Plate 26 A) Worked Neolithic red deer antler from the watching brief at 35.255km, Swanscombe; B) detail of cut marks on the beam

seven from context 11), all plain sherds, in flint-tempered, shelly and sandy fabrics, could be of similar date. These include a probable neck sherd and what could be a lower vessel sherd from a cup. A further neck sherd was recovered from the upper alluvial deposits (watching brief context 001/002), although it is possible that this is of non-Neolithic date.

The rolled form of the two rims as well as the profile of the larger sherd in particular indicate affiliation with the Plain Bowl tradition of the mid-4th millennium BC (Barclay 2007, 342 and table 15.1). This type of pottery has a widespread distribution across much of Britain, occurring in occupation deposits, pits and in association with some monuments (eg, causewayed enclosures such as Staines (Robertson-Mackay 1987, figs 43–4)). The overall range of fabrics and type of temper are fairly typical for the region and it is not unusual to find similar vessels in different fabrics (eg, the rolled rims in fabrics S1/EN and FA1/EN), while the choice to manufacture

the possible cup in a sandy fabric has been noted elsewhere. The relatively small assemblage has a wide range of fabrics, which could suggest that deposition was more than a single event and certainly that the 'life' assemblage was composed of vessels with different histories of manufacture. Charred residue on the illustrated vessel and two other sherds indicate use as cooking pots.

The only non-Neolithic sherd is part of a base in a flint and possible shell-tempered fabric (FS1/LBAEIA) from a vessel of probable Late Bronze Age or Early Iron Age date based on fabric. As the sherd is from the bottom of the base no further comment can be made.

Animal bone

Animal bone recovered from the surface of the sandy silt during the watching brief (context 3) was examined by Jessica Grimm. A possible partial skeleton of a sheep/goat comprised scapulae, a right humerus, right femur and left tibia. Based upon epiphiseal fusion this animal was older than 15–20 months but less than 42 months when it died. A complete fused left radius belonged to an animal older than 42 months when it died and the estimated height at the withers is c 0.61m (Teichert 1975). Four cattle bones comprise a left costa fragment, a complete fused left humerus (GL 295mm), a right humerus shaft fragment and a fused distal tibia fragment. A withers height of c 1.22m could be estimated using the factors proposed by Matolcsi (1970). The complete fused right radius of a red deer (GL 294mm) indicates an animal over 30 months when it died, while a beam and tine fragment was radiocarbon dated to the Early Neolithic, 3790–3650 cal BC (NZA-28891, 4948±30 BP) and exhibited cut marks on the beam (Pl 26A–B). The cut is clearly in its early stages (Pl 26B); not very deep or broad, and was probably made by repeatedly striking the antler with a knife (ie, parallel cuts).

Nineteen fragments (158g) of bone recovered from the base of the peat (context 388004) in 3880TT included two small fragments of bone classified as large mammal and the remaining fragments belonged to a right cattle scapula; as the processus coracoideus had fused, the animal was over 7–10 months when it died (Habermehl 1975). Bone from the upper part of the peat recovered during the watching brief (context 2) included a cranium fragment of a large mammal, a probable right ulna fragment of a red deer, and cattle bones comprising a complete fused right radius, a metacarpus shaft fragment, the fused distal part of a right metatarsus (>24–30 months) and a right tibia shaft fragment. Based on the complete cattle radius a height at the withers of c 1.15m was estimated (Matolcsi 1970). At the interface between the peat and overlying alluvial deposits (context 1/2) cattle bones were also recovered which included a fragment from the left side of an adult skull, the corpus of a lumbal vertebra with unfused epiphyses indicating an animal younger than 48–60 months (Habermehl 1975) and the distal part of an unfused tibia (animal <24 months), as well as the complete unfused right tibia of a juvenile pig. Of particular interest is the recovery of a complete tooth row of a right mandibula of adult cattle. Only the teeth survive and no mandibular bone. According to Grant (1982), the wear stage of this mandible is 43, indicating an older but not aged animal.

Discussion

The flint assemblage from the Thames Crossing excavation and watching brief results from two distinct episodes of activity on the headland as predicted in the original model. The scatter of flint in context 388006 dates from the Upper Palaeolithic. The industry was orientated on the production of blades up to 100mm in length, generally removed from bi-polar blade cores maintained by tablet rejuvenation. The retouched tool assemblage was dominated by short end scrapers on flakes and burins; a curve-backed blade was also present. These attributes and tools are most characteristic of Final Upper Palaeolithic assemblages, although penknife points are absent from the assemblage. Only a few radiocarbon dates are available for comparable assemblages, but they indicate a date probably in the Windermere interstadial (c 12,000–11,000 BC, Barton 1999, 18, table 2.2, 25). An arctic hare bone from the archaeological deposits at Broken Cavern, Devon, was AMS dated to 11,540–11,010 cal BC (OxA-3887, 11,380±120 BP). Three radiocarbon dates on animal bones related to a hearth at Pixie's Hole, Devon, produced dates around c 12,210–11,310 cal BC (OxA-5794–6; the three dates were statistically inconsistent so the range of the calibrated means is quoted here), while charcoal (species not given) from a hearth at Mother Grundy's Parlour, Derbyshire dated to 11,890–11,460 cal BC (OxA-5858, 11,790±901 BP) (Barton 1999, 25). The assemblage is also comparable to the open sites at Hengistbury Head, Dorset and Brockhill, Surrey. The date of these open sites is not clear, but broad TL date of 12,500±1150 years ago was obtained on burnt flint artefacts from the former site (Huxtable 1992, 60). Unfortunately the date of 3790–3650 cal BC (NZA-28891, 4948±30 BP) from the Thames River Crossing, Swanscombe obtained on a worked antler among the flints indicates that it is intrusive to the unit.

The interpretation of the scatter is hindered by archaeological and methodological issues. The Late Upper Palaeolithic scatter in the silts (contexts 388006 and 3) appears to have been preserved in situ, but the upper levels of the deposit have been truncated and finds reworked into later deposits, prior to the peat formation. The location of all of the finds was, however, not subject to detailed recording during the excavation and the lack of sieving resulted in the recovery of only the largest and most obvious flints. The nature of recording means that it is not possible to consider artefact distribution or activity areas. The scatter was clearly quite diffuse and spread over an area over measuring over 53m long; the lateral width is not known. The scatter contained significantly different densities of flint, with a particular focus of activity around 35.250km. A complete flint knapping sequence was present from the dressing of flint nodules to the abandonment of cores. Only a limited number of knapping refits could be made, indicating that significant elements of the sequence are missing, but this may reflect the method of excavation rather than an archaeological pattern. It is probable that many of the tools in the scatter were also manufactured at this location. This could not be demonstrated by refitting, but the presence of burin spalls indicates the manufacture of burins in the scatter. The presence of scrapers, burins and other retouched pieces indicate that several activities were performed at this location. The presence of a significant quantity of burnt unworked flint and burnt worked flints, including a high proportion of the scrapers, indicate the presence of a fire or fires. There is little evidence to suggest the that scatter resulted from prolonged or repeated activity at this location, but in the absence of detailed artefact distributions it is not possible to explore this issue further.

The Neolithic flint from the overlying horizon (contexts 388004 and 11) is likely to be of mixed character with no evidence for *in situ* activity. It indicates probable reuse and a presence in this part of the landscape during the Neolithic.

An Integrated History of Landscape Change and Human Activity

The evidence from both on- and off-site sequences investigated record a series of changes to the landscape that have largely been controlled by the process of flooding of the Early Holocene topographic template as a result of rising sea-levels. However, the initial occupation of the headland area took place in the Late Upper Palaeolithic period. Little evidence from the site exists to allow the archaeology to be dated directly and as the onset of sedimentation upon the Shepperton Gravel surface beneath the floodplain did not begin until around 6610–6430 cal BC (NZA-27599, 7669±50 BP) we do not have any evidence from the vicinity to contextualise the archaeology. The flints recovered indicate that human activity (in all probability associated with hunting and of a transitory nature) occurred at this location which would have provided a good vantage point across the lower lying floodplain. Possible contemporary deposition of sediments may have occurred (11 from watching brief) as a result of small channels crossing the headland.

The deposition of more extensive sediments upon the valley occurred around *c* 6500 cal BC with accumulation of fresh water deposits before intertidal mudflats were established. Up profile, gradually reducing relative water levels are attested in a change towards mid- to upper saltmarsh faunas prior to development of the alder carr woodland. Despite careful examination no evidence for exposure or drying of the minerogenic surface exists beneath the peat. Conditions on the headland at this time (or at least towards the end of this phase) appear to indicate local fresh water reedswamp and grassland conditions with deciduous tree growth on dry ground and significant quantities of charcoal to suggest small-scale clearings in woods. The onset of a major phase of fresh water fen carr becoming reed swamp up profile is recorded both on- and off-site. The Neolithic flint and pottery finds from the lower parts of the peat are probably broadly contemporary with the earlier fen carr phases but the diversity of the finds suggests that a number of episodes of activity are represented. These finds appear to be representative of a lower level of activity that the older Upper Palaeolithic finds and perhaps attest to intermittent visits to the water edge by people throughout an extended period of time. Significantly there was sparse evidence for artefacts and human activity within the large tract of peat exposed in the cutting of the box and we can, therefore, conclude that, based on the absence of material, evidence for human activity in the fen carr and reedswamp in this location was restricted.

Chapter 12

The Ebbsfleet Valley

with contributions by Hugo-Anderson Whymark, Alistair J Barclay, Catherine Barnett, Edward Biddulph, Nigel Cameron, Denise Druce, Damian Goodburn, Elizabeth Huckerby, Sylvia Peglar, Mark Robinson, Rob Scaife, David Smith, Wendy Smith, Chris J Stevens, Lucy Verrill and John Whittaker

The Ebbsfleet Valley (Zones E1–E3)

The line of HS1, after exiting the Thames tunnel on the Swanscombe Marshes, continues southwards through the Ebbsfleet Valley (Fig 78). Initially the line passes through the Pleistocene deposits on the western side of the lower part of the valley and then skirts the western edge of the alluvial floodplain in the vicinity of Northfleet Roman villa. It then continues southwards through the Upper Ebbsfleet Valley to Springhead. The results of the extensive archaeological excavations carried out in the Ebbsfleet Valley are published in detail elsewhere (Andrews *et al* 2011a; Wenban-Smith *et al* forthcoming). The following is a summary of the results and is largely focused on the investigation of the extensive Holocene alluvial sequences preserved in the lower reaches of the valley. It should be noted, however, less extensive freshwater alluvial and peat sequences along with valley side colluvium exist in the upper reaches in the vicinity of Springhead which are associated with archaeological remains.

Construction Impacts

Considerable development impacted on the sequences through the construction not only of the rail corridor but also the major international station at Ebbsfleet and the cross valley line linking HS1 with the North Kent Line (Fig 78). Construction of the rail and associated station complex involved considerable excavation of the Pleistocene sediments while the construction of the North Kent Line Link involved excavation of the alluvial sediments of the floodplain floor. Linked into the development impact within the valley was the construction of a new road corridor on the eastern side of the valley; South Thameside Development Route 4 (STDR-4), funded by Kent County Council (KCC). This road also impacted on the valley floor sediments and the sequences are included in the following synopsis of results.

Key Archaeological Issues

Today it is recognised that this area is of national importance for the Pleistocene sands, gravels and chalk-rich sediments present on the valley sides (Wenban-Smith 1995; Oxford Archaeological Unit 1997) (Fig 79). In places these are associated with rich archaeological remains, for example, the Levallois site at Baker's Hole and the elephant and associated archaeology at Southfleet Road (Wenban-Smith *et al* 2006). Less well known are the rich prehistoric archaeological remains associated with the alluvium in the valley bottom (Burchell 1938; Burchell and Piggott 1939; Sieveking 1960; Barham and Bates 1995; Oxford Archaeological Unit 1997; URL 1997). Later evidence for human activity comes from the Late Iron Age and Roman periods with a villa at Northfleet and temple complex and extensive town at Springhead (Detsicas 1983; Millet 2007; Andrews *et al* 2011a).

Previous work demonstrated that complex alluvial stratigraphies exist in the valley base consisting of clay-silt and organic silts/peats. A peat complex forms the main sediment body resting between two clay-silt units. The peat consists of a basal woody peat and an upper reed peat. The archaeological potential of these deposits has previously been described and both Mesolithic and Neolithic remains have been found (Burchell 1938; Burchell and Piggott 1939; Sieveking 1960; Barham and Bates 1995; Oxford Archaeological Unit 1995, 1997; URL 1997). Towards the valley sides these units probably interdigitate with colluvial sediments derived from the valley margins. The unconsolidated Holocene sediments overlie basal sand and gravel units of probable Late Pleistocene age. Complex sequences of Pleistocene sediments lie beneath the valley sides. However, some uncertainty regarding the precise location of the boundary between the valley sides and alluvium exists.

Today the challenge that faces archaeologists and geologists working in the valley is a function of the recent quarrying history of the area. Extensive quarrying activity up until the middle of the 20th century has resulted in the wholesale removal of large parts of the valley (Fig 79). Small patches, linear strips and unknown extents of elements of the formerly more extensive Pleistocene and Holocene sediments certainly exist in the landscape, however relating these patches to each other and placing them within the framework of the local and regional development of the valley remains a significant challenge.

Strategy, Aims and Objectives

The aims and objectives of the investigation were to identify the location of buried archaeological remains within the floodplain and near floodplain area. Specifically, attempts were to be made to focus investigation on those sequences thought to be of high archaeological potential and those where correlations may be attempted with the previously noted archaeological sequences. Additionally, focus was to be made on the extensive palaeoenvironmental remains recognised to be present within the valley.

A number of phases of investigation were conducted that included works on both HS1 and STDR-4 (Table 74; Figs 80–85) These formed part of the phased response to sequences, construction and the findings of previous investigations. As the archaeological programmes for both HS1 and STDR-4 ran concurrently, the opportunity was taken at an early stage to utilise and integrate data from both projects to inform each phase of work.

Methodologies

Geoarchaeological investigation of the Holocene sequences in the valley bottom and sides was led by Martin Bates and included a range of remote and direct investigations during the early evaluation stages. Some geophysical investigation (Richard Bates) were undertaken using Direct Current electrical soundings along a single transect (Figs 81–82) while borehole and test pit/trench excavations were undertaken to directly view sequences and contained archaeology (Figs 83–85).

Post-excavation work included the analysis of a number of sample profiles in order to characterise the environments of deposition associated with the sediments and the artefactual evidence. The selection of sequences and samples took into account all material recovered from both HS1 and STDR-4 in order to target resources efficiently and avoid duplication between the two projects. It was also agreed between HS1 and KCC at the beginning of the post-excavation analysis that the results related to the prehistoric periods

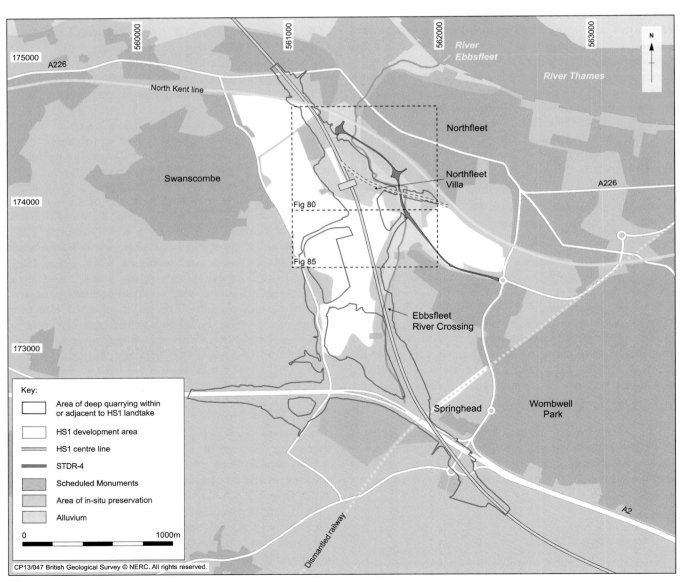

Figure 78 Site location plan of the HS1 and STDR-4 land take within the Ebbsfleet Valley

Table 74 Summary of fieldwork events, Lower Ebbsfleet Valley

Event name	Event code	Type	Zone	Number Interventions	Archaeological contractor
Ebbsfleet Valley, Northfleet	ARC EFT97	Evaluation	E1–E2	7BH (CP), 7TP, 68TT	Oxford Archaeology
Northfleet Rise	EBBS97	Evaluation	E1	11BH(CP), 3TP Geophysical survey	Oxford Archaeology
Ebbsfleet Sportsground	ARC ESG00	Evaluation	E1–E2	45TT	Oxford Archaeology
Ebbsfleet Valley detailed Mitigation	ARC EBB01	Excavation	E1–E2	Multiple area excavation plus 7TT, 1BH(MOS)	Oxford Archaeology
North Kent Line (Reedbeds)	ARC NKL02	Mostap survey	E2	13BH(MOS)	Oxford Archaeology
Ebbsfleet Valley detailed Mitigation	ARC 342W02	Watching Brief	E1–E3		Oxford Archaeology
Ebbsfleet Valley detailed Mitigation	ARC 342E02	Watching Brief	E1–E3		Wessex Archaeology
South Thameside Development Route 4	STDR400	Evaluation	E1–E2	20BH(CP), 15TP	Oxford Archaeology
South Thameside Development Route 4	STDR401	Excavation		4COFF (Areas 1–4)	Oxford Archaeology
South Thameside Development Route 4	STDR401	Watching brief	E1–E2		Oxford Archaeology

BH = borehole   (CP) = Cable percussion   (MOS) = Mostap   TP = testpit   TT = trench   COFF = cofferdam excavation

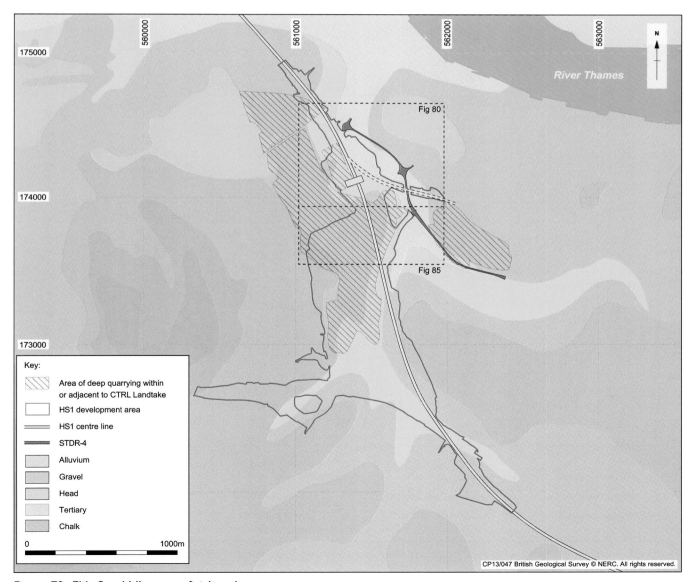

Figure 79 Ebbsfleet Valley superficial geology map

from both projects (geoarchaeology, environment and archaeology) would be most effectively disseminated if integrated into a single publication (Wenban-Smith *et al* forthcoming).

Much of the detailed analysis in the lower reaches of the valley has targeted the deep and most complete sample sequences recovered from borehole, trench and cofferdam excavations during the STDR-4 works, the latter producing considerable evidence of stratified Neolithic activity. Due to the fact the HS1 excavations were located along the shallower floodplain edge which did not produce such well-preserved sequences; the post-excavation analysis of one of the STDR-4 evaluation boreholes (BH7) was funded by HS1. The analysis of sequences from STDR-4 Trench 9 and cofferdam Area 4 were funded by KCC.

Overall interpretation of the sedimentary sequences was carried out by Martin Bates and Elizabeth Stafford. The palaeoenvironmental work was carried out by Denise Druce, Elizabeth Huckerby, Sylvia Peglar and Lucy Verrill (pollen), John Whittaker (ostracods and foraminifera), Nigel Cameron (diatoms), Wendy Smith and Chris Stevens (charred and waterlogged plant remains), Mark Robinson and David Smith (insects) and Catherine Barnett (charcoal and waterlogged wood species). The radiocarbon dating programme was coordinated by Elizabeth Stafford and Catherine Barnett. The following sections provide a summary of the sediment sequences and associated palaeo-environmental evidence, reported in detail elsewhere (Andrews *et al* 2011a–b; Barnett *et al* 2011; Wenban-Smith *et al* forthcoming).

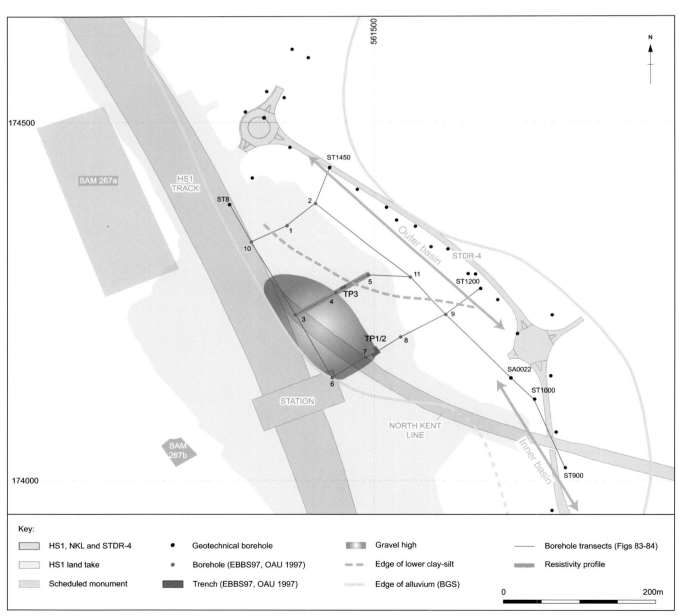

Figure 80 Ebbsfleet Valley showing location of borehole transects and geophysical profile from the Northfleet Rise evaluation (EBBS97)

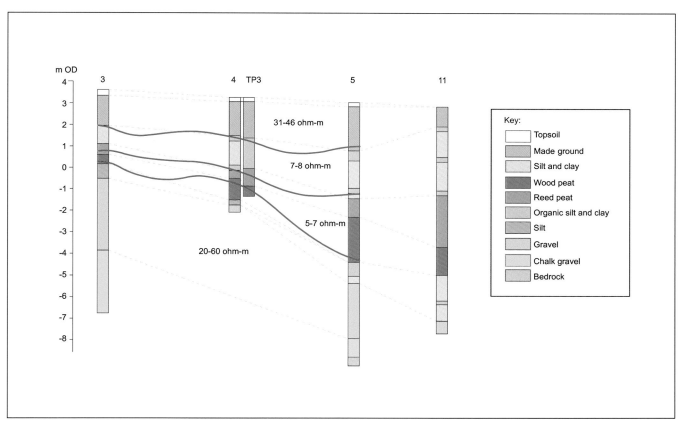

Figure 81   Borehole transect with geophysical profile from the Northfleet Rise evaluation (EBBS97) (Bates and Bates 2000)

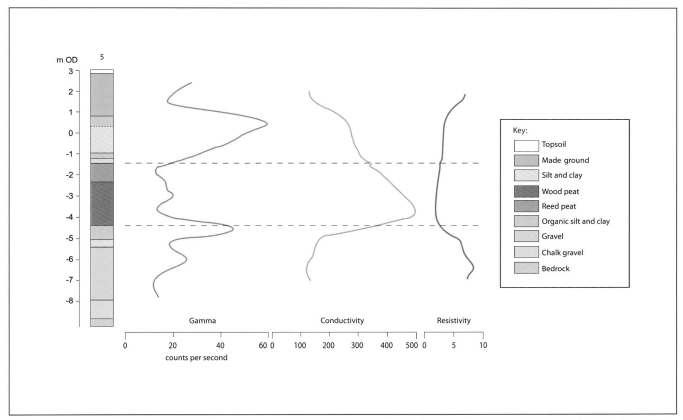

Figure 82   Borehole 5 lithology and gamma, conductivity and resistivity logs from the Northfleet Rise evaluation (EBBS97) (Bates and Bates 2000)

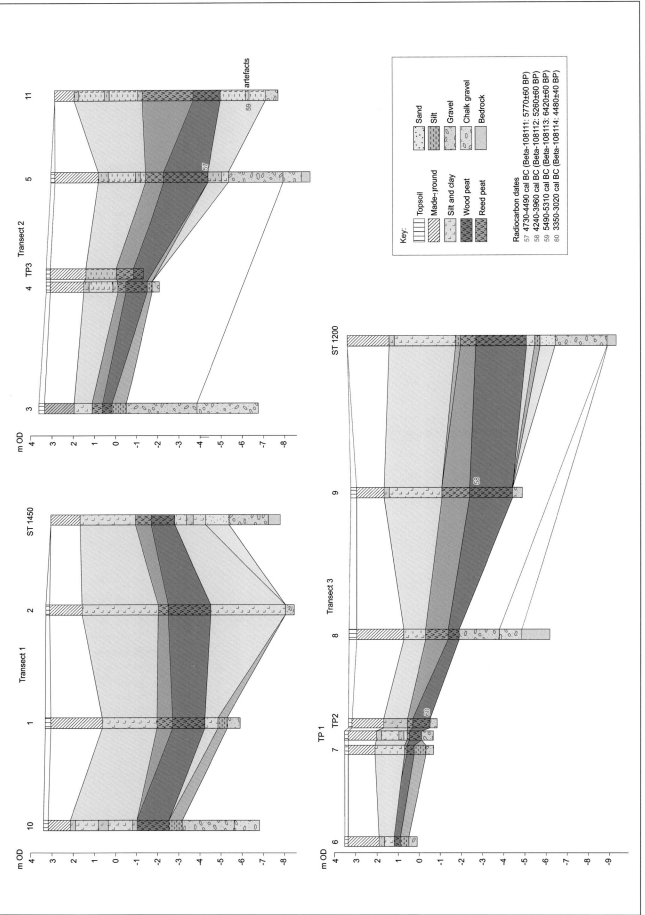

Figure 83 Transects 1–3, from the Northfleet Rise evaluation (EBBS97)

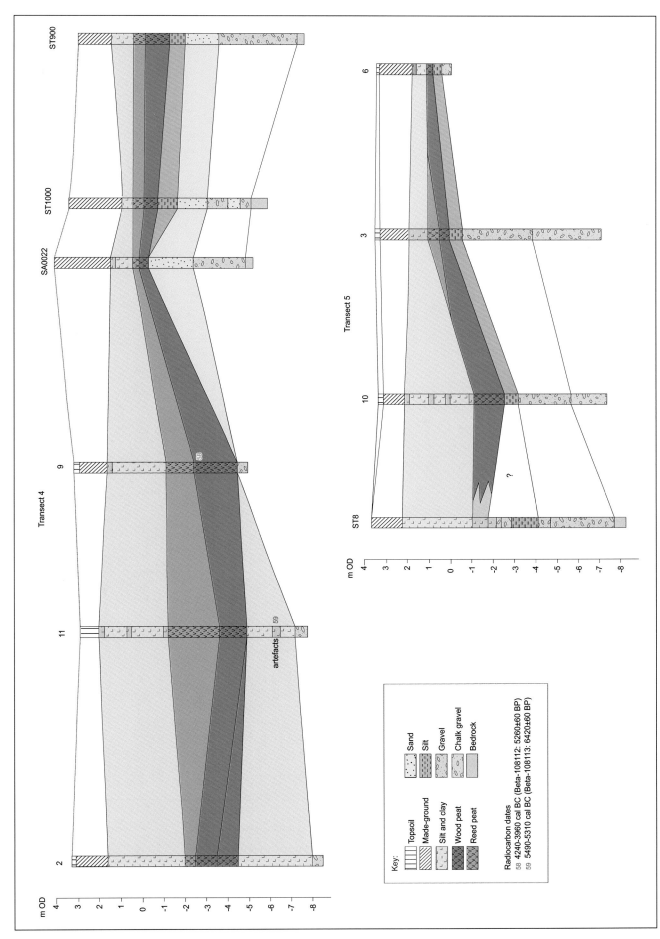

Figure 84 Transects 4–5, from the Northfleet Rise evaluation (EBBS97)

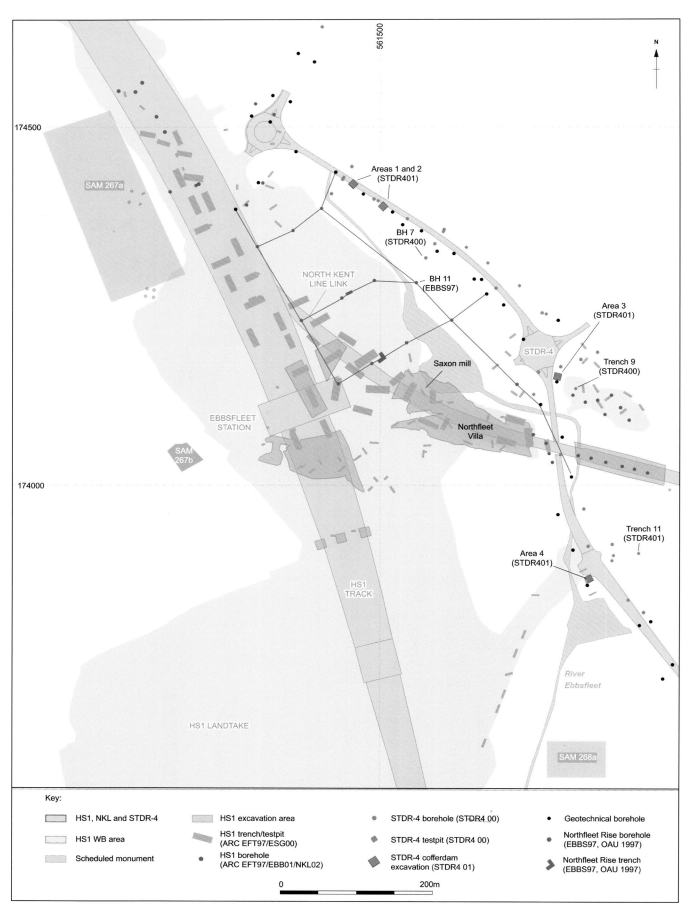

Figure 85 Lower Ebbsleet Valley (excluding Brook Vale) showing distribution of all interventions

Results of the Investigations

In addition to historical boreholes, 27 boreholes, 22 test pits and 113 trenches (including those for the STDR-4) were excavated within the valley floor area during the various evaluation stages (Pl 27). Aside from the large open area excavations for HS1 focused on the Roman site associated with Northfleet villa (Pl 28), a further 17 boreholes and 11 deep trenches were excavated during the mitigation stages. The latter included four cofferdams (Areas 1–4) carried out to mitigate the effects of the STDR-4 (Pl 29). Overall, this amounts to 190 separate interventions (excluding the open area excavations) into the sediments of floodplain and adjacent valley slopes to add to historical borehole records and data from earlier investigations (Fig 85).

The 'off-site' sequences

The results of the numerous phases of investigation (Table 74) have revealed a consistent but complex picture of sediments buried beneath the main Ebbsfleet Valley floor (Table 75). The Holocene alluvial sediments in the Lower Ebbsfleet Valley are underlain by sands, chalky solifluction and fluvial gravel deposits of Pleistocene age, over chalk bedrock in many places. The surface of these deposits formed the Early Holocene topography that dictated patterns of later sediment accumulation. Reconstruction of this surface revealed a deep Outer Basin downstream of Northfleet villa, forming a low lying marshy environment and later a tidally-influenced estuarine inlet (Fig 86). The sequences filling this basin consist of more than 10m of fine-grained sediments. A shallower Inner Basin is located upstream of the villa site. The site of Northfleet villa itself is located on a promontory or 'spur' extending from the western slopes of the valley. This would have remained an area of higher drier ground throughout much of the Holocene. Prior to the investigations associated with HS1 and STDR-4 the only published data on the sedimentary history of the valley infill derived from the limited 1930s excavation undertaken by Burchell (Burchell and Piggott 1939), which included analysis of the pollen from a 'peaty alluvium' containing Neolithic artefacts. Two master palaeoenvironmental sequences have been analysed in detail (Wenban-Smith et al forthcoming). STDR-4 Borehole 7 was located in the Outer Basin approximately 160m north of Northfleet villa (Figs 85 and 87) and STDR-4 Trench 9 in the Inner Basin 60m to the north-west (Figs 85 and 88). Palaeoenvironmental analysis was also been carried out from the sequence in STDR-4 Area 4 cofferdam, 190m to the south-west (Fig 85).

Deposits of Early Holocene age are represented in places by a discontinuous unit of organic sandy silt identified in a number of boreholes and deep trench excavations across the valley bottom. These deposits represent fresh water infilled creeks, radiocarbon dated in Borehole 7 (STDR-4) to 8540–8240 cal BC (NZA-28766, 9122±55 BP). Pollen assemblages (Huckerby et al forthcoming) were dominated by tree and shrub

Plate 27   Evaluation trenching in the Ebbsfleet Valley

Table 75   Main lithological units identified in valley floor area

Unit	Inferred environment of deposition
Made ground	Recent dumping/landfill
Upper peat	Reedswamp
Upper clay-silt	Inter-tidal/estuarine mudflats
Reed peat	Reedswamp
Wood peat	Alder carr wetland
Lower clay-silt	Inter-tidal/estuarine mudflats
Organic silts	Freshwater infilled creeks
Sand	Fluvial channel
Sandy flint gravel	Braided fluvial channel
Chalky gravel	Cold climate slope (solifluction) deposits
Chalk	Bedrock

pollen and suggest rather open scrubby deciduous woodland with Betula (birch), Corylus (hazel) and an understorey of grasses and ferns growing on the banks of the river. More closed deciduous woodland probably grew further away from the site. There is very little evidence of any human impact on the landscape at this time. A few microscopic charcoal particles noted during the pollen analysis may have come from some distance, having been blown or carried into the site by wind or water. Although this could be interpreted as evidence of human activity in the catchment, for example the use of fire to create woodland clearings for grazing (Mellars 1976; Simmons and Innes 1997; Simmons 1996), it could equally be the result of natural events such as forest fires (see Whitehouse and Smith 2004).

Evidence for an early influx of estuarine waters (the 'Lower Clay Silts') during the Late Mesolithic period was found in a number of sequences examined from the Outer Basin. Deposition was dated in Borehole 7 (STDR-4) to between 5480–5070 cal BC (WK-8801, 6340±80 BP) and 4370–4240 cal BC (NZA-28974, 5464±35 BP). Pollen and diatom (Huckerby et al forthcoming; Cameron forthcoming) evidence suggests the local development of saltmarsh and reedswamp environments in the tidally affected Outer Basin. Values

Plate 28 Northfleet villa under excavation (ARC EBB01), Roman quayside in the foreground

Plate 29 Area 4 cofferdam excavation in the Ebbsfleet Valley (STDR4 01)

of microscopic charcoal particles were quite high, including pieces of charred grass, and are evidence for local, possibly man-made, fires in the catchment. In a regional context this early marine transgression into the Lower Ebbsfleet Valley can be broadly correlated with the first phase of estuary expansion on the Thames floodplain (Long *et al* 2000).

Towards the end of the 5th millennium BC minerogenic sedimentation was replaced by peat formation in the Outer Basin, commencing in Borehole 7 (STDR-4) at 4370–4240 cal BC (NZA-28974, 5464±35 BP). Initially, the Inner Basin remained relatively dry land and it is here that significant evidence of human activity, in the form of *in situ* Early Neolithic flint scatters, was identified during the investigations associated with the STDR-4 (Anderson-Whymark forthcoming). These occupation horizons were, however, rapidly inundated as the wetland front expanded into

more marginal areas In Trench 9 (STDR-4) this occurred at 3780–3640 cal BC (NZA-29080, 4926±35 BP) and in Area 4 (STDR-4) at 3800–3650 cal BC (NZA-29247, 4945±35 BP). Pollen, macroscopic plant remains, diatoms and Coleoptera (Wenban-Smith *et al* forthcoming) from the peat indicate that, locally, fresh water alder carr environments predominated in the valley bottom during the Neolithic period, along with marsh/fen and an understorey of ferns and sedges. Fresh water mollusc assemblages included *Bithynia tentaculata*, suggesting that episodes of flooding occurred. Trees and shrubs continued to dominate the pollen assemblages with *Quercus* (oak), *Tilia* (lime), *Ulmus* (elm), *Fraxinus* (ash) and *Corylus* values suggesting that the regional vegetation was deciduous woodland during the period of peat formation. There was, however, some indication of small clearances, possibly for domestic animals on areas of drier ground. A temporary decline in values of *Tilia* pollen noted in the lower part of the peat sequence from Trench 9 (STDR-4), and commensurate with the first appearance of cereal-type pollen, may be related to human activity within the catchment. In a number of sequences, particularly within the more marginal Inner Basin, deposits of micritic tufa, containing rich assemblages of ostracods (Whittaker forthcoming), were noted within the upper part of the peat suggesting the presence locally of freshwater springs. This period of tufa formation, occurring at some point between 3340–2940 cal BC (NZA-28869, 4448±30 BP (date from top of the main peat), and 2470–2140 cal BC (NZA-28971, 3836±50 BP (date from top of the peat with tufa)) in Borehole 7 (STDR-4), Trench 9 (STDR-4) and Area 4 (STDR-4) appears to have been a relatively synchronous event across the valley bottom, occurring between the Early Neolithic and Early Bronze Age periods. Within the wider context, the prehistoric peat in the Lower Ebbsfleet Valley generally occurs at similar elevations, stratigraphic position and date to Devoy's Tilbury III peat on the Thames floodplain (Devoy 1979). The dates are also consistent with Long's proposed phase of mid-Holocene estuary contraction (Long *et al* 2000).

The cessation of tufa formation is probably related to the onset of a further phase of marine incursion into the Lower Valley, which eventually caused the cessation of peat formation and the accumulation a further unit of clay silts (the 'Upper Clay Silts'). Towards the top of the

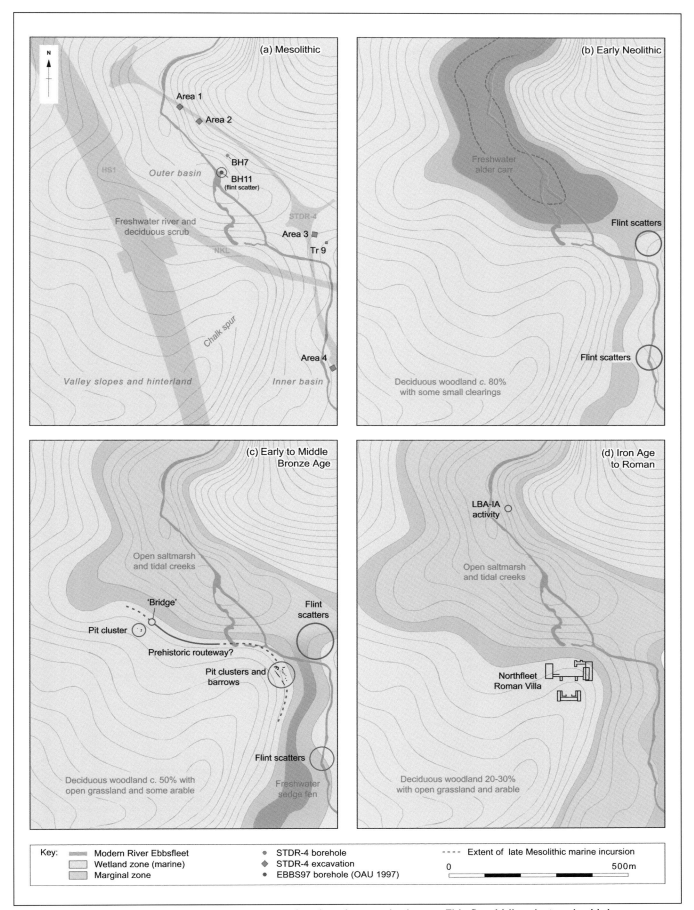

Figure 86 Summary of topography, environment and archaeology in the Lower Ebbsfleet Valley during the Holocene

Thames Holocene

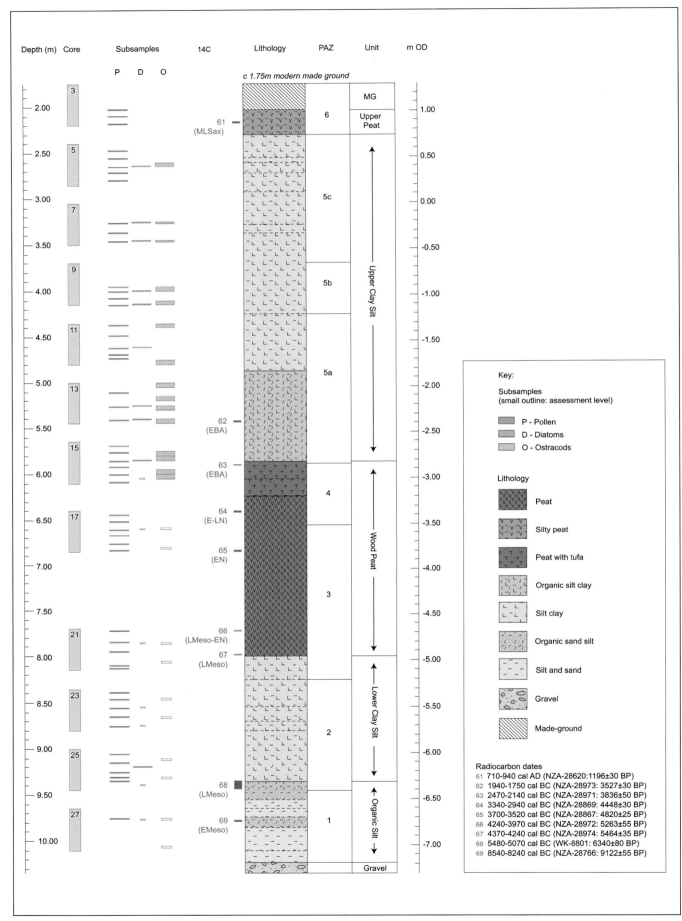

Figure 87 Lithological log and sample locations from Borehole 7 (STDR4 00)

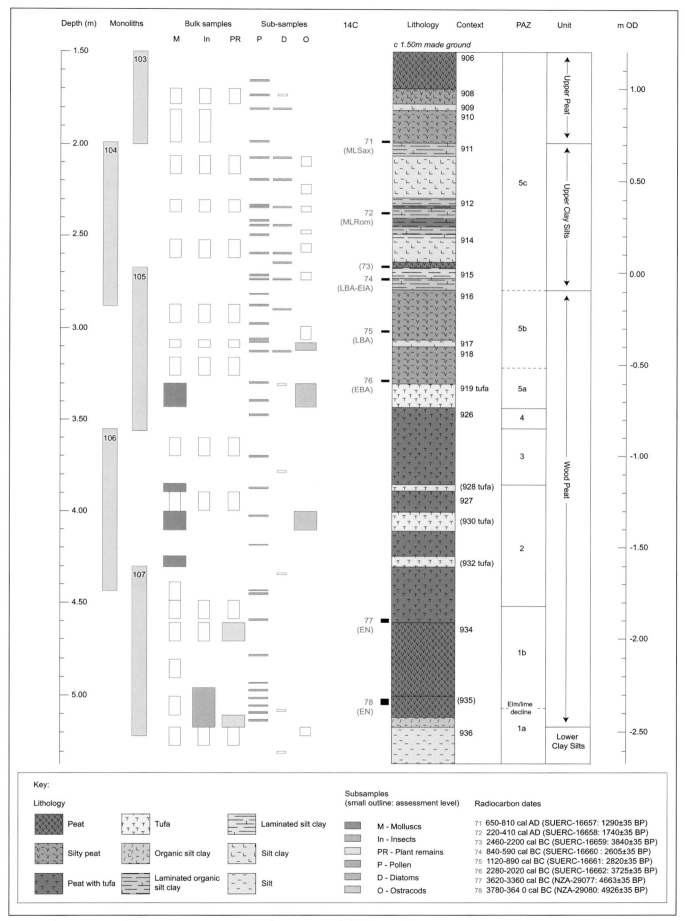

Figure 88 Lithological log and sample locations from Trench 9 (STDR4 00)

peat profile, there is evidence locally for an increase in marsh/sedge fen environments with abundant ferns, indicating increased wetness in the valley bottom. The change to minerogenic sedimentation is dated in Borehole 7 (STDR-4) in the Outer Basin to the Early Bronze Age between 2470–2140 cal BC (NZA-28971, 3836±50 BP) and 1940–1750 cal BC (NZA-28973, 3527±30 BP), although the earlier date may represent an eroded peat surface. In the Inner Basin in Trench 9 the change is dated to the Late Bronze Age or Early Iron Age at 840–590 cal BC (SUERC-16660, 2605±35 BP), discounting the anomalous early date immediately above which is possibly a result of contamination by old carbon (SUERC-16659). However, in this trench the upper part of the peat became increasingly silty from 2280–2020 cal BC (SUERC-16662, 3725±35 BP). The microfossil analysis indicates the presence of a tidal river with mudflats and fringing saltmarsh, fen and reedswamp environments associated with the upper minerogenic units. This phase of marine transgression into the Ebbsfleet Valley in the later prehistoric and historic periods is mirrored at many sites previously investigated up and down the Lower Thames Estuary. It can be broadly correlated with the second phase of estuary expansion on the Thames floodplain (Long *et al* 2000). The regional pollen assemblages suggest that the environment beyond the valley bottom was much more open during the later prehistoric period. Woodland cover decreased significantly at the beginning of the Bronze Age and may be related to human activity in the catchment. The landscape is likely to have comprised open grassland with arable cultivation and some stands of oak and hazel woodland.

Accumulation of the 'Upper Clay Silts', both in the Inner and Outer Basins in the Lower Ebbsfleet Valley, continued throughout the later prehistoric and into the historic period. An organic lens in Trench 9 (STDR-4), at +0.33m OD, produced a mid–late Roman date of cal AD 220–410 (SUERC-16658, 1740±35 BP). Locally the pollen, diatoms, ostracods and foraminifera suggest that environments of middle and upper saltmarsh had developed by this period. This is supported by the recovery of Chenopodiaceae (goosefoots), *Plantago maritima* (sea plantain) and occasional grains of *Armeria/Limonium* (thrift/sea lavender). Away from the valley bottom the landscape, as in the later prehistoric period, probably comprised open grassland pasture with arable cultivation and some stands of *Quercus* and *Corylus* woodland. However, woodland cover continued to decrease from the Early Bronze Age. By the late Roman period arboreal pollen values were 20–30%, as recorded in the sequence from Trench 9 (STDR-4).

Towards the top of the 'Upper Clay Silt' unit there is evidence in both the Borehole 7 (STDR-4) and Trench 9 (STDR-4) sequences that saltmarsh was gradually replaced by fresh water reedswamp, with some areas of open water. The 'Upper Clay Silts' are generally overlain in the valley bottom by a laterally extensive fresh water peat unit (the 'Upper Peat'), suggesting a further

episode of negative sea-level tendency. Radiocarbon determinations suggest peat accumulation during the middle or late Saxon period. This unit was dated in Borehole 7 (STDR-4), at +0.88 m OD, to cal AD 710–940 (NZA-28620, 1196±30 BP), and in Trench 9 (STDR-4) at +0.72m OD, cal AD 650–810 (SUERC-16657, 1290±35 BP). There is no evidence for further marine incursion in these sequences following the Saxon period. However, it is possible the upper parts of the sequence at these locations have been truncated by modern disturbance. The 'Upper Peat' in both Borehole 7 (STDR-4) and Trench 9 (STDR-4) was sealed by varying thicknesses of modern made ground. Pollen evidence from the 'Upper Peat' suggests locally fresh water marsh and sedge fen environments. The pollen data suggest that some woodland was extant in the area (AP <10%), but that the landscape was largely cleared; pollen evidence suggests pasture and particularly arable fields increases in the Saxon period.

The 'on-site' historical sequences

Useful information on the local environment in vicinity of Northfleet villa (ARC EBB01) during the Roman period has also been gained from the analysis of waterlogged well deposits located on the higher ground of the gravel 'spur' during the HS1 investigations (Stevens 2011a, 84–7). The plant assemblages included species associated with wasteland and human occupation; such as *Urtica dioica* (nettle) and *Conium maculatum* (hemlock). There was also some indication of areas of rough, perhaps wet, grassland with, for example, *Ranunculus* (buttercup), *Rumex conglomeratus* (clustered dock) and *Stellaria palustris* (marsh stitchwort). Taxa such as *Ranunculus sardous* (hairy-buttercup), *Chenopodium vulvaria* (stinking goosefoot), *Atriplex littoralis* (grass-leaved orache) and *Atriplex prostrate/portulacoides* (spear-leaved orache/sea purslane), while common on cultivated ground and grassland, are more frequently found in coastal areas. More significant were frequent finds of *Juncus gerardii* (saltmarsh rush). Coleoptera included *Geotrupes*, *Onthophagus* and *Aphodius* dung beetle, suggesting the presence of grazing herbivores and pasture. Several ground beetles identified, such as *Dyschirus salinus*, *Bembidion normannum* and *B. minimum*, and the water beetle, *Octhebius dilatus*, are all associated with muddy areas or saline pools in saltmarshes or along the coast (D Smith 2011, 88–90).

A wide range of taxa is represented in the charcoal assemblages at Northfleet (Barnett 2011, 113–8) and exploitation of a rich variety of open woodland and scrub wood for domestic/everyday fuel use is indicated by the mid-Roman period. There was, however, some indication of a shift in the exploitation of woodland resources during the late Roman period, with perhaps a greater local reliance on trees typical of scrub or hedges, such as hawthorn and/or non-wood fuels such as malting waste (spelt chaff and sprouts).

Evidence of cereal cultivation was well represented. Cereal-type pollen in the basal fills of the wells was quite high (up to 26% TLP, Scaife 2011a, 68–76) and Coleoptera also included taxa associated with stored cereal grain (D Smith 2011, 88–90). In the charred plant assemblages across the villa site the majority of the weed/wild taxa typically comprised weeds of arable crops or cultivated/disturbed ground. The four most consistently recovered taxa were dock, scentless mayweed, rye-grass and wild or cultivated oat. The dominance of spelt remains suggests that the weed flora recovered is directly associated with cultivation conditions for this cereal crop (W Smith 2011, 105–113).

Data from the post-Roman period is largely derived from minerogenic alluvial deposits associated with a Saxon tidal mill which was located in the low-lying area immediately north of villa site during the HS1 investigations (ARC EBB01). Information on changes in salinity levels within the deposits derive from analysis of ostracods, foraminifera (Whittaker 2011, 80–85) and diatoms (Cameron 2011, 75–80) from sequences infilling the mill wheelhouse and millpond. The assemblages were relatively diverse and despite the homogeneous appearance of the lithostratigraphy in places, show some variation through the profiles. Initially the evidence suggests the presence of a tidal creek and mudflats with the occurrence of brackish ostracod species such as *Leptocythere porcellanea*, also common in the Borehole 7, and the abundance of marine plankton. Over time the mudflats, exposed at low tide, appear to have become vegetated by encroaching saltmarsh and experienced increased silting. The agglutinating foraminifera in particular, which build their shells (tests) from grains of sediment, are an important ecological marker species for low, mid- and high saltmarsh. All three recorded in the sequences (*Jadammina macrescens*, *Haplophragmoides* sp. and *Tiphotrocha comprimata*) are herbivores and detrivores living both on the surface (epifaunal) and in the substrate of the water body (infaunal) and are widespread on mid- to high saltmarsh. The diatom samples were initially dominated by brackish water epipelic species that live in or attached to sediments in the water (*Nitzschia navicularis, Diploneis didyma*) and planktonic marine-brackish species (*Cyclotella striata*). This evidence suggests the site of the mill was clearly tidal for at least medium and high water spring tides. Higher up the sedimentary profiles the diatom assemblages indicate a period where freshwater input increased. This is seen by an increase in the number of fresh water diatom species and a decline in brackish and marine species, associated with slightly darker, more humic, laminations within the clay silts. In the mill wheelhouse deposits of organic and peaty detritus accumulating within and adjacent to the penstocks were initially dominated by brackish water aerophile diatoms (air-loving). The overlying, more minerogenic deposits, however, contained high numbers of freshwater diatoms and, in particular, opportunistic early colonisers such as *Fragilaria* spp. with wide salinity tolerance (but with optimal growth in freshwaters). These non-planktonic, shallow water, freshwater diatoms included *Fragilaria brevistriata* and *Fragilaria pinnata*, often associated with less stable conditions and rapidly changing environments.

Broadly the deposits indicate increased freshwater influence occurred at similar elevations to the 'Upper Peat' in Borehole 7 (STDR-4) and Trench 9 (STDR-4) and may be related to a general period of marine regression dated to the mid–late Saxon period (see above). The evidence for a regression in the Ebbsfleet Valley contrasts somewhat with the evidence presented for changing river levels on the Thames floodplain at this time. In the Outer Thames Estuary, Greensmith and Tucker (1973) present evidence of sea transgression between AD 800 and 1000. In Central and East London the River Thames appears to rise in the post-Roman and medieval periods (Sidell *et al* 2000, 17), although a brief period of regression has been suggested between the mid-10th and late 12th centuries at Thames Court in Central London (*ibid*, 17). The regression in the Ebbsfleet Valley may well be related to very local factors and as such may not be entirely comparable to the sequences from the Thames floodplain. As previously stated, the Ebbsfleet Valley has in the past acted rather like a sump. In the absence of a major fluvial system, accretionary processes have tended to dominate. It is possible that accumulation of the 'Upper Clay Silts' reached a point where the valley was simply choked with sediment, inhibiting the flow of tidal waters into the upper reaches. The pollen profiles provide evidence for a reduction in woodland cover and an increase in arable activity during this period that may have resulted in a significant increase in the amount of colluviation and sediment run-off into the channel system. Human interference related to the building of sea-walls and land reclamation cannot be entirely ruled out as a mechanism for environmental change during the mid–late Saxon period, although on social and economic grounds it is thought unlikely and there is no direct archaeological evidence for this. Furthermore, evidence from the onsite sequences at Northfleet show a further phase in marine incursion after the period of peat/organic silt formation. The upper part of the alluvial sequence in the millpond and wheelhouse was not dated but it is likely deposition occurred sometime during the medieval period and may be related to the period of increased storminess and flooding that affected the whole of the eastern seaboard *c* AD 1250–1450 (Galloway and Potts 2007). This event was not apparent in many of the sequences examined during both the evaluation and excavation stages in the valley bottom and deposition may have been very localised and restricted to former creek systems in the Outer Basin.

Historical records suggest marshland in the Thames Estuary and North Kent was being embanked and drained immediately after the Norman Conquest and it is possible that sea banks downstream of Gravesend, at Sittingbourne and on the Cliffe Marshes, date to this period (Spurrell 1885b; Whitney 1989, 33; Hallam 1981, 76). Historical records suggest, however, that by the late 13th century the River Ebbsfleet had silted up sufficiently to allow a bridge or causeway to be built close to its confluence with the Thames at Stonebridge (see above). This enabled a direct route for passengers disembarking from the Long Ferry at Gravesend to rejoin Watling Street at Brent, Dartford (Hiscook 1968, 255). Mention in historical records of flood protection measures in place in the Ebbsfleet Valley dates to the post-medieval period when the low-lying marshes close to the confluence of the Rivers Ebbsfleet and Thames frequently flooded at high tides. The embanked London Road which dissects the valley east–west close to Robins' Creek, and probably followed the line of the earlier causeway, provided protection for a large part of the valley bottom marshland. Sluice gates on the bridge at the junction of London Road and Stonebridge Road controlled the flow of both tidal water from the Thames and fresh water from the River Ebbsfleet (Parishes: Northfleet, 302–18).

The on-site pollen data (Scaife 2011b, 66–69) providing information on the vegetation for the Saxon and medieval periods are again largely based on a sequence through the fills of the mill wheelhouse (ARC EBB01). This is supported by data from waterlogged plant remains and insects from a range of alluvial deposits associated with the mill. Overall the environmental evidence suggests that a relatively open landscape prevailed in the vicinity during the mid–late Saxon and medieval periods. The range of tree taxa was diverse, however, total tree pollen numbers were generally small with the lowest values at <10%. *Quercus* was the most important tree. *Alnus* was also significant but is a high local pollen producer and the values obtained do not reflect any substantial local growth. There were also occasional occurrences of *Betula*, *Pinus* and *Ulmus* that probably derived from the region as a whole. *Tilia*, *Fraxinus*, *Fagus* (beech) and *Salix* (willow) were not generally well represented and may be of more local origin. *Corylus* was the dominant shrub probably growing locally. Poaceae were the dominant pollen taxa in all samples examined from the wheelhouse. This pollen may derive from various habitats from arable, pastoral and local fen. *Plantago lanceolata* (ribwort plantain) and a range of other taxa; *Ranunculus*, *Medicago* sp. (medicks), *Vicia* sp. (vetches), *Rumex* sp. and Asteraceae-types (aster), are strongly indicative of important areas of local grassland. As seen in the Roman period, the waterlogged plant remains provide evidence for rough grassland, which was possibly grazed, with some patches of barer wasteland (Stevens *et al* 2011b, 85–89). The samples provided less evidence for disturbed soils than seen in the Roman period, and it might be assumed that the level of activity associated with settlement, for example middens and trampling by animals, was lower in the Saxon and later periods. Grazing is most clearly suggested by the presence of a limited number of *Onthophagus* and *Aphodius* 'dung beetles' which are associated with animal dung, often lying in open pasture (D Smith 2011b, 89–91). Marshland, with brackish water and saltmarsh, is well

presented in the environmental assemblages. Reedswamp taxa included Cyperaceae (sedges), *T. latifolia* (reedmace) and *Sparganium* (bur-reed). Evidence of standing water comes from seeds of *Potamogeton* sp. (pondweed), *Callitriche palustris* (water starwort) and *Lemna* sp. (duckweed).

Summary of Archaeological Evidence

As stated above, prior to the investigations associated with HS1 and STDR-4, the Ebbsfleet Valley was known to contain important prehistoric archaeology dating to the Mesolithic and Neolithic periods. The results of the HS1 and STDR-4 investigations have added significantly to the archaeological record for these periods. However, they have also provided evidence dating to the Bronze Age and Iron Age, suggesting activity in the valley over much of the prehistoric period. The following sections provide a summary of the archaeological evidence, presented in detail elsewhere (eg, Andrews *et al* 2011a; Wenban-Smith *et al* forthcoming).

Early Post-glacial and Mesolithic
Evidence recovered during the HS1 investigations attests to groups visiting the Ebbsfleet Valley from the very earliest part of the Holocene and is an important addition to that recovered from earlier investigations in the valley. Unfortunately the absence of *in situ* land surfaces or faunal assemblages associated with the more significant assemblages has precluded detailed interpretation. An assemblage of 176 Early post-glacial worked flints (Anderson-Whymark forthcoming) recovered from the Springhead excavations (ARC SPH00; Fig 89) largely represents residual material within Early and Middle Bronze Age contexts, although mostly from a single colluvial sequence.

Catalogue of illustrated flint
(Fig 89)
1. Long blade bipolar core with refitting blade (ARC SPH00, 5876)
2. Long blade, 152mm long, with two areas of bruising (ARC SPH00, 5875)
3. Bruised flake with a con-joining fragment, broken by burning (ARC SPH00, 6553)
4. Bruised flake (ARC SPH00, 5899)
5. Blade with basal retouch which removes bulb (ARC SPH00, 6553)
6. Obliquely retouched flake, burnt and broken (ARC SPH00, 6553)

The flint was in a relatively fresh condition and a number of refitting pieces indicate it had not moved far from the original place of deposition. Diagnostic elements included bruised flakes and blades, and a long blade core. The deposits also contained a quantity of debitage, apparently contemporary with the diagnostic elements. The flint fulfils the criteria established by

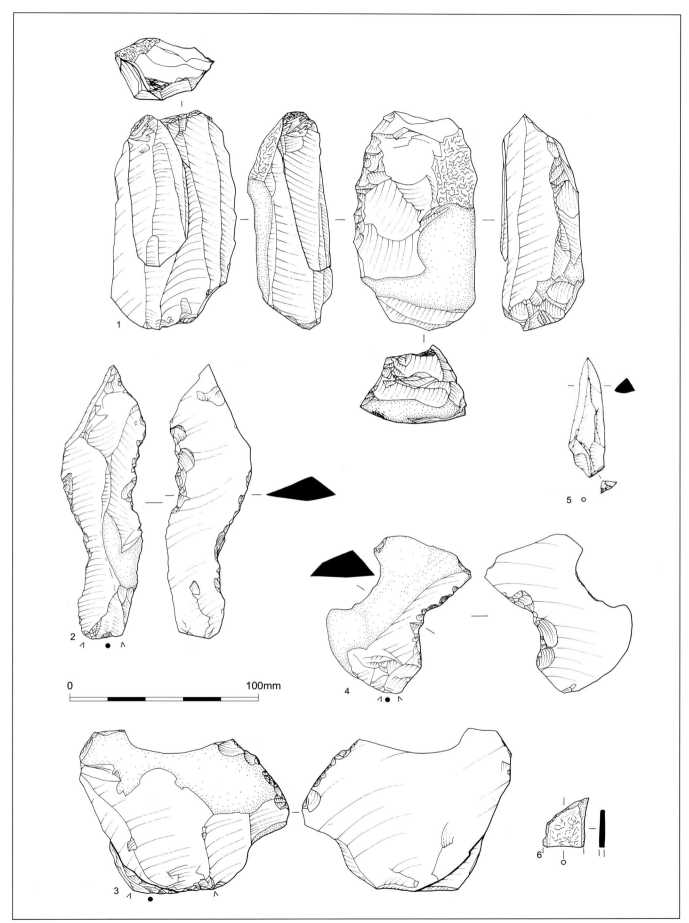

Figure 89 Early post-glacial worked flint from Springhead

Barton (1998) for a long blade assemblage. A number of long blade find spots have been identified along the Thames corridor including Burchell's excavations in the Ebbsfleet Valley (Burchell 1938) where a 'Mesolithic floor' sealed within alluvium produced blades considered by Barton to represent a long blade industry. Associated dating of technologically similar assemblages, for example at Three Ways Wharf, Uxbridge (Lewis 1991; Lewis and Rackham 2011) and Avington VI (Barton *et al* 1998), suggest long blade industries date from the very end of the Late Glacial period but also the beginning of the Post-glacial (*c* 10,000 BC). The function of long blade sites is subject to some debate, but it has been argued that they represent short term sites associated with the processing and butchery of large herbivores, such as red deer and horse (Barton 1995, 64).

Very little direct evidence for human occupation was recovered immediately following this activity and, again, consisted almost entirely of occasional worked flint as residual finds in later archaeological features and layers. The majority of diagnostic flint artefacts, and several blades and flakes, can be broadly attributed to the Mesolithic period on the basis of technological attributes and reflects a general background scatter of activity during this period. A coherent assemblage of 755 flints was, however, recovered from the lower portion of the colluvial sequence containing the redeposited Early post-glacial flintwork at Springhead (Anderson-Whymark forthcoming). These contexts contained debitage resulting from blade production, including several refitting flakes, but the only diagnostic artefacts were a burin and a distal micro-burin. The assemblage reflects the exploitation of local deposits for flint nodules and their primary preparation as blade cores. It is likely these cores were removed for further working, and presumably tool production and use elsewhere. Dating of this assemblage from the colluvial deposits is problematic due to the absence of diagnostic artefacts. The use of the micro-burin technique suggests a Mesolithic date; a date also appropriate for the burin. The presence of a large crested blade, measuring 96mm long, suggests the production of relatively substantial blades characteristic of the earlier Mesolithic.

A small assemblage (26 pieces) of Late Mesolithic worked flint; consisting of reasonably fresh flakes, chips and burnt fragments, was retrieved from an organic silt sampled in a Borehole 11 on the floodplain of the Lower Valley at a depth of 9.1–9.0m (BH11 EBBS97, Oxford Archaeological Unit 1997). Radiocarbon dating of the organic sediment produced a date of 5480–5310 cal BC (Beta-108113, 6420±50 BP). In addition two complete Late Mesolithic microliths (Fig 90A, 1–2) and a third broken example were recovered from the interface of the minerogenic alluvial silt and the main overlying peat body in a 10 x 10m cofferdam excavation for STDR-4 (Area 4, STDR401). A radiocarbon date of 4350–4070 cal BC (NZA-29246, 5405±35 BP, Oxford Archaeological Unit 1997) was obtained on a charred hazelnut shell from the context in which one of the

microliths was recovered, and may date the Mesolithic activity. However, the microliths and hazelnut shell occurred with flint of Early Neolithic character on the same extant land surface (see below).

Catalogue of illustrated flint
(Fig 90A)
1. Late Mesolithic microlith comparable to Jacobi's type 5 (1978) (4044, STDR401)
2. Late Mesolithic rod-like backed bladelet comparable to Jacobi's type 5 (1978) (4054, sf 2018, STDR401)
3. Early Neolithic leaf-shaped arrowhead (300042, SF 340000, ARC EBB01)
4. Early or Middle Neolithic chisel arrowhead (11071, SF 15283, ARC SHN02)
5. Early or Middle Neolithic chisel arrowhead (11207, ARC SHN02)
6. Late Neolithic/Early Bronze Age barbed and tanged arrowhead, Sutton type B (11739, SF 15275, ARC SHN02)
7. Late Neolithic/Early Bronze Age roughout of barbed and tanged arrowhead (16238, ARC EBB01)
8. Late Neolithic/Early Bronze Age piercer (5875, ARC SPH00)
9. Late Neolithic/Early Bronze Age knife (16794, ARC SHN02)
10. Late Neolithic/Early Bronze Age knife (16967, ARC SHN02)
11. Late Neolithic/Early Bronze Age Levallois-style discoidal core (5643, ARC SPH00)
12. Bronze Age? crude pick or chisel-like implement (3797008, ARC ESG00)
13. Middle Bronze Age end scraper (5774, ARC SPH00)
14. Middle Bronze Age denticulated end and side scraper (5774, ARC SPH00)
15. Middle Bronze Age waisted tool (5775, ARC SPH00)
16. Middle Bronze Age waisted tool (2910, ARC SPH00)

Neolithic and Early Bronze Age
During the Neolithic and Bronze Age periods, from about 4000 BC, the valley appears to have held special focus for local communities. There was little evidence for areas of extensive settlement during this period, farming, or indeed the monument building such as that which occurred in the Medway Valley. The type of activity in the Ebbsfleet Valley is of quite different character. Water and watery places play a central role during the later prehistoric period, and the springs themselves, at the head of the valley, appear to have been held with some reverence well before the establishment of the Roman temple complex and town of *Vagniacae*.

The investigations in the earlier part of the 20th century identified a series of Neolithic sites (scatters of pottery and worked flint) stratified within the floodplain deposits where a distinctive style of pottery was first identified; decorated with incised patterns, fingernail and, vertical cord impressions (Burchell and Piggott 1939). The sites are now designated Scheduled Ancient Monuments (SAMs Kent 268A and 268B) and the valley provide the type-site for Ebbsfleet Ware pottery.

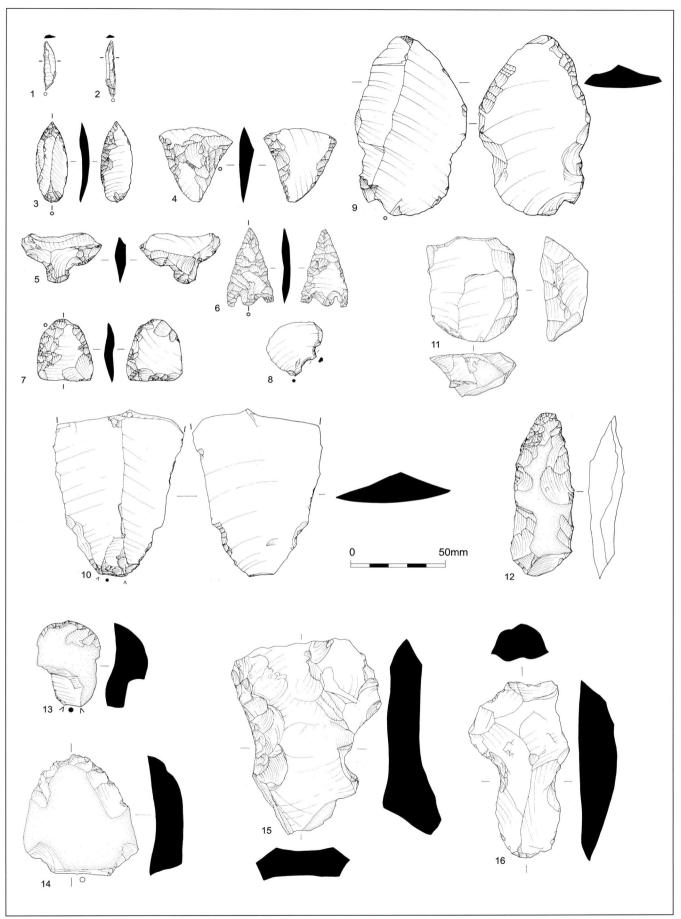

Figure 90A Neolithic and Bronze Age worked flint recovered from the Ebbsfleet Valley for HS1 and STDR4

Plate 30 Reconstruction of the Ebbsfleet Ware bowl from Trench 9 in the Ebbsfleet Valley (STDR4 00)

Along the line of HS1 and STDR-4 further evidence of activity was recovered which included scatters of burnt and worked flint (Fig 90A), butchered animal remains and pottery fragments.

The finds included part of an Ebbsfleet Ware bowl recovered from the lower part of the main peat unit in the valley bottom during the STDR-4 evaluation (Trench 11, STDR400, Pl 30). The bowl consisted of over 50 fragments, although less than a quarter of the original vessel survived, with simple decoration of closely spaced finger-tip impressed neck pits and a continuous finger-tip impressed row on the rim (Barclay forthcoming). Traces of black residue on the rim and neck could be from cooking and the lower part of the vessel also has signs of heat damage, probably from use as a cooking pot. Two further Ebbsfleet Ware vessels were also recovered from the same context, represented by single body sherds, one of which also preserved a thin deposit of charred residue on the interior surface. Two radiocarbon measurements were obtained from samples of charred residue that adhered to the interior surfaces of two of the vessels. A sample from the bowl was dated to 3640–3370 cal BC (NZA-29079, 4723±35 BP) and one of the plain body sherds to 3370–3100 cal BC (NZA-29155, 4547±35 BP). The date on the bowl is as expected and approximates well to the suggested range of 3500/3550–3350/3300 cal BC for this style of pottery (Barclay 2007, 343 and table 15.1; Barclay 2002, 90; Cotton 2004, 133; Gibson and Kinnes 1997). The second vessel date is later than expected for this style of pottery, perhaps suggesting that the vessels were not contemporaneous.

Two additional radiocarbon dates from hazelnut shell and roundwood fragments from the peat around the Ebbsfleet Ware bowl provided similar dates (WK-8799 and WK-8800). Found within the same context as the

pottery were two fish bones identified as *Gadus* sp. (cod), although it is impossible to determine whether the fish had been cooked (R Nicholson, pers comm). The recovery of the bones from fresh water peat deposits is intriguing and clearly indicates that the fish was brought to the site from a distance. Cod is often associated with deep-sea fishing, although it can also be caught closer to land. Although usually caught using hook and line, on Danish Mesolithic sites it has been suggested the fish may have been caught in stationary traps (Enghoff 1995).

In situ scatters of Early Neolithic worked flint along with a small assemblage of animal bones showing signs of butchery were found at a number of locations, particularly along the margins of the Inner Basin concentrated towards the base of the main peat unit (Anderson-Whymark forthcoming; Strid forthcoming). The largest assemblages were recovered from 10 x 10m cofferdam excavations associated with the STDR-4 (Areas 3 and 4, STDR401). Detailed analysis of the worked flint assemblage from Area 4 (1606 items, Fig 90B) suggests episodes of knapping utilised the locally abundant flint and the range of activities included working of unseasoned woods, fibrous plants or dry hide. The fact that many of the flints recovered had been burnt and were found in association with unworked burnt flint suggests that the activities involved the use of fire, although no clear hearth features of areas of burning were identified. The small faunal assemblage included the usual range of domesticated species: pig, sheep/goat and cattle, with cattle the most frequently identified. Due to its larger size, cattle are likely to have been the main meat provider of the three species. While not all skeletal elements were represented in the assemblage, bones from meat-rich body parts as well as meat-poor body parts were present, suggesting these species were

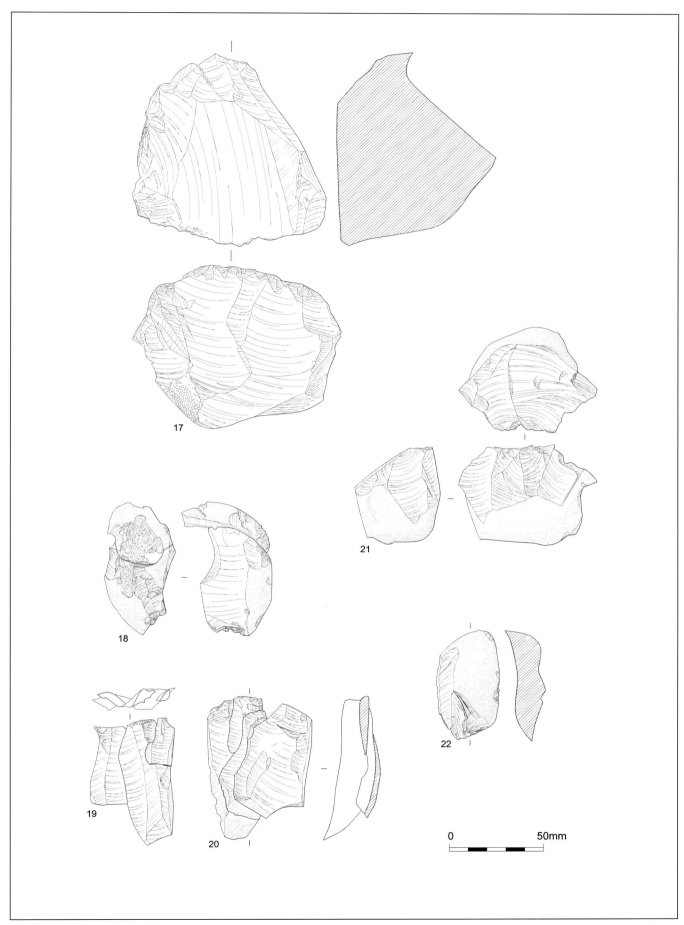

Figure 90B Early Neolithic flint from Area 4 (STDR4 01)

Plate 31   Late Neolithic log and pole trackway from Area 4 in the Ebbsfleet Valley (STDR4 00)

butchered in the vicinity. Butchery marks found on bones from cattle and sheep/goat derive from filleting and/or disarticulation. The faunal assemblage included a number of wild species such as auroch, red and roe deer whose meat would have complemented the diet.

Catalogue of illustrated flint
(Fig 90B)

17. Multi-platform flake core (4044, SF 1994, STDR401)
18. Refit between a hammerstone reworked as a flake core and flake (4042/4044, STDR401)
19. Refit between three utilised flakes (4045/4043, SF 1347/1519/1528, STDR401)
20. Refit between four flakes (4043/4044, SF1537/1872/1747/1538, STDR401)
21. Single platform flake core (4044, SF 1755, STDR401)
22. End and side scraper (4043, SF 1984, STDR401)

The evidence recovered from the Ebbsfleet Valley during the HS1 and STDR-4 works provides little direct evidence for the cultivation of cereals during this period. No charred cereal assemblages were recovered and the pollen evidence indicates only limited opening of the woodland on the Lower Valley slopes or further upstream at Springhead until the beginning of the

Bronze Age. As previously noted, the pollen evidence indicated that during the Early Neolithic the area would have been predominantly wooded, although more open clearings probably existed within this woodland and it is likely that these areas were used for grazing domesticates. The insect assemblages from the basal (Early Neolithic) part of the peat sequence in both Area 4 and Trench 9 (STDR-4) contained a small component dependent upon grassland habitats, probably located on the well-drained soil of the valley side rather than in the valley bottom. Also present in abundance were scarabaeoid dung beetles which feed on the droppings of larger herbivorous mammals and it is likely that the grazing extended from the grassland into partly wooded areas (Robinson forthcoming).

Concentrations of large oak timbers at the base of the peat in an STDR-4 evaluation trench (Trench 9, STDR400) dated to 3780–3640 cal BC (NZA-29080, 4926±35 BP), may represent the remains of some form of Early Neolithic trackway, although no evidence of working was identified in the small area exposed and the evidence remains equivocal (Wenban-Smith *et al* forthcoming). It is, however, noteworthy a concentration of large timbers was also interpreted as a possible trackway at the base of the peat at Burchell's original site to the south-west of Area 4 (SAM 268A, Sieveking 1960); radiocarbon dated to 3750–2900 cal BC (BM-113, 4660±150 BP). More convincing, perhaps, was a section of a Late Neolithic log and pole trackway recorded in the STDR-4 Area 4 cofferdam excavation (Pl 31). The structure was identified within the upper part of the main peat unit sealing the Early Neolithic activity and comprised a NW–SE linear arrangement with clearly defined edges, 1.1–1.2m wide, with the log and pole elements laid along the long axis of the structure. The material used was quite varied and included cleft and charred log sections and identified species included oak, alder and hazel (Wenban-Smith *et al* forthcoming). The edges of several lifted items, examined by Damian Goodburn, bore traces of weathered axe trimming but no clear cut ends were lifted. A piece of alder roundwood from the structure was radiocarbon dated to 2870–2570 cal BC (SUERC-19950, 4120±30 BP).

A number of timber trackway structures have been identified within the Lower Thames floodplain area in recent years; although the majority appear to date to the later Bronze Age period (for recent reviews see Stafford *et al* 2012; Waller and Grant 2012, fig 7). An example recently excavated from the base of a peat deposit at Belmarsh on the Plumstead Marshes contained two possible timber structures, with the earliest dated to *c* 3960–3710 cal BC (WK-25955, 5039±30 BP; and WK-25954, 5023±44 BP; Hart 2010), constructed of tangentially split timber planks alder and hazel laid side by side. A later Neolithic structure at Fort Street, Silvertown, provided a single date of 3030–2700 cal BC (GU-4409, 4280±50 BP), also utilised timber planks with vertical anchoring posts (Crockett *et al* 2002). However, a second date of 2280–1940 cal BC (GU-

4408, 3700±50 BP) on an alder retaining post associated with this trackway may cast some doubt over its true age. Parallels for the log and pole trackway from Area 4 include two structures along the A13 East London at Woolwich Manor Way (Stafford *et al* 2012) and at the Beckton Golf Driving Range (Carew *et al* 2009), although both of these structures were dated to the Early–Middle Bronze Age.

Distributed along the banks of the Ebbsfleet, from Springhead to the valley bottom, a series of features were identified during the HS1 investigations, variously comprising small spreads of burnt flint and pits also containing large quantities of burnt flint (Wenban-Smith *et al* forthcoming). Radiocarbon dating of associated charcoal fragments mostly produced Early Bronze Age dates. Where the HS1 line crosses the current Ebbsfleet Stream, in the middle

Plate 32 'Sauna' feature from the Ebbsfleet River Crossing near Springhead (ARC ERC01)

reaches of the valley, groups of burnt flint filled pits sealed beneath colluvium were found associated with a structure (ARC ERC01). The structure comprised a shallow kidney-shaped pit flanked by two curvilinear slots, each of which contained three substantial post-holes (Pl 32). A shallow gully led from the front of the pit towards the former edge of the river channel. The fill of the pit comprised a dark grey silty clay with frequent burnt flint and charcoal and a sample of *Prunus* sp. roundwood charcoal was radiocarbon dated to the Early Bronze Age, 1760–1530 cal BC (NZA-28445, 3379±35 BP).

Concentrations of burnt flint are a feature of prehistoric settlement sites and provide evidence for the use of heated stones for various activities such as cooking (Lambrick 2009, 179–80). However, some sites produce much larger quantities of burnt flint and include the much debated class of monuments commonly referred to as 'burnt mounds'. Burnt mounds are more generally dated to the Middle to Late Bronze Age and remains of this date were found associated with the Bronze Age barrows during the HS1 works at Springhead (see below). They are often found adjacent to water courses and in the classic form appear as a crescent-like or circular mound of burnt stone often associated with a central trough, probably used to boil water with heated stones (Raymond 1987; O'Neill 2009). Activities that have been suggested for these features include cooking, perhaps large pieces of meat for communal gatherings (O' Kelly 1954; Barber 1990), the processing of fleeces (Jeffery 1991), salt production (Barfield 1991) or the creation of large amounts of steam for the use in sweat lodges (Barfield and Hodder 1987). The only other published 'burnt mound' sites in Kent include the Late Neolithic feature at Crabble Paper, near Dover (Parfitt 2006) and a Late Bronze Age example excavated during the A282/M25 road improvements at Dartford (Simmonds *et al* 2010). Further afield a few examples have been found in the

Greater London area, for example at Phoenix Wharf on the Isle of Dogs (Bowsher 1991; Sidell *et al* 2002; 27–29) and Campden Hill Road, Kensington (Moore *et al* 2003). In common with many other sites, the Early Bronze Age remains identified during the HS1 works did not produce any quantity of faunal remains or midden-type deposits one would perhaps expect of domestic settlement activity. The Early Bronze Age feature group at the Ebbsfleet River Crossing was particularly enigmatic; the identification of a series of possible post-holes within the gullies flanking the central pit or hollow suggests some form of enclosing structure which may point to the sauna hypothesis of Barfield and Hodder (1987). If this interpretation is correct, the absence of any evidence for *in situ* burning within the main pit or hollow might suggest stones were heated from outside the structure, perhaps on the hearths identified a little further to the south. The central gully could have fed water from the nearby River Ebbsfleet to pour on the hot stones that had been brought into the structure to create steam.

Middle Bronze Age

During the Middle Bronze Age a number of barrows were constructed in the valley. At Springhead (ARC SPH00) two intersecting ring-ditches were found at the head of the valley, immediately adjacent to the former springs (Wenban-Smith *et al* forthcoming). The earliest of these lay almost entirely within the excavated area, while the majority of the later ring-ditch (including any central burial) extended beyond the limit of excavation to the south-west. The earlier ring-ditch had a diameter of *c* 18m, although only just less than half of the ditch survived, the north-western part having been eroded away by an advancing spring line. The remains of a central, urned cremation burial survived, though this had been substantially truncated by a later Roman road which had been cut through the area down to the water's edge. Insufficient of the later ring-ditch survived to calculate its diameter, but the ditch was of similar width and depth to the earlier example. Further down the valley, beneath the later Roman villa, on an area of slightly higher ground overlooking what would have been the wetland zone, two ring-ditches surrounded by an enclosure were excavated (ARC EBB01). As at Springhead, they may also represent barrows, one of these ditches, albeit smaller at 5m diameter, contained a central cremation burial dated to 1450–1300 cal BC (NZA-28208, 3113±30 BP). Although the other ring-ditch was only partially preserved, two other cremation deposits of similar date were identified nearby.

In the floodplain zone of the Lower Valley the HS1 investigations revealed contemporary activity represented by a number of wooden structures (Wenban-Smith *et al* forthcoming). This includes a wattle panel of intertwined hazel branches and several concentrations of (coppiced) roundwood laid on the surface of the peat deposits. On the whole these structures are of lightweight construction, perhaps the remains of temporary walkways or trackways linking areas of drier ground. They are located along the line of former wetland edge and may provide evidence of prehistoric routeway through the Lower Valley (Fig 86c). A number of similar Bronze Age structures have been identified in recent years along the edges of the Thames floodplain, particularly in the East London wetlands between the Rivers Lea and Ingrebourne (Carew *et al* 2009; Meddens 1996; Meddens and Beasley 1996; Stafford *et al* 2012) where it has been suggested they may be associated with the movement of stock for seasonal grazing.

One structure recorded during the HS1 watching brief, however, was more substantial and comprised a double row of large timber piles driven into alluvial clay. A total of five oak pile tips and one peaty void of a pile tip were recorded. The diameter of the piles ranged between *c* 100mm and 150mm, with the largest surviving to a length of 520mm. Although the exposure in plan was small, there was a clear deliberate pattern; the piles were set in pairs *c* 3m from each other, and each pile was *c* 1m apart within the pair. The size and layout of the structure suggests it could have supported a walkway, perhaps even a bridge, traversing an ancient water course. Unfortunately the piles were made from rather fast-grown oak and no more than 40 tree-rings could be found; insufficient for tree-ring dating. A sample of the outer rings of one of the piles was radiocarbon dated to the Middle Bronze Age, 1410–1220 cal BC (NZA-28703, 3055±30 BP). The pile alignment can be compared with a number of other similar structures excavated in the Thames Valley. The closest parallel based on form is the Early Bronze Age pile group found along the A13 at Freemasons Road, Newham (Stafford *et al* 2012). Obvious comparisons can also be drawn with the Middle and Late Bronze Age pile groups excavated at Vauxhall (Haughey 1999) and further upstream at Eton (Lambrick 2009; Allen *et al* forthcoming).

Late Bronze Age and Iron Age

Evidence for human activity dating the Late Bronze Age–Iron Age is sparser although potsherds attest to occasional visits. In the Outer Basin excavations for the STDR-4 (Area 1) recorded a series of small wooden structures, possibly revetting the edge of a channel (Wenban-Smith *et al* forthcoming). The structures comprised fragmented wooden stakes, on occasion roughly joined by thin horizontal 'bundles' of rods or 'withies'. The form of the structures is not clear however and it is likely, in part, that they represent repairs, additions or replacements of one or more former structures, as the channel silts accumulated against them. An alder stake from one of the structures produced a radiocarbon date of 835–765 cal BC (SUERC-19949, 2615±30 BP). Fragments of briquetage, a coarse ceramic material used to make evaporation vessels, were found buried in the estuarine silts sealing the wooden structures and may suggest salt production was carried out nearby. The briquetage was found in association with a quantity of Iron Age pottery and animal bone; cattle, sheep, pig and horse. A radiocarbon date on a cattle femur produced an Early–Middle Iron Age date of 730–390 cal BC (SUERC-19947, 2385±30 BP). A cetacean vertebrate bone, from a dolphin or porpoise, along with remains of gannet further emphasises the maritime influence on the Ebbsfleet Valley during this period.

Roman and Saxon Northfleet

Northfleet villa, 1.5km downstream of Springhead Roman town, was originally excavated by W H Steadman in 1909–11. He uncovered evidence for agricultural buildings, a limekiln, and traces of the east wing of the main house, including hundreds of *tesserae* that pointed to the existence of a tessellated floor or mosaic (Steadman 1913). A bath-house was revealed by subsequent fieldwork by the Thameside Archaeological Group between 1979 and 1983 (Ansell 1981; 1982; 1983; Smith 1979; Smith 1980), but the 2001 excavation by Oxford Archaeology for HS1 was the most extensive, exposing a large part of the main complex and the villa's hinterland (Biddulph 2011, 135–88).

Although the main house could not be re-examined, a number of finds recovered from the excavation suggested that the villa estate accommodated the town's elite. A piece of white marble *opus sectile* paving, possibly Carrara marble, was of the sort found at luxury buildings, for example at Fishbourne Palace and a building in Southwark thought to have been used by the provincial administration (Crowley 2005, 91). A seal-box in the shape of a *beneficarius* lance suggested the movement of documents between the villa owners and the legionary staff of the provincial governor (Schuster 2011, 298). And a life-size theatrical face-mask imported from the Rhineland and associated with religious festivals or processions may have been a badge of office. The rarity of such pieces in Britain suggests that the mask was more a symbol of status than merely a practical prop, and provides a tantalising clue that the town's elite lived at the villa and took a leading role in civic and religious life (Biddulph 2011, 229).

However, Northfleet villa was also a working farm. The earliest-known building was a timber rectangular building, erected after AD 70. Something of its use is suggested by the clay- or wood-lined tanks that surrounded it. Some of these were connected to pipes and drains, while another contained large quantities of germinated spelt wheat. The evidence points to the production of malt, which may have been stored or processed in the building ready for on-site brewing, or export. The earliest timber building was replaced by a building with stone footings after AD 120. This was itself replaced with a larger aisled barn after AD 160, which was joined by a second aisled building after AD 200. Like the earliest structure, these later buildings or barns were used for malting or storage. A technological advance arrived in AD 350 with the construction of a malting oven (*cf* Reynolds and Langley 1979). The structure was used to generate moisture to encourage the grain to sprout. Heated subsequently, the oven dried the grain to arrest germination, and the greater control of temperature permitted variation of flavour.

The extraordinary range of evidence recovered from Northfleet – not recorded on such a scale anywhere in Roman Britain – identifies the villa as a major malting and brewing centre. Quantities were vast; the largest brewing tank held up to *c* 10,800 litres. How far the malt or ale was exported is unknown, but it may well have been loaded onto rivercraft from a quayside immediately north of the villa complex (Pl 28) and sent down the Ebbsfleet into the Thames. The waters were shallow at this point, restricting access to flat-bottomed barges or lighters. Once out in the Thames, the cargoes were probably transferred to larger vessels or merchantmen for onward distribution. The quay was built during the late 2nd century at the mouth of a backwater. In its first phase, the quay comprised a wooden revetment and platform, which extended into the water. In the 4th century, the wooden staging was replaced by a more robust structure of timber piles and rubble dumps, which raised the height of the quayside, possibly in response to rising water levels.

A bath-house was built after AD 160. The structure took a simple form initially, being provided with a warm room (*tepidarium*) and hot room (*caldarium*). More rooms were added over the years, so that a more complete range of rooms was present, including changing room (*apodyterium*), cold room (*frigidarium*), sweat room (*sudatorium*) and cold bath. In its final incarnation in the first half of the 3rd century, two sets of cold baths and hot rooms were provided, suggesting perhaps that men and women were segregated.

The villa was abandoned by AD 380. Occupation of sorts continued in the area; quarries were dug for the underlying chalk, while the crumbling villa walls were robbed of their masonry, and it is possible that people living in the area continued to receive new pottery and

Plate 33 Remains of the Saxon tidal mill at Northfleet (ARC EBB01)

other goods. However, in time this too ceased, and there was no occupation until the late 5th or early 6th centuries AD (Biddulph 2011, 215).

The first evidence of Saxon activity at Northfleet occurs perhaps by the middle of the 5th century (Hardy and Andrews 2011, 249–305). A number of sunken featured buildings (SFBs) were excavated in the vicinity of the villa buildings. Each building probably had a suspended wooden floor set over a square pit, which served as storage space and ventilation. One of the buildings was more elaborate: the sides of the pit were lined with planks to prevent the sides collapsing. In one of the SFB pits was a collection of seven lead loomweights. The walls of these buildings were probably light wooden screens plastered with clay and the roofs were probably thatched. The settlement was scattered along the higher and drier ground to the south of the Ebbsfleet channel. There were no divisions of the land, no property boundaries. Although there was no evidence for re-use of the Roman buildings, for a time spelt wheat continued to be cultivated in the surrounding fields. After perhaps a century signs of occupation vanished at Northfleet. This area of the valley was probably slowly getting wetter and probably became a less attractive area to live.

A unique discovery during the 2001 excavations was the remains of a Saxon tidal mill immediately adjacent to the old Roman waterfront (Pl 33; Hardy *et al* 2011, 307–49). Dendrochronological dating of one of the planks from the mill provided a construction date in the spring of AD 692. Detailed analysis of the sediments, palaeoenvironmental remains and structural evidence confirmed the mill had clearly operated in tidal conditions; capturing water in a pond at high tide and then releasing it through the mill at low tide. The mill appeared to operate two millwheels, possibly for up to three hours, producing around 30kg of flour. The water ran from the pond through two square funnels, or pentroughs, made of hollowed-out tree trunks, and the jets probably drove two horizontal paddle wheels. Each wheel was connected by a shaft to a pair of millstones on the milling floor above. Once the water had passed the wheel, it ran along the mill tailrace and joined the main stream channel. There was also evidence that a system of levers may have been used to raise the waterwheel and shaft in order to separate the upper and lower stones while they were turning. At high tide, when the waterwheel would be under water and the mill would not be operating, a boat would perhaps load the flour from a jetty alongside the tailrace, and head off downstream before the tide ebbed again. The wood used to construct the mill was entirely axe-hewn, almost all oak and mostly from quite young trees. The design was quite sophisticated and would have been built by a skilled and experienced builder, possibly one brought over especially from the continent. The structure is likely to have stood on its own in a landscape of open tidal creeks, mudflats and saltmarsh.

The Northfleet structure is virtually alone in England as an example of a middle and late Anglo-Saxon tidal mill with a horizontal wheel; the evidence is otherwise slim and conflicting. Better parallels come from Ireland. The earliest securely dated example is the first phase tide mill at Nendrum, on the shore of Strangford Lough, County Down, which has been dated by dendrochronology to AD 619–21 (McErlean and Crothers 2007). The site at Nendrum, together with Northfleet, provides a growing body of evidence for the use of salt water as well as fresh water for powering early medieval mills.

Part IV
Synthesis

Chapter 13

Discussion

Prehistoric Archaeology and the Floodplain

Evidence for prehistoric use of the floodplain area by humans has been documented through a number of sources of information in the course of the study (Fig 91). Substantial evidence for human activity was identified at Swanscombe Marsh (Thames River Crossing, Chap 11), Rainham Marsh (East of Ferry Lane, Chap 9) and Aveley Marsh (Tank Hill Road, Chap 10) where HS1, or diversionary works associated with the rail corridor, impacted on floodplain marginal sequences on gravel surfaces or highs. At Swanscombe Marsh the evidence consisted of two distinct groups of material, the more substantial representing a Late Upper Palaeolithic site of unknown extent but probably representing single visit activity. By contrast the evidence for Neolithic activity is probably lower intensity use of the site but over a prolonged period of time. On Rainham Marsh the small Early Neolithic flint scatter, although apparently isolated and probably representing a single knapping episode, is quite possibly associated with more extensive occupation evidence recorded at the nearby Brookway site on the higher terrace (Meddens 1996). At Tank Hill Road on Aveley Marsh a small amount of material was recovered dating to the early Post-glacial period, as well as the Neolithic and Early Bronze Age attesting to occasional visits, but the major phase of activity here is dated to the Late Mesolithic period representing repeated and intensive use of the site for the manufacture of microliths, microburins and tranchet axes.

One of the key horizons associated with human activity on the main Thames floodplain appeared to be the interface between the underlying sands and gravels and the overlying clay-silts or organic sediments associated with the Holocene alluvial wedge. Thus artefacts are resting on a surface that has been exposed for a considerable duration since at least the Late Pleistocene up until inundation has taken place across the surface. Similar situations have also been documented at Slade Green (Bates and Williamson 1995) and Erith (Bennell 1998). What remains unclear, however, is the frequency with which artefacts occur on the sand/gravel to alluvium interface. It is interesting to note that this pattern is similar across the floodplain with the exception of the Neolithic artefacts discovered at Purfleet close to the mouth of the Mar Dyke by

Wilkinson and Murphy (1995) where a few artefacts (possibly the result of specialist activity) were located in the clay-silts immediately below the main peat associated with the phase of estuary contraction.

Where significant exposures were observed, little or no direct evidence for human activity was located along the HS1 route on the Thames floodplain within the main body of the thick floodplain peat sequences. This includes geoarchaeological zones previously identified as low, medium and high priority (Chap 6), for example,

- watching briefs on major diversionary works (eg, the Goresbrook diversion and Lamsdon Road at Rainham Creek, Chap 8);
- watching briefs on deep pipeline excavations at road, rail, watercourse and drainage ditch locations from Ripple Lane to Mar Dyke (open cut trenches, cofferdams and caisson chambers)
- archaeological evaluation trenching (eg, Goresbrook, Chap 8; Rainham Marsh, Chap 9);
- where large transects of the alluvial corridor have been impacted on by the construction of the tunnel approaches (eg, Ripple Lane Portal, Chap 8; the Thames River Crossing at Swanscombe, Chap 11).

This is an important observation because of the extensive nature of the works associated with HS1. No evidence for timber structures (eg, trackways, jetties, bridges) or structural remains associated with permanency was detected in the study at any of the locations examined in the main Thames floodplain area. This is perhaps surprising as Bronze Age timber structures have been recorded at several sites in the East London area. Many of these structures commonly occur towards the top of the peat sequences abutting areas of higher ground, often in tributary locations such as the River Roding (eg, Stafford et al 2012, fig 10.3; Carew 2009; Meddens 1996). The absence of similar structures over the HS1 route corridor between the River Roding and Mar Dyke might indicate differential use of the floodplain in the later prehistoric period, where contrasts exist between that part of the floodplain associated with trackways and that part without (see Meddens et al 2012, 149). Although this pattern may, in part, reflect the extent and level of archaeological visibility along this part of the route, especially for the more deeply buried

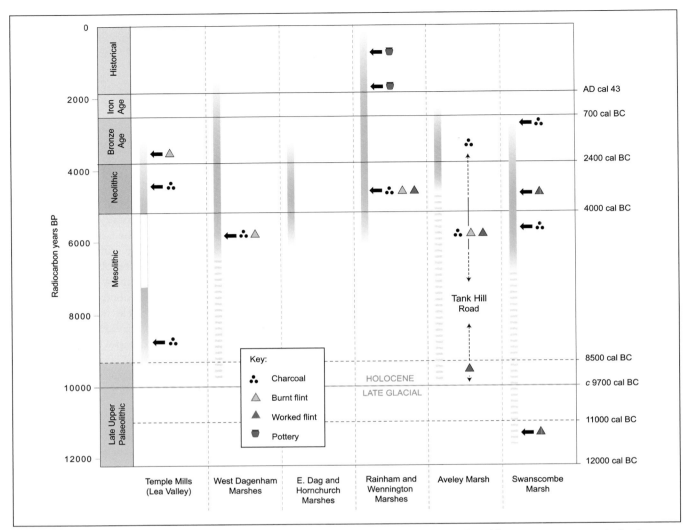

Figure 91 Summary distribution of sequence duration and associated archaeological and human proxy records for key sites and interventions along the route corridor

sequences, it should be noted the upper part of the peat was frequently exposed during the watching brief on service diversions across Dagenham and Hornchurch (Mudlands and Rainham Creek); Rainham Wennington and Aveley Marshes (Chaps 8–10). Here, the excavation of *c* 5.2km of open pipe trench, essentially a linear transect running parallel to the terrace edge, was monitored by a team of archaeologists continually over a period of two years. Trenches were entered frequently in order to carefully inspect the deposits for artefactual and structural remains, as well as for sediment recording and sampling by a geoarchaeologist. The peat often contained large quantities of wood which was consistently checked for evidence of wood working. On occasion, where natural accumulations of wood appeared to resemble some form of linear structure, an ancient wood-working specialist (Damian Goodburn) visited the site to confirm the accumulation to be of natural origin. Exposure of the more deeply buried peat sequences was less frequent but was monitored during the numerous deep excavations at road, rail, watercourse and drainage ditch crossings (see 28.800km, Wennington Marsh, Fig 49).

In contrast to the HS1 route across the main Thames floodplain, investigations in the Ebbsfleet Valley recorded prehistoric material within the alluvial stack. Here, the complex and shifting ecotonal zones of the wetland margins appear to have been a focus of activity during the prehistoric period. The evidence includes a section of a possible Late Neolithic trackway found within the peat during the STDR-4 works, discrete concentrations of coppiced roundwood within the upper part of the main peat body, and in one case a wattle hurdle that was laid down on the peat surface during a period of rising water tables. Radiocarbon dating suggests these concentrations could be contemporary and appear to follow an alignment along the wetland edge during the Middle Bronze Age. A double row of substantial timber piles dating to the Middle Bronze Age were also recorded that may represent the remains of a timber walkway or footbridge traversing a channel. The concentrations of activity may simply be a reflection of the extensive construction impacts and consequently larger scale intensive investigations carried out here (it is perhaps notable a number of the Bronze Age wooden structures were recorded under general watching brief

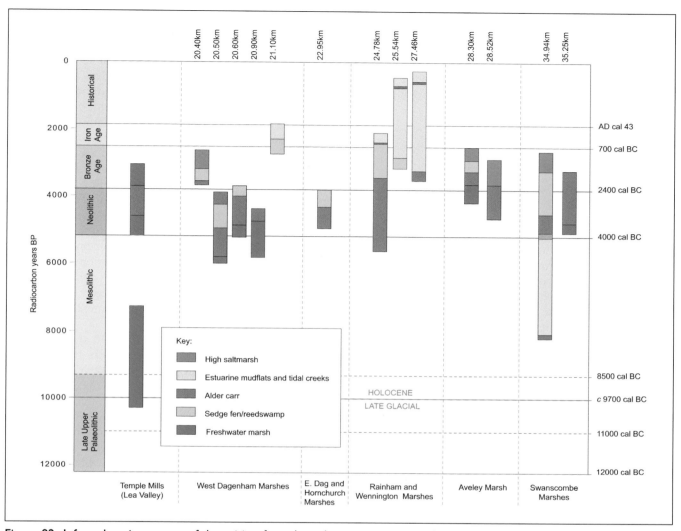

Figure 92 Inferred environments of deposition for selected sequences across the study area

conditions suggesting visibility was sufficient in this case to positively identify such remains). However, it is also clear the unique topography of the valley exerted a huge influence over patterns of sedimentation, hydrological and vegetation successions as well as preservation environments. It might, however, be that the valley was a focal point for activity (a feature that is certainly the case with the establishment of ritual activities at Springhead in the Late Iron Age and Roman periods, Andrews *et al* 2011a).

In addition to direct evidence for human activity, proxy records have been identified in the palaeoenvironmental record at a number of sites. At the Thames River Crossing microscopic charcoal at two horizons in the sequence indicate the possible impact of human activity in the environment that may have been associated with vegetation change and either temporary openings in the forest or more prolonged clearance. Similar evidence, as well as a horizon with burnt flint, was discovered at Temple Mills. It is noticeable that a number of sites contain evidence for elevated levels of charcoal in the Late Mesolithic (Fig 91) as well as in the Neolithic period.

Recent Archaeology and the Near Surface Zone of the Alluvium

Most of the sites investigated in this study, apart from the Ebbsfleet Valley, produced little archaeological evidence for the later prehistoric and historical periods and this is probably a reflection of the low level, seasonal use of the floodplain areas during these periods. Roman activity was detected on Rainham Marsh in the form of an assemblage of redeposited pottery and faunal remains associated with channel deposits. This material probably represents a dump deposit associated with more permanent settlement on the higher drier ground. On Wennington Marsh there is evidence of episodic, probably seasonal, occupation occurring during the medieval period possibly associated with a period of marsh reclamation.

Again the paucity of information from this study contrasts with that from Ebbsfleet where Roman activity is well established in the form of farming and brewing activities associated with the Northfleet villa as well as constructions associated with a waterfront. Saxon occupation is attested to be a series of sunken featured buildings while within the alluvium is the remains of a unique tidal mill (Andrews *et al* 2011a). Without a doubt the abundance of occupation evidence from the Roman and Saxon periods within the Ebbsfleet is in part a function of the ritual activities at Springhead and the urban settlement that grew up around the springs.

Landscape Heterogeneity and Development

Sequences impacted and recorded during the project typically conform to the well-known lithologies and stratigraphies previously documented by Devoy (1977; 1979), Long *et al* (2000), Corcoran *et al* 2011, Powell 2012 and others. These are summarised in Fig 92. However, it is clear from other studies that the nature of the alluvial stack at different locations in the estuary (including the Medway) varies across space (Fig 93, see Fig 94 for profile locations). Devoy himself noted that the peats become less persistent east of Tilbury (Devoy 1977; 1979). This indicates that consideration needs to be given on a site by site basis to the nature of the sequences and their environmental and archaeological relevance.

The evidence gathered at the different locations (*Table 76* and *Table 77*) indicates that, in addition to the well-described alder carr and reedswamp wetland sequences associated with the major peat units of the floodplain, a number of other environments of deposition can be identified within the rivers entering the Thames Estuary. The biological characteristics of these depositional environments in the floodplain vary but the lithologies are strikingly similar (at least in the field situation) and, consequently, have rarely been examined and recorded in detail; particularly where there remains a general perception that the grey clay-silts are of low archaeological potential. Comparison with data gathered from elsewhere within the Thames Estuary (Fig 94) downstream of the Thames River Crossing (eg, at Shellhaven and within the Medway Estuary at Grain (*Table 76*) and the Medway Tunnel (*Table 77*) is interesting. During the HS1 works it has been found that clear differences in the nature of the environments of deposition of minerogenic sediments occur across space and also within a single sequence above and below the main mid-Holocene peat (estuary contraction phase). At the Thames River Crossing this difference is between mudflats below and saltmarsh above the peat. At other locations (Shellhaven/Medway Tunnel) the difference is more marked with mudflats characterised by access to marine waters below and saltmarsh above the main peat units. Furthermore, within the Medway system tidal river sequences are present at depth within the floodplain close to the Isle of Grain; this represents a facies as yet unidentified in the Thames. This evidence suggests that heterogeneity within the floodplain is common and that factors such as proximity to the active channels as well as the relative balance between sediment input and sea-level change

are important. For example, at the Thames River Crossing it appears likely that the development of mudflats following initial flooding of the topographic template gradually gave way to saltmarsh development just prior to contraction of the estuary. Here this shift may well be a function of a near balance of sedimentation rates and change in sea-level. Comparison with other areas of the estuary such as Shellhaven/Medway Tunnel), in which marine access to the mudflats was maintained, suggests flooding and deepening of the waters in the estuary may initially have outpaced the ability of the system to infill the basin. The differing interpretations of these signals raise important questions about the precise nature of local palaeogeography, the nature and position of intertidal zones at different times and the distribution of resources in this patchwork environment. This not only influences how we think about resource distribution across such patchwork environments but also communication pathways through this landscape. At present such issues have rarely been articulated in the context of the later prehistory of the Thames Estuary area.

The dating of the sequences (Figs 95 and 96) is also significant. Although the data conform to the broad model suggested by Long *et al* (2000) and Bates and Whittaker (2004), data collected from the HS1 scheme suggest that onset and cessation of peat formation (indicated at a single site in Figure 95 as joined start and end dates for peat formation) varies along the route corridor. Thus, although there is a trend downstream to younger dates for onset of peat formation after 6000 BP, there is considerable variation that is a result of the nature of the topographic template onto which peat has grown.

Processes of Change in the Floodplain

The processes associated with the evolution of the floodplain have, for many years, been driven by the desire to understand regional vegetation changes and the impact, or nature, of sea-level change in terms of transgressions and regressions across the floodplain surface. This has resulted in a tendency to examine sequence and change at an individual site in terms of considering the landscape at the semi-regional scale; where study at a local level has occurred (eg, Sidell 2003), the focus has tended to be on the process of sea-level change but where this might have an effect on tidal regime, etc. Until recently (eg, Powell 2012; Stafford *et al* 2012; Carew *et al* 2009), the exception to this was the work at Purfleet by Wilkinson and Murphy (1995). It is becoming increasingly apparent that, in order to understand human behaviour and, indeed, the reasons for human activity at a particular point in the landscape (or indeed their absence at other locations), more local environmental reconstructions are required that focus on spatial variation in the depositional environment. In this study we have attempted to shift the focus of attention towards the local scale rather than pursuing the well-trodden path utilising the vegetation record to

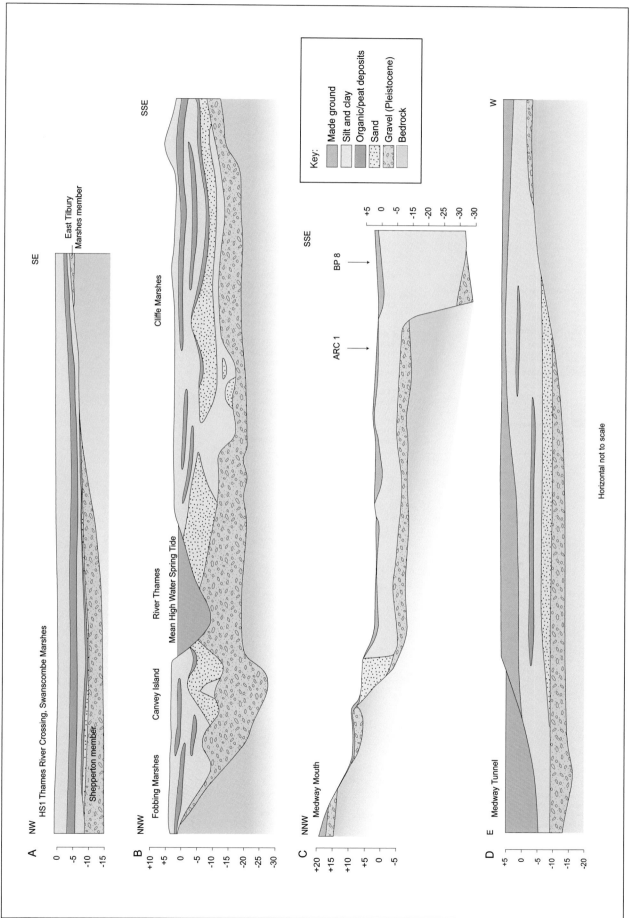

Figure 93 Schematic cross sections based on data from the Thames River Crossing (this study), Canvey Island/Cliffe Marshes (BGS), Medway mouth including the Isle of Grain (Bates unpublished) and the Medway Tunnel site (Bates and Bates 2000)

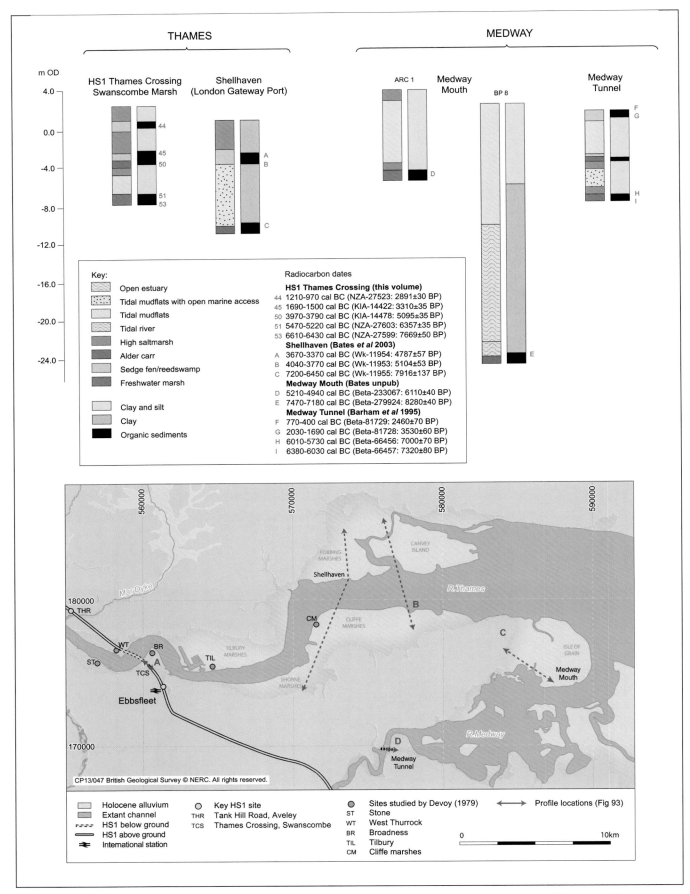

Figure 94 Distribution of lithologies and inferred environments of deposition from key sites in the Thames and Medway Estuaries

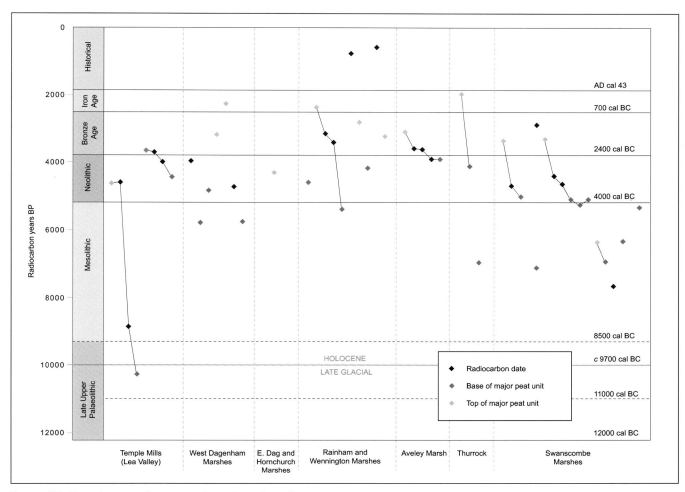

Figure 95   Distribution of route-wide radiocarbon dates

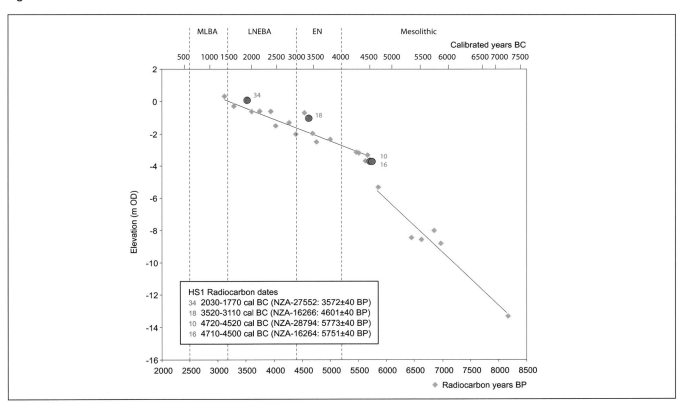

Figure 96   Age versus depth models for onset of sedimentation onto gravel surface in Lower Thames during the Early to Middle Holocene, including data from HS1 investigations

examine the regional signals. In particular, this has focused attention on change in the floodplain with reference to shifts in depositional environment as recorded in sedimentary facies. In other words careful examination of the boundaries between specific units has been undertaken in some cases in order to attempt to document change across that boundary (eg, BH3751 and BH3748 at the Thames River Crossing (Swanscombe), Chap 11). Such an approach is entirely justified, even where artefacts are absent, if we accept the premise that it is likely to be spatial heterogeneity in vegetation, terrain, etc, that significantly influences human behaviour in the landscape (or allows humans the possibility to make decisions about what they are going to do where). The use of this argument is one that is commonly assumed but rarely articulated and is often the basis for justification of investigation of Pleistocene age sites within the framework of developer-led archaeological investigations (Bates and Wenban-Smith 2011).

At the Thames River Crossing, sequences were examined in order to better understand the changes associated with initial flooding of the topographic template and establishment of the tidal mudflat regime as well as the subsequent transformation to alder carr associated with the mid-Holocene phase of estuarine contraction (*sensu* Long *et al* 2000). The shift from estuarine to fresh water within the phase of estuary contraction is of considerable potential significance because it falls around about the time in which the transition from Mesolithic to Neolithic occupation of southern England occurs and hence the context and landscape setting for the earliest Neolithic in the estuary is framed by this event. The progressive shift, as evidenced in the diatom and foraminifera/ostracod record up-profile, from tidal mudflats to mid- and high saltmarsh, within the minerogenic sediment sequence is strong evidence for relative shallowing water depths and the progressive shift towards the river of the intertidal zone (or the progressive creep of fresh water wetlands in a seaward direction) during the Late Mesolithic. The sudden shift to organic sedimentation at the top of the minerogenic requires explanation in order to consider the significance of the transformation. The progressive shift to environments of deposition higher in the tidal envelope (ie, up sequence in BH3751) might indicate that a tidal or fresh water reedswamp should precede the development of an alder carr wetland (as seen in reverse at the top of the main peat deposit). This is not the case here (and at many locations in the Thames) however and, consequently, conditions must have switched quite rapidly towards those suitable for the growth of trees associated with alder carr following the phase of upper saltmarsh development. The concept of a progressive spread of alder carr conditions across the saltmarsh surface suggests unusual conditions pertaining within the estuary for a time. An alternative scenario, based on the evidence from Purfleet (Wilkinson and Murphy 1995), was also examined where the possibility of drying of the saltmarsh surface was considered prior to a return to wetter conditions associated with inundation and formation of alder carr. No evidence was present at the top of the minerogenic sequence for weathering or soil ripening and consequently a phase of emergence of the former saltmarsh surface does not appear to have occurred prior to colonisation by alder carr.

Within the peats the transition towards the phase of estuary re-expansion appears to be associated with the presence of a minerogenic horizon within the peat sequence that indicates a local temporary flooding event. Microfossil data from this organic clay indicate this was probably brackish in nature. This brackish incursion appears to have been of limited duration and its extent, beyond the limits of the Thames River Crossing site, remain to be determined. However, a return to peat formation under freshwater reedswamp subsequently occurred prior to the gradual expansion of the estuary again perhaps in the Middle–Late Bronze Age (Fig 95).

Chapter 14
Conclusions

The results of the investigation of the archaeology of the HS1 route corridor through the Thames alluvium are significant, not only because of the direct results of the field and laboratory investigations, but also in terms of the success of the project in predicting and identifying the location of areas of human activity within the route corridor. The corollary, the identification of those areas in which human activity did not occur, was also, to an extent, a success within the project context. In general the most detailed investigations were undertaken where the direct impact from construction was greatest, in zones where archaeological potential was considered high and confirmed through preliminary field investigations (eg, Tank Hill Road, Thames Crossing and Ebbsfleet). However, field evaluations (eg, Goresbrook, Rainham and Wennington Marshes) and watching briefs were also carried out in lower priority zones and the results proved either negative or the archaeology recorded was relatively insubstantial. Success within the project was also based and assessed through minimising the risk and impact to the engineering programme and schedule of works.

In all cases the results of the investigation appear to have been positive and beneficial with respect to locating and mitigating archaeology. Furthermore, the investigations had little impact on the engineering programme as all aspects of the work were carefully arranged within the overall programme of works. As a result, it is felt that the methods and approaches to the investigation provide a suitable framework for future projects, particularly large-scale infrastructure projects, where management issues are paramount and where a successful project design will be sensitive, not only to the archaeology, but also the engineering and cost limitations. Indeed, the common goal of archaeology and geotechnical ground investigation is to identify the nature of the sub-surface conditions to ensure that adequate provision is put in place at an early stage in the project. A geoarchaeological approach at an early stage in the construction programme, where direct involvement with the geotechnical team can inform both parties on the nature of ground conditions, was fundamental to success on this part of the route corridor. It should be remembered that the very detailed nature of archaeological investigations can place an archaeological team in a position of holding significant information on ground conditions, at a level of detail rarely available to the geotechnical teams on a project.

Archaeology and the HS1 Corridor

The phased approach to evaluating the archaeological resource, where the distribution of sites was buried beneath significant depths of alluvium, allowed the response to evaluation and mitigation to be both appropriate and justified. The weakness of the adopted methodology lies principally in the difficulties in operating within an environment of deep alluvial stratigraphy in which, without costly and time-consuming trenching impacts on our ability to adequately assess the danger to archaeology buried at depth. A second weakness is also inherent in the strategy of rapid assessment of samples and inadequate 'thought time' between stages. This is, however, a minor criticism of the approach given the nature of the project. With the exception of the works at Thames River Crossing (Swanscombe), the location and nature of the investigation strategy was entirely dictated by the location and nature of the impact. The strategy adopted to investigate the route corridor focused on the likely archaeological signatures and proxy records as they overlapped with a range of engineering impacts.

The ephemeral nature of the archaeological signal (predominantly prehistoric in character), as single artefacts and low density scatters lying within sedimentary units, or more substantial remains resting on buried surfaces (eg, at Tank Hill Road), made its identification unlikely prior to intrusive ground works. In many cases, only a reactive response to the watching brief was possible. Furthermore the geoarchaeological approach was vital for assessing significance of single or low numbers of artefacts as potential indicators of significant human activity. For example, the discovery of a single artefact in a test pit where the artefact lay on a boundary interpreted as representing a former landsurface was given higher significance than a similar artefact lying within a sedimentary context. This contextualisation of the archaeology was facilitated through the early common goal of both the geotechnical engineering side of the project and the geoarchaeological approach:

1. Where the understanding of the landscape at a site specific scale was fundamental.
2. Where this scale of investigation was nested within a hierarchical framework of the regional geology and environment.

3. Where factors such as slope aspect and bedrock geology adjacent to the route corridor may have a profound influence on the nature of processes operating within the route corridor.

For the geotechnical engineers this was necessary in order to design the structure of the route corridor, where it was realised that mapping of the route and its surroundings were paramount to a complete understanding of the likely geomorphological history. For the archaeologists this was significant in order to understand the reasons why a particular site may have been occupied (at a regional scale) as well as understanding site formation and transformation processes (at a local scale).

However, it was not only the remains that were discovered, but also those that were absent, that is an important outcome of the project and of significance to our understanding of the regional occupation of the Lower Thames Valley. The ability to survey and monitor excavations across a broad transect of the floodplain provides support to previous notions of presence/absence within the landscape in terms of sites etc. For example, previous surveys of the floodplain have been relatively limited in scope and where detailed investigation has been undertaken it has been typically restricted to expensive cofferdams or remote investigations (through the application of boreholes), without recourse to ascertaining whether or not archaeological evidence is associated with such sequences. The abundance of archaeological evidence from Ebbsfleet, as well as that of parts of the north bank associated with trackways, contrasts with the paucity of evidence along the HS1 route on the main Thames floodplain. This suggests that use of the floodplain may have varied and that places such as Ebbsfleet may certainly have had some significance. It is also possible that taphonomic processes operate differently in the Ebbsfleet to that of the main Thames floodplain leading to enhanced preservational potential. It is important that these issues are considered in the future in order to aid development control in the region. Currently, responses to development impact in alluvial corridor archaeology may be predicated by experience within one area of the floodplain, the results of which are subsequently rolled out across wide tracts of floodplain, but without the empirical data existing to validate such an approach.

Successes of the Project

The overall success of the project can be judged in a number of ways, from both the perspective of increasing our understanding of the evolution of the landscape, but also in terms of testing models and criteria adopted in order to develop a programme of works to investigate the route corridor. The latter is, of course, of particular interest to archaeological practitioners including the curatorial services.

Within the alluvial corridor of HS1 the implementation of the project as designed (URN and URS 1999) had two fundamental principles in order to be judged a success:

1. That the archaeological resource was considered, identified and mitigated in an appropriate way.
2. That the archaeological works did not impede the development programme and cause unacceptable delays to construction.

The evidence presented in this report has demonstrated that the successful implementation of a plan, against an archaeological model that predicted the distribution of the archaeological resource along the route corridor, was achieved. Radiocarbon dates from contexts in which peat bottomed onto uncompressible substrate (Fig 96) indicate that the age/depth model used in the initial project design has been reinforced by the findings of the study. Where the model predicted high potential of archaeological remains, the purposive field investigations produced evidence for human activity (eg, at Tank Hill Road and the Thames River Crossing (Swanscombe). By contrast, those areas of the route corridor deemed of low or no potential did not produce material, either during purposive site investigation or through subsequent watching briefs. In this case, the adopted programme of works was suitable to address the issues that arose during construction. Predicting the location of archaeological remains is significant because of the way in which this will focus attention on particular areas of the landscape in future investigations along similar tracts of the landscape. Hence, the discovery of nearly all major concentrations of archaeology in association with floodplain edge environments, topographic highs overlooking wetlands and dryland/wetland interfaces, substantiated our hypothesis, particularly where we were also able to view those areas thought to be of low potential away (eg, Ripple Lane Portal, Thames River Crossing (Swanscombe).

The approach adopted also caused minimal delay to construction because areas of high archaeological potential were identified early in the development programme and were flagged up for investigation. This was particularly the case with Thames River Crossing (Swanscombe), where a costly cofferdam was required in order to allow excavation to take place to the depth at which archaeology might be expected.

Lessons for the Future

It is clear from the strategy adopted that the designed programme of works successfully integrated the archaeological investigation within the design and build framework of the HS1 construction. This worked well because at all stages of the project the adopted strategy was flexible enough to cope with changing engineering constraints and new opportunities for investigation through the lifetime of the project. Commencing in 1994 the field time duration of 10 years or more from start to finish was impacted on by new technologies and indeed new insights regarding the nature of both natural environmental change within the region as well as human in the Thames Estuary and southern England (Cotton and Field 2004). The success of the project involved the implementation of a route-wide review of the archaeological potential integrated with site by site investigation of areas of impact. The basis for this approach operated within a standardised, route-wide approach to investigation but where an overview of the context of all discoveries was maintained by participant staff. This included adopting and managing the methods and techniques used in a flexible fashion depending on ground conditions and engineering necessities. Furthermore a hierarchical framework was successfully adopted where the methodology and results could integrate with and be tested by further geotechnical investigations, archaeological purposive investigations or observations/recording made. The methods used maximised information gain, minimised costs, and specifically targeted information unavailable at the start of the project (as required for evaluative purposes). This was continued into the assessment phase of the project where a shift from assessment to analysis was simplified in order to reduce costs and reporting between stages. Among the outcomes from the project a number of issues have been forthcoming that perhaps should be considered in the future:

1. Transitions. We have targeted transitions within the floodplain for investigation here and these are likely to have been important tipping points in the landscape that would have impacted on human activity significantly in the past. Further investigation is needed of these at a site specific scale in the future. Particular focus should be put on the timing and speed of transitions as well as the precise nature of those transitions.

2. Full sequence investigation. The variability in environments of deposition associated with the minerogenic sediments (typically clay/silts) suggest that in order to consider resource distribution within the estuary rather than focusing on peat stratigraphies, full sequence characterisation should routinely be undertaken. Furthermore the demonstration that archaeology is associated with a wide range of sediment types rather than simply peats (Fig 10) reinforces this approach.

3. Development control. The spatial variability in evidence for human activity in the floodplain appears to suggest that humans in the past were using the floodplain in different ways at different times. Consequently, our response to development in different parts of the floodplain should vary. At present models from localised areas are used to inform strategies in other parts of the floodplain which may not be justified. Further research into spatial variability in human activity should be undertaken to clarify these issues.

4. Methods and techniques. Some of the approaches used in this study were novel within British archaeology when implemented in the middle 1990s (eg, use of CPT data and some of the geophysical techniques) but are now, if not routinely used, at least available to projects. It is important that new methods and techniques for investigating the subsurface are adopted and tested against future projects (eg, HS 2).

Appendix A
Radiocarbon Dating

The radiocarbon dating results referred to in this volume are presented below. The dates were processed during various stages of post-excavation assessment and analysis between 2001 and 2007. Seeds or waterlogged wood were the preferred material selected for dating, but in some cases where preservation was poor a sample of bulk sediment was submitted. The majority of the dates are AMS measurements processed at the Rafter Radiocarbon Laboratory, Institute of Geological and Nuclear Science, New Zealand (NZA-), and the Leibniz-Laboratory for Radiometric Dating and Isotope Research, Christian-Albrechts-University of Kiel, Germany (KIA-). Some dates, mainly in the Ebbsfleet Valley, were also processed at Waikato Radiocarbon Dating Laboratory, New Zealand (WK-), Beta Analytic Inc. Florida USA (Beta-) and the Scottish Universities Environmental Research Centre, East Kilbride (SUERC-). Four of the dates are radiometric measurements from bulk sediment or waterlogged wood (denoted in the table *).

The radiocarbon results are quoted in accordance with the international standard known as the Trondheim convention (Stuiver and Kra 1986). They are conventional radiocarbon ages, where 0 BP is the year 1950 (Stuiver and Polach 1977; Mook 1986). All dates have been calibrated using datasets published by Reimer *et al* (2004) and the computer program OxCal (v3.10) (Bronk Ramsey 1995; 1998; 2001) with the end points rounded out to 10 years. The calibrated date ranges cited in the tables, as in the text, are those for 95.4% (2σ) confidence.

Radiocarbon results from Temple Mills, Stratford

No	Chainage/ Trench no	Sample no	Cxt no	Depth (m OD)	Sample material	Lab code	Radiocarbon date (BP)	δ¹³C (‰)	Calibrated date (2σ range)
1	4042TT	4201006/7	420003	+2.62	*Phragmites australis* stem	KIA-24052	4610±35	-24.57	3520–3130 cal BC
2	4042TT	4201006/7	420003	+2.49	Twig fragment (indet.)	NZA-30301	4589±30	-25.60	3500–3120 cal BC
3	4042TT	4201006/7	420003	+2.29	Wood (indet.)	NZA-30332	8865±30	-25.60	8220–7830 cal BC
4	4042TT	4201006/7	420003	+1.84	*Phragmites australis* stem	KIA-24051	10305±50	-28.35	10450–9850 cal BC
5	4044TT	441016	420004	+2.73	3 outer rings of mature wood (indet.)	KIA-24588	3650±35	-31.91	2140–1920 cal BC
6	4044TT	441016	420004	+2.67	Horizontal root (indet.)	KIA-24589	3690±35	-26.67	2200–1960 cal BC
7	4044TT	441016	420004	+2.39	Wood (indet.)	KIA-24590	3980±30	-26.75	2580–2450 cal BC
8	4044TT	441016	420006	+2.22	Wood (indet.)	KIA-24591	4435±40	-26.15	3330–2920 cal BC

Radiocarbon results from West Dagenham Marshes

No	Chainage/ Trench no	Sample no	Cxt no	Depth (m OD)	Sample material	Lab code	Radiocarbon date (BP)	δ¹³C (‰)	Calibrated date (2σ range)
9	20.500km	1025	2043	-2.49	Roundwood (*Betula*)	NZA-28798	3952±35	-28.10	2570–2340 cal BC
10	20.500km	1026	2044	-3.75	Peat	NZA-28794	5773±40	-28.70	4720–4520 cal BC
11	20.600km	1031	2061	-1.70	Seeds (*Carex*)	NZA -28710	-413±30	-24.80	1952 cal AD onwards

Radiocarbon results from West Dagenham Marshes continued

No	Chainage/ Trench no	Sample no	Cxt no	Depth (m OD)	Sample material	Lab code	Radiocarbon date (BP)	δ¹³C (‰)	Calibrated date (2σ range)
12	20.600km	1033	2062	-3.38	Seeds (*Rananculus ficaria*)	NZA-28769	4841±60	-26.00	3770–3380 cal BC
13	3780TT	21	8004	-1.75	Peat	WK-11595	3177±49	-27.70	1610–1310 cal BC
14	21.090km	123	105	-1.39	Seeds (*Rubus, Cirsium, Euonymus, Ranunculus, Carex, Eleocharis*)	NZA-16262	2270±45	-27.64	410–200 cal BC
15	20.970km	273	126	-3.30	Seeds (*Alnus*)	NZA-16263	4733±40	-24.68	3640–3490 cal BC
16	20.970km	275	128	-3.88	Roundwood (*Alnus*)	NZA-16264	5751±40	-26.51	4710–4500 cal BC

Radiocarbon results from East Dagenham and Hornchurch Marshes

No	Chainage/ Trench no	Sample no	Cxt no	Depth (m OD)	Sample material	Lab code	Radiocarbon date (BP)	δ¹³C (‰)	Calibrated date (2σ range)
17	22.950km	289	199	-1.32	Seeds (*Rubus, Alnus, Rannunculus*)	NZA-16265	4297±40	-29.38	3030–2870 cal BC

Radiocarbon results from Rainham and Wennington Marshes

No	Chainage/ Trench no	Sample no	Cxt no	Depth (m OD)	Sample material	Lab code	Radiocarbon date (BP)	δ¹³C (‰)	Calibrated date (2σ range)
18	24.455km	253/256	193	-0.98	Seeds (*Alnus, Urtica, Rannunculus*)	NZA-16266	4601±40	-28.66	3520–3110 cal BC
19	3972TT	129	5	-0.70	Peat	WK-11596	2352 ±46	-28.70	750–200 cal BC
20	3972TT	145	7	-0.93	Seeds and bud scale (*Rubus, Carex*)	NZA-16267	3150±50	-29.65	1530–1300 cal BC
21	3972TT	137	9	-1.87	Seeds and catkin fragments (*Alnus*)	NZA-16268	3424±40	-28.23	1880–1620 cal BC
22	3972TT	112	13	-3.86	Seeds and cone axis (*Alnus*)	NZA-16269	5378±40	-26.36	4340–4050 cal BC
23	26.535km	372	234	-0.26	Charred cereal grains (undif.)	NZA-16270	766±40	-23.52	1180–1300 cal AD
24	26.535km	369	236	-0.96	Seeds (*Rannunculus*)	NZA-16271	2815±45	-26.63	1120–840 cal BC
25	26.800km	402	273	-3.20	Seeds and catkin axis (*Alnus*)	NZA-16272	4171±45	-27.60	2890–2620 cal BC
26	27.460km	431	269	-0.47	Seeds (*Potentilla patustris*)	NZA-16273	584±40	-27.31	1290–1420 cal AD
27	27.460km	429	271	-0.92	Seeds (*Eleocharis, Carex*)	NZA-16299	3217±40	-26.90	1610–1410 cal BC

Radiocarbon results from Aveley Marsh

No	Chainage/ Trench no	Sample no	Cxt no	Depth (m OD)	Sample material	Lab code	Radiocarbon date (BP)	δ¹³C (‰)	Calibrated date (2σ range)
28	28.518km	530	375	-0.72	Roundwood (*Alnus*)	NZA-27527	3090±30	-28.5	1430–1270 cal BC
29	28.518km	529	376	-1.25	*Alnus* cones	NZA-27522	3601±30	-27.9	2040–1880 cal BC
30	28.518km	529	377	-1.48	Roundwood (indet.)	NZA-27534	3629±30	-29.9	2130–1900 cal BC
31	28.518km	528	378	-1.63	Roundwood (*Alnus*)	NZA-27625	3912±40	-27.1	2560–2230 cal BC

Radiocarbon results from Aveley Marsh continued

No	Chainage/ Trench no	Sample no	Cxt no	Depth (m OD)	Sample material	Lab code	Radiocarbon date (BP)	δ¹³C (‰)	Calibrated date (2σ range)
32	28.518km	528	378	-1.88–1.91	Roundwood (indet.)	NZA-27528	3909±30	-28.8	2480–2290 cal BC
33	3984TT	8224	8450005 Gp 10004	+0.15	Roundwood (indet.)	NZA-27551	3757±35	-29.5	2290–2030 cal BC
34	3984TT	8424	8450005 Gp 10004	+0.02	Roundwood (indet.)	NZA-27552	3572±40	-28.2	2030–1770 cal BC

Radiocarbon results from the Thames River Crossing, Thurrock

No	Chainage/ Trench no	Sample no	Cxt no	Depth (m OD)	Sample material	Lab code	Radiocarbon date (BP)	δ¹³C (‰)	Calibrated date (2σ range)
35	BH 3742	-	-	-1.66	Plant stem	KIA-14419	1970±30	-26.79	50 cal BC – 110 cal AD
36	BH 3742	-	-	-6.01	Roundwood (*Alnus*)	KIA-14420	4115±30	-29.02	2870–2570 cal BC
37	BH 3742	-	-	-11.02	Roundwood (*Alnus*)	KIA-14421	6960±40	-29.41	5980–5740 cal BC

Radiocarbon results from Thames River Crossing, Swanscombe

No	Chainage/ Trench no	Sample no	Cxt no	Depth (m OD)	Sample material	Lab code	Radiocarbon date (BP)	δ¹³C (‰)	Calibrated date (2σ range)
38	3880TT	17	3880–4	-1.95	Roundwood (indet.)	NZA-29088	5004±40	-25.30	3950–3690 cal BC
39	3880TT	17	3880–4	-1.65	Roundwood (indet.)	NZA-29087	4707±35	-26.20	3640–3370 cal BC
40	3880TT	2	3880–4	-0.75	Roundwood (indet.)	NZA-29086	3372±35	-27.00	1750–1530 cal BC
41	3880TT	21	3880–4	-1.5	Bulk sediment	NZA-29085	7112±40	-30.50	6070–5900 cal BC
42	35.255km	-	3	-	Red deer antler	NZA-28891	4948±30	-20.50	3790–3650 cal BC
43	BH 3751	-	-	-0.20	Bulk sediment	NZA-27529	4497±30	-27.80	3350–3090 cal BC
44	BH 3751	-	-	-0.85	Seeds (*Schoenoplectus lacustris/tabarnaemontani*)	NZA-27523	2891±30	-24.50	1210–970 cal BC
45	BH 3751	-	-	-3.2 to -3.3	Plant stem	KIA-14422	3310±35	-25.46	1690–1500 cal BC
46	BH 3751	-	-	-3.81	Bulk peat	NZA-27530	4402±30	-28.10	3270–2910 cal BC
47	BH 3751	-	-	-4.39	*Phragmites* stem	NZA-27602	4655±30	-26.20	3520–3360 cal BC
48	BH 3751	-	-	-4.63	*Phragmites* stem	NZA-27636	5091±35	-25.20	3970–3790 cal BC
49	BH 3751	-	-	-4.71	*Phragmites* stem	NZA-27605	5244±35	-26.20	4230–3970 cal BC
50	BH 3751	-	-	-4.97	Plant stem	KIA-14478	5095±35	-25.48	3970–3790 cal BC
51	BH 3751	-	-	-8.61	Roundwood (*Betula*)	NZA-27603	6357±35	-28.20	5470–5220 cal BC
52	BH 3751	-	-	-8.77	Plant stem	KIA-14479	6935±35	-25.88	5900–5730 cal BC
53	BH 3751	-	-	-8.89	*Phragmites* stem	NZA-27599	7669±50	-27.00	6610–6430 cal BC
54	BH3852	-	-	-6.61	Wood/seeds (indet.)	KIA-14480	6325±35	-26.98	5380–5210 cal BC
55	BH 3862	-	-	-3.53 to -3.63	Wood (indet.)	KIA-14481	5035±35	-29.63	3950–3710 cal BC
56	BH 3864	-	-	-2.68	*Corylus* nutshell	KIA-14882	5330±45	-29.54	4330–4040 cal BC

Thames Holocene

Radiocarbon results from the Ebbsfleet Valley

No	Chainage/ Trench no	Sample no	Cxt no	Depth (m OD)	Sample material	Lab code	Radiocarbon date BP	δ¹³C (‰)	Calibrated date (2σ range)
	EBBS97								
57	BH5	-	-	-4.37	Roundwood (indet.)	Beta-108111	5770±60	-28.3	4730–4490 cal BC
58	BH9	-	-	-2.66	Roundwood (indet.)	Beta-108112	5260±60*	-28.3	4240–3960 cal BC
59	BH11	-	-	-6.18 to -6.23	Charred *Corylus* nutshell	Beta-108113	6420±60	-25.5	5490–5310 cal BC
60	Tr 2	-	211	3.80/ 0.40	*Corylus* nutshell	Beta-108114	4480±40	-28.9	3350–3020 cal BC
	STDR4								
61	BH7	Core 3	-	+0.88	*Sambucus* seeds	NZA-28620	1196±30	-25.3	710–940 cal AD
62	BH7	Core 13	-	-2.38	*Carduus/Cirsium* sp. seed	NZA-28973	3527±30	-27.2	1940–1750 cal BC
63	BH7	Core 15	-	-2.86	*Rubus* sp. seed	NZA-28971	3836±50	-27.0	2470–2140 cal BC
64	BH7	Core 17	-	-3.36	*Alnus glutinosa* twig	NZA-28869	4448±30	-29.2	3340–2940 cal BC
65	BH7	Core 17	-	-3.79	*Alnus glutinosa* mature wood, outer rings	NZA-28867	4820±25	-23.0	3700–3520 cal BC
66	BH7	Core 21	-	-4.68	2 *Alnus glutinosa* seeds	NZA-28972	5263±55	-27.2	4240–3970 cal BC
67	BH7	Core 21	-	-4.94	3 *Alnus glutinosa* seeds	NZA-28974	5464±35	-26.6	4370–4240 cal BC
68	BH7	Core 25	-	-6.30 to -6.39	Bulk sediment	WK-8801	6340±80*	-28.6	5480–5070 cal BC
69	BH7	Core 27	-	-6.73	Bulk sediment	NZA-28766	9122±55	-30.3	8540–8240 cal BC
70	BH8	-	-	-6.34 to -6.43	Bulk sediment	WK-8802	5880±60*	-	4910–4580 cal BC
71	Tr 9	103	910	+0.72	Bulk sediment	SUERC-16657 (GU-16003)	1290±35	-28.2	650–810 cal AD
72	Tr 9	104	912	+0.33	Bulk sediment	SUERC-16658 (GU-16004)	1740±35	-28.4	220–410 AD
73	Tr 9	104	914	+0.04	Bulk sediment	SUERC-16659 (GU-16005)	3840±35	-27.2	2460–2200 cal BC
74	Tr 9	105	916	-0.03	Bulk sediment	SUERC-16660 (GU-16006)	2605±35	-28.7	840–590 cal BC
75	Tr 9	105	916	-0.31	Bulk sediment	SUERC-16661 (GU-16007)	2820±35	-28.1	1120–890 cal BC
76	Tr 9	105	918	-0.58	Bulk sediment	SUERC-16662 (GU-16008)	3725±35	-26.7	2280–2020 cal BC
77	Tr 9	107	934	-1.89	*Alnus glutinosa* roundwood	NZA-29077	4663±35	-27.7	3620–3360 cal BC
78	Tr 9	107	934	-2.32	*Alnus glutinosa* roundwood	NZA-29080	4926±35	-27.8	3780–3640 BC
79	Tr 11		1119		Waterlogged roundwood from peat around Ebbsfleet Ware pot	WK-8799	4730±70 *	-28.4	3640–3360 cal BC
80	Tr 11	Ves1	1119		Charred residue from Ebbsfleet Ware pot	NZA- 29079	4723±35	-26.1	3640–3370 cal BC
81	Tr 11		1119		Waterlogged *Corylus* nutshell from peat around Ebbsfleet Ware pot	WK-8800	4696±75	-28.6	3650–3340 cal BC
82	Tr 11	Ves2	1119		Charred residue from Ebbsfleet Ware pot	NZA- 29155	4547±35	-28.5	3370-3100 cal BC

* Radiometric measurements from bulk sediment or waterlogged wood

Radiocarbon results from the Ebbsfleet Valley continued

No	Chainage/ Trench no	Sample no	Cxt no	Depth (m OD)	Sample material	Lab code	Radiocarbon date BP	δ¹³C (‰)	Calibrated date (2σ range)
83	Area 1	-	1071	-	Roundwood (cf *Frangula alnus*)	SUERC-19949	2615±30	-26.4	835–765 cal BC
84	Area 1	-	1012	-	Cattle femur	SUERC-19947	2385±30	-21.8	730–390 cal BC
85	Area 4	-	Str 4027 (4033)	-0.59	*Alnus glutinosa*, waterlogged roundwood	SUERC-19950 (GU-17164)	4120±30	-27.9	2870–2570 cal BC
86	Area 4	432	4043	-2.19	*Corylus* nutshell	NZA-29247	4945±35	-23.6	3800–3650 cal BC
87	Area 4	491	4053	-2.24	*Corylus* charred nutshell	NZA-29246	5405±35	-24.3	4350–4070 cal BC
	ARCERC01								
88	-	134	466	-	*Prunus* sp. roundwood charcoal	NZA-28445	3379±35	-25.8	1760–1530 cal BC
	ARCEBB01								
89	-	11153	15086	-	Cremated human bone	NZA-28208	3113±30	-22.0	1450–1300 cal BC
	ARC342W 02								
90	-	-	246	-	*Quercus* sp. waterlogged wooden pile tip, mature outer rings	NZA- 28703	3055±30	-25.9	1410–1220 cal BC

Soil micromorphology: Samples and counts

Location	Thin section (from monolith)	Context number	Depth in monolith (cm)	Micro-facies	SMT	Voids (%)	Fe-roots traces	Roots	Fine organic matter	Burnt flint	Coarse quartzite	Charcoal	Humified peat	More humus	Moder humus	Textural clay
20.5km Ripple Lane Portal, West Dagenham Marsh	1026A	2044/2045	110–110.5	C2	3b–3c	30		aa	aaaaa			a	aaa	aaa	aaa	
	1026A	2045	110.5–118	C1	3a–3b	40		aaaaa	aa (aaaa)	a–1			aa	aaaa		
24.455km East of Ferry Lane, Rainham Marsh	256A	193a	0–6.5	B4	2a–2b	35		aaaaa	aaaaa			a★	aaa			
	256B	193b	9.5–11.5	B1	2a	25		aaa	aaaa	a★		a★				
	256B	192	11.5–17	A3	1	5–15		a	aa	aaaa	a–2	a(aa)				
26.535km Wennington Marsh	366	233	28–30	E2	5a	25	a★		aaa	(a–1)		(aaa)				
	366	234	30–36	E1	5a	5–10	a★		aaa		1xFlint	(aaa)				
27.460km Wennington Marsh	438	268	7–9	E1	5a/5ac	20	a★	a★	aaa(aaaa)			(aaaaa)	(aaaa)			
	438	269	9.0–9.5	B1	2a	20	a	aa	aaaaa				aaaaa			
	438	269	9.5–15	E2	5b, 5c	35	a	a	aaaa			(aaa)	(aaa)			
BH3748 Thames Crossing Swanscombe	3748A	na	24–32	D8/D7	2c/4b2	30	a	aa	aaaa			a★				
	3748B	na	32–40	D7	4b2	30	a★	aaaaa	aaaa			a★				
3880TT Thames Crossing Swanscombe	17A	388004/6	42–50	D3	4c	45		aaaaa	aaaa			a★				
	17B	388006	50–54	D2	4b	5–20		aaa	aa	aaa		a★				
	17B	388006/5	54–57.5	D1	4a	20		aaa	a★							aa
	21A	388004/6	0–7.5	D6	4e, 4f1, 4f2	5–25		aaaaa	a★(aa/aaaa)	aa		a	aa			a★
	21B	388006	7.5–15	D6	4e, 4f1, 4f2	5–25		aaaaa	a★(aa/aaaa)	a★?		a★	aa			a
	21C	388006	38.5–43.5	D5	4d	30		aa	a★							aaaaa
	21C	388005	43.5–46.5	D4	4a	25		aaa	a★							

★ – very few 0–5%   f – few 5–15%   ff – frequent 15–30%   fff – common 30–50%   ffff – dominant 50–70%   fffff – very dominant >70%,
a – rare <2% (a★1%; a–1, single occurrence)   aa – occasional 2–5%   aaa – many 5–10%   aaaa – abundant 10–20%   aaaaa – very abundant >20%

Soil micromorphology: samples and counts continued

Location	Thin section (from monolith)	Context number	Depth in monolith (cm)	Micro-facies	SMT	Textural intercal	Textural silt	Bedding	2ndry Fe	Pyrite	Gypsum	Nodular carbonate	<500 um burrows	Broad burrows	Granule
20.5km Ripple Lane Portal, West Dagenham Marsh	1026A	2044/2045	110–110.5	C2	3b–3c			f	a				aa	aa	
	1026A	2045	110.5–118	C1	3a–3b			f	a				aaa	aa	
24.455km East of Ferry Lane, Rainham Marsh	256A	193a	0–6.5	B4	2a–2b			ff	a				aaaa	aaaa	
	256B	193b	9.5–11.5	B1	2a				a–1				aa		
	256B	192	11.5–17	A3	1		aaa		a*						
26.535km Wennington Marsh	366	233	28–30	E2	5a	a			aa(aaaa)					aaa	a–1 (slug?)
	366	234	30–36	E1	5a	aa	a	(fffff)	aa(aaaa)					aaa	a–2
27.460km Wennington Marsh	438	268	7–9	E1	5a/ac			fffff	aaa				a	aa	
	438	269	9.0–9.5	B1	2a			(fffff)	aaaa				aa		
	438	269	9.5–15	E2	5b, 5c				aa	a*	a*		aa	aaaaa	
BH3748 Thames Crossing Swanscombe	3748A	na	24–32	D8/D7	2c/4b2			fff	aa		aa	aa			
	3748B	na	32–40	D7	4b2			fff	a		aa	aa			
3880TT Thames Crossing Swanscombe	17A	388004/6	42–50	D3	4c	aaa	aa					aaaa			
	17B	388006	50–54	D2	4b	aaa					a*	a			
	17B	388006/5	54–57.5	D1	4a					aa		a*			
	21A	388004/6	0–7.5	D6	4e, 4f1, 4f2	aaa	aaaaa		aa		a*	aaa			
	21B	388006	7.5–15	D6	4e, 4f1, 4f2	aaaa	aaaaa		aa			aaa			
	21C	388006	38.5–43.5	D5	4d	aaaaa		(ff)	aaa		a*	aaa			
	21C	388005	43.5–46.5	D4	4a				aa		aa				

* – very few 0–5%   f – few 5–15%   ff – frequent 15–30%   fff – common 30–50%   ffff – dominant 50–70%   fffff – very dominant >70%,

a – rare <2% (a*1%; a–1, single occurrence)   aa – occasional 2–5%   aaa – many 5–10%   aaaa – abundant 10–20%   aaaaa – very abundant >20%

20.5km Ripple Lane Portal, West Dagenham Marsh

Microfacies type (MFT) and Soil microfabric type (SMT)	Thin section	Depth (from top of monolith) and Soil micromorphology (SM)	Interpretation and Comments
MFT C2 SMT 3b and 3c	1026A	110–110.5cm: Homogeneous bedded and layered *Microstructure:* massive with fine (2–4mm) layering; 30%, simple and complex packing voids and poorly formed planar voids *Coarse mineral:* C:F, 35:65 (F= SMT 3b; amorphous organic matter); moderately well sorted coarse silt-very fine sand *Coarse organic and anthropogenic:* very abundant flattened coarse horizontal plant tissues and organs (leaves, lignified plant remains, roots); occasional sand-size charcoal/charred plant remains in lower thinly layered beds *Fine fabric:* SMT 3b (as below, but with abundant tissues and organs) in lower beds; upwards – SMT 3c: pale yellowish brown to brown (PPL), isotic (undifferentiated b-fabric, XPL), very dark yellowish to blackish brown (OIL); layered plant fragments and pellety amorphous organic matter (poorly humified moder) *Pedofeatures:* very abundant very thin to thin (100–500µm) aggregated organic excrements. Sloping and irregular boundary	2044: Above sloping and irregular boundary, there are initially bedded fine sands and silts and humified organic matter (mor humus), which includes rare charcoal/charred organic fragments; upwards – layers of horizontal compact plant fragments and intercalated pellety amorphous organic matter *Renewed colluviation (possibly of anthropogenic origin) containing charcoal within humic fine sands and silts – and associated erosion of 2045?, becoming a moder humus under presumed woodland (producing coarse roots present here and in 2045)*
MFT C1 SMT 3a and 3b		110.5–118cm: Heterogeneous (common SMT 3a and 3b) *Microstructure:* massive with weak layering; 40% voids, few very fine (0.5mm) and dominant very coarse (max 20mm) root channels, complex packing voids *Coarse mineral:* C:F, 95:05 (SMT 3a) and 80:20 (SMT 3b); SMT 3a: moderately poorly sorted very fine and medium sand-size subangular to rounded quartz (and feldspar), with coarse silt; SMT 3b: moderately sorted coarse silt, with fine and medium sand; also fragments of thin (0.5mm) bands mixed silt and sand *Coarse organic and anthropogenic:* very abundant coarse (max 20mm) woody roots, occasional horizontal very fine (0.5mm) fleshy roots; examples of sand-size calcined flint and other whitened mineral grains *Fine fabric:* SMT 3a: as SMT 3b (pellety and coated); SMT 3b: blackish brown (PPL), isotic (pellety [microaggregates], coated and bridged, undifferentiated b-fabric, XPL), very dark reddish to blackish brown (OIL); very abundant amorphous fine organic matter, with occasional tissues and organs; spores/pollen present *Pedofeatures:* Amorphous: very weak ferrugination of some roots. Fabric: many thin to broad (1–2mm) burrows. Excrements: very abundant very thin to thin (100–500µm) aggregated organic excrements	2045: Bioturbated sands and humic silts, with fine to very coarse (woody) roots; fine amorphous organic matter is as highly humified microaggregates (excrement pellets); rare traces of fine sand-size burnt flint and other minerals *Once-bedded sands and humic silts formed as accreting sands and humic silts, with contemporary weathering and biological activity forming a Ah/mor horizon acidic topsoil; possibly colluvial sediments include rare traces of burnt flint from nearby (upslope) occupation; subsequently coarsely rooted*

24.455km East of Ferry Lane, Rainham Marsh

Microfacies type MFT) and Soil microfabric type (SMT)	Thin section	Depth (from top of monolith) and Soil micromorphology (SM)	Interpretation and *Comments*
MFT B4 SMT 2a–2b	256A	0–6.5cm: Heterogeneous (layered and burrowed) *Microstructure:* massive, burrowed and channel; 35% voids, coarse (5mm) root channels and simple packing voids *Coarse mineral:* C:F, 85:15 (fragments coarse silt sediment) to 65:35 (minerogenic peat) *Coarse organic and anthropogenic:* very abundant coarse (max 6mm) plant roots (possible woody roots) and lignified/bark(?) fragments, with abundant coarse patches of burrowed humified amorphous organic matter and wood/plant fragments; rare traces of sand-size charcoal *Fine fabric:* SMT 2a and 2b (coarsely mixed) *Pedofeatures:* Amorphous: rare ferruginisation of some plant fragments and peat. Fabric: abundant to thin to broad burrows; very broad burrow/root mixing. Excrements: abundant thin to broad organic excrements, some associated with humified peat fragments	193a: Coarsely biologically mixed broadly layered peat and minerogenic peat, with patches and fragments of humified peat and plant/woody fragments *Finely and coarsely mixed minerogenic peat and humified (wood?) peat layers, by both rooting and mesofauna activity; implies fluctuating water tables and exposure episodes*
MFT B1 SMT 2a	256B	9.5–11.5cm: Homogeneous; as thin section 1C, SMT 2a, MFT B1 (described below), with rare traces of fine burnt flint and charred OM and charcoal M1C, SMT 2a, MFT B1 *Microstructure:* massive, with ~8mm layering/bedding; channel; 25% voids, medium to coarse (2–10mm) channels, simple packing voids *Coarse mineral:* C:F, 65:35, thin beds of well sorted coarse silt, with very fine sand; patches and thin beds of very poorly sorted coarse silt to medium sand (mineralogy as below) *Coarse organic and anthropogenic:* very abundant coarse (2–10mm) plant roots (possible woody roots) and fragments, some showing horizontal orientation *Fine fabric:* SMT 2a: speckled reddish brown (PPL), isotropic (open to close porphyric, undifferentiated b-fabric, XPL), brown with reddish brown (OIL); very abundant amorphous organic matter, with organ and tissue fragments; parenchymatous cells etc; rare traces of phytoliths *Pedofeatures:* Amorphous: rare example of iron hypocoating on a fine sub-vertical channel. Moderately sharp, gently sloping boundary; very finely burrowed junction	193b: minerogenic peat with trace amounts of burnt fine flint and charcoal present; thin burrowing *Biologically worked base of minerogenic peat, with trace amounts of anthropogenic inclusions (picked up locally?)*
MFT A3 SMT 1		11.5–17cm: Moderately heterogeneous (silt inwash) *Microstructure:* massive, with crack/channel; <5%, 15% open vughs, fine (3mm) channels and coarse (1mm) cracks; simple packing voids *Coarse mineral:* C:F, 80:20, with frequent gravel-size angular quartzite and flint (see below); example of fragmenting weathered glauconite *Coarse organic and anthropogenic:* rare coarse root; abundant coarse (11mm) burnt (rubefied and calcined) flint, with 2 coarse (12mm) angular quartzite fragments; rare 2mm charcoal *Fine fabric:* SMT 1 (with trace of fine charcoal) (occasional rounded fine charcoal/blackened organic matter in silt inwash) *Pedofeatures:* Textural: many coarse silt inwash as 2–3mm wide fills (ex-burrows/root channels?) – merging boundaries with surrounding 'soil'; include fine rounded charcoal and amorphous organic matter. Amorphous: rare traces of fine weak iron impregnations	Context 192: Artefact- (burnt coarse and fine flint with coarse quartzite) rich poorly sorted coarse silt-medium weakly humic sands, with rare 2mm size charcoal; compact (collapsed structure with probable loss of fines); broad burrow/channel infills of coarse silt and fine charcoal; rare coarse roots *Possible truncated in situ occupation soil rich in burnt artefacts, with inundation causing loss of structure (loss of fines), associated with coarse silt inwash carrying fine detrital charcoal*

26.535km Wennington Marsh

Microfacies type (MFT) and Soil microfabric type (SMT)	Thin section	Depth (from top of monolith) and Soil micromorphology (SM)	Interpretation and *Comments*
MFT E2/SMT 5a	366	28–30cm Mainly homogeneous (with burrows) *Microstructure:* massive, channel and vughy, 25% voids, very fine (<1mm) vughs and channels, very few 1mm size root channels *Coarse mineral:* C:F, 40:60, moderately poorly sorted coarse silt-very fine sand- and medium and coarse sand-size subangular quartz (quartzite), with examples of flint *Coarse organic and anthropogenic:* rare root traces; rare fine (200μm) charcoal and rare to occasional plant fragments; example of coarse sand-size (1mm) weakly burnt (calcined) ferruginous chert and partially weathered biogenic calcite (slug plate) *Fine Fabric:* SMT 5a *Pedofeatures:* as below, with burrowed boundary – two broad 2mm wide burrows	233: Moderately poorly clayey sediment containing coarse silt, very fine to coarse sand, including burnt coarse sand-size chert and much fine charred and amorphous organic matter fragments; burrowed with example of possible slug plate; rooted, depleted and iron stained as below; sharp but burrowed boundary to clayey 234 *Moderately poorly sorted very fine to coarse sandy loam sediment, that was possibly erosive (removing weathered/ripened clay surface from 234; see below), and which contains anthropogenic inclusions (burnt mineral and charcoal); fine sand inwash/sedimentation infiltrated 234 below; probable biological homogenisation of sediment; burrowing affected boundary to 234*
MFT E1/SMT 5a		30–36cm: Mainly homogeneous (30–33cm) and mainly clayey, and moderately heterogeneous (partly burrowed) laminated (33–36cm: silty and clayey, with 1mm thick coarse silt/very fine sand bed/injection/inwash – associated with 4mm wide fill – from 233? *Microstructure:* massive (30–33cm) and laminar (33–36cm; 350–500μm thick, even, parallel beds, with minor wavy, parallel at base), 5–10% voids, fine sub-horizontal planar voids and very fine vughs, simple packing voids; trace examples of fine vesicles; very few fine channels *Coarse mineral:* C:F (Coarse:Fine limit at 10μm), 60/90: 40/10 (silty) and 10:90 (clayey), well sorted medium and coarse silt-size quartz (and mica), with few very fine sand-size quartz, very few fine and medium sand-size subrounded clasts of reddish brown clay; example of gravel-size (3mm) flint *Coarse organic and anthropogenic:* many very fine (max 250μm) charred organic matter and sub-horizontally oriented plant fragments, fine sand-size amorphous organic matter present; two egs of 1mm size earthworm granules, 3mm size flint; rare 1mm root traces (Fe stained channels) *Fine fabric:* SMT 5a: finely speckled, pale to darkish brown (PPL), low to moderately high interference colours (mainly open to very open porphyric, speckled and weakly developed uni-strial b-fabrics (patches of weak crystallitic), XPL), grey to pale reddish brown (OIL); very thin to moderate humic staining, with rare to occasional very fine charred and amorphous OM); pollen/spores, calcite and phytoliths present *Pedofeatures: Textural:* rare intercalations and associated vesicles, associated clayey void coatings (500μm at base of burrow). *Depletion:* patchy probable iron depletion, especially in upper 3cm (later? rooting?) moderately strongly impregnative Fe. *Fabric:* many thin to broad (1–2 mm) burrows, associated with unistrial b-fabric in places, contain mixed clay, iron-stained fragmented clay and organic matter	234: Finely (350–500μm thick) laminated (mainly even, parallel beds), silt (with very fine sand) & clay, becoming massive clayey upwards, with thin to broad burrows and a 3mm example of flint, with two earthworm granules; much detrital very fine charred and amorphous organic matter (oriented in lower laminated part); burrowed areas include clay fragments with included clay clasts and organic matter; vesicles, intercalations, part burrow clayey void coatings; much weak iron staining (more Fe depleted in massive upper part); later fine root iron staining/depletion features. (BD: organic content reflected by 3.85% LOI, iron staining by χ_{max}) *Laminated silt and clay estuarine sediment became more massive clayey upwards (diminished energy – cut-off from sea/reclaimed marsh?); earthworm working & ripened humic clay surface (now truncated) worked down profile. Relative 'high' 2.37% χ_{conv} may reflect relict (post-waterlogging) magnetic susceptibility of in sediment fine burnt material* *Both 233 and 234 can be associated with human landscape management and activities* 235: Bulk data evidence of probably similar origins to 234
		BD 234: 3.85% LOI, 0.766 mg g⁻¹ Phosphate-P, 14.6 x 10⁻⁸ SI χ_3 2.37% χ_{conv}, BD 235: 3.30% LOI, 0.810 mg g⁻¹ Phosphate-P, 14.6 x 10⁻⁸ SI χ_3 1.727% χ_{conv},	

27.460km Wennington Marsh

Microfacies type (MFT) and Soil microfabric type (SMT)	Thin section	Depth (from top of monolith) and Soil Micromorphology (SM)	Interpretation and *Comments*
MFT E1 SMT 5a/5ac	438	7–9cm: Heterogeneous/layered (a: clayey, b: very fine sandy, c: fine charcoal-rich). *Microstructure:* laminar (2–4mm thick laminates); Coarse Mineral: C:F, a: 05:95, b: 90:10, c: 15:85 *Coarse organic and anthropogenic:* rare fine root remains; laminae with very abundant fine 'peat' and OM fragments, and laminae with very abundant fine charred OM *Fine fabric:* a and c: as in M234; c: speckled and very heavily dotted (PPL), moderate interference colours (open porphyric, speckled b-fabric, XPL), greyish brown with very abundant black inclusions; humic stained with very abundant humified, blackened and charred fine OM and tissues *Pedofeatures:* Amorphous: many weak to moderate iron staining. Fabric: occasional broad burrows (eg. mixing fine sands)	268: multiple thin (2–4mm) laminations of very fine sand, humic clay containing silt and very fine sand, with high concentrations of blackened and charred fine organic matter *Alluviation, depositing clean very fine sand, and clayey silts rich in detrital and locally(?) eroded weathered peat and background fine charcoal*
MFT B1 SMT 2a		9–9.5cm: Homogeneous *Microstructure:* very fine laminar with fine planar; 20% voids, very fine planar and fine chambers *Coarse mineral:* C:F, 05:95, well sorted coarse silt, very fine sand *Coarse organic and anthropogenic:* occasional medium (1000–1250µm) fleshy roots (post-peat?), abundant sub-horizontal monocotyledonous plant fragments and very abundant amorphous organic matter (reddish brown, humified) *Fine fabric:* SMT 2a *Pedofeatures:* Amorphous: many fine strong and abundant moderate iron impregnation of amorphous OM and plant tissues. Fabric: occasional thin (400µm) burrows and chambers. Excrements: occasional very thin (50µm) organic excrements	269 upper: Uppermost 5mm of dark reddish brown layered humified peat (15.9% LOI, amorphous organic matter and layered plant fragments), with small biochannels containing very thin organic excrements
MFT E2 SMT 5b and 5c		9.5–15cm: Moderately heterogeneous *Microstructure:* fine angular blocky (massive, burrowed, channel), 35% voids, fine (<1 mm) angular curved planar voids and fine (1–2mm) chambers and fine channels; Coarse Mineral: C:F, 25:75, well sorted silt to medium sand-size quartz *Coarse Organic and Anthropogenic:* rare root remains, *in situ* and in fragments abundant fine humified plant fragments and fine charred and amorphous OM *Fine Fabric:* SMT 5b and SMT 5c, as humic and poorly humic variants of SMT 5a (grano-striate examples) *Pedofeatures:* Crystalline: rare traces of gypsum. Amorphous: rare traces of pyrite; occasional iron impregnation. Fabric: very abundant broad (2mm) burrows. Excrements: rare thin (<500µm) organic excrements	269 lower: Heterogeneous humic and poorly humic clays (with silt and very few sand), showing un-oriented blackened, humified and charred organic matter inclusions, with burrows and channels, and angular blocky structures; iron staining (and trace amounts of pyrite and gypsum *Ripened peaty clay–humic clay, burrowed and rooted, with formation of pedological structures (angular blocks) – lowering of water table; original oriented organic content was homogenised (cf horizontal oriented detrital OM in unworked peaty clays of 268); renewed rise in water table and laminated peat formation – affected by minor ripening (chamber fills of organic excrements), prior to flooding and renewed alluviation (268)*
		BD 269: 15.9% LOI, 0.978 mg g^{-1} Phosphate-P, 7.40 x 10^{-8} SI χ, 0.836% χ_{conv}, BD 270: 4.32% LOI, 0.690 mg g^{-1} Phosphate-P, 12.7 x 10^{-8} SI χ, 1.51% χ_{conv},	270: bulk data suggests probable humic clays, similar to lower part of 269

BH3748 Thames Crossing Swanscombe

Microfacies type MFT) and Soil microfabric type (SMT)	Thin section	Depth (from top of core) and Soil micromorphology (SM)	Interpretation and *Comments*
MFT D8 SMT 2c over MFT D7 SMT 4b2	3748A	24–32cm: SM: as below (with fewer [occasional] roots and many iron impregnations), becoming more organic (horizontally oriented plant fragments and long [5mm] plant fragments in dominantly organic laminae at 26cm SMT 2c: pale brown, horizontal oriental plant-dominated (PPL), moderately low interference colours (very open porphyric, plant-associated pseudo-unistrial b-fabric, XPL), brown to darkish brown (OIL); very abundant plat tissues	Horizontally layered monocotyledonous plant fragments, with humic clayey matrix and very sparse silt, over (sharp boundary) laminated humic clays with detrital organic matter content (as below) *Laminated in situ-formed peat over probable low energy mudflat deposits. (No evidence of sediment ripening/soil formation)*
MFT D7 SMT 4b2	3748B	32–40cm: Homogeneous *Microstructure:* massive with relict fine (1–2mm) laminae; 30% fine to very coarse (1–6mm) channels *Coarse mineral:* C:F, 10:90, well sorted coarse silt with very few fine sand-size quartz *Coarse organic and anthropogenic:* very abundant medium to coarse flattened horizontal and vertical (browned & blackened) roots & traces; very abundant sub-horizontally oriented monocotyledonous plant fragments and amorphous organic matter; trace amounts of very fine charcoal *Fine Fabric:* SMT 4b2: heavily speckled dark yellowish brown (PPL), moderately high interference colours (very open porphyric, speckled and pseudo-unistrial b-fabric (root and plant fragment-associated), XPL), darkish brown (OIL); patchy humic staining many to abundant amorphous OM and tissue fragments *Pedofeatures: Textural:* many intercalations, some associated with relict rooting/root traces. Fabric: many areas of slickensides/preferred orientation (associated with rooting?). *Crystalline:* occasional gypsum crystals throughout, rare carbonate void infills *Amorphous:* rare weak iron impregnations	Laminated (1–2 mm) humic clays with sparse coarse silt and generally horizontally oriented very abundant detrital plant fragments, with very abundant coarse roots producing sediment disruption and working; minor iron staining, probable carbonate concentrations, with occasional fine gypsum crystal formation throughout *Very low energy humic clays with silt, which are finer and better sorted compared to peaty silts at Thames Crossing coffer excavation at Swanscombe (M17A-B, M21A-C), consistent with mudflat deposition*

3880TT Thames Crossing Swanscombe

Microfacies type (MFT) and Soil microfabric type (SMT)	Thin section	Depth (from top of monolith) and Soil micromorphology (SM)	Interpretation and *Comments*
MFT D3 SMT 4c	M17A	42–50cm: SM as upper M17B/SMT 4b *Microstructure:* massive and channel; 45% voids, very coarse (10mm) vertical channels; simple packing voids *Coarse organic and anthropogenic:* very abundant very coarse fleshy roots; rare traces of charcoal *Fine fabric:* SMT 4c, as SMT 4a, with very abundant fine amorphous organic matter and tissues *Pedofeatures:* as upper M17B. *Textural:* occasional silt infillings of root channels. *Crystalline:* abundant thick (1–2mm) calcium carbonate hypocoatings affecting vertical root channels. Fabric: very abundant mixing and slickenside/preferred orientation – from rooting	388004/6: Very humic poorly sorted coarse silt and fine sand, with very abundant coarse roots and root fragments, with strong fabric mixing and disturbance by roots and marked secondary carbonate hypocoating formation; trace amounts of charcoal present *Successive rooting and root mixing/disturbance of wet soil/sediment, with calcareous substrate leading to much secondary carbonate nodular formation along root channels – fluctuating water tables*

3880TT Thames Crossing Swanscombe continued

Microfacies type (MFT) and Soil microfabric type (SMT)	Thin section	Depth (from top of monolith) and Soil micromorphology (SM)	Interpretation and *Comments*
MFT D2 SMT 4b	M17B	50–54cm: Heterogeneous *Microstructure:* massive with relict broad bedding; compact – 5%, with 20% very to very coarse (7mm) channels *Coarse mineral:* C:F, 90:10, poorly sorted coarse silt to medium sand (and gravel size flint), as SMT 1, but with angular feldspar *Coarse organic and anthropogenic:* many medium to coarse flattened horizontal and vertical roots and traces; many burnt (calcined and rubefied) angular flint (3+ – max 24mm); rare trace of fine charcoal *Fine Fabric:* SMT 4b, as SMT 1, but with grano- and parallel striate b-fabrics in places *Pedofeatures: Textural:* many intercalations, some associated with relict rooting/root traces Fabric: many areas of slickensides/preferred orientation (associated with rooting?) Crystalline: rare traces of coarse dense CaCO₃ nodular formation and gypsum crystals Semi-horizontal boundary	388006: Massive poorly mixed humic silt and medium sand, containing many very coarse burnt flint, and trace of charcoal; all affected by abundant semi-aquatic plant(?) rooting, many intercalations, preferred orientation and some nodular (calcium?, sodium?) carbonate formation *Short-lived weakly biologically worked and weathered poorly sorted silts and medium sands, containing plant fragments; occupied (local burnt rock midden?); inundation and rooting through slaking and collapsing 'soil'*
MFT D1 SMT 4a		54–55cm: laminated silts and very fine sand with yellow clay matrix (see Textural Pedofeature, below), silts and silty fine sands 55–57.5cm: Heterogeneous *Microstructure:* massive/poorly layered(?); 20% voids, fine to medium (0.5–4mm) root channels, fine horizontal planar voids *Coarse mineral:* C:F, 80:20, very poorly sorted rounded chalk clasts (gravel ~10mm) with coarse silt fine sand and sand-size chalk clasts in matrix *Coarse organic and anthropogenic:* many blackened fine to medium roots (0.5–4mm); *Fine Fabric:* SMT 4a: cloudy grey (PPL), high interference colours (close porphyric, crystallitic b-fabric, XPL), white (OIL); rare traces of fine amorphous organic matter and tissues *Pedofeatures: Textural:* many thin to coarse (0.2–1.0mm) yellow poorly oriented limpid clay inwash (see above). Crystalline: rare traces of fine dense CaCO₃ nodular formation. Amorphous: occasional patches of pyrite framboids associated with roots	388005: 10mm of finely bedded silts and silty clay over weakly bedded chalk gravel in calcareous silt and sand loam, with inwashed yellow clay from base of context 6; rooting and localised pyrite and traces of nodular carbonate (CaCO₃, NaCO₃) formation *Soliflual chalky deposit, with declining energy – low energy becoming fluvial/colluvial silts*
MFT D6 SMT 4e, 4f1, 4f2	M21A	0–7.5cm: Heterogeneous (common palaeosol SMT 4e [context 388004]) and common estuarine silts – SMT 4f [context 388004]): as M21B, with rare to occasional gravel-size (5mm) flint and burnt flint and fine charcoal; SMT 4e as SMT 4e in M21B, with thin humic staining and rare fine charred and blackened organic matter	388004–6 (peat-silty soil interface) *Strongly root-mixed boundary between weakly humic palaeosol (context 388006) with occasional burnt flint and fine charcoal, and peaty, carbonate and iron stained context 388004*

MFT D6 SMT 4e, 4f1, 4f2	M21B	7.5–15cm Heterogeneous (dominant palaeosol SMT 4e and common estuarine silts – SMT 4f) *Microstructure:* massive and channel; 5–25%, fine to coarse (12mm) root channels *Coarse mineral:* C:F, SMT 4e, 70:30, SMT 4f, 60:40, SMT 4e, as SMT 4d; SMT 4f moderately well sorted fine to coarse silt *Coarse organic and anthropogenic:* rare traces of fine charcoal, possible very fine calcined mineral; very abundant fine to very coarse (12mm), often woody (lignified cells) roots *Fine Fabric:* SMT 4e: speckled and dotted pale brown (PPL), low interference colours (close porphyric, speckled and grano-striate b-fabric, XPL), grey (OIL); very thin organic staining, rare traces of blackened (and charred) organic matter; SMT 4f1: speckled and dotted brownish (PPL), low interference colours (close porphyric, speckled b-fabric, XPL), pale brown (OIL); humic staining with occasional fine amorphous and tissue fragments, phytoliths and fungal material present; SMT4f2 – as SMT 4f1 (relict fleshy root channel fill); strong humic staining, very abundant amorphous organic matter and tissues, occasional fungal material, phytoliths present *Pedofeatures:* Textural: abundant intercalations and rare associated moderately thick (300μm) very finely dusty and laminated void coatings and infills. Depletion: probable strong iron depletion of matrix. Crystalline: many dense CaCO$_3$ (or possibly Na$_2$CO$_3$) nodular formation and broad (7mm) void (root channel) hypocoatings. Amorphous: occasional iron root and matrix impregnations. Fabric: very abundant fabric mixing of silt dominated 'soil', with slickenside-like features/preferred orientation of clay	388006: Compact silt-medium sand loam, with strong (woody) root mixing of weakly humic silt and humic silty clay (rich in plant tissues and fungal material – fleshy semi-aquatic rooting? [context 388004]). Compact soil with rare scatter of charcoal and possible fine burnt mineral, localised intercalations and dusty clay void infills; secondary iron and carbonate impregnations associated with roots and relict coarse root channels *Weakly humic palaeosol with included rare fine charcoal, undervent inundation and structural collapse and partial elutriation (washing into M21C); some mixing of initial estuarine silts, and ensuing complicated history of probable woody root impact and mixing, followed by fleshy root mixing-in of peat; fluctuating water tables also recorded by calcium carbonate and later iron impregnation (along channels)*
MFT D5 SMT 4d	M21C	38.5–43.5cm: Homogeneous (relict bedding) *Microstructure:* massive with weak channel; 30%, fine to coarse root channels, with fine closed vughs and vesicles; *Coarse Mineral:* C:F, 70:30, patches of moderately sorted silt-very fine sand, and moderately poorly sorted silt to medium sand *Coarse organic and anthropogenic:* occasional very fine (<0.5mm) to coarse (5mm) roots; rare traces of possible calcined mineral grains *Fine fabric:* SMT 4d (similar to SMT 4b, but non-humic), finely speckled pale yellowish brown (PPL), moderately low interference colours (close porphyric, speckled and grano-striate [see intercalations] b-fabric, XPL), grey (OIL); rare traces of fine blackened organic matter *Pedofeatures:* Textural: very abundant intercalations and associated thick (100–300μm) very finely dusty void coatings and infills. Depletion: probable strong iron depletion of matrix. Crystalline: many dense CaCO$_3$ (Na$_2$CO$_3$) nodular formation and broad (2–3mm) void (root channel) hypocoatings; rare traces of gypsum at boundary between contexts 388005 and 388006. Amorphous: many iron root and matrix impregnations. Fabric: very abundant fabric mixing of silt dominated 'soil' Irregular boundary	388006: massive, partially mixed silt and medium sandy loams, dominated by textural pedofeatures (intercalations and void infills) of structural collapse and mixing and 'bedding'; secondary features include occasional roots and rare gypsum, and many ferruginous and calcareous (sodic) impregnations with some finely dusty clay void coatings being associated with rooting *Non-calcareous solifluction/solifual poorly bedded silt and medium sandy loam (Head) deposits, as evidence of Late Glacial (possibly Zone III, Loch Lomond Stadial?) slope erosion and deposition – see WHS and Folkestone; down-profile clay movement and slickenside-like fabric features related to rooting and structural collapse higher up (eg, M21B) and in situ thixotrophic (water saturated condition); iron and calcium carbonate impregnation linked to Holocene rooting into calcareous gravels below, and ensuing oxygenation (iron movement)*
MFT D4 SMT 4a		43.5–46.5cm: as MFT D1, but with rounded coarse ironstone (7mm) and flint (18mm) gravel; relict 388005: ironstone and flint gravel-rich bed, with traces remains of calcareous SMT 4a – root mixing with overlying SMT 5a *Pedofeatures:* Crystalline: occasional gypsum laths. Amorphous: occasional iron impregnation and void hypocoatings	388005: ironstone and flint gravel-rich bed, with traces of original calcareous matrix mixed with silty clay from above; gypsum and root traces present *Solifual gravel (coarse Head deposits)*

Bulk analysis

Wennington Marsh	Context	LOI (%)	Phosphate-P_i (mg g^{-1})	Phosphate-P_o (mg g^{-1})	Phosphate-P (mg g^{-1})	Phosphate-P_i:P (%)	Phosphate-P_o:P (%)	χ (10^{-8} SI)	χ_{max} (10^{-8} SI)	χ_{conv} (%)
26.535km	234	3.85	0.554	0.212	0.766	72.3	27.7	14.6	617	2.37
	235	3.30	0.621	0.189	0.810	76.7	23.3	14.6	847	1.72
27.460km	269	15.9	0.667	0.311	0.978	68.2	31.8	7.40	885	0.836
	270	4.32	0.493	0.197	0.690	71.4	28.6	12.7	842	1.51

Appendix C

Tables

Table 8 Route corridor Windows and Zone descriptors

Window	Chainages (km)	Zones	Zone distances (km)	Description	Priority
6	17.3–18.92	T1	17.3–17.66	This zone is characterised by thin alluvial sequences of Holocene clay-silts and peats overlying the Pleistocene gravels at datums of c -1.5m OD	Medium
		T2	17.66–18.04	This zone is characterised by a steep descent in the rockhead datums from c -5.0m OD to c -9.0m OD and a corresponding, although less marked, decrease in the elevation of the upper surface of the Pleistocene sands and gravels. Holocene sediments consist of peat immediately overlying the Pleistocene sediments and a thin sequence of clay-silts above the peat. Holocene sediments are thicker than that within Zone T1	Low
		T3	18.04–19.06	This zone, which extends into Window 7, is characterised by rockhead datums of -9.0m OD with the upper surface of the Pleistocene deposits typically resting at -4.0m OD. Holocene sediments consist of thick sequences of peats, above a thin minerogenic basal unit, and a thick cover of clay-silts. Only at 18.287km does a second peat appear in the sequence. Some lateral variability in sequence type is noted particularly where organic silts replace peats at about 18.6km	Low
7	18.92–21.40	T3	18.04–19.06	As above	Low
		T4	19.06–19.83	This zone contains Pleistocene gravels resting on bedrock between -9.0m and -10.0m OD, with upper surface datums for the gravels between -4.5m and -6.0m OD. The upper surface of the gravels undulates with a major topographic low (possibly marking the position of a former floodplain channel tributary) at 19.325km. A major peat unit extends across this zone between -0.5m and -4.0m OD. Upper and lower contacts appear to dip gently from west to east along route corridor. Thin basal minerogenic deposits exist below the peat with coarser grained elements (including gravels and silts) in association with the low described at 19.325km (strengthening arguments suggesting this may represent the course of a floodplain tributary)	Low
		T5	19.83–19.94	This zone is defined by the sharp rise in the upper surface of the Pleistocene gravels from -6.0m OD to -3.5m OD. Peats exist immediately above the gravel surface here. The rockhead datum shows no comparable rise	Medium
		T6	19.94–20.75	Rockhead datums lie below -10.0m OD. The upper surface of the gravels dips gently eastwards from c -3.5m OD to in excess of -4.0m OD. Peat units, comparable in elevation to those in Zone 5, exist and dip towards the east following the underlying gravel contours. Thin clay-silt and sand units underlie the peat. Typically made ground extends from the ground surface to the top of the peat through much of this area	Low
		T7	20.75–21.65	This zone shows a dip in rockhead datums from -10.5m OD to -12.0m OD. A similar dip is noted in the gravel surface. Peat units exist in the western part of this zone but are replaced eastwards by organic silts. Sediments underlying the peat consist of sands or clay-silts	Low
8	21.40–24.39	T7	20.75–21.65	As above	Low
		T8	21.65–22.06	Rockhead datums lie at -10.0m OD with the upper gravel contact at c -4m OD. Internal variation is noted within the gravel where sand bodies exist within the gravel at 22km. This may indicate the presence of a major relict channel within the sequence. A thin peat/organic silt directly overlies the gravels. Thick sequences of made ground exist at this point in the route corridor	Low

Table 8 Continued

Window	Chainages (km)	Zones	Zone distances (km)	Description	Priority
		T9	22.06–22.73	Rockhead datums vary through this zone from -13.0m OD to -11.0m OD. The upper surface of the Pleistocene deposits undulate and fluctuate between -6.0m OD and -4.0m OD. Considerable internal variation in grain size of sediments exists within the gravel body. This may indicate channel activity within the depositional episode responsible for gravel sequence accumulation. Holocene sediments consist of a major peat unit between -2.0m OD and -4.0m OD. The peat is underlain by organic silts and clays. Organic silts and clays overlie the peat. Made ground exists along the length of the route corridor	Low
		T10	22.73–23.03	Rockhead datums lie at about -11.0m OD. The upper surface of the gravel extends to *c* -3.0m OD. Considerable grain size variation exists within the sand and gravel body. Holocene peats immediately overlie the Pleistocene deposits at about 22.9km. At this point two peat units are noted to exist, extending upwards to datums of *c* 1.5m OD	Low
		T11	23.03–23.46	Rockhead datums obtain maximum depths of -14.0m OD in this area. The upper surface of the gravels outcrops at *c* -5.0m OD. Holocene sediments consist of silts overlain by peats, capped by clay-silts	Low
		T12	23.46–24.13	This zone corresponds with the Rainham Wharf area. Rockhead datums vary from -14.0m OD to -6.0m OD at the eastern end of the route corridor. Marked variation in the elevation of the upper surface of the gravels is also noted with rapidly changing topographic variation at 23.8km and 24km. These gravels thin rapidly to the east	High
		T13	24.13–24.73	Rockhead datums are unknown for this zone as boreholes only penetrated the upper surface of the Pleistocene sequences. The base of the Holocene sequences lies at -7.0m OD within this zone. Holocene sediments consist of a thin sequence of sand, silts and clays overlain by a thin peat unit at *c* -6.0m OD. A major peat unit exists at the eastern end of this zone, but to the west only clay-silts exist	Low
9	24.39–27.78	T13	24.13–24.73	As above	Low
		T14	24.73–26.05	Within this zone rockhead datums dip from -10.0m OD to -14.0m OD. The upper surface of the Pleistocene deposits undulate and show considerable topographic variation from -5.0m OD to -8.5m OD and attain maximum elevations at 25.750km. Holocene sediments consist of a major peat unit between -2.0m OD and *c* -5.0m OD. In places this peat subdivides into three units. A basal organic unit resting at *c* -7.0m OD exists at the eastern end of the zone resting directly on the Pleistocene surface. Clay-silts and silts with some organic material both overlie and underlie these peat units	Low
		T15	26.05–28.00	Rockhead datums within this zone are typically between -13.0m OD and -17.0m OD. The upper surface of the gravels lies below -10.0m OD. Peat units within this area lie between -2.0m OD and -5.0m OD and overlie a thick sequence of organic and inorganic silts across much of the zone. Thick sand sequences are noted at the 26.5km mark. These sands may mark the position of an active channel within the floodplain through much of the Holocene. Inorganic silts cap the sequence	Low
10	27.78–28.93	T15	26.05–28.00	As above	Low
		T16	28.00–28.20	Rockhead datums rest at *c* -5.0m OD. The rockhead is overlain by sediments interpreted in the borehole logs as Head units. Head deposits lie below approximately 4m of sand and gravel with an upper contact with the overlying made ground at *c* 1.0m OD. These deposits are thought to be floodplain remnants of older Pleistocene sediments isolated as 'islands' within the floodplain. No Holocene sediments exist within this zone	High
		T17	28.20–28.93	Rockhead datums within this zone dip from -5.0m OD to -10.0m OD at 28.6km before rising steeply to -2.0m OD at the eastern end. This surface is overlain by a complex of different sediments varyingly described as Head deposits, gravels and sands. These deposits are considered to represent a complex of probable Late Pleistocene periglacial solifluction deposits and interbedded fluvial sequences. The Pleistocene sediments are overlain by Holocene deposits probably infilling the valley of the Mar Dyke. Complex lateral variation in facies is to be expected where the Mar Dyke was discharging into the Thames system. This complexity is revealed in the cross profile	Medium

Table 8 Continued

Window	Chainages (km)	Zones	Zone distances (km)	Description	Priority
11	30.50–33.15	T18	30.50–31.00	Rockhead datums dip steeply from north to south in this zone dipping from 9.0m OD to -13.0m OD. Pleistocene gravels overlying bedrock only occur in two locations to the north between datums of 2.0m OD and 4.0m OD around 30.6km and at the southern end of the zone between -13.0m OD and -8.0m OD. Holocene sediments are noted to be present thinning and disappearing northwards against the rising chalk bedrock. Two peat units are present that consist of a basal peat at -8.0m OD overlying the basal gravels and a thicker, higher peat between -1.0m OD and -5.0m OD clay-silt units occur above and below the main (upper) peat unit	High
		T19	31.00–31.50	Rockhead datums lie at about -15.0m OD and the upper surface of the gravels rests at -9.0m OD. Holocene clay silts with organic inclusions overlie the gravel. Thick sequences of made ground cap the sequence. Made ground may have removed any traces of peat in this area	Low
		T20	31.50–32.25	Within this zone rockhead contours descend to *c* -16.0m OD. This reflects a similar dip to the upper surface of the Pleistocene deposits. These deposits contain substantial thicknesses of sand possibly indicative of a former, sand filled, channel through the floodplain. Holocene sediments overlie the basal gravels between -9.0m OD and -10.0m OD. Two peat complexes are present within the Holocene stack. The lower complex typically lies between -8.0m OD and -9.0m OD. These peats overlie thin organic silt units. The uppermost peat is of considerable thickness and lies between -1.0m OD and -5.0m OD. Organic silts are present between the two peat units. Made ground rests directly on the surface of the upper peat in most cases	Medium
		T21	32.25–32.85	Rockhead datums lie at about -16.0m OD and the upper surface of the gravels exist at -9.0m OD. Holocene clay silts with organic inclusions overlie the gravel. The lowermost peat seen in Zone T20 is only present at the northern end of this zone. The upper peat seen in Zone T20 peat is of considerable thickness and lies between -1.0m OD and -5.0m OD. Thick sequences of made ground cap the sequence	Low
		T22	32.85–33.25	Rockhead datums vary between -17.0m OD and -15.0m OD. This trend is mirrored by a similar rise in the upper surface of the gravels where elevations between -11.0m OD and -10.0m OD are attained. Holocene sediments overlie the basal gravels and two peat complexes are present within the Holocene stack. The lower complex typically lies between -9.0m OD and -10.0m OD. These peats overlie thin organic silt units or rest directly on the underlying gravels. The uppermost peat is of considerable thickness and lies between -1.0m OD and -7.0m OD. In places this peat may be divided into various sub-units. Organic silts are present between the two peat units. Made ground exists through much of this zone	Medium
		T23	33.25–34.10	This zone corresponds with the modern position of the Thames channel. Rockhead datums vary between -17.0m OD and -15.0m OD. Similar trends in the elevation of the upper surface of the gravels have been noted. Some variation in the nature of the gravel sequences is noted to the south of the main channel. At 34.0km organic sediments have been noted within the gravels. Within this zone beneath the modern Thames channel, it is likely that sequence truncation has taken place. Holocene sediments can be seen to thin rapidly towards the modern channel. Holocene sediments are similar to those in zones landward of the main channel	Low
12	33.15–36.30	T23	33.25–34.10	As above	Low
		T24	34.10–34.95	Rockhead datums vary between -16.0m OD and -18.5m OD in this zone. The upper surface of the Pleistocene sequence also undulates, varying between -14.0m OD and -9.5m OD. The Pleistocene sediments are highly variable with chalk gravels infilling a possible incised channel at the base of the sequence and sands and gravels making up the majority of the sediment body. Evidence exists for a possible sand filled channel within the upper part of the gravel sequence (an alternative interpretation would suggest this represents a channel cut into the gravels and dates to a younger phase). Holocene sediments consist of two peat units interstratified with organic silts. Thick made ground sequences are present here	Medium
		T25	34.95–35.23	Within this zone rockhead datums lie at about -15.0m OD. The upper surface of the Pleistocene sequence lies at about -7.5m OD. A major sand body appears as part of this aggradation and may infill a channel within or cut into the gravels. Holocene sediments consist of up to two peats interbedded with organic silts. Made ground is minimal within this zone	Medium

Table 8 Continued

Window	Chainages (km)	Zones	Zone distances (km)	Description	Priority
		T26	35.23–35.28	This zone contains a small outcrop of gravel resting on a rockhead surface at -7.5m OD and exhibiting an upper surface datum of -4.5m OD. This gravel clearly forms a remnant gravel body at a very different elevation to those elsewhere within the transect. Holocene sediments consist of peat and organic silts. No made ground is present here	High
		T27	35.28–35.65	This zone consists of a rockhead surface at or above 0.0m OD. No Pleistocene gravel is recorded here and fill immediately overlies made ground	High
13	35.90–37.55	E1	35.90–36.70	This zone coincides with the valley margin situation on the western side of the Ebbsfleet Valley. Previous work in this area (Oxford Archaeological Unit 1997) has illustrated the broad nature of the stratigraphic sequence through this part of the route corridor. However some uncertainty regarding the precise location of the boundary between the valley sides and alluvium exists. In particular the interface between the Pleistocene sediments, forming a complex of last interglacial and last glacial deposits (Boreholes 0018SA–0021SA), and the Holocene wedge thinning from the west towards the sports pavilion remains difficult to evaluate. Edge marginal situations to the south, adjacent to the Roman building, have been shown to contain complex archaeological remains. Furthermore prehistoric ecotonal zones may contain archaeological artefacts	Medium
		E2	North Kent Link Line	This zone defines a cross-valley profile through the main stratigraphic units identified from borehole and test pit records. The Holocene valley bottom consists of sands and gravels forming a raised area to the west and a deeper 'basin-like' area to the east. A peat complex forms the main sediment body resting between two clay-silt units. The peat consists of a basal woody peat and an upper reed peat that rises and thins to the west over the gravel high. The organic sediments are unusual in that they contain both plant remains and molluscs in places. The archaeological potential of these deposits has previously been described and both Mesolithic and Neolithic remains have been located within this zone (Oxford Archaeological Unit 1997)	High
		E3	37.30–37.55	This zone contains the main line crossing of the Ebbsfleet river downstream of the Roman town of Springhead. Sediments within this stretch of the valley are poorly understood although previous work has indicated that important waterlogged sediments of Neolithic age are present within the area (Burchell 1938; Burchell and Piggot 1939)	High

Table 13 Temple Mills sedimentary descriptions from monoliths analysed in Trenches 4042TT and 4044TT

	Height (m OD)	Context	Description
Trench 4042TT, monoliths <421005–7>	3.65–3.22	420001	10YR 5/2 greyish brown smooth amorphous gleyed clay. Substantial coarse mottling with iron (7.5YR 5/6 strong brown) and iron redeposition in root voids. *Oxidised alluvial clay: the movement of iron through the profile indicates terrestrialisation of waterlogged deposits.* Diffuse boundary to lesser iron redeposition below
	3.22–2.77	420002	10YR 5/2 greyish brown smooth amorphous gleyed clay. Some mottling with iron (7.5YR 5/6 strong brown). *Alluvial clay.* Gradual transition to:
	2.77–2.65	420003	10YR 2/2 very dark brown peaty clay, clay content increasing to top. Gradual transition to:
	2.65–1.78		2.65–2.57m OD: 10YR 2/3 very dark brown humified silty clay peat. *Phragmites australis* (common reed) stem common. 2.62m OD: *Phragmites* stem dated to *3520–3330 cal BC (4610±35BP, KIA-24052). Diffuse boundary to: 2.57–2.47m OD: 10YR 2/3 very dark brown peaty clay. No discernible inclusions or structure. Clear boundary to: 2.4–2.34m OD: 10YR 3/2 very dark greyish brown silty peat (silt increasing up the unit). Contains wood fragments (less than underlying unit), 2.49m OD twig fragments dated to *3500–3120 Cal BC (4589±30BP, NZA-30301). Diffuse boundary to: 2.34–1.92m OD: 10YR 2/2 very dark brown woody peat, reduced silt and clay content than underlying stratum, 2.29m OD wood dated to 8220–7830 cal BC (8865±30BP, NZA-30332). 1.92–1.78m OD: 10YR 3/2 dark brown woody silty clay peat. Clear horizontal layers of plant material, notably *Phragmites*. 1.84m OD: *Phragmites* stem dated to 10,800–9800 cal BC (10,305±40BP, KIA-24051). *Woody fen peat and peaty clays.* Diffuse boundary to:
	1.78–1.60	420004	1.78–1.75m OD: 5Y 4/3 olive calcareous silt with very fine horizontal bedding. Mollusc rich, no other visible inclusions. 1.75–1.66m OD: 5Y 4/2 olive grey silty clay streaked with black organic matter. Mollusc rich, rare (<1%) angular flint gravel 1cm and twig wood at 1.93m OD. Vertical root marks filled with overlying peat material. Seemingly from plants growing on lower peat when it was an exposed surface, no evidence of deep modern root penetration. Gradual boundary to: 7.5YR 3/2 (N3/) very dark grey 75% rounded gravel (0.1–0.5cm +5cm) in coarse sandy humic clay. *Fluvial sands and gravels*
Trench 4044TT, monolith <441016>	3.44–3.27	440001	10YR 5/6 yellowish brown amorphous stiff sticky silty clay with coarse black mottles (including a 5mm black band at 3.31m OD) which include rare fragments of possible coke. *Disturbed alluvium/made ground.* Clear wavy slanting boundary to:
	3.27–2.74	440002	3.27–2.99m OD: 10YR 5/3 brown silty clay alluvium with laminations and lenses of black organic clay silt (7.5YR 2/0 black (N2/)). Occasional mollusc shells, monocot stems including possible straw. Charred seed *Nuphar/Nymphaea* at 3.22m OD. Thin band of 10YR 5/8 yellowish brown slightly crumbly clay silt at 2.97–2.96m OD. *Alluvium and organic alluvium.* Gradual-diffuse boundary to: 2.99–2.74m OD: 10YR 4/3 brown/dark brown massive slightly fibrous and organic greasy silty clay. Occasional fine humified vertical and horizontal fine stems and rootlets. *Alluvium.*Sharp (erosional?) boundary:
	2.74–2.68	440003	2.73m OD: 3 outer rings mature wood dated to 2140–1910 cal BC (3650±35BP, KIA-24588). 2.74–2.72m OD: band of woody peat as below (unit D1) clear-abrupt boundary. 2.72–2.69m OD: 10 YR 5/4 yellowish brown organic silty sand with molluscs, including operculum of *Bithynia tentaculata*, whole hinged bivalve (*Spherium* sp.) and *Trichia* sp. Sand white, medium-coarse. Contained 30mm degraded branch wood and a 40mm fire cracked flint (both in direct contact with the overlying peat). *Old land surface on fluvial sands.* Clear boundary to:
	2.68–2.37	440004	2.69–2.47m OD: 10YR2/1 black highly humified silty clay peat. Minerogenic component increasing to top, becoming peaty silty clay in top 20mm. Occasional molluscs include large *Cepaea* sp. at 2.57m OD. Large wood fragment, 130mm diameter (including bark to heartwood) crossing nearly whole width and depth of monolith from 2.57–2.43m OD. 2.68m OD, horizontal root dated to 2200–1950 cal BC (3690±35BP, KIA-24589). Gradual boundary to: 2.46–2.37m OD: 10YR 2/1 black peaty silty clay with numerous molluscan remains and occasional wood and root fragments. 2.39m OD, two fragments of twig dated to 2580–2400 cal BC (3980±30BP, KIA-24590). *Peat and peaty alluvium.* Gradual boundary to:
	2.37–2.26		2.37–2.29m OD: 10YR 4/3 brown/dark brown silty clay thinly bedded/laminated with black organic bands. Rare wood fragments, abundant molluscs. *Alluvium.* Clear boundary to:
	2.29–2.26	440005	2.29–2.26m OD: 10YR 7/2 light grey, white medium-coarse sand band in organic silt with molluscs. *Alluvium/fluvial sands.* Clear boundary to:
	2.26–2.19	440006	10YR 2/1 black sandy woody peat, slightly loose and degraded/humified. Wood fragments common, large humified *in situ* woody root. 2.22m OD, two fragments of twig wood dated to 3340–2920 cal BC (4435±40BP, KIA-24591). *Peat*

* Dates suspected as being erroneous (too young)

Table 14 Insect remains from Temple Mills Trenches 4042TT and 4044TT

		Context	420004	440005
		Sample number	421003B	441022B
		Volume of sediment (litres)	5	5
		Ecological codes		

COLEOPTERA

Carabidae	*Dyschirus globosus* (Hbst.)		-	2
	Bembidion doris (Panz.)		-	1
	B. guttula (F.)		1	-
	Bembidion spp.		2	-
	Pterostichus spp.		1	1
	Calathus fuscipes (Goeze)		1	-
Halididae	*Haliplus* spp.	a	2	-
Dytiscidae	*Hygrotus decoratus* (Gyll.)	a	2	-
	Hydrophorus spp.	a	1	-
	Stictotarsus duodecimpustulatus (F.)	aff	2	-
	Acilius pp.	a	1	-
Gyrinidae	*Gyrinus* spp.	a	1	-
Hydraenidae	*Hydraenariparia* Kug.	aff	1	5
	Hydreana spp.	a	9	-
	Ochthebius minimus (F.)	a	1	-
	Octhebius spp.	a	8	6
	Helophorus spp.	a	8	-
Hydrophilidae	*Cercyon tristis* (Ill.)	a	-	2
	Megasternum boletophagum (Marsh.)	df	-	2
	Hydrobius fusipes (L.)		3	-
	Enochrus spp.	a	3	-
Liodidae	*Agathidium* spp.		1	-
Ptiliidae	Ptilidae Genus & spp. indet.		-	2
	Acrotrichis spp.		-	3
Staphylinidae	*Olophrum* spp.	ws	2	-
	Lesteva spp.	ws	2	3
	Trogophloeus spp.		1	-
	Oxytelus rugosus (F.)	df	-	2
	Platystethus corntus (Grav.)	ws	1	-
	Stenus spp.		1	2
	Stilicus spp.		-	1
	Lathrobium spp.	ws	1	1
	Philonthus spp.		2	-
	Tachyporus spp.		2	-
	Aleocharinidae Genus & spp. indet.		5	-
Cantharidae	*Cantharis* sp.		1	-
Dryopidae	*Dryops* spp.	a	-	1
	Esolus parallelepipedus (Müll.)	aff	1	-
	Oulimnius spp.	aff	-	4
	Macronychus quadrituberculatus Müll	aff	-	2
Nitidulidae	*Meligethes* spp.		1	-
Rhizophagidae	*Rhizophagus* spp.		-	1
Lathridiidae	*Corticaria/corticarina* spp.		1	-
Mordellidae	*Anaspis* spp.		1	-
Chyrsomelidae	*Donacia vulgaris* Zschach	ws	2	-
	Plateumaris braccata (Scop.)	ws	-	1
	Prasocuris phellandri (L.)	ws	1	-
	Lochmaea suturalis (Thoms.)	m	2	-
	Phyllotreta spp.		2	1
	Haltica spp.	p	2	-
Scolytidae	*Hylesinus crenatus* (F.)	t	-	1
Cuculionidae	*Phyllobius* sp.	p	1	-
	Phleoephagus lignarius (Marsh.)	t	-	1
	Bagous spp.	ws	1	-
	Notaris spp.	ws	1	-
	Ceutorhynchus spp.	p	1	-

Total number of individuals		83	45
Total number of species		41	22
% aquatic (a)		43.4	20.0
% aquatic fast flowing (aff)		4.8	24.4
% waterside (ws)		13.3	11.1
% rotting foul/terrestrial (df)		0.0	20.0
% tree/terrestrial (t)		0.0	10.0
% moorland/terrestrial (m)		6.3	0.0
% grassland and pasture/terrestrial (p)		12.5	0.0

Table 15 Waterlogged plant remains from Temple Mills

		Trench	4042	4044
		Lithology	Shelly silt	Sand within peat
		m OD	1.78–1.66	2.26–2.29
		Context	420004	440005
		Sample	441003	441022
Taxa	**Common name**			
Chara sp. (gametes)	stonewort		+++	-
Musci (fragments)	moss		++	-
Nymphaea alba	white water-lily		-	2
Ceratophyllum demersum	rigid hornwort		17	-
Ranunculus subg. *arb*	buttercup		-	2
Ranunculus subg. *Batrachium*	water-crowfoot		3	1
Thalictrum cf *minus/flavum*	meadow-rue		1	-
Betula cf *nana* (seed)	dwarf birch		1	-
Alnus glutinosa (catkins)	alder catkins		-	10
Alnus glutinosa (cones)	cones		-	11
Alnus glutinosa (fruit)	alder seeds		-	15
Alnus incana (seed)	alder fruit		1	-
Rumex sp.	dock		1	-
Filipendula ulmaria	meadow sweet		1	-
Crataegus monogyna (stone)	hawthorn		-	1 gnawed
Myriophyllum cf *verticillatum/spicatum*	water-milfoil		21	-
Lycopus europaeus	gypsywort		-	1
Mentha cf *arvensis*	corn mint		-	1
Mentha cf *aquatica*	water mint		-	1
Sambucus nigra	elder		-	1
Valeriana dioica	marsh valerian		5	-
Cirsium/Carduus sp.	thistle/knapweed		5	-
Baldellia ranunculoides ssp. *ranunculoides*	lesser water plantain		cf. 1	-
Alisma plantago-aquatica	water-plantain		2	-
Potamogeton sp. (<2mm)	pondweed		48	-
Potamogeton sp. (>2mm)	pondweed		13	-
Potamogeton cf natans	pondweed		21	-
Potamogeton sp. (c. 2mm)	pondweed		14	-
Carex sp. (seed)	sedge		19	-
Schoenoplectus lacustris/tabernaemontani	common/grey club rush		31	-
Sparganium erectum inner kernels	Branched bur-reed		-	cf 5
cf *Carex sylvatica* type	wood sedge		-	1
Twigs and branch wood			-	+++

+ 5–25   ++ 25–50   +++ 50–100

Table 16 Ostracods from Temple Mills, 4042TT

| **Context** | 420003 | | | 420004 | | |
m OD	2.77–1.78	1.78–1.76	1.76–1.741	1.74–1.72	1.72–1.70	1.70–1.68
* *Candona candida*		x	xx	xx	xx	xx
Cyclocypris ovum (RV>LV)		x	x	x	x	x
* *Pseudocandona* cf *rostrata*		o	x	x	x	x
Ilyocypris sp.		o	x	x	o	o
Candona neglecta		x	x	x	x
* *Fabaeformiscandona protzi*		x	x	o	
Herpetocypris sp.			o	x	o	x
Eucypris pigra			o			o
Ecology	fen		weedy cold/cool permanent pool			

* cold stenothermal forms (species linked to permanently cold water)   o – one specimen   x – present (several specimens)   xx – common

Table 17 Molluscs from Temple Mills

		4042TT	4044TT
Trench		4042TT	4044TT
Lithology		Shelly silt	Sand within peat
Context		420004	440005
Sample		421003	441022
Volume of sediment (litres)		30	2
LAND			
Carychium minimum Müller		-	3
Carychium tridentatum (Risso)		-	1
Carychium spp.		-	4
Succinea oblonga (Draparnaud)		1	5
Cochlicopa spp.		-	1
Pupilla muscorum (Linnaeus)		4	-
Discus rotundatus (Müller)		-	3
Aegopinella nitidula (Draparnaud)		-	5
Trichia hispida (Linnaeus)		-	1
Cepaea/Arianta spp.		-	2
FRESH- /BRACKISH-WATER			
Theodoxus fluviatilis (Linnaeus)		-	15
Valvata cristata Müller		1	122
Valvata piscinalis (Müller)		655	455
Bithynia tentaculata (Linnaeus)		4	79
Bithynia leachii (Sheppard)		4	36
Bithynia spp.		7	202
Bithynia operculum		196	89
Lymnaea truncatula (Müller)		2	4
Lymnaea peregra (Müller)		2	2
Lymnaea spp.		10	18
Planorbis planorbis (Linnaeus)		-	1
Planorbis carinatus (Müller)		2	-
Anisus leucostoma (Millet)		-	48
Anisus vortex (Linnaeus)		-	3
Gyraulus laevis (Alder)		451	-
Gyraulus albus (Müller)		17	72
Gyraulus crista (Linnaeus)		157	103
Hippeutis complanatus (Linnaeus)		2	2
Planorbids		66	-
Ancylus fluviatilis (Müller)		-	20
Acroloxus lacustris (Linnaeus)		-	4
Pisidium cf *amnicum* (Müller)		-	1
Pisidum cf *casertanum* (Poli)		3	-
Pisidium cf *milium* (Held)		3	-
Pisidium cf *nitidum* (Jeyns)		12	16
Pisidium spp.		36	29
Taxa		16	24
TOTAL		1438	1257
Shannon Index		1.345	2.092
Brillouin Index		1.324	2.054
Shannon Index – Brillouin Index		0.021	0.039
Delta 2		0.6571	0.8100
Delta 4		1.9204	4.2800
% Shade-loving species		0.0	1.3
% Intermediate species		0.0	0.3
% Open country species		0.3	0.0
% Marsh		0.1	0.4
% Amphibious		0.1	4.1
% Catholic		13.4	15.5
% Slum		0.2	10.1
% Moving water		46.8	64.3
% Unassigned		39.2	4.0

Table 20 Pollen from evaluation Trenches 3778TT and 3780TT at the Goresbrook diversion (ARC GOR00)

Trench	3778TT								3780TT						
Lithology	Peat	Organic silty clay			Upper silty clays				Peat			Upper silty clays			
Context	7808	7807	7807	7807	7806	7804	7805	7803	8004	8004	8004	8004	8003	8003	8002
Trees															
Picea	-	-	-	-	1	2	-	-	-	-	-	-	-	-	-
Pinus sylvestris	1	2	4	2	2	4	1	3	-	-	1	1	-	1	3
Ulmus	1	1	3	2	2	-	3	-	-	2	2	1	2	1	2
Fagus sylvatica	-	-	-	-	-	-	-	-	-	1	-	-	-	-	-
Quercus	4	5	2	7	3	10	5	6	-	1	5	1	2	1	3
Betula	1	-	3	-	3	-	1	-	-	4	5	2	1	2	1
Alnus glutinosa	3	65	115	14	17	9	7	12	5	15	4	3	6	10	2
Carpinus betulus	-	-	-	-	-	1	-	-	-	-	-	-	-	-	-
Tilia cordata	-	-	-	-	1	2	-	-	-	1	-	-	1	-	-
Fraxinus excelsior	-	1	1	1	-	-	-	1	-	-	2	1	2	-	6
Shrubs															
Corylus avellana-type	2	3	7	15	13	13	4	8	2	15	5	3	6	6	8
Salix	-	1	-	-	1	1	-	-	-	-	1	1	1	-	-
Ericaceae	-	-	-	-	1	-	-	-	-	1	-	-	-	-	-
Sorbus-type	-	-	-	1	-	-	-	-	-	-	-	-	-	-	-
Hedera helix	-	-	-	-	-	-	-	1	-	-	-	-	1	-	-
Herbs															
Ranunculaceae	-	-	-	-	-	-	1	-	-	-	-	-	-	-	-
Ranunculus acris-type	-	-	-	-	-	-	-	1	-	-	-	-	-	-	-
Chenopodiaceae	2	1	1	11	8	20	6	21	-	-	-	1	1	7	3
Caryophyllaceae	-	-	-	-	-	-	-	-	-	-	-	-	-	-	1
Plumbaginaceae	-	-	-	1	-	-	-	-	-	-	-	-	-	-	-
Limonium	-	-	-	1	-	1	-	-	-	-	-	-	-	-	-
Filipendula	-	-	-	-	-	2	-	-	-	-	-	-	-	-	-
Saxifraga granulata-type	-	-	-	-	-	-	-	-	-	-	-	-	-	-	1
Apiaceae	-	1	-	-	-	1	-	-	-	-	-	1	-	-	-
Plantaginaceae	-	2	1	1	7	11	51	22	-	-	-	1	1	13	2
Plantago maritima	-	2	-	-	-	-	9	2	-	-	-	-	-	5	-
Plantago lanceolata	-	-	1	-	-	-	-	-	-	-	-	-	-	-	-
Scrophulariaceae	-	-	-	-	-	-	-	-	-	-	-	-	-	-	1
Veronica	-	-	-	-	-	1	-	-	-	-	-	-	-	-	-
Rubiaceae	-	-	-	-	-	1	-	-	-	-	-	-	-	-	-
Valerian adioica	-	-	1	-	-	-	-	-	-	-	-	-	-	-	-
Arctium-type	-	-	-	-	1	-	-	-	-	-	-	-	-	-	-
Lactuceae	-	-	-	-	1	1	6	3	-	-	-	1	3	13	5
Solidago virgaurea-type	1	-	-	3	1	1	1	3	-	-	-	-	-	1	3
Artemisia-type	-	-	-	-	-	-	2	-	-	-	-	-	-	-	-
Cyperaceae undiff.	11	1	1		2	5	-	11	2	5	1	10	2	11	6
Poaceae undiff.	8	3	7	18	22	10	31	9	1	8		16	13	32	65
Aquatics															
Potamogetonaceae	-	-	-	-	-	-	-	-	-	-	1	-	-	-	-
Potamogeton filiformis-type	-	-	-	-	-	1	-	-	-	-	-	-	-	-	-
Sparganium emersum-type	-	-	-	-	-	-	-	-	-	-	-	-	-	4	-
Typha latifolia	-	-	-	-	1	-	-	-	-	1	-	-	-	-	-

Table 20 Continued

Trench	3778TT								3780TT						
Lithology	Peat	Organic silty clay			Upper silty clays				Peat				Upper silty clays		
Context	7808	7807	7807	7807	7806	7804	7805	7803	8004	8004	8004	8004	8003	8003	8002
Spores															
Osmunda regalis	-	-	-	-	-	-	-	-	5	1	4	1	11	-	-
Polypodium	-	1	-	2	6	1	-	1	-	-	-	1	-	-	-
Pteridium aquilinum	1	-	2	10	16	5	1	3	-	-	2	4	-	-	1
Thelypteris palustris	13	1	-	-	-	-	-	-	-	2	-	-	-	-	-
Pteropsida(monolete) indet.	80	17	-	32	24	12	9	15	5	10	21	86	51	38	15
Sphagnum	1	-	-	3	1	-	-	-	-	-	-	-	2	-	2
Charcoal	64	40	68	328	246	306	105	243	7	10	160	69	800	632	771
Others															
Fungal spores	-	+	+	+	+	+	+	+	+	+	+	+	-	+	+
Foraminifera	-	-	-	-	-	-	1	-	-	-	-	-	-	-	-
Amphitrema flavum	-	1	-	-	-	-	-	-	-	-	-	-	-	-	-
Other rhizopods	1	-	-	-	-	-	-	-	-	-	-	1	-	-	-
Dinoflagellates	-	-	-	-	2	-	-	-	-	-	-	-	-	-	-
Type 143 fungal spore	-	-	-	-	1	-	-	-	-	-	-	1	-	-	-

Table 21 Waterlogged plant remains from evaluation Trenches 3778TT and 3780TT at the Goresbrook diversion (ARC GOR00)

Trench		3778TT							3780TT		
Lithology		Peat	Organic clay	Upper silts and clays					Peat	Upper silty clays	
Context		7808	7807	7806	7805	7804	7803	7803	8004	8003	8002
Sample		7	6	5	4	3	2	1	20	19	18
Weight of sediment (kg)		0.2	0.2	0.2	0.2	0.2	0.2	0.2	0.2	0.2	0.2
Taxa	**Common name**										
Ranunculus cf *repens*	creeping buttercup	-	-	+	-	-	-	-	-	+	-
R. sceleratus	celery-leaved crowfoot	-	-	-	+	++	+	-	-	+	-
Viola S. *Viola* sp.	violet	-	-	-	-	-	-	-	-	-	-
Lychnis flos-cuculi	ragged robin	-	-	-	-	-	-	-	+	-	-
Moehringia trinervia	sandwort	-	-	-	-	-	-	-	+	-	-
Rubus fruticosus agg.	blackberry	-	-	+	-	+	-	-	+	-	-
Potentilla cf *reptans*	creeping cinquefoil	-	-	-	-	-	+	-	-	-	-
Epilobium sp.	willowherb	-	-	-	-	+	-	-	+	-	-
Hippuris vulgaris	mare's tail	-	-	-	-	-	-	-	-	-	-
Hydrocotyle vulgaris	marsh pennywort	+	-	-	-	-	-	-	-	-	-
Berula erecta	water parsnip	+	-	-	-	-	-	-	+	-	-
Rumex sp.	dock	-	-	-	-	+	-	-	-	+	-
Alnus glutinosa	alder	-	+	-	-	-	-	-	-	-	-
Galium sp.	bedstraw	-	-	-	-	-	-	-	+	-	-
Eupatorium cannabinum	hemp agrimony	-	-	-	-	-	-	-	+	-	-
Carduus sp.	thistle	-	-	-	-	+	+	-	-	+	-
Sonchus oleraceus	sowthistle	-	-	-	-	-	-	-	-	-	+
S. asper	sowthistle	-	-	-	-	+	-	-	-	-	-
Potamogeton sp.	pondweed	-	-	-	-	-	-	-	+	-	-
Juncus sp.	rush	-	-	-	-	-	+	+	+	+	-
Schoenoplectus lacustris	bulrush	-	-	-	-	-	-	-	+	-	-
Carex sp.	sedge	+	+	-	-	-	-	-	+	+	-
Gramineae indet.	grass	-	-	-	-	-	+	-	-	-	-

+ present   ++ many

Table 22 Insects from evaluation Trench 3780TT at the Goresbrook diversion (ARC GOR00)

	Lithology	Peat	Silty clay
	Context	8004	8003
	Sample	20	19
Weight of sediment (kg)		2	2
Taxa			
Bembidion sp.		-	+
Colymbetes fuscus		+	-
Hydrobius fuscipes		-	+
Aphodius sp.		+	+
cf *Cyphon* sp.		+	-
Dryops sp.		+	-
Plateumaris braccata		+	-
Longitarsus sp.		-	+
Apion sp.		-	+
Thryogenes sp.		+	-

+ present

Table 23 Pollen from Chainage 20.5km, Ripple Lane tunnel portal (ARC 25001)

Lithology	Basal sandy deposits			Peat								
Context number	2053	2045	2045	2044	2044	2044	2044	2044	2043	2043	2043	2043
Trees & shrubs												
Acer campestre-type	-	-	-	-	-	-	-	-	-	-	-	1
Alnus glutinosa	81	1	10	14	5	124	7	44	11	41	54	52
Betula	4	5	5	2	3	11	1	65	19	100	93	3
Corylus avellana-type	7	1	3	10	3	12	1	12	4	5	26	1
Fraxinus excelsior	2	-	-	-	-	2	1	-	-	-	2	-
Hedera helix	-	-	-	-	-	-	-	-	-	1	1	1
Ilex aquifolium	-	-	-	-	-	-	-	1	1	1	-	-
Pinus sylvestris	1	1	-	-	-	-	-	-	-	1	-	-
Quercus	15	-	1	8	1	23	3	14	4	19	33	27
Salix	3	-	-	-	1	3	1	4	-	11	48	1
Sambucus	-	-	-	-	1	-	-	-	-	-	-	-
Taxus baccata	1	-	-	-	1	-	-	-	-	-	-	-
Tilia cordata	4	-	3	6	1	3	1	4	-	-	6	-
Ulmus	3	-	1	3	-	1	1	1	-	2	6	-
Crops												
Cereal-type	-	-	-	-	-	-	1	-	-	-	-	-
Herbs												
Poaceae	3	24	4	4	1	2	2	2	3	5	8	22
Cyperaceae	34	-	3	-	1	11	3	23		19	15	20
Apiaceae	2	-	-	-	-	-	1	-	-	-	-	-
Solidago virgaurea-type	1	-	-	-	-	-	-	-	-	-	-	-
Artemisia-type	-	-	-	-	-	-	-	-	-	1	-	-
Lactuceae	-	-	-	-	-	-	-	-	-	-	-	3
Hypericum perforatum-type	-	-	-	-	-	-	-	-	-	-	-	1
Plantago lanceolata	1	-	-	-	-	-	-	1	-	-	-	1
Rubiaceae	2	-	-	-	-	2	-	-	-	-	-	-
Rumex	-	-	-	-	-	-	-	-	-	-	1	-
Pteridophytes												
Athyriumfilix-femina	1	-	1	2	-	9	2	-	-	-	2	-
Dryopteris	-	-	-	-	-	3	-	-	-	-	-	-
Osmunda regalis	-	-	-	-	1	-	-	-	4	51	53	-
Polypodium vulgare-type	-	-	-	-	-	2	-	1	-	1	-	-
Pteridiuma quilinum	2	1	3	-	2	-	-	-	-	-	-	6
Thelypteris palustris	51	-	-	-	-	86	1	-	-	-	-	-
Pteropsida (monolete) indet.	98	4	4	7	20	660	36	13	2	17	15	38
Sphagnum	-	-	-	-	-	-	-	-	8	1	12	-
Aquatics												
Potamogeton	-	-	1	1	-	3	1	3	-	-	-	3
Typha angustifolia	2	-	-	-	-	8	-	-	-	-	-	3
Typha latifolia	-	-	-	-	-	21	-	-	-	-	-	-
Unidentifiable	9	6	6	8	2	5	3	25	3	16	24	15
Charcoal	54	960	665	126	48	55	30	50	20	110	160	4500

Table 24 Pollen from Chainage 20.6km, Ripple Lane tunnel portal (ARC 25001)

Lithology	SC	Peat											SC
Context number	2064	2062	2062	2063	2062	2062	2062	2062	2061	2061	2061	2061	2060
Trees & shrubs													
Alnus glutinosa	159	149	45	6	6	30	27	23	53	5	18	55	89
Betula	15	6	4	-	2	3	3	69	29	4	16	3	8
Carpinus	1	-	-	-	-	-	-	-	-	-	-	-	-
Corylus avellana-type	10	7	1	1	4	3	6	4	7	-	11	5	7
Fraxinus excelsior	2	1	-	1	-	1	-	-	1	-	-	-	-
Hedera helix	-	-	1	-	1	-	-	1	-	-	-	-	-
Ilex aquifolium	-	-	-	-	-	-	-	-	-	-	-	1	-
Pinus sylvestris	1	1	2	-	-	-	2	1	1	-	-	1	2
Quercus	41	33	1	6	-	8	8	20	13	2	17	14	5
Rosaceae	-	-	-	-	-	-	-	1	-	-	-	-	-
Salix	-	-	-	-	-	-	2	1	-	-	-	1	3
Taxus baccata	-	-	-	1	-	-	-	-	-	-	-	-	1
Tilia cordata	6	4	12	3	1	1	2	2	5	-	-	1	
Ulmus	2	6	1	1	3	-	-	2	1	-	-	-	3
Vaccinium	-	-	-	-	-	-	-	-	1	-	-	-	1
Sambucus	-	-	-	-	-	-	-	-	-	-	-	1	-
Crops													
Cereal-type	-	-	-	-	-	-	-	-	-	-	-	-	2
Herbs													
Poaceae	3	2	1	-	1	4	2	1	1	-	4	6	33
Cyperaceae	42	12	2	-	-	10	42	28	8	-	19	5	1
Apiaceae	-	-	1	-	-	-	-	-	-	-	-	-	-
Anthemis-type	-	-	-	-	-	-	-	-	-	1	-	-	2
Solidago virgaurea-type	-	-	-	-	-	-	-	-	-	1	-	-	1
Cirsium-type	-	-	-	-	-	-	-	-	-	-	-	-	3
Lactuceae	-	-	-	-	-	-	-	-	-	-	-	2	11
Brassicaceae undiff	-	-	-	-	-	-	-	-	-	-	-	-	1
Chenopodiaceae	-	-	-	-	-	-	-	-	-	-	-	2	4
Plantago lanceolata	-	-	-	-	-	-	-	-	-	-	-	-	1
Rubiaceae	-	-	-	-	-	-	-	1	-	-	-	-	-
Succisa pratensis	-	-	-	-	-	-	-	-	-	-	-	-	1
Urtica	1	-	-	-	-	-	-	-	-	-	-	-	-
Pteridophytes													
Athyrium filix-femina	-	2	1	3	8	-	4	-	16	-	1	-	-
Polypodium vulgare-type	3	2	1	-	-	1	2	-	2	-	2	3	1
Pteridium aquilinum	3	3	4	-	-	-	-	-	1	-	-	5	8
Thelypteris palustris	-	-	1	-	-	1	4	54	172	-	38	-	-
Osmunda regalis	-	-	-	-	-	-	-	-	3	-	4	-	-
Pteropsida (monolete) indet.	300	252	35	6	17	13	87	44	907	20	217	15	18
Sphagnum	1	-	-	-	-	1	-	-	-	-	-	-	2
Aquatics													
Potamogeton	1	1	-	-	-	-	-	1	-	-	-	-	1
Typha angustifolia	1	-	-	-	-	1	2	4	-	-	-	-	-
Typha latifolia	1	-	-	-	-	-	8	-	-	-	-	-	-
Unidentifiable	11	12	3	2	1	6	5	6	2	2	16	8	16
Charcoal	131	105	450	40	28	18	50	81	80	330	78	750	470

Table 25 Ostracods from Chainage 20.6km, Ripple Lane tunnel portal (ARC 25001)

	Lithology	Upper silty clay
	Sample	Monolith 1031
	Context	2060
Weight of sediment (kg)		0.2
Brackish water ostracods		
Cyprideis torosa (smooth)		+++
Cytherura gibba		++
Loxoconcha elliptica		+
Leptocythere porcellanea		+

+ present (a few specimens)   ++ common   +++ abundant

Table 26 Waterlogged plant remains from Chainages 20.97km and 21.09km, Dagenham Vale (ARC 36100)

		20.97km			21.09km		
Chainage							
Lithology		Organic sandy silt	Organic silt	Peat	Peat	Organic silty clay	Silty clay
Context		128	127	126	105	104	103
Sample		275	274	273	123	122	119
Weight of sediment (kg)		1	1	1	1	1	1
Taxa	**Common name**						
Ranunculus cf *repens*	buttercup	-	+	-	-	-	-
Stellaria neglecta	greater chickweed	-	+	-	-	-	-
Rubus fruticosus agg.	blackberry	+	-	-	+	-	-
Potentilla anserina	silverweed	-	-	-	+	-	-
Callitriche sp.	starwort	-	-	-	-	+	-
Oenanthe aquatica gp.	water dropwort	-	-	+	-	-	-
Alnus glutinosa	alder	+	+	++	-	-	-
A. glutinosa	alder (female catkin)	-	-	+	-	-	-
Mentha sp.	mint	-	-	-	+	-	+
Lycopus europaeus	gipsy-wort	-	+	+	-	-	-
Alisma sp.	water-plantain	-	+	-	+	-	+
Juncus spp.	rush	-	-	-	+	-	+
Scirpus sylvaticus	wood club-rush	+	-	-	-	-	-
Carex spp.	sedge	+	-	-	-	-	-

+ present   ++ many

Table 27 Insects from Chainages 20.97km and 21.09km, Dagenham Vale (ARC 36100)

	20.97km		21.09km
Chainage			
Lithology	Organic silt	Peat	Peat
Context	127	126	105
Sample	274	273	123
Weight of sediment (kg)	1	1	1
Coleoptera			
Agonum sp.	+	-	-
Agabus sp. (not *bipustulatus*)	+	-	-
Megasternum obscurum	-	+	-
Anacaena sp.	+	-	-
Ochthebius cf *minimus*	-	+	-
Hydraena testacea	+	-	-
Limnebius nitidus	+	-	-
Silpha atrata	-	+	-
Geotrupes sp.	-	-	+
Aphodius sp.	-	-	+
cf *Cercyon* sp.	+	+	-
Ctenicera sp.	-	+	-
Corylophus cassidoides	-	+	-
Phymatodes alni	-	+	-
Prasocuris phellandrii	+	-	-
Chrysomela aenea	-	+	-
Rhynchaenus testaceus	+	-	-
Other insects			
Homoptera indet.	+	-	-
Trichoptera larva indet.	+	+	-
Hymenoptera indet.	+	-	-
Chironomid larva indet.	+	-	-

+ present

Table 28　Pollen from Chainages 20.97km and 21.09km, Dagenham Vale (ARC 36100)

Chainage	20.97km			20.09km					
Lithology	Sand	Org SS	Peat	Peat	Org SC		Upper silty clays		
Context	130	127	126	105	104	103	103	102	102
Trees and shrubs									
Betula	-	1	13	3	-	2	1	1	1
Pinus	1	1	-	-	1	2	4	7	11
Picea	-	-	-	-	-	-	1	-	-
Ulmus	-	1	-	1	-	1	1	-	1
Quercus	-	15	50	16	19	17	14	21	9
Tilia	-	-	16	-	-	1	-	-	-
Fraxinus	-	-	-	-	1	-	1	-	-
Corylus avellana-type	-	13	12	22	6	1	15	13	6
Viburnum	-	1	-	-	-	-	-	-	-
Herbs									
Ranunculus-type	-	-	1	1	1	-	-	1	-
Sinapsis-type	-	-	-	-	-	1	5	4	2
Hornungia-type	-	-	-	-	-	-	-	1	-
Dianthus-type	-	-	-	1	-	-	-	-	-
Chenopodium-type	-	-	-	-	11	-	7	5	17
Rosaceae	-	-	-	1	-	-	-	-	-
Filipendula	-	-	-	1	-	-	-	-	-
Agrimonia	-	-	-	-	-	-	1	-	-
Scrophulariaceae	-	-	-	1	-	-	-	1	-
Apiaceae	-	-	1	1	-	-	-	-	-
Lamiaceae	-	-	-	-	-	-	-	-	1
Plantago major-type	-	-	-	-	1	-	-	-	-
Plantago lanceolata	-	-	-	6	-	1	-	-	1
Bidens-type	-	-	-	-	-	-	1	-	7
Anthemis-type	-	-	-	-	-	-	1	-	-
Cirsium-type	-	-	-	-	-	-	-	1	-
Lactucoideae	-	-	-	3	7	8	1	3	-
Poaceae	6	2	7	37	49	53	22	35	13
Cerealia-type	1	-	-	-	1	2	2	-	9
Large Poaceae	-	-	-	-	1	-	-	1	-
Unident/degraded	-	-	-	1	-	-	3	5	1
Marsh									
Alnus	4	65	1026	94	6	15	26	68	20
Salix	-	-	-	18	-	-	-	-	-
Alisma-type	-	-	-	-	1	-	-	-	-
Myriophyllum spicatum	-	-	-	-	1	-	-	-	-
Potamogeton	-	-	-	-	-	2	1	1	-
Typha angustifolia-type	-	-	-	-	8	3	19	1	1
Cyperaceae	1	1	57	33	9	11	9	14	3
Caltha-type	1	-	-	-	-	-	-	-	-
Spores									
Pteridium aquilinum	4	2	-	4	1	6	12	12	18
Dryopteris-type	-	4	58	28	9	9	9	27	22
Polypodium vulgare	-	1	-	1	-	-	-	-	1
Sphagnum	-	-	-	-	-	1	-	-	-
Misc									
Pediastrum	-	-	-	-	-	-	-	-	1
Zygnemataceae	-	-	-	-	-	-	-	-	-
Hystrichospheres	-	-	-	-	-	3	1	2	7
Pre-Quaternary	-	-	-	-	-	3	9	17	5

Table 29 Ostracods and foraminifera from Chainage
21.09km, Dagenham Vale (ARC 36100)

Lithology		Upper silty clays		
Sample	116	117	118	121
Context	102	102	102	103
Weight of sediment (kg)	0.2	0.2	0.2	0.2
Brackish water ostracods				
Cyprideis torosa	+++	+	+	++
Loxoconcha elliptica	-	-	+	-
Cytherura gibba	-	-	+	-
Leptocythere porcellanea	-	-	+	-
Marine ostracods				
Pontocythere elongata	-	-	+	-
Hirschmannia viridis	-	-	+	-
Semicytherura nigrescens	-	-	+	-
Semicytherura acuticostata	-	-	+	-
Heterocythereis albomaculata	-	-	+	-
Elofsonella concinna	-	-	+	-
Robertsonites tuberculatus	-	-	+	-
Freshwater ostracods				
Candona spp.	-	-	+	+
Limnocythere inopinata	-	-	+	-
Foraminifera				
Haynesina germanica	++	-	++	+
Ammonia limnetes	++	+	++	+
Elphidium williamsoni	+	-	++	-
Elphidium margaritaceum	+	-	+	-
Lagena spp.	-	-	+	+

+ present (a few specimens)   ++ common   +++ abundant

Table 31 Pollen from Chainage 22.95km, Mudlands (ARC 36100)

Lithology	Peat		Upper silty clays		
Context	199	199	198	197	197
Trees and shrubs					
Betula	1	1	-	-	1
Pinus	-	2	3	5	9
Ulmus	-	2	1	-	-
Quercus	69	62	39	8	18
Tilia	14	4	6	5	6
Fraxinus	3	-	3	-	-
Corylus avellana-type	10	26	37	13	9
Herbs					
Ranunculus-type	-	1	-	3	-
Chenopodium-type	-	-	3	3	3
Hedera helix	1	1	1	-	-
Apiaceae	1	-	1	-	-
Rumex	1	-	-	-	-
Scrophulariaceae	1	-	1	-	-
Mentha-type	-	-	-	1	-

Table 31 Continued

Lithology	Peat		Upper silty clays		
Context	199	199	198	197	197
Plantago lanceolata	-	1	-	7	-
Bidens-type	-	-	-	1	-
Artemisia	-	-	1	-	-
Lactucoideae	-	-	-	-	5
Poaceae	1	2	5	45	39
Large Poaceae	-	-	-	9	-
Cerealia-type	-	-	-	-	2
Unident/degraded	-	-	-	1	7
Marsh					
Alnus	192	196	166	41	10
Salix	1	-	-	-	-
cf *Littorella uniflora*	-	-	-	1	-
Potamogeton	-	-	1	1	-
Iris	-	-	-	1	-
Typha angustifolia-type	-	-	1	2	1
Cyperaceae	2	2	11	10	12
Spores					
Pteridium aquilinum	-	-	5	23	69
Dryopteris-type	49	10	14	10	23
Polypodium vulgare	2	-	-	1	1
Sphagnum	-	-	-	1	1
Liverworts	-	-	-	1	-
Misc					
Pediastrum	-	-	-	7	-
Hystrichospheres	-	-	3	-	-
Pre-Quaternary	-	-	2	-	-

Table 32 Waterlogged plant remains from Chainage 22.95km, Mudlands (ARC 36100)

		Lithology	Peat			Upper silty clays	
		Context	199	199	199	198	197
		Sample	286	287	288	293	294
		Weight of sediment (kg)	1	1	1	1	1
Taxa	**Common name**						
Rubus fruticosus agg.	blackberry		+	-	-	-	-
Oenanthe aquatica gp.	water dropwort		-	-	+	-	-
Alnus glutinosa	alder		++	+	-	-	-
A. glutinosa	alder (female catkin)		+	-	-	-	-
Lycopus europaeus	gipsy-wort		+	+	-	-	-
Juncus spp.	rush		-	-	-	++	-
Lemna sp.	duckweed		-	-	+	-	-

+ present   ++ common

Table 33 Ostracods from Chainage 22.95km, Mudlands (ARC 36100)

	Lithology	Peat	
	Context	199	197
	Sample	289	294
	Weight of sediment (kg)	0.2	0.2
Brackish water ostracods			
Cyprideis torosa		-	+
Leptocythere porcellanea		-	+
Fresh water ostracods			
Cypria opthalmica		+	-
Foraminifera			
Haynesina germanica		-	+
Ammonia limnetes		-	+

+ present (a few specimens)

Table 35 Waterlogged plant remains and charcoal from Chainage 25.455km, East of Ferry Lane, Rainham Marsh (ARC 36100)

		Sand	Peat	Channel	
	Lithology				
	Context	192	193	194	195
	Weight of sediment (kg)	1	1	1	1
Taxa	**Common name**				
Ranunculus acris/repens/bulbosus	buttercup	-	-	-	+
Ranunculus sceleratus	celery-leaved crowfoot	-	-	+	+
Ranunculus subg. *Batrachium*	crowfoot	-	-	+	+
Stellaria media agg.	chickweed	-	-	+	+
Atriplex sp.	orache	-	-	+	-
Chenopodium album	fat hen	-	-	+	-
Rubus sp.	bramble	-	-	+	-
Apium nodiflorum	fool's watercress	-	-	-	+
Umbelliferae		-	-	-	+
Rumex sp.	docks	-	-	-	+
Urtica dioica	stinging nettle	-	+	-	-
Compositae		-	-	-	+
Alisma plantago-aquatica	water-plantain	-	-	-	+
Juncus sp.	rush	-	-	-	-
Eleocharis palustris	common spikerush	-	-	+	-
Carex spp.	sedges	-	-	+	+
Gramineae	grass, large seeded	-	-	-	-
Wood Fragments		+	+++	+++	++
Quercus sp.	oak charcoal fragments	+	-	-	-
Indet	indeterminate charcoal	-	-	+	-

+ present   ++common   +++ abundant

Table 36 Pollen from Chainage 25.455km, East of Ferry Lane, Rainham Marsh (ARC 36100)

	Sand	Peat		Channel				SC
Lithology	Sand	Peat		Channel				SC
Context	192	193	193	194	194	194	195	166
Sample	253	253	253	253	253	254	255	255
Trees and shrubs								
Betula	1	1	-	4	1	3	1	1
Pinus	3	1	-	1	-	2	2	1
Acer	-	-	1	-	-	-	-	-
Ulmus	-	3	-	1	3	1	2	-
Quercus	20	49	57	35	26	13	12	15
Tilia	12	36	11	3	5	-	4	-
Fraxinus	-	1	3	-	-	-	2	-
Sorbus-type	-	-	1	-	-	-	-	-
Corylus avellana-type	12	14	28	5	11	2	8	12
Erica	-	-	-	-	1	-	-	-
Calluna	-	-	-	-	1	-	-	1
Herbs								
Ranunculus-type	-	-	-	-	-	1	-	1
Sinapis-type	-	-	-	1	-	-	1	-
Hornungia-type	-	-	-	-	1	-	1	-
Dianthus-type	-	-	-	-	-	-	-	1
Chenopodium-type	-	-	-	1	3	5	7	5
Trifolium-type	-	-	-	-	-	-	1	-
Filipendula	-	-	-	-	1	-	-	-
Hedera	-	-	-	1	-	-	-	-
Apiaceae	-	-	-	-	-	-	-	-
Rumex	-	-	-	4	2	2	-	-
Myosotis	-	-	1	-	-	-	-	-
Plantago major-type	-	-	-	-	1	-	-	-
Plantago lanceolata	-	-	1	3	-	2	-	4
Plantago maritime-type	-	-	-	-	-	1	1	-
Plantago coronopus-type	-	-	-	-	1	-	3	-
Galium	-	-	-	1	-	-	-	-
Bidens-type	-	-	-	-	1	3	1	-
Anthemis-type	-	-	-	-	-	1	-	-
Aster-type	-	-	-	-	-	1	-	-
Cirsium-type	-	-	-	-	-	-	-	1
Lactucoideae	1	1	-	4	2	9	1	1
Poaceae	4	2	1	36	41	57	52	56
Cerealia-type	-	-	-	-	1	1	-	4
Large Poaceae	-	-	-	-	-	-	2	-
Unident/degraded	3	-	-	-	1	-	-	-
Marsh								
Alnus	46	124	214	117	38	46	34	1
Salix	-	-	-	3	-	-	-	-
Alisma-type	-	-	-	-	-	-	-	1
Potamogeton	-	-	-	-	1	-	-	-
Typha angustifolia-type	-	-	-	-	-	-	3	10
Cyperaceae	11	2	2	12	22	24	23	25
Spores								
Equisetum	-	1	-	-	-	-	-	-
Pteridium aquilinum	10	3	1	5	7	9	6	8
Dryopteris-type	22	24	40	16	24	37	8	4
Polypodium vulgare	-	4	1	1	1	-	-	1
Sphagnum	1	1	-	-	1	-	1	-
Liverworts	-	-	-	-	-	-	-	-
Misc								
Pediastrum	-	-	-	-	7	-	1	-
Pre-Quaternary	1	-	-	-	-	-	-	2

Table 37 3972TT lithostratigraphy

Stratigraphy	Elevation (mOD)	Depth (m)	Context number	Description
Topsoil	+0.68 to +0.54	0.00–0.14	1	TOPSOIL: Friable, brownish grey (10YR 4/1) silty clay, well rooted
Upper alluvium	+0.54 to -0.64	0.14–0.70	2	SILTY CLAY: Firm oxidised silty clay, greyish yellow brown (10YR 5/2) in upper 0.45m. Massive and structureless, heavily bioturbated, frequent fine modern roots. Below 0.6m increase in Fe mottling (bright yellowish brown 10YR 6/6 and light grey 10Y 7/1). 5% white carbonate flecks concentrated at the contact with (3)
		0.70–0.82	3	SILTY CLAY: Very firm, tenacious mid-grey (10Y 6/1) silty clay. Massive and structureless, 5% white carbonate flecks at upper contact, occasional fine roots
		0.82–1.32	4	SILTY CLAY: Firm, tenacious, bright yellowish brown (10YR 6/6) and grey (10Y 6/1) mottled, silty clay. Massive and structureless, occasional fine roots. Rare white carbonate flecking
Organic complex	-0.64 to -3.86	1.32–1.38	5a	ORGANIC SILTY CLAY: Friable, soft brownish grey (7.5YR 4/1) silty clay. Massive and structureless. Frequent fine roots and faint Fe oxidation
		1.38–1.46	5b	PEATY CLAY: Firm, dense, brownish black (7.5YR 3/1), well humified peaty clay silt, occasional fine roots and plant fibres
		1.46–1.61	6	ORGANIC SILTY CLAY: Soft, tenacious, brownish grey (10YR 4/1) and bright yellowish brown (10YR 6/8) mottled silty clay. 10% organic material, occasional woody detritus (10mm D x 10mm L) frequent plant fibres and rootlets
		1.61–1.66	7a	PEATY SILT: Firm dark reddish brown (5YR 3/2) well humified peaty silt. Root boles identified at interface with (6) extending 0.10–0.20m into (7) and contained a higher % of woody root material
		1.66–1.89	7b	ORGANIC SILTY CLAY: Soft, tenacious brownish grey (7.5 YR 4/1) fibrous silty clay with frequent small roots
		1.89–2.55	8	ORGANIC SILTY CLAY: Very tenacious, soft, greyish brown (7.5Y 5/2), fibrous silty clay, 15–20% organic material, dominated by reeds rooted *in situ* (5–10mm D), very occasional woody detritus (10–20mm D x 20–40mm L)
		2.55–2.63	9	PEAT: Dry, friable, brownish black (5YR 3/1) oxidizing to black (5YR 1.7/1), well humified, rooted (5–10%) slightly silty (15%) amorphous peat. Woody fragments frequent (5–10mm D x 10–40mm L)
		2.63–2.93	10	SILTY PEAT: Soft, dry, friable, greyish brown (5YR 3/2) oxidising to brownish black (5YR 2/1), 25% silt. Frequent woody roots and bark (5–20mm D x 20–50mm L), plant fibres and rare hazelnut shell. Occasional very large timber with root balls attached and branches lying horizontally; *Taxus baccata* (yew), *Alnus glutinosa* (alder) *Quercus* (oak) and *Fraxinus* (ash).
		2.93–3.8	11	SILTY PEAT: Soft, tenacious, brownish grey (5YR 4/1) poorly humified, slightly clayey, very silty peat, fibrous, very few woody fragments, some bark detritus, predominately vertically, well rooted reed type material (3–5mm D x 50mm L)
		3.8–4.47	12	PEAT: Soft, dark reddish brown (5YR 3/3) oxidising to brownish black (5YR 2/1), peat. Frequent woody inclusions (10–50mm D x 100mm L). Occasional horizontal trunks/branches with root balls attached. Frequent fibres (<1mm), occasional reedy material noted
		4.37–4.54	13	SILTY PEAT: Soft, dark reddish brown (2.5YR 3/2) slightly silty (15%) peat, oxidising to brownish black (5YR 2/1). Roots (5mm–10mm D X 20–50mm L), Frequent plant fibres.
Lower alluvium	-3.86 to -3.99	4.54–4.60	14	ORGANIC CLAYEY SILT: Soft, tenacious, yellowish grey (2.5Y 4/1) to greyish yellow (2.5Y 4/2) organic fibrous clay silt, 20–25% organic material, frequent reeds, occasional woody detritus
		4.60–4.67	15	CLAYEY SILT: Soft, very tenacious grey (7.5 Y 5/1) to greyish olive (7.5Y 5/2), clay silt, 15% organic material, fibrous, *in situ* reeds (5mm–10mm D)

Table 38 Waterlogged plant remains from Trench 3972TT, Rainham Marsh (ARC TAM01)

Lithology		Organic complex (lower)								Organic complex (upper)				
Context		14	13	12	12	11	11	11	10	9	8	8	6	5b	5a
Weight of sediment (kg)		1	1	1	1	1	1	1	1	1	1	1	1	1	1
Taxa	**Common name**														
Ranunculus cf *repens*	buttercup	-	-	-	-	-	-	-	+	-	-	-	-	-	-
R. sceleratus	celery-leafed crowfoot	-	-	-	-	-	-	-	-	-	-	+	-	-	-
Rubus fruticosus agg.	bramble	-	-	-	-	+	-	+	-	-	-	-	-	-	-
Cornus sanguinea	dogwood	-	-	-	+	-	-	-	-	-	-	-	-	-	-
Oenanthe aquatica gp.	water dropwort	-	-	-	-	-	+	-	-	-	-	-	-	-	-
Polygonum hydropiper	water-pepper	-	-	-	-	-	-	-	-	-	-	+	-	-	-
Rumex sp.	dock	-	-	-	-	-	-	-	-	-	-	+	-	-	-
Urtica dioica	stinging nettle	-	-	-	-	-	-	-	+	-	-	-	-	-	-
Alnus glutinosa	alder	+	+	+	+	+	-	-	++	++	+	++	-	-	-
A. glutinosa	alder (female catkin)	-	+	+	-	-	-	-	+	+	+	-	-	-	-
A. glutinosa	alder (bud scale)	-	-	-	-	-	-	-	-	-	-	+	-	-	-
Corylus avellana	hazel	+	-	-	-	-	-	-	-	-	-	-	-	-	-
Quercus sp.	oak	-	-	-	-	-	-	+	-	-	-	-	-	-	-
Quercus sp.	oak (bud scale)	-	-	-	-	-	-	+	-	-	-	-	-	-	-
Alisma sp.	water-plantain	-	-	-	-	-	-	-	-	-	-	+	-	-	-
Juncus spp.	rush	-	-	-	-	-	-	-	-	-	-	-	+	+	+
Sparganium erectum	bur-reed	-	-	-	-	-	-	-	-	-	-	+	-	-	-
Eleocharis palustris	common spikerush	-	-	-	-	-	-	-	-	-	-	+	-	-	-

+ present   ++common   +++ abundant

Table 39 Pollen from Trench 3972TT, Rainham Marsh (ARC TAM01)

Lithology	Lower SC		Organic complex (lower)								Organic complex (upper)						Upper silty clays				
Context	15	14	13	12	12	11	11	11	10	9	8	8	8	7	6	5	4	4	3	2	2
Trees and shrubs																					
Betula	-	-	-	1	-	1	3	1	-	-	-	-	-	-	1	-	13	5	1	-	1
Pinus	-	-	1	1	1	-	1	-	-	-	2	-	5	3	3	1	-	11	1	4	2
Ulmus	3	3	3	1	3	3	-	1	-	-	12	2	-	1	1	1	-	-	-	-	1
Quercus	63	59	20	73	73	73	76	57	17	37	40	12	28	29	27	12	68	10	-	21	12
Tilia	3	1	5	1	8	2	6	2	-	-	5	-	1	-	1	1	10	1	-	3	1
Fraxinus	1	1	-	3	2	2	4	-	1	-	4	-	-	1	-	-	-	-	-	-	-
Ilex aquifolium	-	-	-	-	-	-	-	-	-	-	2	-	-	-	-	-	-	-	-	-	-
Sorbus-type	1	-	-	-	-	-	-	1	-	-	-	-	-	-	-	-	-	-	-	-	-
Frangula alnus	-	-	-	-	-	1	-	-	-	-	-	-	-	-	-	-	-	-	-	-	-
Rhamnus cathartica	-	-	-	-	-	1	-	-	-	-	-	-	-	-	-	-	-	-	-	-	-
Corylus avellana-type	27	31	11	18	8	22	12	-	4	7	24	21	9	11	12	6	5	-	1	15	10
Viburnum	-	-	-	-	-	1	-	-	-	-	-	-	-	-	-	-	-	-	-	-	-
Herbs																					
Ranunculus-type	-	-	-	-	-	-	-	-	-	-	1	-	-	-	1	-	2	-	-	-	-
Sinapis-type	-	1	-	-	-	-	-	-	-	-	-	-	1	1	-	-	-	17	1	7	4
Hornungia-type	1	-	-	-	-	-	-	-	-	-	-	-	-	-	-	-	-	-	-	-	-
Chenopodium-type	1	-	-	-	-	-	-	-	-	1	6	7	3	8	17	1	1	4	1	9	14
Fabaceae undiff.	-	-	1	-	-	-	-	-	-	-	-	-	-	-	-	-	-	-	-	-	-
Filipendula	-	1	-	-	-	-	-	-	-	-	-	1	-	-	1	-	-	-	-	-	-
Potentilla-type	-	-	-	-	-	-	-	-	-	-	-	-	-	-	1	-	-	-	-	-	-
Hedera	1	1	-	-	-	1	-	-	-	1	2	-	-	-	-	-	-	-	-	-	-
Apiaceae	-	-	1	-	-	4	-	1	-	-	-	-	-	-	1	-	-	-	-	-	-
Polygonaceae undiff.	-	-	-	-	-	-	-	-	-	-	-	-	1	-	-	-	-	-	-	-	-
Rumex	-	-	-	-	-	-	1	-	-	-	1	-	1	-	-	-	-	-	-	-	-
Urtica-type	-	-	-	-	-	-	-	-	-	-	-	1	-	-	-	-	-	-	-	-	-
Armeria 'A' line	-	-	-	-	-	-	-	-	-	-	-	-	-	-	-	-	-	1	-	1	-
Plantago lanceolata	-	-	-	-	-	-	-	-	-	-	2	1	5	5	-	-	-	5	2	-	-
Galium	-	-	-	-	-	-	-	-	-	-	-	-	-	-	1	-	-	-	-	-	-
Succisa-type	-	-	-	-	-	-	-	-	-	-	-	-	-	-	1	-	-	-	-	-	-
Aster-type	-	-	-	-	-	-	-	-	-	-	1	-	-	-	1	1	-	-	-	-	-
Artemisia	-	-	-	-	-	-	-	-	-	-	-	-	-	1	-	-	-	-	-	-	-
Centaurea nigra-type	-	-	-	-	-	-	-	-	-	-	-	-	-	-	-	-	-	-	-	1	-
Lactucoideae	-	-	-	-	-	-	-	-	-	-	-	-	-	-	-	1	-	3	63	3	6
Poaceae	3	4	1	-	-	2	1	-	-	1	1	17	15	23	30	58	2	26	26	8	28
Cerealia-type	-	-	-	-	-	-	-	-	-	-	-	1	-	-	-	-	-	-	-	1	1
Large Poaceae	-	-	-	-	-	-	-	-	-	-	1	1	1	-	1	-	-	-	-	-	-
Unident/degraded	1	-	1	-	3	-	-	2	-	1	-	2	5	1	-	-	-	6	-	8	9
Marsh																					
Alnus	106	309	316	520	102	253	242	202	85	107	836	32	31	12	55	32	101	12	1	25	9
Salix	-	-	-	2	2	-	1	3	-	-	1	-	-	-	3	9	-	-	-	-	-
Lythrum salicaria	-	1	-	-	-	-	-	-	-	-	-	-	-	-	-	-	-	-	-	-	-
Myriophyllum spicatum	-	3	-	-	-	-	-	-	-	-	-	-	-	-	-	-	-	-	-	-	-
cf *Lemna*	-	-	-	-	-	-	-	-	-	-	1	-	-	-	-	-	-	-	-	-	1
Potamogeton	-	-	-	1	-	-	-	-	-	-	-	-	-	-	-	-	-	-	-	1	-
Iris	-	-	-	-	-	-	-	-	-	-	-	-	-	-	1	-	1	-	-	-	-
Typha latifolia-type	-	-	-	1	-	1	-	-	-	-	-	-	-	-	-	-	-	-	-	-	-
Typha angustifolia-type	-	-	1	-	-	-	-	-	1	4	-	5	4	30	1	3	-	7	-	1	1
Cyperaceae	-	-	-	5	16	9	1	-	-	-	4	37	28	17	22	52	14	11	26	4	12
Spores																					
Equisetum	-	-	-	-	-	-	-	-	-	-	-	1	-	-	-	-	-	-	-	-	-
Osmunda regalis	-	-	-	-	-	-	-	1	-	1	-	-	-	-	-	-	-	-	-	-	-
Pteridium aquilinum	-	-	-	-	-	-	-	1	-	-	-	19	85	-	48	70	-	24	5	13	14
Dryopteris-type	-	2	-	43	53	11	36	16	3	3	2	16	5	-	44	130	65	22	23	30	15
Polypodium vulgare	-	-	-	-	1	1	-	2	-	4	1	1	-	-	-	-	2	-	-	-	1
Sphagnum	-	-	-	-	-	-	-	-	-	1	-	-	1	-	-	-	-	-	-	-	2
Misc																					
Pediastrum	-	-	-	-	-	-	-	-	-	-	-	-	-	-	-	-	-	1	1	1	1
Zygnemataceae	-	-	-	-	-	-	-	-	-	-	-	-	-	-	-	3	-	-	-	-	-
Hystrichospheres	-	-	-	-	-	-	-	-	-	-	-	-	-	-	-	-	-	3	1	1	3
Pre-Quaternary	-	-	-	-	-	-	-	-	-	-	1	-	-	-	-	-	-	8	2	14	32

Table 40 Insects from Trench 3972TT, Rainham Marsh (ARC TAM01)

Lithology	Organic complex (lower)		Organic complex (upper)
Context	12	11	8
Sample	107	117	140
Weight of sediment (kg)	1	1	1
Coleoptera			
Helophorus sp. (*brevipalpis* size)	-	-	+
Ochthebius cf *minimus*	+	-	+
Anobium cf *Punctatum*	+	-	-
Donacia sp.	-	-	+
Plateumaris sericea	-	-	+
Donacia or *Plateumaris* sp.	-	-	+
Prasocuris phellandrii	-	-	+
Agelastica alni	-	+	-
Apion sp.	-	-	+
Ceutorhynchus erysimi	-	-	+
Other Insects			
Trichoptera larva indet.	-	-	+

+ present

Table 41 Ostracods and foraminifera from Trench 3972TT, Rainham Marsh (ARC TAM01)

Lithology	Organic complex		Upper silty clays			
Context	8	5	4	3	2	2
Sample	140	148	149	152	153	155
Weight of sediment (kg)	0.2	0.2	0.2	0.2	0.2	0.2
Brackish water ostracods						
Cyprideis torosa	-	++	++	-	+	+++
Loxoconcha elliptica	-	+	-	+	++	++
Cytherura gibba	-	-	-	-	+	-
Leptocythere porcellanea	-	-	-	+	++	++
Leptocythere castanea	-	-	-	-	+	-
Freshwater ostracods						
Cypria opthalmica	++	-	-	-	-	-
Candona spp.	-	-	-	-	+	-
Limnocythere inopinata	-	-	-	-	+	-
Foraminifera						
Haynesina germanica	-	-	+	-	+	-
Ammonia limnetes	-	-	-	-	-	+
Elphidium williamsoni	-	-	-	-	+	-

+ present (a few specimens)   ++ common   +++ abundant

Table 42 Waterlogged plant remains from Chainage 26.535km and 26.540km, Wennington Marsh (ARC 36100)

Chainage		26.535km		26.54km		
Lithology		Peat	UCS	Ditch 253		
Context		236	233	257	256	255
Sample		369	373	397	398	399
Weight of sediment (kg)		1	1	1	1	1
Taxa	**Common name**					
Ranunculus cf *repens*	buttercup	+	-	-	-	-
Alisma sp.	water-plantain	-	-	-	+	-
Juncus spp.	rush	-	+	-	-	-
Lemna sp.	duckweed	-	-	+	+	+
Typha sp.	reedmace	-	+	+	-	+

+ present   ++ common   +++ abundant

Table 43 Pollen from Chainage 26.535km and 26.54km, Wennington Marsh (ARC 36100)

Chainage	26.535km							26.54km						
Lithology	Peat		Upper silty clays					Ditch 253					Upper SC	
context	236	236	235	235	234	232	232	257	256	255	254	254	252	250
Trees and shrubs														
Betula	1	3	1	-	3	-	1	-	1	-	3	-	-	1
Pinus	2	-	6	6	5	-	3	1	2	3	3	3	2	4
Picea	-	-	-	-	1	-	-	-	-	-	-	-	-	-
Ulmus	-	-	-	-	-	-	5	-	1	-	-	-	-	-
Quercus	12	9	14	7	21	3	25	22	2	20	8	9	9	12
Tilia	1	-	-	2	1	-	1	1	-	-	-	-	-	-
Fraxinus	-	-	-	-	-	-	1	-	-	-	-	-	-	-
Carpinus betulus	-	-	-	-	-	-	1	-	-	-	-	-	-	-
Rhamnus cathartica	1	-	-	-	-	-	-	-	-	-	-	-	-	-
Corylus avellana-type	10	14	20	9	16	5	24	8	3	10	5	3	3	13
Viburnum	-	-	-	1	-	-	-	-	-	1	-	-	-	-
Herbs														
Ranunculus-type	1	-	-	-	-	-	-	1	-	-	-	-	-	1
Sinapsis-type	-	1	-	23	-	25	5	12	7	7	13	25	63	5
Hornungia-type	-	-	-	-	-	-	-	-	-	-	-	-	-	1
Malvaceae	-	-	-	1	-	-	-	-	-	-	-	-	-	-
Dianthus-type	-	-	-	-	-	-	1	-	-	-	1	-	-	-
Chenopodium-type	8	1	18	19	16	23	6	17	11	20	15	11	9	11
Filipendula	-	1	-	-	-	-	-	-	-	-	-	-	-	-
Trifolium-type	-	-	-	-	-	-	-	-	-	-	-	-	-	1
Hedera helix	1	-	-	-	1	-	-	-	-	-	-	-	-	-
Apiaceae	-	-	-	-	-	-	-	-	1	-	-	-	-	-
Scrophulariaceae	-	-	-	-	-	-	-	1	-	1	-	-	-	-
Pedicularis	-	1	-	-	-	-	-	-	-	-	-	-	-	-
Plantago lanceolata	-	1	-	-	-	-	2	-	-	-	-	-	-	2
Galium	1	-	-	-	-	-	-	-	-	-	-	-	-	-
Valeriana officinalis	-	-	-	-	-	-	-	-	-	-	-	1	-	-
Bidens-type	1	-	1	-	-	-	2	-	-	-	-	-	-	-
Aster-type	-	-	-	-	-	-	1	-	-	-	-	-	-	4
Anthemis-type	-	-	-	-	-	-	2	-	-	-	1	-	-	-
Cirsium-type	1	-	-	1	-	-	-	-	-	-	-	-	1	-
Artemisia	1	-	1	-	1	-	-	-	-	-	-	-	-	1
Centaurea sp.	-	-	-	-	-	-	-	-	-	-	-	1	-	-
Lactucoideae	10	3	5	7	5	15	1	3	11	1	13	17	5	5
Poaceae	48	38	25	28	30	17	16	30	34	24	28	29	9	34
Cerealia-type	-	1	2	-	-	1	3	-	1	-	5	2	1	3
Large Poaceae	-	1	-	-	-	-	-	1	1	3	4	-	-	-
Unident/degraded	-	-	1	-	1	8	3	2	2	1	2	1	-	1
Marsh														
Alnus	86	26	11	9	17	13	54	10	23	14	19	7	17	28
Salix	1	-	-	-	-	-	-	-	-	-	-	1	-	-
Myriophyllum spicatum	-	-	-	-	-	-	1	-	-	-	-	-	-	-
Alisma-type	-	1	-	-	-	-	-	-	-	-	-	-	1	-
Potamogeton	1	-	2	-	-	-	1	-	-	-	-	-	-	-
Typha latifolia	-	-	3	-	-	-	-	-	-	1	5	-	-	-
Typha angustifolia-type	3	-	2	1	-	1	5	-	1	-	-	-	-	3
Cyperaceae	40	32	35	14	5	10	4	24	27	12	5	3	6	8
Spores														
Equisetum	-	-	-	-	-	-	-	-	1	-	-	-	-	-
Pteridium aquilinum	26	19	23	23	18	13	5	21	6	16	20	-	-	6
Dryopteris-type	128	356	30	22	21	20	11	36	121	63	75	31	34	9
Polypodium vulgare	-	2	-	-	-	1	-	-	1	-	1	1	1	1
Osmundaregalis	-	-	-	-	-	-	-	-	-	1	-	-	-	-
Sphagnum	-	-	-	-	-	-	2	-	-	-	-	1	-	1
Liverworts	-	2	-	-	-	1	-	1	-	-	-	-	1	-
Misc														
Pediastrum	-	-	2	1	3	-	10	1	-	-	-	-	-	-
Zygnemataceae	-	7	-	1	-	-	-	-	-	1	1	-	-	-
Hystrichospheres	-	-	-	1	2	-	5	1	-	-	-	1	1	-
Pre-Quaternary	-	-	2	9	19	-	5	6	-	2	-	1	4	11

Table 44 Ostracods and foraminifera from Chainage 26.535km and 26.54km, Wennington Marsh (ARC 36100)

	Chainage		26.535km						26.54km						
	Lithology		Upper silty clays					Sand	Ditch 253					Upper SC	
	Context	235	235	234	233	232	232	248	257	256	255	254	254	252	250
	Sample	370	371	372	373	374	376	394	395	395	395	396	396	396	396
	Weight of sediment (kg)	0.2	0.2	0.2	0.2	0.2	0.2	0.2	0.2	0.2	0.2	0.2	0.2	0.2	0.2
Brackish water ostracods															
Cyprideis torosa		++	+++	–	+	+++	+++	+++	++	+	++	+	–	+	++
Loxoconcha elliptica		–	–	–	++	+	+	–	–	–	–	+	+	+	++
Cytherura gibba		+	–	–	++	–	–	+	+	–	–	–	–	–	++
Leptocythere porcellanea		+	++	–	–	+++	++	–	–	–	–	–	–	+	++
Leptocythere castanea		–	–	–	–	+	–	–	–	–	–	–	–	–	–
Marine ostracods															
Pontocythere elongata		–	–	–	–	+	–	+	–	–	–	–	–	–	–
Freshwater ostracods															
Candona spp.		+	+	–	+	–	–	–	–	–	–	–	–	–	–
Cypria opthalmica		–	–	–	–	–	–	–	–	–	–	–	–	–	–
Heterocypris salina		–	+	–	–	–	–	+	+	–	–	–	–	–	–
Limnocythere inopinata		–	–	–	–	–	–	+	–	–	–	–	–	–	–
Ilyocypris sp.		–	–	–	–	–	–	+	–	–	–	–	–	–	–
Pseudocandona sp.		–	–	–	+	–	–	+	–	–	–	–	–	–	–
Foraminifera															
Haynesina germanica		++	+	–	+	+	+	+	++	–	+	–	–	–	++
Ammonia limnetes		+	+	–	+	+	+	+	++	–	+	–	–	–	+
Elphidium williamsoni		++	–	–	+	++	–	+	++	–	+	–	–	–	+
Elphidium margaritaceum		+	–	–	–	–	–	–	+	–	–	–	–	–	+
Lagena spp.		+	–	–	–	–	–	–	+	–	+	–	–	–	–
Glabratella millettii		–	+	+	–	–	–	–	–	–	–	–	–	–	–

+ present (a few specimens)   ++ common   +++ abundant

Table 45 Waterlogged plant remains from Chainage 26.8km and 27.46km, Wennington Marsh (ARC 36100)

		Chainage	26.8km			27.46km		
		Lithology	LCS	Peat		Peat		USC
		Context	274	273	273	272	271	269
		Sample	405	403	402	428	429	431
		Weight of sediment (kg)	1	1	1	1	1	1
Taxa	**Common name**							
Rubus fruticosus agg.	blackberry		-	-	+	+	+	-
Potentilla anserina	silverweed		-	-	-	-	-	++
Urtica dioica	stinging nettle		-	-	-	+	-	-
Alnus glutinosa	alder		++	-	++	-	-	-
A. glutinosa	alder (female catkin)		+	-	+	-	-	-
Corylus avellana	hazel		-	-	-	-	+	-
Quercus sp.	oak (bud scale)		-	+	-	-	-	-
Populus sp.	poplar (bud scale)		-	-	-	+	-	-
Lycopus europaeus	gipsy-wort		-	-	-	+	-	-
Juncus spp.	rush		-	-	-	-	-	+
Carex spp.	sedge		-	-	-	+	-	-

+ present   ++ common   +++ abundant

Table 46 Insects from Chainage 26.8km and 27.46km, Wennington Marsh (ARC 36100)

	Chainage	26.8km	27.460km
	Lithology	LCS	Peat
	Context	274	272
	Sample	405	428
	Weight of sediment (kg)	1	1
Coleoptera			
Ochthebius cf *minimus*		+	+
Hydraena testacea		+	-
Stenus sp.		+	-
Agelastica alni		+	-
Dryocoetinus alni		+	-

+ present

Table 47 Pollen from Chainage 26.8km and 27.46km, Wennington Marsh (ARC 36100)

| Chainage | 26.8km | | | | 27.46km | | | | | | | | | |
| Lithology | Org SC | Peat | | | Peat | | | | Upper silty clays | | | | | |
Context	274	273	273	273	272	272	272	271	270	269	269	268	268	268
Trees and shrubs														
Betula	1	3	-	-	1	-	-	-	1	-	1	3	3	1
Pinus	4	-	1	1	3	-	-	1	2	-	2	1	3	6
Picea	-	-	-	-	-	-	-	-	-	-	-	-	1	-
Taxus baccata	-	-	-	-	-	-	-	2	-	-	-	-	-	-
Ulmus	3	-	-	1	1	-	-	-	-	-	-	13	4	-
Quercus	42	63	74	72	35	25	21	32	8	4	13	26	26	9
Tilia	5	8	6	4	1	4	7	9	1	2	-	2	1	-
Fraxinus	-	-	-	-	1	1	1	-	-	-	-	3	-	-
cf *Populus*	-	-	-	1	-	-	-	-	-	-	-	-	-	-
Sorbus-type	-	-	1	-	-	-	-	-	-	-	-	-	-	-
Prunus-type	-	-	-	-	-	-	1	-	-	-	-	-	-	-
Corylus avellana-type	23	19	14	22	12	12	3	24	4	-	1	19	15	3
Erica	-	-	-	-	-	-	-	-	-	-	-	-	1	-
Herbs														
Ranunculus-type	-	-	-	-	-	-	-	-	-	-	-	-	-	1
Sinapsis-type	-	-	-	-	-	-	-	-	11	1	-	-	1	3
cf *Hypericum*	-	-	-	-	-	-	-	-	-	-	-	-	1	-
Malvaceae	-	-	-	-	-	-	-	-	1	-	-	-	-	-
Spergula-type	-	-	-	-	-	-	-	-	1	-	-	-	-	1
Chenopodium-type	11	-	-	1	-	-	-	1	-	-	3	9	7	12
Trifolium-type	-	-	-	-	-	-	-	-	-	-	2	-	-	-
Rosaceae	-	-	1	-	-	-	-	-	-	1	-	-	-	-
Filipendula	-	-	1	-	-	-	-	-	-	-	-	-	-	-
Filipendula ulmaria	-	-	-	-	-	-	1	-	-	-	-	-	-	-
Hedera helix	-	-	-	-	-	-	1	-	-	-	-	-	-	-
Apiaceae	-	1	2	-	-	-	-	-	-	1	-	-	1	-
Mercurialis	-	-	-	-	-	-	1	-	-	-	-	-	-	-
Polygonum sp.	-	-	-	-	-	-	-	-	-	1	-	-	-	-
Rumex	-	-	-	-	-	-	1	-	-	1	-	-	-	-
Cynoglossum	-	-	-	-	-	-	-	-	-	1	-	-	-	-
Scrophulariaceae	-	-	-	-	-	-	-	1	-	1	-	-	-	-
Plantago major-type	-	-	-	-	-	-	-	1	-	-	-	-	-	-
Plantago lanceolata	3	-	-	-	1	-	-	-	-	-	-	-	-	3
Plantago coronopus	-	-	-	-	-	-	-	-	-	-	-	-	-	1
Lysimachia	1	-	-	-	-	-	-	-	-	-	-	-	-	-
Bidens-type	-	-	-	-	-	-	-	-	-	1	-	-	-	-
Aster-type	-	-	-	-	-	-	-	-	-	-	-	3	1	-
Anthemis-type	-	-	-	-	-	-	-	-	-	-	-	-	-	1
Cirsium-type	-	-	-	-	-	-	-	-	-	1	1	-	-	-
Centaurea nigra-type	-	-	-	-	-	-	-	-	-	-	-	-	1	-
Centaurea scabiosa-type	-	-	-	-	-	-	-	-	-	1	-	-	-	-
Lactucoideae	-	-	-	-	-	-	-	5	-	41	7	-	1	3
Poaceae	6	-	-	1	25	4	6	16	28	48	56	32	35	35
Cerealia-type	-	-	-	-	-	-	-	-	3	-	-	-	4	6
Large Poaceae	-	-	-	-	-	-	-	1	1	-	6	1	-	-
Unident/degraded	1	-	1	1	-	2	-	2	2	-	-	-	-	-
Marsh														
Alnus	123	73	105	148	20	52	65	116	13	4	2	86	14	18
Salix	-	9	-	1	-	-	-	-	-	-	-	1	-	-
Caltha-type	-	-	-	-	-	-	-	-	-	-	1	-	-	-
Potamogeton	-	-	-	-	-	-	-	-	-	-	-	-	-	1
Lemna	-	-	-	-	-	-	-	-	-	-	1	-	-	-
cf *Callitriche*	-	-	-	-	-	1	-	-	-	-	-	-	-	-
Typha angustifolia-type	-	-	-	1	1	-	-	1	-	-	-	-	3	3
Cyperaceae	-	16	33	10	48	2	3	17	15	62	22	6	7	8
Spores														
Equisetum	-	-	-	-	-	-	-	-	-	1	1	-	-	-
Pteridium aquilinum	1	3	1	2	10	3	-	-	1	10	12	7	8	4
Thelypteris palustris	-	11	-	-	-	1	-	-	-	-	-	-	-	-
Dryopteris-type	11	114	16	24	129	9	19	0	33	24	6	21	29	14
Polypodium vulgare	1	4	3	3	4	0	1	0	1	0	0	0	0	1
Sphagnum	0	0	0	0	0	0	0	0	0	0	0	0	0	0
Liverworts	0	0	0	0	9	0	0	0	0	0	0	0	0	0
Misc														
Pediastrum	0	0	0	0	0	0	0	0	1	0	0	0	0	1
Zygnemataceae	0	0	2	0	5	0	0	0	1	0	1	0	0	0
Hystrichospheres	1	0	0	0	0	0	0	0	0	0	0	0	5	4
Pre-Quaternary	0	0	0	0	0	0	0	0	2	0	0	0	2	5

Table 48 Ostracods and foraminifera from Chainage 27.46km, Wennington Marsh (ARC 36100)

	Lithology		Upper silty clays		
	Context	270	268	268	268
	Sample	430	432	434	436
Brackish water ostracods					
Cyprideis torosa		++	++	++	+++
Loxoconcha elliptica		-	++	++	++
Cytherura gibba		-	+	-	-
Leptocythere porcellanea		-	-	+	-
Freshwater ostracods					
Limnocythere inopinata		-	-	-	+
Cyclocypris sp.		-	-	+	-
Foraminifera					
Haynesina germanica		-	++	++	++
Ammonia limnetes		+	+	+	+
Elphidium williamsoni		-	+	+	+
Lagena spp.		-	+	-	-

+ present (a few specimens)   ++ common   +++ abundant

Table 49 The worked flint assemblage from Rainham Marsh (ARC 36100)

Category type	Context	
	192	193
Flake	30	1
Sieved chips 10–4mm	31	-
Rejuvenation flake core face/edge	1	-
Tested nodule/bashed lump	1	-
Core on a flake	1	-
Microlith	1	-
Total	65	1
Burnt unworked flint No./wt (g)	103/459	1/34
No. burnt worked flints (%)*		1
No. broken worked flints (%)*	3 (8.8)	
No. retouched flints (%)*	1 (2.9)	

*percentage excludes chips

Table 50 Roman pottery from context 194, Rainham Marsh (ARC 36100)

Fabric*	Count	Weight
'Early' shell-tempered ware (B6)	26	74
Flint-tempered ware (no code)	4	23
Sandy grey ware (R7)	7	11
Grog-tempered ware (B2/B5)	7	10
Unidentified (no code)	2	4
'Upchurch'-type oxidised ware (R17)	1	1
Total	47	123

*Fabric code from the Canterbury Archaeological Trust

Table 51 Medieval and post-medieval pottery from Wennington Marsh

Context	SHEL No.	SHEL Wt	EMSS No.	EMSS Wt	Micaceous No.	Micaceous Wt	Sandy No.	Sandy Wt	LOND No.	LOND Wt	KING No.	KING Wt	MG No.	MG Wt	RE No.	RE Wt	Date
U/S	-	-	-	-	-	-	2	2	2	7	-	-	1	5	4	27	U/S
234	-	-	-	-	-	-	-	-	-	-	1	28	-	-	-	-	L13C
239	-	-	2	14	-	-	-	-	-	-	-	-	2	26	-	-	L13C
240	8	99	3	16	-	-	-	-	1	56	-	-	1	1	-	-	M12C
252	-	-	-	-	-	-	2	8	-	-	-	-	-	-	3	24	16C
254	-	-	1	12	-	-	42	255	-	-	-	-	1	1	-	-	L13C
256	-	-	1	8	-	-	-	-	-	-	-	-	-	-	-	-	E11C
257	-	-	-	-	1	87	-	-	-	-	-	-	-	-	-	-	12C
Total	8	99	7	50	1	87	46	265	3	63	1	28	5	33	7	51	

Table 52 Charred plant remains from Wennington Marsh (ARC 36100)

		Context 252	254	255	256	257
		Sample 401	400	399	398	397
Taxa	**Common name**					
Hordeum sp. – hulled grain	hulled barley	-	-	+	+	-
Avena sp. – grain	oats	-	-	+	-	-
cereal indet. – grain		+	+	+	+	-
Avena sp. – awn	oats	+	-	-	-	-
Chenopodium album – seed	fat hen	-	-	+	-	-
Galium aparine – seed	goosegrass	-	-	+	-	-
Anthemis cotula – seed	stinking mayweed	-	+	-	-	-
Gramineae indet. – seed	grass	-	-	+	-	-

+ present

Table 54 Waterlogged plant remains from Chainage 28.517km, Aveley Marsh (ARC 36100)

		Lithology LCS	Peat	Organic silts and clay				Upper SC	
		Context Number 379	378	377	376	376	375	374	373
		Sample Number 532	533	534	536	537	538	539	540
		Volume of sediment (litres) 1	1	1	1	1	1	1	1
		Proportion scanned (%) 30	30	30	30	100	100	100	100
Taxa	**Common name**								
Taxus baccata	yew	-	-	-	+	-	-	-	
Caltha palustris	marsh-marigold	-	-	-	+	-	-	-	-
Ranunculus repens/R. acris/R. bulbosus	creeping/meadow/bulbous buttercup	-	-	+	++	-	-	-	-
Ranunculus subg. *Ranunculus*	buttercup	-	+	+	-	-	-	-	-
Fagus sylvatica – mast fragment	beech	-	-	-	+	-	-	-	-
Alnus glutinosa – seed	alder	-	++	++	+++	-	-	-	-
Alnus glutinosa – intact inflorescence	alder	-	-	+	-	-	-	-	-
Alnus glutinosa – stalk of inflorescence	alder	-	+++	+	++	+	-	-	-
Alnus cf *glutinosa* – stalk of inflorescence	possible alder	-	+	-	-	-	-	-	-
Polygonum hydropiper	water-pepper	-	-	+	-	-	-	-	-
Brassica cf *nigra*	black mustard	-	-	-	+	-	-	-	-
Rubus subg. *Rubus* section 1 *Rubus*	bramble	-	+	+	-	-	-	-	-
Mentha sp. – possible aquatic type	mint (possible water mint)	-	-	+	-	-	-	-	-
Solanum sp.	nightshades	-	+	+	-	-	-	-	-
cf *Scripus sylvaticus*	possible wood club-rush	-	+	-	-	-	-	-	-
cf *Iris pseudacorus* – fragment	yellow iris	-	-	+	-	-	-	-	-
Unidentified bud	bud	-	+	-	+	-	-	-	-
Unidentified bud scar	bud scar	-	++	+	++	++	-	-	-
Unidentified moss fragments	moss fragments	-	-	-	+	-	-	-	-
Unidentified wood fragments	wood fragments	++++	-	-	-	++++	++	++	+

+ < 3   ++ 3–9   +++ 10–25   ++++ >25

Table 56 Summary of main lithological units identified in Stage I Thames River Crossing investigation

Unit Number	Stratigraphic description	Inferred environment of deposition	Age ascription	Archaeological and palaeoenvironmental potential
X	5Y 3/2 dark olive grey slightly organic clay-silt. Structureless and moderately firm. Modern roots present. Laterally this may include some or significant quantities of recent material	Topsoil/made ground	Recent	Low
IX	5Y 5/2 olive grey clay-silt with 7.5YR 4/4 dark brown mottles. Very firm and compact. Occasional small, sub-rounded clasts (<3mm). Modern roots This unit also includes sediments that are 10YR 6/4 light yellowish brown clay-silt becoming 5Y 5/1 grey with depth. Strong 7.5YR 4/4 dark brown mottles. Structureless and massive. Very firm becoming softer with depth. Occasional plant fragments present Deposit may also contain 10YR 3/2 very dark grey organic silt becoming a 10YR 2/1 black woody peat with depth. Moderately firm and compact. Structureless. Well preserved wood and root fragments. Very well humifed ground mass	This sequence is indicative of deposition within intertidal or upper-tidal mudflat situations (clay-silt dominated zones) alternating with periods of organic accumulation in saltmarsh surface zones. Rooted horizons and weathered surfaces within sequences suggest periodic drying of areas and pedogenic activity	< 1500 cal BC	Archaeological artefacts discovered within these fine grained sediments are unlikely to have been transported any distance due to the fine grained nature of the substrate. The presence of surfaces may be indicative of horizons on which occupation may have occurred Palaeoenvironmental material may exist within these contexts. Better preservation may exist of pollen/plant fragments within organic sub-units
VIII	Black to very dark brown reed peat containing moderately well preserved reed fragments. Slightly pliable and plastic Can vary to dark brown laminated peat or organic silt. With common reed fragments. Relatively soft and unconsolidated. Bedded with 1–2mm thick laminae of sub-parallel aspect. Locally wood peat also present. A noticeable clay-silt horizon (20–20cm thick in places) is present within some peat sequences	Freshwater or saltmarsh reed swamp. Locally alder carr wetland may also be present Clay-silt horizon within peat may be indicative of local channelling or the presence of a short lived phase of tidal channel activity	c 4000– 1500 cal BC	Archaeological artefacts discovered within these deposits may be *in situ* or close to *in situ* Artefacts are commonly associated with the upper surface of peats (trackways) or within the peats Palaeoenvironmental potential may be high in unhumified parts of the sequence with good plant, pollen and insect preservation
VII	Grey to dark grey clay-silt. Common black reduced organic fragments and fresher reed fragments. Laminated in places with 1–3mm thick wavy, sub-parallel laminations. Numbers of laminae increase towards base. Moderately soft and unconsolidated	Intertidal or upper tidal mudflats or channel fills	c 5900/5200– 4000 cal BC	Archaeological artefacts discovered within these fine grained sediments are unlikely to have been transported any distance due to the fine grained nature of the substrate. Some well preserved palaeoenvironmental material may exist within these contexts including pollen, plant macrofossils, foraminifera/ostracoda and diatoms.

Table 56 Continued

Unit Number	Stratigraphic description	Inferred environment of deposition	Age ascription	Archaeological and palaeoenvironmental potential
VI	5Y 2.5/1 black organic silt. Very dense and compact with reed fragments present. May also vary to a 5YR 2.5/1 black woody peat that is loose and unconsolidated. Occasional flint clasts (<2cm, angular). Structureless	? freshwater reed swamp or channel marginal infill with local trees	5900–5200 cal BC	Any artefacts found in this sequence would be *in situ* to slightly reworked artefacts. Palaeoenvironmental material may be well persevered in this sequence
V	Light blue-grey silt to sandy-silt. Very dense and compact Occasional black wood fragments. Common shell fragments. May grade downwards into dark greenish-grey medium sand. Common shell fragments. Possibly some crude bedding noted. Gravel clasts increase with depth	Freshwater channel fills, edge channel or channel Marginal situations	>5900 cal BC	Any artefacts present may be considered to have been subject to post-depositional movement. Palaeoenvironmental potential may include pollen and ostracod remains
IV	Blue-grey bedded sands. Beds 1–2cm thick and consisting of alternating bands of medium and coarse sand. Beds and parallel and sub-horizontal. Unit is dense and compact and contains shell fragments. Chalk clasts are present and increase in frequency with depth. Locally coarser gravel units may exist	High energy braided channel environments	10–15ka BP	Considerable post-depositional transportation may have occurred to any artefacts. Palaeoenvironmental potential is low
III	5Y 5/2 olive grey silty and. Very firm and compact. Structureless and massive. Occasional roots noted (1–3mm wide). Grades downward into more silty deposit with some gravel. Becomes 5G 5/1 greenish-grey colour. 5G 4/1 dark greenish-grey medium to coarse sand with flint and chalk clasts. Chalk becomes very coarse towards base of unit. Clearly bedded in places	High energy braided channel environments	>25ka BP	Considerable post-depositional transportation may have occurred to any artefacts. Palaeoenvironmental potential is low
II	Angular chalk rubble and chalky paste matrix. Moderately dense and compact	Periglacial solifluction or *in situ* weathering and breakup of chalk	>10ka BP	Low archaeological and palaeoenvironmental potential
I	Fresh, dense clean chalk	Tropical sea	65mya	None

Table 57 Diatoms from Borehole BH3751

Lithology	Organic silt	LCS	Peat						Upper clay silts		
m OD	-8.53	-8.43	-4.81	-4.57	-4.47	-4.35	-3.53	-3.29	-3.19	-0.72	-0.35
Polyhalobous											
Biddulphia aurita	-	-	-	-	-	-	-	-	+	-	-
Cymatosira belgica	-	-	-	-	-	-	-	-	-	-	+
Paralia sulcata	-	+	-	-	-	-	-	-	++	+	++
Podosira stelligera	-	-	-	-	+	-	-	-	-	-	-
Rhaphoneis sp.	-	-	-	-	-	-	-	+	+	-	+
Rhaphoneis minutissima	-	-	-	-	-	-	-	-	-	-	+
Rhaphoneis surirella	-	-	-	-	-	-	-	+	+	-	+
Thalassionema nitzschiodes	-	-	-	-	-	-	+	-	+	-	-
Polyhalobous to mesohalobous											
Diploneis smithii	-	-	-	-	-	-	-	-	-	+	++
Navicula flanatica	-	-	-	-	-	-	-	-	+	-	-
Thalassiosira decipiens	-	-	-	-	-	-	-	-	+	-	-
Mesohalobous											
Campylodiscus echeneis	-	+	-	+	-	-	-	-	-	+	-
Cyclotella striata	-	-	+	-	-	-	-	+	++	-	-
Diploneis aestuari	-	-	-	-	-	-	-	-	+	-	-
Diploneis didyma	-	-	-	-	+	-	-	-	-	-	-
Diploneis interrupta	-	-	-	-	-	-	-	-	-	++	++
Nitzschia granulata	-	-	-	-	+	-	-	-	++	-	-
Nitzschia navicularis	-	+	-	+	++	-	-	-	++	+	+
Nitzschia sigma	-	-	-	-	-	-	-	-	+	-	-
Synedra fasciculata	-	+	-	-	-	-	-	-	+	-	+
Mesohalobous to halophilous											
Actinocyclus normanii	-	-	-	-	-	-	-	-	+	-	-
Nitzschia levidensis	-	-	-	-	-	-	-	-	+	-	+
Halophilous											
Navicula cincta (& v. *minor*)	-	-	-	-	-	-	-	-	-	+	+
Navicula pusilla	-	-	-	-	-	-	-	-	-	-	+
Navicula slesvicensis	-	-	-	-	-	-	-	-	-	+	-
Halophilous to oligohalobous indifferent											
Diploneis ovalis	-	-	-	-	-	-	-	-	-	+	-
Gomphonema olivaceum	+	-	-	-	-	-	-	-	-	-	-
Oligohalobous indifferent								-	-	-	-
Achnanthes minutissima	-	-	-	-	-	-	-	+	-	-	-
Amphora ovalis	-	-	-	-	-	-	-	-	-	+	-
Caloneis bacillum	-	-	-	-	-	-	-	-	-	-	+
Fragilaria pinnata	-	-	-	-	-	-	-	-	-	-	+
Meridion circulare	+	-	-	-	-	+	-	-	-	-	-
Navicula rhyncocephala	-	-	-	-	-	-	-	-	-	++	+
Unknown salinity preference											
Diploneis sp.	-	-	-	+	-	-	-	-	-	-	-
Nitzschia sp.	-	-	-	-	-	-	-	-	-	+	-
Pinnularia sp.	-	-	-	-	-	-	-	-	-	+	-
Indeterminate centric diatom	-	+	-	+	-	-	-	-	-	-	-
Indeterminate fragment	-	-	-	+	-	-	-	-	-	-	-

+ present   ++ common

Table 58 Waterlogged plant remains from Borehole BH375I

Taxa	Common name	Peat and organic silt			LCS			Peat								Upper clay silts		
Lithology (m OD)		-8.81 to -8.87	-8.63 to -8.73	-8.53 to -8.63	-8.03 to -8.13	-6.13 to -6.23	-5.18 to -5.28	-4.73 to -4.83	-4.50 to -4.58	-4.38 to -4.48	-4.03 to -4.13	-3.60 to -3.70	-3.26 to -3.36	-3.03 to -3.13	-1.93 to -2.03	-0.98 to -1.08	-0.33 to -0.43	0.27 to 0.17
Weight of sediment (kg)		0.208	0.217	0.245	0.416	0.638	0.418	0.251	0.191	0.285	0.254	0.327	0.300	0.603	0.333	0.402	0.200	0.427
Proportion of sample scanned		25%	25%	25%	25%	25%	25%	25%	25%	25%	25%	25%	25%	25%	50%	50%	25%	No flot
Ranunculus sceleratus	celery-leaved buttercup	-	-	-	-	-	-	-	-	-	-	-	-	+	-	+	++	-
Urtica dioica	common nettle	-	-	-	-	-	-	-	-	-	-	-	-	-	-	-	-	-
Alnus glutinosa – seed	alder	-	++++	++	-	+	-	-	-	-	-	-	-	-	-	-	-	-
Alnus glutinosa – stalk of inflorescence	alder	-	-	+	-	-	-	-	-	-	-	-	-	-	-	-	-	-
Persicaria hydropiper	water-pepper	-	-	-	-	-	-	-	-	-	-	-	-	-	-	-	+	-
Rumex spp.	dock	-	-	-	-	+	-	-	-	-	-	-	-	-	-	-	-	-
Lycopus europaeus	gypsywort	-	-	-	-	+	-	-	-	-	+	-	-	-	-	-	-	-
Eleocharis palustris/uniglumis	common/slender spike-rush	-	-	-	-	-	-	-	-	+	-	-	-	-	-	-	-	-
cf *Eleocharis palustris/uniglumis*	possible common/slender spike-rush	-	-	-	-	-	-	-	-	-	-	-	-	-	-	-	+	-
Bolboschoenus maritimus/ Schoenoplectus spp.	club rushes	-	-	-	-	-	-	-	-	-	-	-	-	+++	-	-	-	-
cf *Scirpus sylvaticus*	possible wood club-rush	-	-	+	-	-	-	-	-	-	-	-	-	-	-	-	-	-
Carex spp. – 3-sided	sedge	-	-	-	-	-	-	-	+	-	+	-	-	-	-	-	-	-
Cyperaceae – unidentified	Sedge Family	-	+	-	-	-	-	-	-	-	-	-	-	-	-	-	-	-
Unidentified bud	bud	-	-	-	-	-	++	-	-	-	-	-	-	-	-	-	-	-
Unidentified bud scar	bud scar	-	++	-	-	-	-	-	-	-	-	-	-	-	-	-	-	-
Unidentified wood fragments (most likely alder)	wood fragments	++	+++++	+++	+	+++	+++++	+++++	+++++	+++++	++++	+++++	+++++	+++	++++	++++	+++++	-
Unidentified vegetative fragments (most likely reed and/or sedge)	vegetative fragments (most likely reed)	++++	++	+++++	+	+++	+++++	+++++	+++++	+++++	+++++	+++++	+++++	+++	++++	++++	+++++	-

+ 1–3   ++ 4–10   +++ 11–25   ++++ 26–50   +++++ >50

Table 59 Foraminifera and ostracods from Borehole BH3751

Lithology	m OD	FORAMINIFERA Trochammina inflata	Jadammina macrescens/ Haplophragmoides spp.	Tiphotrocha comprimata	Ammonia spp. (small)	Haynesina germanica	Elphidium williamsoni	Arenoparrella mexicana	OSTRACODS Cyprideis torosa (smooth)	Loxoconcha elliptica	Leptocythere porcellanea	Candona sp. (juvs.)	Cytheromorpha fuscata	Ecology	Tidal access	[regression]
Upper clay silts	0.44 to 0.39													Weathered horizon		
	0.13 to 0.07													Weathered horizon		
	-0.08 to -0.15													?Freshwater, reed beds; decalcified		[regression]
	-0.28 to -0.33													?Freshwater, reed beds; decalcified		[regression]
	-0.78 to -0.83													?Freshwater, reed beds; decalcified		[regression]
	-0.93 to -0.98													?Freshwater, reed beds; decalcified		[regression]
	-1.21 to -1.26		x											?Freshwater, reed beds; decalcified		[regression]
	-1.61 to -1.65	xxx	xxx	x	x									Mid–low saltmarsh, tidal flats and creeks	Tidal access	
	-2.01 to -2.06	o			x	x	x							Mid–low saltmarsh, tidal flats and creeks	Tidal access	
	-2.38 to -2.43		x		xx	o	o							Mid–low saltmarsh, tidal flats and creeks	Tidal access	
	-2.83 to -2.88		x		xx				x	o				Mid–low saltmarsh, tidal flats and creeks	Tidal access	
	-3.22 to -3.27	x	x	x	x				x					Mid–low saltmarsh, tidal flats and creeks	Tidal access	
Peat	-4.58 to -4.63		x											Mid–high saltmarsh		
Lower clay silts	-5.08 to -5.13													Freshwater; reedbeds		[regression]
	-5.43 to -5.48													Freshwater; reedbeds		[regression]
	-6.03 to -6.08		o		xx				x		x	x	o	Saltmarsh and tidal mudflats	Tidal access	
	-6.43 to -6.48		x		xxx						x		o	Saltmarsh and tidal mudflats	Tidal access	
	-6.93 to -6.98	xx	xx		xxx		o	x	o		x			Saltmarsh and tidal mudflats	Tidal access	
	-7.53 to -7.58		x		xxx	x		x						Saltmarsh and tidal mudflats	Tidal access	
	-7.93 to -7.98			x	xxx			xx						Saltmarsh and tidal mudflats	Tidal access	
Basal peat and organic silt	-8.43 to -8.51													?Freshwater		
	-8.85 to -8.93													?Freshwater		

o – one specimen   x – several specimens   xx – common   xxx – abundant/superabundant

Foraminifera
- Calcareous foraminifera of low–mid saltmarsh and tidal flats
- Agglutinating foraminifera of mid–high saltmarsh

Ostracods
- Brackish ostracods of tidal flats and creeks
- Freshwater ostracods (FW OS)

Table 60 Foraminifera and ostracods from Borehole BH3748

Lithology	m OD	*Jadammina macrescens*	*Trochammina inflata*	*Ammonia* spp. (small)	*Elphidium williamsoni*	*Cyprideis torosa* (smooth)	Ecology		
Lower clay silts	-5.88 to -5.93						freshwater; reedbeds	tidal access	regression
	-5.98 to -6.03						freshwater; reedbeds		
	-6.08 to -6.13						freshwater; reedbeds		
	-6.18 to -6.23	x					mid–high saltmarsh		
	-6.28 to -6.33	x					mid–high saltmarsh		
	-6.38 to -6.43	x					mid–high saltmarsh		
	-6.48 to -6.53	x	x	x			saltmarsh and tidal mudflats		
	-6.58 to -6.63	x		x			saltmarsh and tidal mudflats		
	-6.68 to -6.73		o	xx	x		saltmarsh and tidal mudflats		
	-6.78 to -6.83			xx		x	saltmarsh and tidal mudflats		
	-6.88 to -6.93			xxx	x	x	saltmarsh and tidal mudflats		

o – one specimen   x – several specimens   xx – common   xxx – abundant/superabundant

Foraminifera

☐ Calcareous foraminifera of low–mid saltmarsh and tidal flats

☐ Agglutinating foraminifera of mid–high saltmarsh

Ostracods

☐ Brackish ostracods of tidal flats and creeks

Table 61 Insects from Borehole BH3751

	Lithology	Peat			UCS
	m OD	-4.5 to -4.58	-4.03 to -4.13	-3.6 to -3.7	-0.33 to -0.43
COLEOPTERA	Ecological codes				
Carabidae					
Pterostichus spp.	oa	-	1	-	-
Hydrophilidae					
Cercyon spp.	rt	-	-	-	2
Chaetarthria seminulum (Hbst.)	oa-w	-	2	-	-
Staphylinidae					
Stenus spp.	pu	-	1	-	-
Philonthus spp.					1
Helodidae Gen. & spp. Indet.	oa-w	-	1	-	-
Colydiidae					
Aglenus brunneus (Gyll.)	rt-h	-	2	-	1
Chyrsomelidae					
Plateumaris braccata (Scop.)	oa-d	1	1	-	-
Cuculionidae					
Gymnetron spp.	oa-p	-	-	-	1
DIPTERA					
Muscinae					
Musca domestica L.		-	1	-	-

Ecological coding (after Kenward and Hall 1995):

oa– species which will not breed in human housing
w – aquatic species
d – species associated with damp watersides and river banks
rt – insects associated with decaying organic matter
p – phytophage species often associated with waste areas or grassland and pasture
pu – species associated with pulses (peas and beans)
h – members of the 'house fauna' this is a very arbitrary group based on archaeological associations (Hall and Kenward 1990)

Table 63 Diatoms from 3880TT, Thames Crossing

	Monolith 1 (420–430mm)	Monolith 2 (20–30mm)
Sample		
Context Number	2	3
m OD	-0.10	-0.57
Polyhalobous		
Campylosira cymbelliformis	-	1
Coscinodiscus sp.	1	-
Cymatosira belgica	-	7
Dimeregramma minor var. *minor*	-	1
Grammatophora sp.	1	-
Paralia sulcata	3	8
Podosira stelligera	-	1
Rhaphoneis sp.	1	-
Rhaphoneis amphiceros	-	2
Rhaphoneis minutissima	-	4
Rhaphoneis surirella	-	4
Polyhalobous to Mesohalobous		
Actinoptychus undulatus	-	1
Diploneis smithii	4	-
Synedra gaillonii	-	1
Mesohalobous		
Achnanthes delicatula	1	-
Caloneis westii	1	-
Cyclotella striata	3	3
Diploneis interrupta	2	-
Fragilaria cf *schulzi*	-	1
Navicula peregrina	1	-
Nitzschia granulata	2	-
Nitzschia navicularis	11	4
Halophilous		
Navicula cincta	-	2
Navicula mutica	-	1
Unknown Salinity Preference		
Diploneis sp.	3	-
Navicula sp.	1	-
Nitzschia sp.	1	-
Unknown Naviculaceae	1	1

Table 64 The flint assemblages from the Thames Crossing excavation and watching brief by context

	Watching brief (ARC 32001)					3880TT (ARC TMS00)		Grand Total
	0	1	2	3	11	388004	388006	
Category type								
Flake	3	2	1	105	80	28	30	249
Blade	1	-	4	36	15	6	5	67
Bladelet	-	-	-	4	6	2	1	13
Blade-like	1	-	2	20	16	5	8	52
Irregular waste	-	-	1	1	1	1	5	9
Sieved chips 10–4mm	-	-	-	-	-	37	17	54
Rejuvenation flake core face/edge	-	-	-	-	1	-	1	2
Rejuvenation flake tablet	-	-	-	3	-	-	-	3
Rejuvenation flake other	-	-	-	5	-	-	1	6
Janus flake (= thinning)	-	-	5	-	-	-	-	5
Thinning flake	-	-	-	-	1	-	-	1
Flake from ground implement	-	-	-	-	1	-	-	1
Core single platform blade core	-	-	-	2	-	-	-	2
Bipolar (opposed platform) blade core	1	-	-	-	1	2	2	6
Other blade core	-	-	-	1	-	-	-	1
Tested nodule/bashed lump	-	-	-	1	-	1	1	3
Single platform flake core	-	-	-	1	2	-	-	3
Multiplatform flake core	1	-	-	1	3	-	-	5
Keeled non-discoidal flake core	-	-	-	-	1	-	1	2
Levallois/other discoidal flake core	-	-	-	-	1	-	-	1
Unclassifiable/fragmentary core	-	-	-	-	-	-	2	2
Core on a flake	-	-	-	-	1	-	-	1
Microlith	-	-	-	-	-	-	-	0
Burin	-	-	-	3	2	-	-	5
Burin spall	-	-	-	-	-	2	3	5
Laurel leaf	-	-	-	-	1	-	-	1
Unfinished arrowhead/blank	-	-	-	-	-	1	-	1
End scraper	-	-	-	4	1	-	5	10
Serrated flake	-	-	-	-	1	-	-	1
Notch	-	1	-	4	-	-	-	5
Backed knife	-	-	-	-	1	-	-	1
Backed blade	-	-	-	-	-	-	1	1
Retouched flake	-	-	-	2	-	-	1	3
Grand total	7	3	13	193	136	85	84	521
Burnt unworked flint No/wt (g)	-	-	44/2161	26/491	71/3021	3/22	158/1846	302/7541
No burnt worked flints	-	-	-	37	16	10	26	89
No broken worked flints	1	-	2	99	65	23	43	233
No retouched flints	-	1	-	13	6	1	7	28

Table 65 The flint assemblages from the Thames Crossing watching brief (contexts 3 and 11), by chainage

Chainage	35.220km to 35.240km		35.250km		35.250km to 35.235km	35.250km to 35.255km	35.255km		35.255km to 35.260km		35.260km to 35.267km		35.267km to 35.273km	35.267km to 35.277km	Grand total
Category type	3	11	3	11	11	11	3	11	3	11	3	11	3	3	
Flake	2	23	93	20	15	9	2	5	-	6	1	1	6	2	185
Blade	-	4	33	8	1	1	1	-	-	-	-	-	2	1	51
Bladelet	-	1	4	1	3	1	-	-	-	-	-	-	-	-	10
Blade-like	3	4	17	3	3	3	1	-	-	-	-	-	2	-	36
Irregular waste	-	-	-	1	-	-	1	-	-	-	-	-	-	-	2
Rejuvenation flake core face/edge	-	-	-	-	1	-	-	-	-	-	-	-	-	-	1
Rejuvenation flake tablet	-	-	3	-	-	-	-	-	-	-	-	-	-	-	3
Rejuvenation flake other	-	-	5	-	-	-	-	-	-	-	-	-	-	-	5
Thinning flake	-	-	-	1	-	-	-	-	-	-	-	-	-	-	1
Flake from ground implement	-	-	-	1	-	-	-	-	-	-	-	-	-	-	1
Core single platform blade core	-	-	2	-	-	-	-	-	-	-	-	-	-	-	2
Bipolar (opposed platform) blade core	-	-	-	-	-	-	-	1	-	-	-	-	-	-	1
Other blade core	-	-	1	-	-	-	-	-	-	-	-	-	-	-	1
Tested nodule/bashed lump	-	-	-	-	-	-	-	-	-	-	1	-	-	-	1
Single platform flake core	-	-	-	-	-	-	-	1	-	1	1	-	-	-	3
Multiplatform flake core	-	-	-	1	-	-	-	-	1	2	-	-	-	-	4
Keeled non-discoidal flake core	-	-	-	-	-	-	-	1	-	-	-	-	-	-	1
Levallois/other discoidal flake core	-	-	-	1	-	-	-	-	-	-	-	-	-	-	1
Core on a flake	-	-	-	1	-	-	-	-	-	-	-	-	-	-	1
Burin	-	-	2	3	-	-	-	-	-	-	-	-	-	-	5
Laurel leaf	-	-	-	1	-	-	-	-	-	-	-	-	-	-	1
End scraper	-	1	4	-	-	-	-	-	-	-	-	-	-	-	5
Serrated flake	-	-	-	1	-	-	-	-	-	-	-	-	-	-	1
Notch	-	-	4	-	-	-	-	-	-	-	-	-	-	-	4
Backed knife	-	1	-	-	-	-	-	-	-	-	-	-	-	-	1
Retouched flake	-	-	1	1	-	-	-	-	-	-	-	-	-	-	2
Grand total	5	34	169	44	23	14	5	8	1	9	3	1	10	3	329
Burnt unworked flint No/wt (g)	9/361	27/945	11/41	37/1855	1/16	-	2/51	-	-	3/164	1/5	-	4/33	4/41	99/3512
No burnt worked flints (%)*	-	5 (14.7)	37 (21.9)	5 (11.4)	5	1	-	-	-	-	-	-	-	-	53 (16.1)
No broken worked flints (%)*	1	12 (35.4)	97 (57.4)	40 (90.9)	5	8	2	-	-	-	-	-	1	-	166 (50.5)
No betouched flints (%)*	-	2 (5.9)	11 (6.5)	6 (13.6)	-	-	-	-	-	-	-	-	-	-	19 (5.8)

*percentage excludes chips

Table 66 Technological attributes of selected flint assemblages: dorsal extent of cortex

Context	Dorsal extent (no=208)					
	0	1–25%	26–50%	51–75%	76–99%	100%
ARC TMS00 – 388006	24 (48)	12 (24)	6 (12)	4 (8)	4 (8)	
ARC 32001 – 3	67 (42.4)	48 (30.4)	20 (12.7)	7 (4.4)	14 (8.9)	2 (1.3)
388006/3 combined	91 (43.8)	60 (28.9)	26 (12.5)	11 (5.3)	18 (8.7)	2 (1.0)

Table 67 Technological attributes of selected flint assemblages: flake types

Context	Flake type (no=208)					
	Preparation	Side trimming	Distal trimming	Misc trimming	Non-cortical	Rejuvenation
ARC TMS00 – 388006	5 (10)	12 (24)	5 (10)	3 (6)	21 (42)	4 (8)
ARC 32001 – 3	14 (8.9)	33 (20.9)	22 (13.9)	20 (12.7)	61 (38.6)	8 (5.1)
388006/3 combined	19 (9.1)	45 (21.6)	27 (12.9)	23 (11.1)	82 (39.4)	12 (5.8)

Table 68 Technological attributes of selected flint assemblages: proportion of blades, presence of platform-edge abrasion and dorsal blade scars

Context	flakes >2:1 L:B ratio (%)	flakes with platform edge abrasion (%)	flakes with dorsal blade scars (%)
ARC TMS00 – 388006	1 (6.6%)	16 (50%)	15 (30%)
ARC 32001 – 3	23 (38.3%)	73 (70.9%)	58 (36.7%)
388006/3 combined	24 (32%)	89 (66%)	69 (33.2%)

Table 69 Technological attributes of selected flint assemblages: butt types

Context	Butt type (no=135)						
	Cortical	Plain	>1 Removal	Facetted	Linear	Punctiform	Other
ARC TMS00 – 388006	3 (9.1)	22 (66.7)	3 (9.1)	1 (3)	2 (6.1)	1 (3)	1 (3)
ARC 32001 – 3	5 (4.9)	45 (44.1)	18 (17.7)	8 (7.8)	6 (5.9)	11 (10.8)	9 (8.8)
388006/3 combined	8 (5.9)	67 (49.6)	21 (15.6)	9 (6.7)	8 (5.9)	12 (8.9)	10 (7.4)

Table 70 Technological attributes of selected flint assemblages: termination types

Context	Hinge	Step	Plunging	Feather	Other
			Termination type (no=137)		
ARC TMS00 – 388006	2 (6.9)		3 (10.3)	24 (82.8)	
ARC 32001 – 3	22 (20.4)	6 (5.6)	25 (23.2)	53 (49.1)	2 (1.9)
388006/3 combined	24 (17.5)	6 (4.4)	28 (20.4)	77 (56.2)	2 (1.5)

Table 71 Technological attributes of selected flint assemblages: hammer mode

Context	Hard	Soft	Indeterminate
		Hammer mode	
ARC TMS00 – 388006	8 (25)	35 (34)	43 (31.9)
ARC 32001 – 3	11 (34.4)	41 (39.8)	38 (28.1)
388006/3 combined	13 (40.6)	27 (26.2)	54 (40%)

Table 72 Prehistoric pottery fabric descriptions

Code	Description
A1/EN	Hard fabric with sparse coarse quartz sand (up to 1mm) and rare flint or quartz grits (up to 3mm) in a slightly micaeous matrix
F1/EN	Hard fabric with sparse ill-sorted angular (calcined) flint (up to 5mm) in a clay matrix that contains rare coarse quartz sand
FA1/EN	As above but with sparse to common coarse quartz sand
FP1/EN	Soft fabric with well-sorted sparse calcined flint (up to 1mm) and rare dark grey clay pellets (up to 1mm)
S1/EN	Soft friable fabric with common shell (sometimes leached) platelets (up to 4mm)
FS1/LBAEIA	Hard fabric with well-sorted sparse calcined flint (1–3mm) and rare lenticular voids (leached shell platelets)

Table 73 Breakdown of the prehistoric pottery assemblage from the Thames Crossing watching brief

Context	Chainage	Count, Wt	Fabric	Comment
001/002	35.240km	1, 21g	FP1/EN	Neck sherd
011	33.250–33.255km	2, 12g	S1/EN	
011	35.250–33.255km	1, 15g	A1/EN	?cup sherd
		1, 2g	S1/EN	Rolled rim
		1, 11g	F1/EN	Neck sherd
	35.220–35.240km	1, 34g	FA1/EN	Rim and neck sherd from a hemispherical bowl
		2, 19g	FA1/EN	Could be from the above vessel
		1, 20g	F1/EN	Body sherd – charred residue on interior surface
		1, 40g	FS1/LBAEIA	From a flat based vessel
Total		11, 174g		

Table 76　Microfossils from Borehole BP 8, Isle of Grain

Depth (m)	ORGANIC REMAINS					Ecology	BRACKISH INDIGENOUS FORAMINIFERA						OUTER ESTUARINE & MARINE FORAMINIFERA								BRACKISH INDIGENOUS OSTRACODS									
	Plant debris & seeds	Brackish/outer estuarine/marine foraminifera	Brackish/outer estuarine/marine ostracods	Molluscs	Freshwater ostracods		*Haynesina germanica*	*Ammonia* spp. (small)	*Elphidium williamsoni*	*Elphidium waddense*	*Trochammina inflata*	*Jadammina macrecens*	*Elphidium excavatum*	lagenids	*Miliolinella subrotunda/Pateoris hauerinoides*	*Cyclogyra involvens*	*Ephidium margaritaceum*	discorbids	*Cibicides lobatulus*	*Planorbulina mediterranensis*	*Leptocythere porcellanea*	*Leptocythere lacertosa*	*Leptocythere psammophila*	*Cytherois fischeri*	*Cyprideis torosa*	*Loxoconcha elliptica*	*Leptocythere castanea*	*Cytherura gibba*	*Xestoleberis nitida*	*Cytheromorpha fuscata*
3.94-3.96	X	X				Estuarine mudflats and saltmarsh; diminishing marine influence	XXX	XX	X	X	X	X	X	X																
4.90-4.92	X	X	X	X			XX	XX	X		X	X	X	X	X	X	X				X	X	X	X						
6.90-6.92	X	X	X	X			XX	XX	XX		X	X	X	X	X	X	X				X	X	X		O					
7.86-7.88	X	X	X				XX	XX	X	X		X	X	X	X	X						X	O							
10.42-10.44	X	X	X	X			XXX	XX	XXX	X	XX	X	X	X	X			X			XX	X		X	X	XX	X			
11.34-11.36	X	X	X	X			XX	XX	X	X	X	X	X	X	X							X		O		X				
12.40-12.42	X	X	X	X		Open-estuarine with fringing saltmarsh; though slightly protected from the strongest marine influences and tidal surges as sea-levels rise	XX	XX	X	X	X	X	X	X	X	X	X	X	O		X	X	O	X		X	X			
13.39-13.41	X	X	X	X			XX	XX	X	X	X	X	X	X	X	X	X				X	X	O	X	X	X	X			
14.43-14.45	X	X	X	X			XX	XX	X	X	X	X	X	X	X	X	X				X	X	O	X		X	O			
15.30-15.32	X	X	X	X			XX	XX	X	X	XX	X	X	X	XX						X	X	X	X		X	X			
16.57-16.59	X	X	X	X	X		XXX	XXX	X	X	X	X	X	X	XX	X	X	X	X	O	X	X	X	X		X			X	X
16.81-16.83	X	X	X	X	X		XX	XX	X	X	X	X	X	X	XX		X	X			X	X	X	X		X	X			
18.30-18.32	X	X	X	X	X		XX	XX	X	X	X	X	X	X	XX	O	O		X		X	X	X		X	X	X			
19.00-19.02	X	X	X	X	X		XX	XX	X	X	X	X	X	X	XX		X	X			X	X	X		X	X	X	X	X	
19.75-19.77	X	X	X	X	X		XX	XX	X	X	XX	O	X	X	XX	O	X	O			X	X	X		X	XX	X		X	X
20.25-20.27	X	X	X	X	X		XX	XX	X	X	XX	X	X	X	XX		O			O	X	X	X	X	X	XX	X	X	O	O
21.05-21.07	X	X	X	X			XX	XX	X	X	X	X	X	X	XX		X	X	X		X	X			X	X			O	
21.55-21.57	X	X	X	X	X		XX	XX	X	X	XX	X		X	X	X		X			X	XX	X	X	XX	X	X	X	X	O
22.45-22.47	X	X	X	X	X		XXX	XXX	X	X	X	X	X	X	XX	X	X				X	X	X		X	XX	X		X	
22.95-22.97	X	X	X	X	X		XX	XXX	X	X	X	X	X	X	X	O	X	O		O	X	X	X		X	X				
23.85-23.87	X	X	X	X	X		XX	XX	X	X	XX	X	X	X	X	X	X	X			X	X	X		X	XX	X			O
24.35-24.37	X	X	X	X	X		XX	XX	X	X	X	X	X	X	X						X	X	X		X	XX	X			
24.53-24.55	X	X	X	X	X		XXX	XXX	XX	X	XX	X	X	X	XX	X	X	X			X	X	XX	X	X	X	X	X	X	X
25.20-25.22	X	X	X	X		Mudflats of tidal river; low salinity initially	XX	XXX	X	XX											O				X	XX		XX	XX	
25.27-25.29	X	X	X	X			XX	XX	X	XX												O				X		X	XX	
25.41-25.43	X	X	X	X			XX	XXX	XX	X															XX	XX		XX	XX	O
25.60-25.62	X	X	X	X			X	XXX	O	XX															X	XXX		XX	XX	
25.76-25.78	X	X	X	X	X		X	XXX	O	X															XXX	XXX		XXX	X	X
25.95-25.97	X	X	X	X	X			XXX																	XX	XXX		XXX	X	XX
26.30-26.32	X					Riverine; freshwater																								
26.40-26.42	X																													
26.51-26.53	X																													

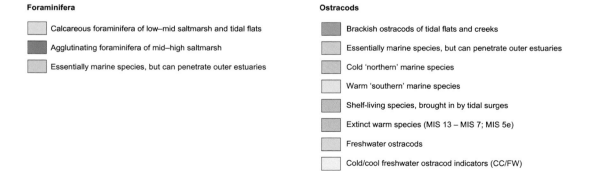

Foraminifera

- Calcareous foraminifera of low–mid saltmarsh and tidal flats
- Agglutinating foraminifera of mid–high saltmarsh
- Essentially marine species, but can penetrate outer estuaries

Ostracods

- Brackish ostracods of tidal flats and creeks
- Essentially marine species, but can penetrate outer estuaries
- Cold 'northern' marine species
- Warm 'southern' marine species
- Shelf-living species, brought in by tidal surges
- Extinct warm species (MIS 13 – MIS 7; MIS 5e)
- Freshwater ostracods
- Cold/cool freshwater ostracod indicators (CC/FW)

	OUTER ESTUARINE & MARINE OSTRACODS																		'EXOTIC' OSTRACODS								FRESHWATER OSTRACODS						CC/FW	
	Pontocythere elongata	*Palmoconcha laevata*	*Semicytherura striata*	*Semicytherura nigrescens*	*Paradoxostoma* spp.	*Loxoconcha rhomboidea*	*Cytheropteron nodosum*	*Leptocythere tenera*	*Hirschmannia viridis*	*Hemicytherura cellulosa*	*Hemicytherura villosa*	*Semicytherura sella*	*Leptocythere pellucida*	*Heterocythereis albomaculata*	*Bonnyannella robertsoni*	*Semicytherura acuticostata*	*Eucythere argus*	*Palmoconcha guttata*	*Finmarchinella finmarchica*	*Finmarchinella angulata*	*Hemicytherura clathrata*	*Aurila convexa*	*Neonesidea globosa*	*Jonesia acuminata*	*Anchistrocheles acerosa*	*Callistocythere curryi*	*Limnocythere inopinata*	*Candona neglecta*	*Darwinula stevensoni*	*Pseudocandona* sp. (juvs)	*Ilyocypris* sp.	*Candona angulata*	*Cytherissa lacustris*	*Limnocytherina sanctipatricii*
	x	x	x	x	x	o	o	o																										
	x	o		o	x		o	x	x	x	o																							
	x		x	x	x			x	x	o	x	x	x	o	o	o			o				o	o										
	x	o		o	x	o		x	x														o			o								
	x		o	x	x			x	x			o					o		o															
	x		x	x	x	x	x	x	x	o	x						o																	
	x	x	x	x	x	x			x	x	x	x											o				o		o				x	
	x	x	x		x	x			x			x	x										x											
	x		x	x	x	x			x	o	x		x	o										o		o							o	
	x	x	x	x	x		o		x	x	x		x														x	x					o	
	x	x	x	o	x	o	x	x	x	o	x		x						o			x					x							x
	x	x	x	x	x	o	x	x	x			x	x		o	o	o			o		x		x		o	x	o						
	x	o			x			x	x	o	x		x			x					o	o	o	o	o									
	x	x	x		x	x			x	x	o	x	o	x					o			o					x	o					o	
	x	x	o	x	x			x	x		x		x					x	o			o					x	o						
	x		x		x			x	x	o	x					o		x				o		o	o		o						x	
	x	x	x	x	x	o		x	x	o	x	o	x					o				x				o	o	o						
	x	x	o	x	x			x	x	o	x		x				o	x					x		x		o	x		o				
	x	x	x	x	x	x		x	x	x	x	x	o	x				o	x		o	x		o	o		o	o			x			
																												x						
																												XX	X			XXX		

Table 77 Microfossils from the Medway Tunnel

mOD	Plant debris & seeds	Insects	Brackish foraminifera	Brackish ostracods	Molluscs	Freshwater ostracods	Ecology	Jadammina macrescens	Trochammina inflata	Miliammina fusca	Haynesina germanica	Elphidium williamsoni	Ammonia sp.	Elphidium waddense	lagenids	miliolids	Leptocythere porcellanea	Loxoconcha elliptica	Leptocythere lacertosa	Cyprideis torosa	Leptocythere psammophila	Leptocythere castanea	Xestoleberis nitida	Cytherura gibba	Cytheromorpha fuscata	Semicytherura sella	Pontocythere elongata	Hemicythere villosa	Paradoxostoma spp.	Hirschmannia viridis	Aurila convexa	Limnocythere inopinata	Candona sp.
+0.04 / 0.01	×	×	×					×																									
-0.71 / -0.76	×	×	×				Mid–high saltmarsh	×	×																								
-0.83 / -0.88	×		×				Mid–high saltmarsh	×																									
-1.01 / -1.06	×		×				Mid–high saltmarsh	×	×																								
-1.14 / -0.19	×																																
-1.53 / -1.58	×		×	×			Low–mid saltmarsh with fringing tidal flats; initially with a small marine influence		×	×	XX	XX	XX				XX																
-2.05 / -2.10	×		×	×					×		XX	XX	XX				XX	×	XX														
-3.18 / -3.23	×		×	×				×		×	XXX	XX	XX				×	×	XX	×													
-3.90 / -3.95	×				×													×		×													
-4.38 / -4.43	×		×	×				×	×		XXX	×	XX	×	×	×	XX	×	XX	XX	×	×											
-5.70 / -5.75	×				×						XXX	XXX	XXX			×	×	XX	XX	×	×	×				×							
-7.43 / -7.48	×		×	×	×	×		×	×		XXX	XXX	XXX	×	×	×	×	×	XX	×	×	×					×	×	×		×	×	×
-7.65 / -7.70	×				×	×			×		XXX	XXX	XXX	×	×	×	×	×	XX	×	×	×	×	×	×	×	×	×	×	×		×	
-7.90 / -7.95		×						×	×																								
-8.38 / -8.43		×						×	×		XXX	XXX	XX	×	×		×	XX		XX													
-9.18 / -9.23		×					Freshwater?																										
-9.67 / -9.72																																	

Foraminifera

- Calcareous foraminifera of low–mid saltmarsh and tidal flats
- Agglutinating foraminifera of mid–high saltmarsh
- Essentially marine species, but can penetrate outer estuaries

Ostracods

- Brackish ostracods of tidal flats and creeks
- Essentially marine species, but can penetrate outer estuaries
- Warm 'southern' marine species
- Freshwater ostracods (FW OS)

Bibliography

Agee, J K, 1998 Fire and pine ecosystems, in D M Richardson (ed) *Ecology and Biogeography of* Pinus. Cambridge University Press, 193–218

Allen, J R L, 1987 Desiccation of mud in the temperate inter-tidal zone: studies from the Severn Estuary and eastern England. *Phil Trans Royal Soc London B* 315, 127–156

Allen, J R L, 1999 Geological impacts on coastal wetland landscapes: some general effects of sediment autocompaction in the Holocene of northwest Europe. *The Holocene* 9, 1–12

Allen, T, Anderson, L and Barclay, A, forthcoming, *The Archaeology of the Middle Thames Landscape: the Eton College Rowing Lake Project and the Maidenhead, Windsor and Eton Flood Alleviation Scheme, Volume 1: Mesolithic to early Bronze Age.* Oxford Archaeology

Allison, J, Godwin, H and Warren, S H, 1952 Late-Glacial deposits at Nazeing in the Lea Valley, North London. *Phil Trans Royal Soc London B* 236, 169–240

Ammerman, A J, 2000 Coring ancient Rome. *Archaeology* 53, 78–83

Amorosi, A and Marchi, N, 1999 High-resolution sequence stratigraphy from piezocone tests: an example from the Late Quaternary deposits of the southeastern Po Plain. *Sedimentary Geology* 128, 67–81

Andersen, S, Th, 1970 *The relative pollen productivity and pollen representation of North European trees, and correction factors for tree pollen spectra.* Danm. Geol. Unders. Ser I 96

Andersen, S, Th, 1973 The differential pollen productivity of trees and its significance for the interpretation of a pollen diagram from a forested region, in H J B Birks and R G West, *Quaternary Plant Ecology.* Blackwell, Oxford, 109–115

Anderson-Whymark, H, forthcoming, Worked flint, in Wenban-Smith *et al* forthcoming

Andrews, P, Biddulph, E, Hardy, H and Brown, R, 2011a *Settling the Ebbsfleet Valley: High Speed 1 Excavations at Springhead and Northfleet, Kent. The Late Iron Age, Roman, Saxon and Medieval Landscape, Volume 1, The Sites.* Oxford Wessex Archaeology Monogr

Andrews, P, Mepham, L, Schuster, J and Stevens, C, 2011b *Settling the Ebbsfleet Valley: High Speed 1 Excavations at Springhead and Northfleet, Kent. The Late Iron Age, Roman, Saxon and Medieval Landscape Volume 4, Saxon and Later Finds and Environmental Reports.* Oxford Wessex Archaeology Monogr

Ansell, R, 1981 Thameside Archaeological Group. *Kent Archaeological Review* 66, 141–2

Ansell, R, 1982 Thameside Archaeological Group. *Kent Archaeological Review* 69, 201–2

Ansell, R, 1983 Thameside Archaeological Group. *Kent Archaeological Review* 74, 85–6

Armour-Chelu, M and Andrews, P, 1994 Some effects of bioturbation by earthworms (Oligochaeta) on archaeological sites. *Journ Archaeol Sci* 21, 433–443

Ashton, N M and Lewis, S G, 2002 Deserted Britain: declining populations in the British late Middle Pleistocene. *Antiquity* 76, 388–396

Atkinson, T C, Briffa, K R and Coope, G R, 1987 Seasonal temperatures in Britain during the past 22,000 years, reconstructed using beetle remains. *Nature* 325, 587–592

Baales, M and Street, M, 1996 Hunter-gatherer behaviour in a changing late glacial landscape: Allerød archaeology in the central Rhineland, Germany. *Journ Anthropological Res* 52, 281–316

Babel, U, 1975 Micromorphology of soil organic matter, in J E Giesking (ed) *Soil Components: Organic Components*, Volume 1. New York, Springer-Verlag, 369–473

Bailey, G and Thomas, G, 1987 The use of percussive drilling to obtain core samples from rock shelter deposits. *Antiquity* 61, 433–439

Baines, D, Smith, D G, Froese, D G, Bauman, P and Nimeck, G, 2002 Electrical resistivity ground imaging (ERGI): a new tool for mapping the lithology and geometry of channe-belts and valley fills. *Sedimentology* 49, 411–449

Bal, L, 1982 *Zoological Ripening of Soils.* Wageningen, Centre for Agricultural Publishing and Documentation, 365

Barber, J, 1990 Burnt mound material on settlement sites in Scotland, in V Buckley (ed) *Burnt Offerings: international contributions to burnt mound archaeology.* Wordwell, Dublin, 92–97

Barclay, A, 2002 *Ceramic Lives, in Prehistoric Britain: the ceramic basis* (A Woodward and J D Hill). Prehistoric Ceramic Research Group Occas Pap 3, Oxbow Books, Oxford, 85–95

Barclay, A, 2007 Connections and networks: a wider world and other places, in D Benson and A Whittle (eds) *Building Memories. The Neolithic Cotswold Long Barrow at Ascott-Under-Wychwood, Oxfordshire.* Cardiff Studies in Archaeology, Oxbow Books, Oxford, 331–344

Barclay, A J, forthcoming, Prehistoric pottery, in Wenban-Smith *et al* forthcoming

Barfield, L, 1991 Hot stones: Hot food or hot baths? in M A Hodder and L H Barfield (eds) *Burnt mounds and Hot Stone Technology: papers from the 2nd international burnt mound conference, Sandwell, 12–14 October 1990*. Sandwell Metropolitan Borough Council, Sandwell, 59–67

Barfield, L and Hodder, M, 1987 Burnt mounds as saunas, and the prehistory of bathing. *Antiquity* 61, 370–379

Barham, A J 1995 Methodological approaches to archaeological context recording: X-radiography as an example of a supportive recording, assessment and interpretative technique, in A J Barham and R I Macphail (eds) *Sediments and Soils: analysis, interpretation and management*. Institute of Archaeology, London, 145–182

Barham, A J, 1999 The local environmental impact of prehistoric populations on Saibai Island, northern Torres Strait, Australia: enigmatic evidence from Holocene swamp lithostratigraphic records. *Quaternary International* 59, 71–105

Barham, A J and Bates, M R, 1994 *Strategies for the Use of Boreholes in Archaeological Evaluations: a review of methodologies and techniques*, Geoarchaeological Service Facility Technical Report 94/01, Institute of Archaeology, University College London. Unpubl Rep

Barham, A J and Bates, M R, 1995 *Method Statement and Proposal for Tasks 2–5 of Union Railways Ltd, Contract No. 194/607*, Geoarchaeological Service Facility Technical Report 95/05, Institute of Archaeology, University College London. Unpubl Rep

Barham, A J, Bates, M R, Pine, C A and Williamson, V D, 1995 Holocene development of the Lower Medway Valley and Prehistoric occupation of the floodplain area, in D R Bridgland, P Allen, and B A Haggart, (eds) *The Quaternary of the Lower Reaches of the Thames. Field Guide*. Quaternary Research Association, Cambridge, 339–350

Barnett, C, 2007 Dating the on-site sequence; and Dating the off-site sequence, in Leivers *et al* 2007, 29, and 33

Barnett, C, 2009 The Chronology of Early Mesolithic Occupation and Environmental Impact at Thatcham Reedbeds, Southern England, in P Combé, M van Strydonck, J Sergant, M Boudin, and M Bats (eds) *Chronology and Evolution within the Mesolithic of North-West Europe: Proceedings of an International Meeting, Brussels, May 30th–June 1st 2007*. Newcastle upon Tyne, Cambridge Scholars Publishing, 57–76

Barnett, C, 2011 Wood charcoal, in Barnett *et al* 2011, 113–118

Barnett, C, and Macphail, R, 2007 Stratigraphy, soils and sediments: on-site sequence, in Leviers *et al* 2007, 5–6

Barnett, C, McKinley, J I, Stafford, E, Grimm, J M and Stevens, C J, 2011 *Settling the Ebbsfleet Valley: High Speed 1 Excavations at Springhead and Northfleet, Kent. The Late Iron Age, Roman, Saxon and Medieval Landscape Volume 3, Late Iron Age to Roman Human Remains and Environmental Reports*. Oxford Wessex Archaeology Monogr

Barnett, C M, Scaife, R G and Stevens, C J, forthcoming. Lateglacial to Holocene alluviation and landscape development: High Speed 1 investigations at Stratford, London Borough of Newham. Oxford Wessex Archaeology online publication

Barton, R N E, 1986 Experiments with long blades from Sproughton, near Ipswich, Suffolk, in D A Roe (ed) *Studies in the Upper Palaeolithic of Britain and northwest Europe*. Brit Archaeol Rep S296, Oxford, 129–141

Barton, R N E, 1992 *Hengistbury Head, Dorset Volume 2: The Late Upper Palaeolithic and Early Mesolithic Sites*. Oxford University Committee for Archaeology Monogr 34

Barton, R N E, 1995 The long blade assemblage, in T G Allen (ed) *Lithics and Landscape: archaeological discoveries on the Thames Water pipeline at Gatehampton Farm, Goring, Oxfordshire 1985–92*. Oxford University Committee for Archaeology, Thames Valley Landscapes Monogr 7, 54–64

Barton, R N E, 1998 Long Blade technology and the question of British Late Pleistocene/Early Holocene lithic assemblages, in N Ashton, F Healy and P Pettitt (eds) *Stone Age Archaeology: essays in honour of John Wymer*. Oxford, Oxbow Books/Lithic Studies Society Occas Pap 6, 158–164

Barton, R N E, 1999 The Lateglacial colonization of Britain, in J Hunter and I Ralston (eds) T*he Archaeology of Britain: an introduction from the Upper Palaeolithic to the Industrial Revolution*. Routledge, London, 13–34

Barton, R N E and Roberts, A J, 1996 Reviewing the British Late Upper Palaeolithic: new evidence for chronological patterning in the Late Glacial record. *Oxford J Archaeol* 15(3), 245–265

Barton, R N E, Antoine, P, Dumont, S and Hall, S, 1998 New OSL dates from the Late Glacial archaeological site of Avington VI, Kennet Valley, Berkshire. *Quaternary Newsletter* 85, 21–31

Batchelor, C R, 2009 *Middle Holocene Environmental Changes and the History of Yew* (Taxus baccata *L.*) *Woodland in the Lower Thames Valley*. Unpubl PhD thesis, Univ London

Bates, M R, 1998 Locating and evaluating archaeology below the alluvium: the role of sub-surface stratigraphical modelling. *Lithics* 19, 4–18

Bates, M R, 2003 Visualising the sub-surface: problems and procedures for areas of deeply stratified sediments, in A J Howard, M G Macklin, and D G Passmore (eds) *Alluvial Archaeology in Europe*. Balkema, Lisse, 277–289

Bates M R, 2004 Thames Gateway Bridge, Environmental Impact Assessment, Chapter 12: Cultural Heritage, Appendix 12D: Deposit Model.

Unpubl Rep prepared by Oxford Archaeology for Scott Wilson

Bates, M R and Barham, A J, 1993 Recent observations of tufa in the Dour Valley, Kent. *Quaternary Newsletter* 71, 11–25

Bates, M R and Bates, C R, 2000 Multidisciplinary Approaches to the Geoarchaeological Evaluation of Deeply Stratified Sedimentary Sequences: Examples from Pleistocene and Holocene Deposits in Southern England, United Kingdom. *Journ Archaeol Sci* 27, 845–858

Bates, M R, Barham, A J, Pine, C A and Williamson, V D, 2000a The use of borehole stratigraphic logs in archaeological evaluation strategies for deeply stratified alluvial areas, in S Roskams (ed) *Interpreting Stratigraphy: site evaluation, recording procedures and stratigraphic analysis.* Brit Archaeol Rep S910, Archaeopress, Oxford, 49–69

Bates, M R, Bates, C R, Gibbard, P L, Macphail, R I, Owen, F, Parfitt, S A, Preece, R C, Roberts, M B, Robinson, J E, Whittaker, J E and Wilkinson, K N, 2000b Late Middle Pleistocene deposits at Norton Farm on the West Sussex coastal plain, southern England. *Journ Quat Sci* 15, 61–89

Bates, M R, Bates, C R and Whittaker, J E, 2007 Mixed method approaches to the investigation and mapping of buried Quaternary deposits: examples from Southern England. *Archaeological Prospection* 14, 104–129

Bates, M R, Bates, C R, Cameron, N, Huckerby, E, Nicholson, R and Whittaker, J E, 2012 A multidisciplinary investigation of the sediments at the London Gateway site, Essex: Geophysics, palaeo-environment and dating. Final deposit model update. Unpubl Rep by Oxford Archaeology for DP World

Bates, M R, Parfitt, S A and Roberts, M B, 1997 The chronology, palaeogeography and archaeological significance of the marine Quaternary record of the West Sussex Coastal Plain, Southern England, UK, *Quat Sci Rev* 16, 1227–1252

Bates, M R, Walker, M J C, Cameron, N, Druce, D and Whittaker, J E, 2003 London Gateway Logistics and Commercial Centre Outline Planning Application. Cultural heritage assessment refinement in respect of the proposed development of London Gateway Logistics and Commercial Centre. Technical Report Volume 2. Appendix O, Unpubl Rep prepared by Oxford Archaeology for P&O

Bates, M R and Wenban-Smith, F F, 2011 Palaeolithic Geoarchaeology: palaeolandscape modeling and scales of investigation. *Landscapes* 12, 69–96

Bates, M R and Whittaker, K, 2004 Landscape evolution in the Lower Thames Valley: implications of the archaeology of the earlier Holocene period, in J Cotton and D Field (eds) *Towards a New Stone Age: aspects of the Neolithic in south-east England.* Counc Brit Archaeol Res Rep 137, York, 50–70

Bates, M R and Williamson, V D, 1995 *A Report on the Stratigraphy, Palaeoenvironmental and Archaeological Significance of the Slade Green Relief Road Site.* Geoarchaeological Service Facility Technical Report 95/03, Institute of Archaeology, University College London. Unpubl Rep

Behre, K E, 1981 The interpretation of anthropogenic indicators in pollen diagrams. *Pollen et Spores* 23, 225–45

Bell, F G, 1969 The occurrence of southern steppe and halophyte elements in Weichselian (full glacial) floras from southern England. *New Phytologist* 68, 913–922

Bell, F G, 1993 *Engineering Geology.* Blackwell Scientific, Oxford

Bell, M, 2007 *Prehistoric Coastal Communities: the Mesolithic in Western Britain.* Counc Brit Archaeol Res Rep 149, York

Bell, M and Boardman, J, 1992 *Past and Present Soil Erosion: Archaeological and Geographical Perspectives.* Oxbow Monogr 22, Oxbow Books, Oxford

Bell, M, Caseldine, A and Neumann, H, 2000 *Prehistoric Intertidal Archaeology in the Welsh Severn Estuary.* Counc Brit Archaeol Res Rep 120, York

Bennell, M, 1998 *Under the Road: archaeological discoveries at Bronze Age Way, Erith.* Bexley Council, London

Bennett, K D, 1984 The Post-Glacial history of *Pinus sylvestris* in the British-Isles. *Quat Sci Rev* 3, 133–155

Bennett, K D, Simonson, W D and Peglar, S M, 1990 Fire and man in Postglacial woodlands of eastern England. *Journ Archaeol Sci* 17, 635–642

Berendsen, H J A and Stouthamer, E, 2001 *Palaeogeographic Development of the Rhine-Meuse Delta, the Netherlands.* Van Gorcum, Assen

Bertrand, S and Baeteman, C, 2005 Sequence mapping of Holocene coastal lowlands: the application of the Streif classification system in the Belgium coastal plain. *Quaternary International* 133–134, 151–158

Biddulph, E, Seager Smith, R and Schuster, J, 2011 *Settling the Ebbsfleet Valley, High Speed 1 Excavations at Springhead and Northfleet, Kent. The Late Iron Age, Roman, Saxon and Medieval Landscape Volume 2, Late Iron Age to Roman Finds Reports.* Oxford Wessex Archaeology Monogr

Biddulph, E, 2011 Northfleet Villa, in Andrews *et al* 2011a, 135–88

Biddulph, E, 2011 The development of Northfleet Villa, in Andrews *et al* 2011a, 213–230

Biddulph, E, Foreman, S, Stafford, E, Stansbie, D and Nicholson, R, 2012 *London Gateway Iron Age and Roman salt making in the Thames Estuary: excavation at Stanford Wharf Nature Reserve.* Oxford Archaeol Monogr 18, Oxford

Bingley, R M, Ashkenasi, V, Ellison, R A, Morigi, A, Penna, N T and Booth, S J, 1999 *Monitoring Changes in Ground Level using High Precision GPS.* Environmental Agency R & D Report, W210

Birbeck, V and Barnes, I, 1995 Prehistory in the pipeline. *London Archaeologist* 7 (12), 313–314

Birks, H H, Birks, H J B, Kaland, P and Moe, D, 1988 *The Cultural Landscape – Past, Present and Future.* Cambridge University Press

Birks, H J B, 1989 Holocene isochrone maps and patterns of tree-spreading in the British Isles. *Journ Biogeography* 16, 503–540

Booth, P, Champion, T, Foreman, S, Garwood, P, Glass, H, Munby, J and Reynolds, A, 2011 *On Track: The Archaeology of the Channel Tunnel Rail Link in Kent.* Oxford Wessex Archaeology

Bouma, J, Fox, C A and Miedema, R, 1990 Micromorphology of hydromorphic soils: applications for soil genesis and land evaluation, in L A Douglas (ed) *Soil Micromorphology*, Elsevier Sci Publ B V Amsterdam, 257–278

Bowden, R A, 2004 Building confidence in geological models, in A Curtis and R Wood (eds) Geological *Prior Information: Informing Science and Engineering.* Geological Society of London Special Publications 239, London, 157–173

Bowsher, J M C, 1991 A burnt mound at Phoenix Wharf, South-East London: A preliminary report, in M A Hodder and L H Barfield (eds) *Burnt Mounds and Hot Stone Technology: papers from the second international burnt mound conference, Sandwell, 12th–14th October 1990.* Sandwell Metropolitan Borough Council, Sandwell, 11–19

Branch, N P, Batchelor, C R, Cameron, N G, Coope, G R, Densem, R, Gale, R, Green, C P and Williams, A N, 2012 Holocene environmental changes in the Lower Thames Valley, London, UK: Implications for woodland *Taxus* understanding the history of *Taxus* woodland. *The Holocene* 22 (10), 1143–1158

Bridgland, D R, 1983 *The Quaternary Fluvial Deposits of North Kent and Eastern Essex.* Unpubl PhD thesis, CNAA City of London Polytechnic

Bridgland, D R, 1988 The Pleistocene fluvial stratigraphy and palaeogeography of Essex. *Proc Geologists' Ass* 99, 291–314

Bridgland, D R, 1993 *The Geoarchaeological Implications of the Union Railway London-Folkestone Link.* Unpubl Client Rep for Cobham Resource Consultants on behalf of Union Railways Ltd

Bridgland, D R, 1994 *Quaternary History of the Thames.* Geological Conservation Review Series, Chapman & Hall, London

Bridgland D R, 1995 The Quaternary sequence of the eastern Thames basin: problems of correlation, in D R Bridgland, P Allen and B A Haggart (eds) *The Quaternary of the Lower Reaches of the Thames. Field Guide.* Quaternary Research Association, Durham, 35–52

Bridgland, D R, 1999 Wealden Rivers north of the Thames: a provenance study based on gravel clast analysis. *Proc Geologists' Ass* 110, 133–148

Bridgland, D R, 2000 River terrace systems in north-west Europe: an archive of environmental change, uplift and early human occupation. *Quat Sci Rev* 19, 1293–1303

Bridgland, D R, 2003 The evolution of the River Medway, S.E. England, in the context of Quaternary palaeo-climate and the Palaeolithic occupation of NW Europe. *Proc Geologists' Ass* 114, 23–48

Bridgland, D R, 2006 The Middle and Upper Pleistocene sequence in the Lower Thames: a record of Milankovitch climatic fluctuation and early human occupation of southern Britain. Henry Stopes Memorial Lecture. *Proc Geologists' Ass* 117, 281–305

Bridgland, D R and Schreve, D C, 2004 Quaternary lithostratigraphy and mammalian biostratigraphy of the Lower Thames terrace system, south-east England. *Quaternaire* 15, 29–40

Bridgland, D R, Schreve, D C, Keen, D H, Meyrick, R and Westaway, R, 2004 Biostratigraphical correlation between the late Quaternary sequence of the Thames and key fluvial localities in Central Germany. *Proc. Geologists' Ass* 115, 125–140

Brigham, T, 1990 The Late Roman waterfront in London. *Britannia* 21, 99–185

British Geological Survey (BGS), 1993 *Solid and Drift Geology, England and Wales*, Sheet 256 North London

Bromehead, C E N, 1925 *The Geology of North London*, Memoir of the Geological Survey of Great Britain, London

Bronk Ramsey, C, 1995 Radiocarbon calibration and analysis of stratigraphy: the OxCal program. *Radiocarbon* 37, 425–30

Bronk Ramsey C, 1998 Probability and dating, *Radiocarbon* 40 (1) 461–474

Bronk Ramsey, C, 2001 Development of the radiocarbon calibration program OxCal. *Radiocarbon* 43, 355–63

Brown, A G, 1997 *Alluvial Geoarchaeology: Floodplain Archaeology and Environmental Change.* Cambridge Methods in Archaeology, Cambridge University Press

Brown, A G and Keough, M, 1992a Palaeochannels, palaeo-landsurfaces and the 3-D reconstruction of floodplain environmental change, in P A Carling and G E Petts (eds) *Lowland Floodplain Rivers: a geomorphological perspective.* Wiley, Chichester, 185–202

Brown, A G and Keough, M, 1992b Palaeochannels and palaeolandsurfaces: the geoarchaeological potential of some Midland floodplains, in S Needham, and M G Macklin (eds) *Alluvial Archaeology in Britain.* Oxbow Monogr 27, Oxbow Books, Oxford, 185–196

Brown, F, 2008 *Archaeology of the A1(M) Darrington to Dishforth DBFO Road Scheme.* Oxford Archaeology North, Lancaster

Burchell, J P T, 1938 Two Mesolithic 'floors' in the Ebbsfleet Valley of the Lower Thames. *Antiquaries Journ* 18, 397–401

Burchell, J PT and Piggott, S. 1939 Decorated prehistoric pottery from the bed of the Ebbsfleet, Northfleet, Kent. *Antiquaries Journ* 19, 405–420

Cameron, N G, 2007 Diatoms, in Leivers *et al* 2007, 35–36

Cameron 2011 Diatoms from Northfleet, in Andrews *et al* 2011b, 75–80

Cameron forthcoming, Diatoms, in Wenban-Smith *et al* forthcoming

Canti, M, 1998, Origin of calcium carbonate granules found in buried soils and Quaternary deposits. *Boreas* 27, 275–288

Carew, F, Meddens, F, Batchelor, R, Branch, N, Elias, S, Goodburn, D, Vaughan-Williams, A, Webster, L and Yeomans, L, 2009 Human-environment interactions at the wetland edge in East London: trackways, platforms and Bronze Age responses to environmental change. *Trans London Middlesex Archaeol Soc* 60, 1–34

Catt, J A, 1979, Soils and Quaternary geology in Britain. *Journ Soil Science* 30, 607–42

Challis, K and Howard, A J, 2003 GIS-based modelling of sub-surface deposits for archaeological prospection in alluvial landscapes, in A J Howard, M G Macklin and D G Passmore (eds). *Alluvial Archaeology in Europe*, Balkema, Lisse, 263–276

Chambers, F M, Mighall, T M and Keen D H, 1996 Early Holocene pollen and molluscan record from Enfield Lock, Middlesex, UK. *Proc Geologists' Ass* 107, 1–14

Chen, W, Xuanqing, Z, Naihua, H and Yongyhong, M, 1996 Compiling the map of shallow-buried palaeochannels on the North China Plain. *Geomorphology* 18, 47–52

Chew, K J, 1995 Data modelling: a general-purpose petroleum geological database, in J R A Giles (ed) *Geological Data Management*. Geological Society Special Publication 97, Geological Society of London, 13– 23

Churchill, D M, 1965 The displacement of deposits formed at sea level, 6500 years ago in Southern Britain. *Quaternaria* 7, 239–247

Clark, C D, Hughes, A L C, Greenwood, S L, Jordan, C and Sejrup, H P, 2012 Pattern and timing of retreat of the last British-Irish Ice Sheet. *Quat Sci Rev* 44, 112–146

Clayton, C R I, Matthews, M C and Simons, N E, 1995 *Site Investigation*, Blackwell Science, Oxford, 584

Coleman, L, Hancocks, A and Watts, M, 2006 *Excavations on the Wormington to Tirley Pipeline, 2000: Four sites by the Carrant Brook and River Isbourne – Gloucestershire and Worcestershire*. Cotswold Archaeology Monogr 3, Cotswold Archaeology, Kemble

Coles, B, 1990 Anthropomorphic wooden figurines from Britain and Ireland, *Proc Prehist Soc* 56, 315–33

Coles, B J, 1995 *Wetland Management*, A survey for English Heritage. WARP Occas Pap 9, Exeter

Coles, B J, 1998 Doggerland: a speculative survey. *Proc Prehist Soc* 64, 45–81

Coles, B and Coles, J, 1986 *Sweet Track to Glastonbury: the prehistory of the Somerset Levels*. Thames & Hudson, London

Coles, J and Coles, B, 1996 *Enlarging the Past: the contribution of wetland archaeology, The Rhind Lectures for 1994–5*. Society of Antiquaries of Scotland Monogr 11

Coope, G R, 1977 Fossil Coleoptera assemblages as sensitive indicators of climatic changes during the Devensian (Last) cold stage. *Phil Trans Royal Soc London B* 280, 313–340

Coope, G R and Brophy, J A, 1972 Late Glacial environmental changes indicated by a coleopteran succession from North Wales. *Boreas* 1, 97–142

Coope, G R and Tallon, P, 1983 A full glacial insect fauna from the Lea Valley, Enfield, north London. *Quaternary Newsletter* 40, 7–10

Corcoran, J and Swift, D, 2004 *Lower Lea Valley Olympic Planning Application: further archaeological information*, Museum of London Archaeology Service. Unpubl Rep

Corcoran, J, Halsey, C, Spurr, G, Burton, E and Jamieson, D, 2011 *Mapping Past Landscapes in the Lower Lea Valley: A Geoarchaeological Study of the Quaternary Sequence*. Museum of London Archaeology Monogr 55, London

Cotton, J, 2004 Two decorated Peterborough bowls from the Thames at Mortlake and their London context, in Cotton and Field 128–147

Cotton, J and Field, D, (eds) 2004 *Towards a new stone age; aspects of the Neolithic in south-east England*. Counc Brit Archaeol Res Rep 137, London

Courty, M A and Fedoroff, N, 1982 Micromorphology of a Holocene dwelling. *Proc Nordic Archaeometry*, 257–277

Cowell, R and Innes, J, 1994 *The Wetlands of Merseyside*. North West Wetlands Survey I, Lancaster Imprints, Lancaster

Crockett, A D, Allen, M J and Scaife, R G, 2002 A Neolithic trackway within peat deposits at Silvertown, London. *Proc Prehist Soc* 68, 185–214

Crowley, N, 2005 Building materials, in B Yule *A Prestigious Roman Building Complex on the Southwark Waterfront: excavations at Winchester Palace, London, 1983–90*. Museum of London Archaeological Service Monogr 23, London, 90–103

Culshaw, M G, 2005 From concept towards reality: developing the attributed 3D geological model of the shallow subsurface. *Quarterly Journ Engineering Geology and Hydrogeology* 38, 231–284

Dalrymple, R W, Zaitlin, B A and Boyd, R, 1992 Estuarine facies models conceptual, basis and stratigraphic implications. *Journ Sedimentary Petrology* 62, 1130–1146

Deeben, J, Hallewas, D P, Kolen, J and Wiemer, R, 1997 Beyond the crystal ball: predictive modelling as a tool in archaeological heritage management and occupation history, in W J H Willems, H Kars and Hallewas (eds) *Archaeological Heritage Management in the Netherlands*. Van Gorcum, Amersfoort, 76–118

Densem, R and Doidge, A, 1979 The topography of North Lambeth. *London Archaeologist* 3 (10), 265–269

Detsicas, A, 1983 *The Cantiaci*. Alan Sutton, Stroud

Devoy, R J N, 1977 Flandrian sea-level changes in the Thames Estuary and the implications for land subsidence in England and Wales. *Nature* 220, 712–715

Devoy, R J N, 1979 Flandrian sea-level changes and vegetational history of the Lower Thames Estuary. *Phil Trans Royal Soc London B* 285, 355–407

Devoy, R J N, 1980 Post-glacial environmental change and man in the Thames estuary: A synopsis, in F H Thompson (ed) *Archaeology and Coastal Change*. Society of Antiquaries, London, 134–148

Devoy, R J N, 1982 Analysis of the geological evidence for Holocene sea level movements in southeast England. *Proc Geologists' Ass* 93, 65–90

Dewey, H and Bromehead, C.E.N. 1921 *The Geology of South London*. Memoir of the Geological Survey of Great Britain, Keyworth

Dewey, H, Bromehead, C E N, Chatwin, C P and Dines, H G, 1924 *The Geology of the Country around Dartford*. Memoir of the Geological Survey of Great Britain, Keyworth

Dines, H G and Edmunds, F H, 1925 *The Geology of the Country around Romford*. Memoir of the Geological Survey of Great Britain, Keyworth

Dinç, U, Miedema, R, Bal, L and Pons, L J, 1976 Morphological and physio-chemical aspects of three soils developed in peat in the Netherlands and their classification. *Netherlands Journ Agricultural Sci* 24, 247–265

Divers, D, 1996 *Archaeological investigation of Hayes Storage Services Ltd Pooles Lane, Ripple Road, Dagenham, Essex* (DA-HS93). Newham Museum Service Archaeology Centre, http://ads.ahds.ac.uk/catalogue/projArch/newham/da-hs93

Dobney, K, Jaques, J and Irving, B 1996 The animal bones from Lincoln, in *Of Butchers and Breeds. Report on Vertebrate Remains from Various Sites in the City of Lincoln*. Lincoln Archaeological Studies 5, Lincoln

Drewett, P L, 1989, Anthropogenic soil erosion in prehistoric Sussex: excavations at West Heath and Ferring, 1984. *Sussex Archaeol Collect* 127, 11–29

Edwards, K J, 1981 The separation of *Corylus* and *Myrica* pollen in modern and fossil samples. *Pollen et Spores* 23, 205–218

Edwards, K J, 1990 Fire and the Scottish Mesolithic: evidence from microscopic charcoal, in P Vermeesch and P van Peer (eds) *Contributions to the Mesolithic in Europe*. University Press, Leuven, 71–79

Edwards, K J and Macdonald, G M, 1991 Holocene palynology: II. Human influence and vegetation change. *Progress in Physical Geography* 15, 364–417

Elias, S A, Webster, L and Amer, M, 2009 A beetle's eye view of London from the Mesolithic to Late Bronze Age. *Geological Journal* 44, 501–626

Ellison, R A, 2004 *Geology of London: Special Memoir for 1:50,000 geological sheets 256 (North London), 257 (Romford), 270 (South London) and 271 (Dartford) (England and Wales)*. British Geological Survey, Keyworth

Emery, P A and Wooldridge, K, 2011 *St Pancras Burial Ground: Excavations for St Pancras International, the London terminus of High Speed 1, 2002–3*. Gifford

Enghoff, I B, 1995 Fishing in Denmark during the Mesolithic period, in A Fischer (ed) *Man and Sea in the Mesolithic. Coastal Settlement Above and Below Present Sea Level*. Oxbow Monogr 53, Oxbow Books, Oxford, 67–74

Fokkens, H, 1998 Drowned landscape: The occupation of the western part of the Frisian-Drentian Plateau, 4400 BC– AD 500. *Rijksdienst voor het Oudheidkundig Bodemonderzoik*, Van Gorcum & Comp, BV, Assen

Foley, R, 1981 A model of regional archaeological structures. *Proc Prehist Soc* 47, 1–17

Ford, S, 1987 Chronological and functional aspects of flint assemblages, in A G Brown and M R Edmonds (eds), *Lithic analysis and later British prehistory: some problems and approaches*. Brit Archaeol Rep, Brit Ser 162, Oxford, 67–81

Fox, C A, 1985, Micromorphological characterisation of histosols, in L A Douglas and R Thompson (eds), *Soil Micromorphology and Soil Classification*. Soil Science Society of America, Special Publication 15, Madison, Wisconsin, 85–104

Fulford, M, Champion, T and Long, A, 1997 *England's Coastal Heritage: A survey for English Heritage and the RCHME*. English Heritage Archaeol Rep 15, London

Gaffney, V, Thomson, K and Fitch, S, 2007 *Mapping Doggerland: the Mesolithic landscapes of the Southern North Sea*. Institute of Archaeology, Birmingham

Gallois, R W, 1965 *The Wealden District*. British Regional Geology, HMSO, London, 4th edition

Galloway, J A and Potts, J S, 2007 Marine flooding in the Thames Estuary and tidal river *c.* 1250–1450: impact and response. *Royal Geographical Society* 39 (3), 370–379

Gdaniec, K, Edmonds, M and Wiltshire, P, 2007 A *Line Across Land: fieldwork on the Isleham-Ely pipeline, 1993–4*. East Anglian Archaeology 121, Cambridge

Gibbard, P L, 1977 Pleistocene history of the Vale of St. Albans. *Phil Trans Royal Soc London B* 280, 445–483

Gibbard, P L, 1985 *Pleistocene History of the Middle Thames Valley*. Cambridge University Press

Gibbard, P L, 1994 *Pleistocene History of the Lower Thames Valley*. Cambridge University Press

Gibson, A and Kinnes, I, 1997 On the urns of a dilemma: radiocarbon and the Peterborough problem. *Oxford J Archaeol* 16 (1), 65–72

Girling, M A, 1989 Mesolithic and later landscapes interpreted from the insect assemblages of West Heath Spa Hampstead, in D Collins and D Lorimer (eds) *Excavations at the Mesolithic Site on West Heath,*

Hampstead 1976–1981. Brit Archaeol Rep 217, Oxford, 72–89

Godwin, H, 1975 *History of the British flora*. Cambridge University Press, 2nd edition

Goldberg, P and Macphail, R I, 2006a *Practical and Theoretical Geoarchaeology*. Blackwell, Oxford

Goldberg, P, and Macphail, R I, 2006b *Playa Vista Archaeological and Historical Project (California): soil micromorphology – preliminary report*. Tucson, Statistical Research Inc 7

Goldberg, P and Macphail, R I, 2012 Gorham's Cave sediment micromorphology in R N E Barton, C Stringer and C Finlayson (eds) *Neanderthals in Context. A report of the 1995–1998 excavations at Gorham's and Vanguard Caves*, Gibraltar, Oxford University School of Archaeology Monogr 75, 50–61; Appendix 52: 314–321; Colour figures at: www.arch.ox.ac.uk/gibraltar

Grant, A, 1982 The use of tooth wear as a guide to the age of domestic ungulates in B Wilson, C Grigson and S Payne (eds), *Ageing and Sexing Animal Bone from Archaeological Sites*. Brit Archaeol Rep 109, Oxford, 91–108

Grant, M J and Dark, P, 2006 *Re-evaluating the Concept of Woodland Continuity and Change in Epping Forest: new dating evidence from Lodge Road*. Unpubl report for the Corporation of London

Grant, M J, Barber, K E and Hughes, P D M, 2009 Early to mid-Holocene vegetation-fire interactions and responses to climatic change at Cranes Moor, New Forest, in R M Briant, M R Bates, R T Hosfield and F F Wenban-Smith (eds), *The Quaternary of the Solent Basin and West Sussex Raised Beaches: Field Guide*. Quaternary Research Association, London, 198–214

Grant, M J and Norcott, D, 2012 Deposit Modelling, in A B Powell, *By River, Fields and Factories: The Making of the Lower Lea Valley – archaeological and cultural heritage investigations on the site of the London 2012 Olympic Games and Paralympic Games*. Wessex Archaeology Monogr 29, Salisbury, 349–358

Grant, M J and Waller, M P, 2010 Holocene fire histories from the edge of Romney Marsh, in M Waller, E Edwards, and L Barber (eds), *Romney Marsh: Persistence and Change in a Coastal Lowland*. Romney Marsh Research Trust, Sevenoaks, 53–73

Grant, M J, Waller, M P and Groves, J, 2011 The *Tilia* decline: vegetation change in lowland Britain during the mid and late Holocene. *Quat Sci Rev* 30, 394–408

Green, L S, (ed) 1999 *The Essex Landscape: In Search of its History, The 1996 Cressing Conference*. Essex County Council Planning

Greensmith, J T and Tucker, E V, 1980 Evidence for differential subsidence on the Essex Coast. *Proc Geologists' Ass* 91, 169–175

Greenwood, M and Smith, D N, 2005 A survey of Coleoptera from sedimentary deposits from the Trent Valley, in D N Smith, M B Brickley and W

Smith (eds) *Fertile Ground: papers in honour of Professor Susan Limbrey*. Association for Environmental Archaeology Symposia 22, Oxbow Books, Oxford, 53–67

Greenwood, P, 1989 Uphall Camp, Ilford, Essex: an Iron Age fortification. *London Archaeologist* 6, 94–101

Greenwood, P, 2001 Uphall Camp, Ilford: an update. *London Archaeologist* 9, 207–16

Groves, J A, 2008 *Late Quaternary Vegetation History of the Acidic Lithologies of South East England*. Unpubl PhD thesis, Kingston University

Guéguen, Y and Palciauskas, V, 1994 *Introduction to the Physics of Rocks*. Princeton University Press

Habermehl, K H, 1975 *Die Altersbestimmung bei Haus- und Labortieren 2. vollständig neubearbeitete Auflage*. Paul Parey, Berlin and Hamburg

Haggart, B A 1995 A re-examination of some data relating to Holocene sea-level changes in the Thames estuary, in D R Bridgland, P Allen and B A Haggart (eds) *The Quaternary of the Lower Reaches of the Thames, Field Guide*. Quaternary Research Association, Cambridge, 329–338

Hall, A R and Kenward, H K 1990 *Environmental evidence from the Colonia: General Accident and Rougier Street*. The Archaeology of York 14/6, Counc Brit Archaeol, London

Hall, D and Coles, J, 1994 *Fenland Survey: an essay in landscape and persistence*. English Heritage, London

Hallam, H E, 1981 *Rural England 1066–1348*, Fontana, London

Hansen, M, 1986 *The Hydrophilidae (Coleoptera) of Fennoscandia and Denmark Fauna*. Fauna Entomologyca Scandinavica 18, Scandinavian Science Press, Leiden

Hardy, A, and Andrews, P, 2011 Saxon, medieval and post-medieval landscape, in Andrews *et al* 2011a, 249–305

Hardy, A, Watts, M and Goodburn, D, 2011 The mid-Saxon mill at Northfleet, in Andrews *et al* 2011a, 307–349

Hart, D, 2010 Excavations at Belmarsh West, Woolwich. *London Archaeologist*, 12 (8), 203–207

Hasted, E, 1797 *The History and Topographical Survey of the County of Kent*, Volume 3

Haughey F, 1999 The archaeology of the Thames: prehistory within a dynamic landscape. *London Archaeologist* 9 (1), 6–21

Haughey, F, 2003 From prediction to prospection: finding prehistory on London's river, in A J Howard, M G Macklin and D G Passmore (eds) *Alluvial Archaeology in Europe*. Balkema, Lisse, 61–68

Haughey, F, 2007 Searching for the Neolithic while it may be found: research in the inter-tidal zone of the London Thames, in E J Sidell and F Haughey (eds) *Neolithic Archaeology in the Intertidal Zone*. Neolithic Studies Group Seminar Paper 8, Oxbow Books, Oxford, 86–94

Hendey, N I, 1964 *An Introductory Account of the Smaller Algae of British Coastal Waters. Part V. Bacillariophyceae (Diatoms)*. Ministry of Agriculture Fisheries and Food, Series IV, London

Hiscook, R H, 1968 The road between Dartford, Gravesend and Strood. *Archaeologia Cantiana* 83, 228–46

Holland, D G, 1972 *A key to the larvae, pupae and adults of the British species of Elminthidae*. Scientific Publication 26, Freshwater Biological Association, Ambleside

Howie, J A, Cavers, D S and Karlen, W S. 1998 Burnaby Lake – A case history of piezocone testing and ground penetrating radar, in P K Robertson and P W Mayne (eds) *Geotechnical Site Characterization*. Balkema, Rotterdam, 1247–1252

Huckerby, E, Druce, D, Scaife, R and Verrill, L forthcoming, Pollen, in Wenban-Smith *et al* forthcoming

Huxtable, J, 1992 Thermoluminesence (TL) dating of burned artefacts from the Hengistbury sites, in Barton 1992, 60–61

Ibrahim, E H, Elgamili, M M, Hassaneen, A G H, Soliman, M N and Ismael, A M 2002 Geoelectrical investigation beneath Behbiet ElHigara and ElKom ElAkhder archaeological sites, Samannud Area, Nile Delta, Egypt. *Archaeological Prospection* 9, 105–113

Ikinger, A, 1990 Verschüttete Landschaft: Das Gelände unter dem Bims im Neuwieder Becken, 89–93, in W Schimer (ed) *Rheingeschichte zwischen Mosel und Mass. Deuqua-Führer 1*. Deutsche Quartärvereinigung, Hannover

Jacobi, R, 1978 The Mesolithic of Sussex, in P L Drewett (ed) *Archaeology in Sussex to AD 1500*. Counc Brit Archaeol Res Rep 29, York, 15–22

Jarvis M G, Allen, R H, Fordham, S J, Hazleden, J, Moffat, A J and Sturdy, R G, 1984 *Soils and Their Use in South-East England*. Soil Survey of England and Wales, Harpenden

Jashemski, W F, 1979 Pompeii and Mount Vesuvius, A.D. 79, 587–622, in P D Sheets and D K Grayson (eds) *Volcanic Activity and Human Ecology*. Academic Press, London

Jeffery, S, 1991 Burnt mounds, fulling and early textiles, in Hodder and Barfield 1991, 97–108

Jones, T A, 1992 Extensions to three-dimensional: Introduction to the sections of 3D geologic block modelling, in D E Hamilton and T A Jones (eds) *Computer Modelling of Geologic Surfaces and Volumes*. AAPG Computer Applications in Geology, 1175–182

Keatinge, T, 1982 Influence of stemflow on the representation of pollen of *Tilia* in soils. *Grana* 21, 171–4

Keatinge, T H, 1983 Development of pollen assemblage zones in soil profiles in southeastern England. *Boreas* 12, 1–12

Kelsey, J, 1972 Geodetic aspects concerning possible subsidence in South-Eastern England. *Phil Trans Royal Society London A* 272, 141–149

Kenward, H K and Hall, A R 1995 *Biological evidence from Anglo-Scandinavian deposits at 16–22 Coppergate*. The Archaeology of York 14/7, Counc Brit Archaeol, York

Kirby, R, 1969 *Sedimentary Environment, Sedimentary Processes and River History in the Lower Medway Estuary, Kent*. Unpubl. PhD thesis, University London

Kirby, R, 1990 The sediment budget of the erosional intertidal zone of the Medway Estuary, Kent. *Proc Geological Ass* 101(1), 63–77

Kraft, J C, Rapp, G, Szemler, G J, Tziavos, C and Kase, E W, 1987 The Pass at Thermopylae, Greece. *Field Archaeol* 14, 181–198

Koch, K, 1992 *Die Kafer Mitteleuropas*. Ökologie Band 3, Goecke and Evers, Krefeld

Kooistra, M J, 1978 *Soil Development in Recent Marine Sediments of the Intertidal Zone in the Oosterschelde – the Netherlands: a soil micromorphological approach*. Soil Survey Institute, Wageningen

Küster, H, 1988 *Vom werden einer kulturlandschaft: vegetationsgeschichtliche studien am auerberg (Südbayern)*. Acta Humaniora, Weinheim

Lambrick, G, 2009 *The Thames Through Time, the archaeology of the gravel terraces of the Upper and Middle Thames: the Thames Valley in late prehistory: 1500 BC–AD 50*. Oxford Archaeology Thames Valley Landscapes Monogr, Oxford

Leivers, M and Barnett, C, 2007 Discussion, in Leivers *et al* 2007, 36–41

Leivers, M, Barnett, C and Harding, P, 2007 Excavation of Mesolithic and Neolithic flint scatters and accompanying environmental sequences at Tank Hill Road, Purfleet, 2002. *Essex Archaeol Hist* 38, 1–44

Lenham, J W, McDonald, R, Miller, S and Reynolds, J M, 2005 Integrated seismic investigations across the Mersey Estuary, Halton District, UK. *Quarterly Journal of Engineering Geology and Hydrogeology* 38, 7–22

Lewis, J S C, 1991 Excavation of a late Devensian and early Flandrian site at Three Ways Wharf, Uxbridge, England: interim report, in N Barton, A J Roberts and D A Roe (eds) *The Late-glacial in North-west Europe: human adaptation and environmental change at the end of the Pleistocene*. Counc Brit Archaeol Res Rep 77, York, 246–255

Lewis, J S C with Rackham, J, 2011 *Three Ways Wharf, Uxbridge: A Late Glacial and Early Holocene Hunter-gatherer Site in the Colne Valley*. Museum of London Archaeology Monogr 51, London

Lewis, J S C, Wiltshire, P E J and Macphail, R I, 1992 A late Devensian/early Flandrian site at Three Ways Wharf, Uxbridge: environmental implications, in S P Needham and M G Macklin (eds) *Alluvial Archaeology in Britain*. Oxbow Monogr 27, Oxbow Books, Oxford, 235–247

Lewis, S G and Roberts, C L, 1998 Location of the buried cliffline using resistivity methods, in M R

Roberts and S A Parfitt (eds) *The Middle Pleistocene Hominid site at ARC Eartham Quarry, Boxgrove, West Sussex, UK.* English Heritage Archaeol Rep 17, English Heritage, London

Lippi, R D, 1988 Palaeotopography and P analysis of a buried jungle site in Ecuador. *Journ Field Archaeol* 15, 85–97

Lister, A M and Sher, A V, 2001 The origin and evolution of the woolly mammoth. *Science* 294, 1094–1097

Long, A J, 1995 Sea-level and crustal movements in the Thames estuary, Essex and East Kent, in D R Bridgland, P Allen and B A Haggart (eds) *The Quaternary of the Lower Reaches of the Thames Field Guide.* Quaternary Research Association, Cambridge, 99–105

Long, A J and Roberts, D H, 1997 Sea-level change, in M Fulford, T Champion and A Long (eds) *England's Coastal Heritage: a survey for English Heritage and the RCHME.* English Heritage Archaeol Rep 15, English Heritage, London, 25–49

Long, A J and Shennan, I, 1993 Holocene relative sea-level and crustal movements in southeast and northeast England, UK. *Quaternary Proceedings 3*, Cambridge, 15–19

Long, A J, Scaife, R G and Edwards, R J, 2000 Stratigraphic architecture, relative sea level and models of estuary development in southern England: New data from Southampton Water, in K Pye and J R L Allen (eds) *Coastal and Estuary Environments: sedimentology, geomorphology and Geoarchaeology.* Geological Society Special Publication 175, London, 253–280

Lyell, C, 1832 *Principles of Geology, being an attempt to explain the former changes of the Earth's surface, by reference to causes now in Operation.* John Murray, London

McErlean, T and Crothers, N, 2007 H*arnessing the Tides: the monastic tide mills at Nendrum Monastery.* Northern Ireland Archaeological Monogr 8 TSO, London

Macphail, R I, 1994 Soil micromorphological investigations in archaeology, with special reference to drowned coastal sites in Essex, in H F Cook and D T Favis-Mortlock (eds). *SEESOIL, Volume 10: Wye*, South East Soils Discussion Group, 13–28

Macphail, R I, 2006 *Star Carr (VP05): soil micromorphology assessment*, Institute of Archaeology, UCL. Unpubl Rep

Macphail, R I, and Crowther, J, 2004 *White Horse Stone: soil micromorphology, phosphate and magnetic susceptibility*, Oxford Archaeology. Unpubl Rep

Macphail, R I and Cruise, G M, 2000 Soil micromorphology, in M Bell, A Caseldine and H Neumann (eds) *Prehistoric Intertidal Archaeology in the Welsh Severn Estuary.* Counc Brit Archaeol Res Rep 120, York, 267–269 and CD-ROM

Macphail, R I, and Crowther, J, 2006 *The soil micromorphology, phosphate and magnetic susceptibility evidence from White Horse Stone, Boxley, Kent.* CTRL specialist report series, ADS 2006

Maddy, D, 1997 Uplift driven valley incision and river terrace formation in southern England, *Journ Quat Sci* 12, 539–545

Marsland, A, 1986 The floodplain deposits of the Lower Thames. *Quarterly Journal of Engineering Geology* 19, 223–247

Martín-Consuegra, E, Chisvert, N, Cáceres, L and Ubera, J L, 1998 Archaeological, palynological and geological contributions to landscape reconstruction in the alluvial plain of the Guadalquivir River at San Benardo, Sevilla (Spain). *Journ Archaeol Sci* 25, 521–532

Matolcsi, J, 1970 Historische Erforschung der Körpergröße des Rindes auf Grund von ungarischen Knochenmaterial. *Zeitschrift für Tierzüchtung und Züchtungsbiologie* 87, 89–137

McGrail, S, 1990 Early boats of the Humber Basin, in S Ellis and D R Crowther (eds) *Humber Perspectives: a region through the ages.* Hull University Press, 109–130

McNeill, J D, 1990 Use of electromagnetic methods for groundwater studies, in S H Ward (ed) *Geotechnical and Environmental Geophysics, Vol. 1. Review and Tutorial.* Society of Exploration Geophysicists, Tulsa

Meddens, F, 1996 Sites from the Thames estuary wetlands, England and their Bronze Age use. *Antiquity* 70, 325–334

Meddens, F and Beasley, M, 1990 Wetland use in Rainham, Essex. *London Archaeologist* 6, 242–248

Meddens, F M and Sidell, J, 1995 Bronze Age trackways in east London. *Current Archaeology* 12(11), 412–16

Meisch, C, 2000 Freshwater Ostracoda of Western and Central Europe, in J Schwoerbel and P Zwick (eds), *Sußwasserfauna von Mitteleuropa Band 8/3.* Spektrum Akademischer Verlag, Heidelberg and Berlin

Mellars, P, 1976 Fire ecology, animal population and man: a study of some ecological relationships in prehistory. *Proc Prehist Soc* 42, 15–45

Mellars, P and Dark, P, 1998 *Star Carr in Context.* Cambridge University Press

Miall, A D, 1977 A review of the braided river depositional environment. *Earth Science Reviews* 13, 1–62

Miall, A D, 1996 *The Geology of Fluvial Deposits: sedimentary facies, basin analysis and petroleum geology.* Springer-Verlag, Berlin

Miedema, R, Jongmans, A G and Slager, S, 1974 Micromorphological observations on pyrite and its oxidation products in four Holocene alluvial soils in the Netherlands, in G K Rutherford (ed) *Soil Microscopy.* Limestone Press, Kingston, Ontario, 772–794

Millett, M, 2007 Roman Kent, in J Williams (ed) *Archaeology of Kent to AD 800*, Boydell & Brewer, Suffolk and Kent County Council, 135–86

Milne, G, Bates, M R and Webber, M D 1997 Problems, potential and partial solutions: an archaeological study of the tidal Thames, England. *World Archaeology* 29, 130–146

Milne, G, Batterbee, R W, Straker, V and Yule, B, 1983 The London Thames in the mid-first century. *Trans London Middlesex Archaeol Soc* 34, 19–30

MoLAS 1996 *West Silvertown Urban Village, Royal Victoria Dock, London E16, London Borough of Newham: A geoarchaeological survey.* Museum of London Archaeological Service. Unpubl Rep

MoLAS, 2000 *The Archaeology of Greater London: An assessment of archaeological evidence for human presence in the area now covered by Greater London.* MoLAS Monogr 4

Mook, W G, 1986 Business Meeting: recommendations/ resolutions adopted by the twelfth international radiocarbon conference. *Radiocarbon* 28, 799

Moore, P, Bradley, T and Bishop, B J, 2003 A Late Bronze Age burnt mound site at The Phillimores, Campden Hill Road, Kensington. *London Archaeologist* 10 (7), 179–186

Murray, J W, 2006 *Ecology and Applications of Benthic Foraminifera.* Cambridge University Press

Nilsson, A N and Holmen, M, 1995 *The Aquatic Adephaga (Coleoptera) of Fennoscandia and Denmark II. Dytiscidae.* Fauna Entomologyca Scandinavica Volume 35. E J Brill, Leiden

Ogden, C G and Hedley, R H, 1980 *An Atlas of Freshwater Testate Amoebae.* British Museum (Natural History), London and Oxford University Press

O'Kelly, M J, 1954 Excavation and experiments in ancient Irish cooking sites. *Journ Royal Soc Antiquaries Ireland* 84, 105–55

Ó'Néill, J J, 2009 *Burnt Mounds in Northern and Western Europe: A study of prehistoric technology and society.* VDM Verlag Dr. Müller, Saarbrücken

Onhuma, K and Bergman, C A, 1982 Experimental studies in the determination of flake mode. *UCL Univ London Inst Archaeology* 19, 161–171

Osborne, P J, 1988 A late Bronze Age insect fauna from the River Avon, Warwickshire, England: Its implications for the terrestrial and fluvial environment and for climate. *Journ Archaeol Sci* 15, 715–727

Ovando-Shelley, E and Manzanilla, L, 1997 An archaeological interpretation of geotechnical soundings under the Metropolitan cathedral, Mexico City. *Archaeometry* 39, 221–235

Oxford Archaeology, 2011 *Dagenham and Washlands, Public Realms Enhancement, Dagenham, Greater London, NGR TQ 5033 836, Archaeological Watching Brief Report and Updated Project Design.* Unpubl Rep for Ove Arup and Partners on behalf of the Environment Agency

Oxford Archaeological Unit, 1995 *South Thames-side Development Route IV, Archaeological Desktop Assessment.* Unpubl Rep for Kent County Council

Oxford Archaeological Unit, 1997 *The Proposed Ebbsfleet Development (Northfleet Rise Area), Archaeological Evaluation Report.* Unpubl

Oxford Archaeological Unit, 2001 *Rainham, Wennington and Aveley Marshes, archaeological desk-based assessment for the RSPB.* Unpubl Rep

Parfitt, K, 2006 A Prehistoric 'Burnt Mound' site at Crabble Paper Mill, near Dover. *Archaeologia Cantiana* 126, 219–238

Peeters, H, 2006 Sites, landscapes and uncertainty: on the modelling of the archaeological potential and assessment of deeply-buried Stone Age landscapes in the Flevoland polders (the Netherlands), in E Rebsink and H Peeters (eds) *Preserving the Early Past: Investigation, selection and preservation of Palaeolithic and Mesolithic sites and landscapes.* National Service for Archaeological Heritage, Amersfoort, 167–184

Pollard, J, 1998 Prehistoric settlement and non-settlement in two southern Cambridgeshire river valleys: the lithic dimension and interpretative dilemmas. *Lithics* 19, 61–71

Powell, A B, Booth, P, Fitzpatrick, A P and Crockett, A D, 2008 *The Archaeology of the M6 Toll 2000–2003,* Oxford Wessex Archaeology Monogr 2, Salisbury

Powell, A B, 2012 *By River, Fields and Factories: The Making of the Lower Lea Valley – archaeological and cultural heritage investigations on the site of the London 2012 Olympic and Paralympic Games.* Wessex Archaeology Monogr 29, Salisbury

Preece, R C and Bridgland, D R, 1998, *Late Quaternary Environmental Change in North-West Europe: Excavations at Holywell Coombe, South-East England.* Chapman & Hall, London

Rackham, J and Sidell, J, 2000 London's landscapes: the changing environment, in M Kendall (ed) *The Archaeology of Greater London.* Museum of London Archaeology Service, London, 11–27

Raymond, F, 1987, *Monument Protection Programme Single Monument Class Description: Burnt Mounds.* London

Reed, N A, Bennett, J W and Porter, J W, 1968 Solid core drilling of Monks Mound: technique and findings. *American Antiquity* 33, 137–148

Reid, C, 1949 The Late-Glacial flora of the Lea Valley. *New Phytologist* 48, 245–52

Reimer, P J, Baillie, M G L, Bard, E, Bayliss, A, Beck, J W, Bertrand, C J H, Blackwell, P G, Buck, C E, Burr, G S, Cutler, K B, Damon, P E, Edwards, R L, Fairbanks, R G, Friedrich, M, Guilderson, T P, Hogg, A G, Hughen, K A, Kromer, B, McCormac, G, Manning, S, Bronk Ramsey, C, Reimer, R W, Remmele, S, Southon, J R, Stuiver, M, Talamo, S, Taylor, F W, van der Plicht, J and Weyhenmeyer, C E, 2004 IntCal04 Terrestrial Radiocarbon Age Calibration, 0–26 cal kyr BP. *Radiocarbon* 46, 1029–1058

Reynolds, J M, 1997 *An Introduction to Applied and Environmental Geophysics.* Wiley, Chichester

Reynolds, P J and Langley, J K, 1979 Romano-British corn-drying ovens: an experiment. *Archaeological Journal* 136, 27–42

Ritchie, K, Allen, M J, Barnett, C, Cooke, N, Crowther, J, Gale, R, Grant, M, Jones, G P, Knight, S, Leivers, M, McKinley, J I, Macphail, R I, Mepham, L, Scaife, R G, Stevens, C J and Wyles, S F 2008 Environment and land use in the Lower Lea Valley *c*. 12,500 BC – *c*. 600 AD: Innova Park and the former Royal Ordnance Factory, Enfield. *Trans London Middlesex Archaeol Soc* 59, 1–38

Roberts, M B and Parfitt, S A 1999 *Boxgrove: A Middle Pleistocene Hominid Site at Eartham Quarry, Boxgrove, West Sussex.* English Heritage Archaeol Rep 17

Robertson-Mackay, R, 1987 The Neolithic causewayed enclosure at Staines Surrey: excavations 1961–63. *Proc Prehist Soc* 53, 23–128

Robinson, M A, 2000a Middle Mesolithic to Late Bronze Age insect assemblages and an Early Neolithic assemblage of waterlogged macroscopic plant remains, in S P Needham (ed) *The Passage of the Thames: Holocene environment and settlement at Runnymede.* British Museum Press, London, 146–167

Robinson, M A, 2000b Coleopteran evidence for the Elm Decline, Neolithic activity in woodland, clearance and the use of the landscape in A S Fairbairn (ed) *Plants in Neolithic Britain and Beyond.* Neolithic Studies Group Seminar Papers 5, Oxbow Books, Oxford, 27–36

Robinson, M A, forthcoming, Insects, in Wenban-Smith *et al* forthcoming

Ryves, D B, Juggins, S, Fritz, S C and Battarbee, R W, 2001 Experimental diatom dissolution and the quantification of microfossil preservation in sediments. *Palaeogeography, Palaeoclimatology, Palaeoecology,* 172, 99–113

Salvany, J M, Carrera, J, Bolzicco, J and Mediavilla, C, 2004 Pitfalls in the geological characterization of alluvial deposits: site investigation for reactive barrier installation at Aznalcóllar, Spain. *Quarterly Journ Engineering Geology and Hydrogeology* 37, 141–154

Scaife, R G, 1987 The Late-Devensian and Flandrian vegetation of the Isle of Wight, in K E Barber (ed) *Wessex and the Isle of Wight Field Guide.* Quaternary Research Association, Cambridge, 156–180

Scaife, R G, 2000 Holocene vegetation development in London, in Sidell *et al* 2000, 111–117

Scaife, R, 2007 Pollen analysis, in Leivers *et al* 2007, 29–32

Scaife, R, 2011a Pollen, in Barnett *et al* 2011, 68–76

Scaife, R, 2011b Pollen from Northfleet, in Andrews *et al* 2011b, 66–69

Schoute, J F T, 1987 Micromorphology of soil horizons developed during semiterrestrial phases in transgressive and regressive sedimentary sequences in the Northern Netherlands, in N Fedoroff, L M Bresson, and M A Courty (eds) *Soil Micromorphology.* Plaisir, Association Française pour l'Étude du Sol, 661–667

Schuster, J, 2011 Northfleet metalwork, in E Biddulph, R Seager Smith and J Schuster (eds) *Settling the Ebbsfleet Valley: High Speed 1 Excavations at Springhead and Northfleet, Kent. The Late Iron Age, Roman, Saxon and Medieval Landscape, Volume 2, Late Iron Age to Roman Finds Reports.* Oxford Wessex Archaeology Monogr 294–307

Seel, S, 2001 *Late Prehistoric Woodlands and Wood Use on the Lower Thames Floodplain.* Unpubl PhD thesis, University College London

Shennan, I, 1983 Flandrian and Late-Devensian sea-level changes and crustal movements in England and Wales, in D E Smith and A G Dawson (eds) *Shorelines and Isostasy.* Academic Press, London, 255–283

Shennan, I, 1987 Holocene sea-level changes in the North Sea, in M J Tooley and I Shennan (eds), *Sea-Level Changes.* Blackwell, Oxford, 109–151

Shennan, I, 1989a Holocene crustal movements and sea-level changes in Great Britain. *Journ Quat Sci* 4, 77–89

Shennan, I, 1989b Holocene sea-level changes and crustal movements in the North Sea Region: an experiment with regional eustasy, in D B Scott, P A Pirazzoli and C A Honig (eds) *Late Quaternary Sea-level Correlations and Applications.* NATO ASI Series C256, Kluwer, Dordrecht

Shennan, I, Milne, G and Bradley, S, 2012 Late Holocene vertical land motion and relative sea-level changes: lessons from the British Isles. *Journ Quat Sci* 27, 64–70

Sherlock, R L, 1947 *London and the Thames Valley, British Regional Geology.* HMSO, London, 2nd edition

Sidell, E J, 2000 Twenty-five years of environmental archaeology in London, in I Haynes, H Sheldon and L Hannigan (eds) *London Underground: the Archaeology of a City.* Oxbow Books, Oxford, 284–294

Sidell, E J, 2003 *Holocene Sea Level Change and Archaeology in the Inner Thames estuary, London, UK.* Unpubl PhD thesis, University Durham

Sidell, E J, Cotton, J, Rayner, L and Wheeler, L, 2002 *The Prehistory and Topography of Southwark.* Museum of London Archaeology Service Monogr 14, London

Sidell, E J, Scaife, R G, Wilkinson, K N, Giorgi, J A, Goodburn, D, Gray-Rees, L and Tyers, I, 1997 *Spine Road Development, Erith, Bexley (RPS Clouston Site 2649): A palaeoenvironmental assessment.* Unpubl Report, Museum of London Archaeology Service

Sidell, E J, Wilkinson, K N, Scaife, R G and Cameron, N, 2000 *The Holocene Evolution of the London Thames.* Museum of London Archaeology Service Monogr 5, London

Sieveking, G, 1960 Ebbsfleet: Neolithic sites. *Archaeologia Cantiana* 74, 192–193

Simmonds, A, Wenban-Smith, F, Bates, M, Powell, K, Sykes, D, Devaney, R, Stansbie D and Score, D,

2010 *Excavations in North-West Kent, 2005–2007: One hundred thousand years of human activity in and around the Darent Valley*. Oxford Archaeology Monogr 11, Oxford

Simmons, I G, 1996 *The Environmental Impact of Later Mesolithic Cultures*. Edinburgh University Press

Simmons, I G and Innes, J B, 1997 Mid Holocene adaptations and the Later Mesolithic forest disturbance in Northern England. *Journ Archaeol Sci* 14, 385–403

Skene, K R, Sprent, J I, Raven J A and Herdman, L, 2000 Biological Flora of the British Isles, *Myrica gale* L. *Journal of Ecology* 88, 1079–1094

Slager, S and van der Wetering, H T J, 1977 Soil formation in archaeological pits and adjacent loess soils in southern Germany. *Journ Archaeol Sci* 4, 259–267

Smith, A G, 1970 The influence of Mesolithic and Neolithic man on British vegetation: a discussion, in D Walker and R G West (eds), *Studies in the Vegetational History of the British Isles*. Cambridge University Press, 81–96

Smith, D N, 1997 The insect fauna, in C Thomas, B Sloane and C Philpotts (eds) *Excavations at the Priory and Hospital of St. Mary Spital, London*. Museum of London Archaeology Service Monogr 1, London, 245–247

Smith, D N, 1999 *Atlas Wharf, Isle of Dogs: Paleoentomological analysis*, The University of Birmingham Environmental Archaeology Services Report 8. Unpubl Rep for Museum of London Archaeology Service

Smith, D N, 2002. Insect remains, in B Barber and C Thomas (eds) *The London Charterhouse*. Museum of London Archaeology Service Monogr 10, London, 113–115

Smith, D N, 2006a The insect remains, in D Seeley, C Phillpotts and M Samuel (eds) *Winchester Palace: excavations at the Southwark residence of the bishops of Winchester*. Museum of London Archaeology Service Monogr 20, London

Smith, D N, 2006b *The Insect remains from the Ikea site at Glover Drive, Edmington, Edfield (GVV 04)*. University of Birmingham Environmental Archaeology Services. Unpubl Rep for AOC Archaeology

Smith, D N and Chandler, G, 2004 Insect remains, in B Sloane and G Malcolm (eds) *Excavations at the Priory of the Order of the Hospital of St John of Jerusalem. Clerkenwell, London*, Museum of London Archaeology Service Monogr 20, London, 389–94

Smith, D N and Howard, A J, 2004 Identifying changing fluvial conditions in low gradient alluvial archaeological landscapes: Can Coleoptera provide insights into changing discharge rates and floodplain evolution? *Journ Archaeol Sci* 31, 109–20

Smith, D, 2011a Insects from Northfleet, in Barnett *et al* 2011, 88–90

Smith, D, 2011b Insects from Northfleet, in Andrews *et al* 2011b, 89–91

Smith, V, 1979 Thameside Archaeological Group. *Kent Archaeological Review* 57, 157

Smith, V, 1980 Thameside Archaeological Group. *Kent Archaeological Review* 62, 43–44

Smith, W, 2011 Charred plant remains from Northfleet, in Barnett *et al* 2011, 105–113

Spurr, G, 2006 *Omega Works Phase III, Crown Wharf, Roach Road, London E3, Site Code OMW05*, London, MoLAS. Unpubl Rep

Spurrell, F C J, 1885a Excursion to Erith and Crayford. *Proc Geologists' Ass* 9, 213–216

Spurrell, F C J, 1885b Early sites and embankments on the margins of the Thames estuary. *Archaeol J* 42, 269–302

Spurrell, F C J, 1889 On the estuary of the river Thames and its alluvium. *Proc Geologists' Ass* 11, 210–230

Stafford, E with Goodburn, D and Bates, M, 2012 *Landscape and prehistory of the East London Wetlands: Investigations along the A13 DBFO Roadscheme, Tower Hamlets, Newham and Barking and Dagenham, 2000–2003*. Oxford Archaeology Monogr 17, Oxford

Steadman, W H, 1913 Excavations on a Roman site at Northfleet. *The Dartford Antiquary* 1, 4–15

Stephenson, A, 2008 Bridging the Lea: excavations at Crown Wharf, Dace Road, Tower Hamlets. *Trans London Middlesex Archaeol Soc* 59, 39–59

Stevens, C J, 2011a Waterlogged plant remains, in Barnett *et al* 2011, 84–87

Stevens, C J, 2011b Waterlogged plant remains from Northfleet, in Andrews *et al* 2011b, 85–89

Stein, J K, 1991 Coring in CRM and Archaeology: a reminder. *American Antiquity* 56, 138–142

Street, M, 1986 Un Pompéi de l'âge glaciaire. *La Recherche* 17, 534–535

Strid, L, forthcoming, Faunal remains, in Wenban-Smith *et al* forthcoming

Stuiver, M and Kra, R S (eds) 1986 Calibration issue, Proceedings of the 12th International 14C conference. *Radiocarbon* 28(2B), 805–1030

Stuiver M, and Polach H A 1977 Discussion: reporting of 14C data. *Radiocarbon* 19(3), 355–63

Sturdy, D, Webly, D and Bailey, G, 1997 The Palaeolithic geography of Epirus, 587–614, in G Bailey (ed) *Klithi: Palaeolithic settlement and Quaternary landscapes in northwest Greece, Volume 2: Klithi in its local and regional setting*. McDonald Institute for Archaeological Research, Cambridge

Sturman, W M, 1961 *Barking Abbey: study in its external and internal administration from the Conquest to the Dissolution*. Unpubl PhD thesis, Queen Mary, University London

Sumbler, M G, 1996 *London and the Thames Valley*. British Regional Geology, British Geological Survey, Keyworth

Teichert, M, 1975 Osteometrische Untersuchungen zur Berechnung der Widerristhöhe bei Schafen in A T Clason (ed), *Archaeozoological studies*. Elsevier, Amsterdam, 51–69

Telford, W, Geldart, L, and Sheriff, R 1990 *Applied Geophysics, 2nd edition*, Cambridge University Press

Thomas, C and Rackham, D J, 1996 Bramcote Green, Bermondsey: a Bronze Age trackway and palaeoenvironmental sequence. *Proc Prehist Soc* 61, 221–253

Timby, J, Brown, R, Biddulph, E, Hardy, A and Powell, A 2007 *A Slice of Rural Essex: Recent archaeological discoveries from the A120 between Stansted Airport and Braintree*. Oxford Wessex Archaeology Monogr 1, Oxford and Salisbury

Tweddle, J C, Edwards, K J and Fieller, N R J, 2005 Multivariate statistical and other approaches for the separation of cereal from wild Poaceae pollen using a large Holocene dataset. *Vegetation History and Archaeobotany* 14, 15–30

URL, 1994 *Channel Tunnel Rail Link: Assessment of Historic and Cultural Effects – Final Report*. Unpubl Rep prepared by Oxford Archaeological Unit for URL

URL, 1997 *The Ebbsfleet Valley, Northfleet, Kent (ARC EFT97)*. Unpubl Rep prepared by Oxford Archaeological Unit for URL

URN, 2002 *Rainham Creek Desk-based Study Report*. Unpubl Rep prepared by E Heppell for URN

URN, 2003 *Rainham Creek, Archaeological Fieldwork Report*. Unpubl Rep prepared by Essex County Council Field Archaeological Unit for URN

URN and URS, 1999 *A Geoarchaeological Evaluation of the Thames/Medway Alluvial Corridor of the Channel Tunnel Rail Link. A Report in accordance with Tasks 2 – 4 of Contract No. 194/607*. Unpubl Rep prepared by Oxford Archaeology for URN and URS

URS, 1997 *CTRL Archaeological Research Strategy*. Unpubl Rep prepared by P Drewett for URS

Valler, H J and Crockett, A D, forthcoming. *Waterside management from the Middle Bronze Age to present day: High Speed 1 investigations at Stratford, London Borough of Newham*. Oxford Wessex Archaeology online publication

Van de Noort, R and Davies, P, 1993 *Wetland Heritage: An archaeological assessment of the Humber Wetlands*. Humber Wetlands Project, Hull

Van de Noort, R and O'Sullivan, A, 2006 *Rethinking Wetland Archaeology*. Duckworth, London

Verart, L, 1996 Fishing for the Mesolithic, the North Sea: a submerged Mesolithic landscape in A Fischer (ed) *Man and the Sea in the Mesolithic*. Oxbow Monogr 53, Oxford, 291–301

Vermeiden, J, 1948 Improved sounding apparatus as developed in Holland since 1936. *Proc 2nd International Conference on Soil Mechanics and Foundation Engineering* 1, 280–287

VCH – *Victoria County History*, 1907 *A History of the County of Essex: Volume 2*. London (eds W Page and J H Round)

Vince A G, 1985 The Saxon and medieval pottery of London: a review. *Medieval Archaeology* 29, 25–93

Vos, P C and de Wolf, H, 1993 Diatoms as a tool for reconstructing sedimentary environments in coastal wetlands; methodological aspects. *Hydrobiologia* 269/270, 285–296

Walker, M, Johnsen, S, Rasmussen, S O, Popp, T, Steffensen, J-P, Gibbard, P, Hoek, W, Lowe, J, Andrews, J, Bjorck, S, Cwynar, L C, Hughen, K, Kerhsaw, P, Kromer, B, Litt, T, Lowe, D J, Nakagawa, T, Newnham, R and Schwander, J, 2009 Formal definition and dating of the GSSP (Global Stratotype Section and Point) for the base of the Holocene using the Greenland NGRIP ice core, and selected auxiliary records. *Journ Quat Sci* 24, 3–17

Walker, M J C, 2005 *Quaternary Dating Methods*. Wiley, Chichester

Walker, R G and Cant, D J, 1984 Sandy fluvial systems, in R G Walker (ed) *Facies models, 2nd edition*. Geoscience Canada, Toronto, 71–90,

Waller, M P, 1993 Flandrian vegetational history of south-eastern England: pollen data from Pannel Bridge, East Sussex. *New Phytologist* 124, 345–369

Waller, M P, 1994 Paludification and pollen representation: the influence of wetland size on Tilia representation in pollen diagrams. *The Holocene* 4, 430–434

Waller, M P and Grant, M J, 2012 Holocene pollen assemblages from coastal wetlands: differentiating natural and anthropogenic causes of change in the Thames estuary, UK. *Journ Quat Sci* 27 (5), 461–474

Waller, M P, Long, A J and Schofield, J E, 2006 Interpretation of radiocarbon dates from the upper surface of late-Holocene peat layers in coastal lowlands. *The Holocene* 16, 51–61

Warren, S H, 1912 On a late glacial stage in the valley of the river Lea, subsequent to the epoch of River-drift Man. *Quarterly Journal of the Geological Society* 68, 213–251

Warren, S H, 1915 Further observations on the Late Glacial or Ponders' End Stage of the Lea Valley. *Quarterly Journal of the Geological Society* 71, 164–182

Weerts, H J T, Westerhoff, W E, Cleveringa, P, Bierkens, M F P, Veldkamp, J G and Rijskijk, K F, 2005 Quaternary geological mapping of the lowlands of the Netherlands, a 21st century perspective. *Quaternary International* 133–134, 159–178

Wenban-Smith, F F, 1995 The Ebbsfleet Valley, Northfleet (Baker's Hole) (TQ 615735), 147–164, in D R Bridgland, P Allen and B A Haggart (eds) *The Quaternary of the Lower Reaches of the Thames Field Guide*. Quaternary Research Association, Cambridge, 147–164

Wenban-Smith, F F, Allen, P, Bates, M R, Parfitt, S A, Preece, R C, Stewart, J R, Turner, C and Whittaker, J E, 2006 The Clactonian elephant butchery site at Southfleet Road, Ebbsfleet, UK. *Journ Quat Sci* 21, 471–483

Wenban-Smith, F F, Stafford, E C and Bates, M R forthcoming, *Prehistoric Ebbsfleet: Excavations and Research in advance of High Speed 1 and South Thameside Development Route 4 1989–2003*. Oxford Wessex Archaeology Monogr

Westaway, R., Bridgland, D R and White, M J, 2006 The Quaternary uplift history of central southern England: evidence from the terraces of the Solent River system and nearby raised beaches. *Quat Sci Rev* 25, 2212–2250

Westaway, R, Maddy, D and Bridgland, D R, 2002 Flow in the lower continental crust as a mechanism for the Quaternary uplift of south-east England: constraints from the Thames terrace record. *Quat Sci Rev* 21, 559–603

Whitaker, W, 1889 *The Geology of London and Parts of the Thames Valley*. Memoir of the Geological Survey of Great Britain, Keyworth

Whitehouse, N J and Smith, D N, 2004 Islands in Holocene Forests: Implications for Forest Openness, Landscape Clearance and Cultural Steppe Species. *Environmental Archaeology* 9, 199–208

Whitney, K P, 1989 Development of the Kentish Marshes in the aftermath of the Norman Conquest. *Archaeologia Cantiana* 107, 29–50

Whittaker, J, 2011, in Andrews *et al* 2011b, 80–85

Widdowson, M, 1997 The geomorphological and geological importance of palaeosurfaces, 1–12, in M Widdowson (ed) *Palaeosurfaces: recognition, reconstruction and palaeoenvironmental interpretation*. Geological Society Special Publication 120, Geological Society, London

Wilkinson, K and Bond, C J, 2001 Interpreting archaeological site distribution in dynamic sedimentary environments, in T Darvill and M Gojda (eds) *One Land, Many Landscapes; papers from a session held at the European Association of Archaeologists, Fifth Annual Meeting in Bournemouth 1999*. Brit Archaeol Rep S987, Oxford, 55–66

Wilkinson, K and Sidell, E J, 2007 London, the backwater of Neolithic Britain? Archaeological significance of Middle Holocene river and vegetation change in the London Thames, in E J Sidell and F Haughey (eds) *Neolithic Archaeology in the Intertidal Zone*. Neolithic Studies Group Seminar Paper 8, Oxbow Books, Oxford, 71–85

Wilkinson, K N, Scaife, R G and Sidell, E J, 2000 Environmental and sea level changes in London from 10,500 BP to the present: a case study from Silvertown. *Proc Geologists' Ass* 111, 41–54

Wilkinson, T J, 1988 *Archaeology and Environment in South Essex: rescue archaeology along the Grays Bypass 1979/80*. East Anglian Archaeology 42

Wilkinson, T J and Murphy, P L, 1995 *The Archaeology of the Essex Coast, Volume 1: the Hullbridge Survey*. East Anglian Archaeology 71, Chelmsford

Wiltshire, P E J, Edwards, K J and Bond, S, 1994 Microbially-derived metallic sulphide spherules, pollen, and the waterlogging of archaeological sites. *Proc American Association of Sedimentary Palynologists* 29, 207–221

Wymer, J J, 1968 *Lower Palaeolithic Archaeology in Britain, as Represented by the Thames Valley*. John Baker, London

Wymer, J J, 1999 *The Lower Palaeolithic Occupation of Britain*. Trust for Wessex Archaeology, Salisbury

Yokoyama Y, Lambeck, K, Beccker, P, de, Johnston, P and Fyfield, L K 2000 Timing of the Last Glacial Maximum from Observed Sea Level Minima. *Nature* 406, 703–706

Zhu, S, Hack, R., Turner, K and Hale, M, 2003 How far will uncertainty of the subsurface limit the sustainability planning of the subsurface? *Proceedings of the Sustainable Development and Management of the Subsurface (SDMS) conference. 5–7th November 2003, Utrecht, Netherlands.* Delft Cluster, Delft, 203–210

Index

by Chris Hayden